Unchecked and Unbalanced

Also by Frederick A.O. Schwarz Jr.

Nigeria: The Tribes, the Nation, or the Race: The Politics of Independence

Unchecked and Unbalanced

Presidential Power in a Time of Terror

FREDERICK A.O. SCHWARZ JR.

& AZIZ Z. HUQ

THE NEW PRESS

NEW YORK
LONDON

BRENNAN
CENTER
FOR JUSTICE
AT NYU SCHOOL OF LAW

Published in the United States by The New Press, New York, 2007
Distributed by W. W. Norton & Company, Inc., New York

LIBRARY OF CONGRESS CATALOGING-IN-PUBLICATION DATA
Schwarz, Frederick A.O.
Unchecked and unbalanced : presidential power in a time of terror / Frederick A.O. Schwarz
and Aziz Z. Huq.
p. cm.
Includes bibliographical references and index.
ISBN-13: 978-1-59558-117-4 (hc.)
1. War and emergency powers—United States.   2. War on Terrorism, 2001—Law and legislation.
3. Executive power—United States.   4. Presidents—United States.   I. Huq, Aziz.   II. Title.
KF5060.S39 2007
342.73'062—dc22   2006028784

The New Press was established in 1990 as a not-for-profit alternative to the large, commercial publishing houses currently dominating the book publishing industry. The New Press operates in the
public interest rather than for private gain, and is committed to publishing, in innovative ways, works
of educational, cultural, and community value that are often deemed insufficiently profitable.

www.thenewpress.com

Composition by NK Graphics, a Black Dot Company
This book was set in Bembo

Printed in the United States of America

2   4   6   8   10   9   7   5   3   1

FAOS:

To Ricky, my beloved wife

AZH:

To my parents

Contents

Unchecked and Unbalanced

Introduction

In the late 1970s, former president Richard Nixon had claimed to the Senate and the American public that a president had power to set aside laws enacted by Congress. Few then accepted Nixon's blunt assertion that "when the president does it, that means that it is not illegal." But his claim was not forgotten. Ten years later, in 1987, the same claim reappeared in the minority section of a congressional report about the Iran-Contra scandal. According to the minority report, "the Chief Executive will on occasion feel duty bound to assert monarchical notions of prerogative that will permit him to exceed the laws." The leading congressional advocate of this view was a new representative from Wyoming by the name of Richard Cheney; when four commercial airplanes became instruments of mass murder on the morning of September 11, 2001, Dick Cheney had become vice president of the United States.[1]

At the onset of a national emergency, Americans understandably turn to the White House for leadership. As head of the executive branch and the security agencies it contains—the FBI, the CIA, and the Department of Defense—the President is best equipped among the three branches of government to respond immediately to crisis. On 9/11, jets scrambled, emergency services rallied, and law enforcement began investigations, as indeed they should have.

More than five years later, however, at the time of this writing, the executive remains the dominant, almost exclusive, branch of government choosing and wielding national security tools in response to terrorist threats. President George W. Bush acts with little deference to or collaboration with Congress or the federal courts on matters he considers relevant to national security. Further, the views of the Iran-Contra minority report are now official policy and practice of the United States. For the first time in American history, the executive branch claims authority under the Constitution to set aside laws permanently—including prohibitions on torture and warrantless eavesdropping on Americans. A frightening idea decisively rejected at America's birth—that a president, like a king, can do no wrong—has reemerged to justify torture and indefinite presidential detention.

This is a book about how this new theory of unchecked presidential power developed and why it is embarrassingly wrong. This theory upsets the delicate balance of our constitutional government, sullies the nation's name, and hurts vital counterterrorism campaigns. The theory is not a response to 9/11, but, as the 1987 minority report suggests, has long been nurtured by the leaders of today's Bush Administration. Moreover, the executive branch's mistakes are uncannily familiar. During the Cold War, intelligence agencies slipped into similar sorts of overreaching and abuse because of a lack of checks and balances. But Cold War errors are multiplied in scale today by the theory of unlimited presidential power.

This "monarchical executive" argument is deployed to many ends: for example, to defeat laws barring both torture and cruel or degrading treatment; to underwrite the "outsourcing" of torture to other countries, such as Syria and Egypt; to detain individuals, including Americans, indefinitely without any due process; to spy on Americans' telephone calls and e-mails in violation of federal statutes and, at times, the Fourth Amendment; and to infiltrate and keep watch on domestic groups protesting government policy.

The framers of the Constitution and those who ratified it were acutely aware of threats both from overseas and from chief executives who wished to set aside the law. They recognized that if democratic government was to persist, no single individual—selected by lineage or popular suffrage—could be blindly trusted to wield power wisely.[2] So they restrained each branch of government from grasping excess power and dominating the others. This system of checks and balances was unique to the new republic. As James Madison explained, arguing for the Constitution's ratification,

> If men were angels, no government would be necessary. If angels were to govern men, neither external nor internal controls on government would be necessary. In framing a government, which is to be administered by men over men, the great difficulty lies in this: *you must first enable the government to control the governed; and in the next place, oblige it to control itself.*[3]

The Constitution entrenched not only a public power to judge leaders at the ballot box but also "auxiliary precautions" to stymie leaders' inevitable efforts to immunize themselves from accountability. Reflecting Madison's insights, the Constitution does not simply divide government power among three separate branches—a lawmaking part in Congress; a law-executing part in the president and his departments and agencies; and an adjudicative part in the federal courts—it also fashions a system of separate institutions *sharing* power, thus restraining each other from power's abuse. No one branch may entirely ignore the others when the nation's interests are at stake. Indeed, in a majority of vital decisions implicating constitutional values of national importance, each of the three branches typically plays some role. Contrary to much recent commentary, questions of national security are no exception to this rule. The Founders also believed this system of "checks and balances" was liberty's first and best defense.[4] The Bill of Rights followed as supplemental protection.

The checks and balances were termed "auxiliary" by the Founders because the American public was to have the final checking power at the ballot box. But democratic accountability at the polls is also intertwined with the checks and balances imposed by separate branches sharing powers. For the public to play its proper checking role at the ballot box, citizens must know what is done by government in their name. Between periodic elections, Congress and the courts are tasked with preventing the executive branch from obscuring policies and their consequences from public scrutiny and thus entrenching itself against electoral testing. Democracy cannot be reduced to a biennial trip to the polling station.

Yet at many points in American history, fear and crisis have temporarily shifted power to executive branch officials who have been tempted to ignore the Constitution's wise restraints. Decisions to ignore the Constitution's system of checks and balances, however, have rarely made the nation safer.[5]

In 1798, a mere decade after the Constitution's passage, President John Adams and his Federalist Party allies in Congress forced through the Alien and Sedition Acts in response to fears of French revolutionary radicalism. These Acts criminalized citizens' speech critical of the government and allowed deportation, by order of the president alone without judicial review, of aliens deemed dangerous. Legal historian Geoffrey Stone explains that the Sedition Act, although defended as a way to strengthen the nation in its impending war with France, in fact "served primarily as a political weapon to strengthen the Federalists in their 'war'" against political opponents led by Vice President Thomas Jefferson. Federalist prosecutors argued that it was criminal for ordinary citizens to "raise surmises and suspicions of the wisdom" of the president's "measures." Thomas Cooper, a publisher and pamphleteer critical of the Adams Administration who was charged under the Sedition Act, argued to a jury that "I know in England their King can do no wrong, but I did not know till now that the President of the United States had the same attribute." Cooper and nine other citizens were nevertheless convicted of the "crime" of criticizing the Administration.[6]

The twentieth century again witnessed executive officers using unilateral security powers for political gain during the Palmer Raids. After World War I, the Department of Justice launched dragnet raids against immigrant communities, arresting and deporting thousands of innocent people without warrants or access to counsel. Eyeing a run for the White House and playing to the ethnic prejudices of the day, Attorney General A. Mitchell Palmer, chief instigator of these raids, condemned the detainees as people with "sly and crafty eyes . . . lopsided eyes, sloping brows and misshapen features."[7] Executive power in the name of national security, operating without accountability, instead serviced political goals.

In February 1942, some twenty years after Palmer's folly, President Franklin Delano Roosevelt issued a presidential order interning 117,000 Japanese Americans on the West Coast in "relocation camps." Initially, this decision was made without congressional approval or judicial input. Cooler heads within the Administration reacted with alarm. Even before the internment, when lesser restraints on aliens were under discussion, Attorney General Robert H. Jackson warned the President not to make "[scape]goats" of all aliens as "Germany has made [scape]goats of all Jews." The FBI and military officials said the "vast majority" of Japanese Americans were "loyal to the United States." In the end, although both Congress and the Supreme Court gave post hoc approval to the internments, not a single documented act of espionage, sabotage, or treasonable activity of a person of Japanese descent living on the West Coast occurred.[8]

It was irrational fear and prejudice—marching in lockstep with Roosevelt's narrow electoral calculations—that propelled the Japanese internment. General John DeWitt, responsible for the army on the West Coast, rendered a report recommending internment of all West Coast Japanese Americans. His report is recognized today as a "travesty" based on "unsubstantiated and even fabricated assertions." DeWitt saw no danger from German Americans or Italian Americans except in "certain cases," but warned, "a Jap is a Jap." He was not alone: the Attorney General of Idaho pressed for internment of Japanese Americans "to keep this a white man's country."[9]

These examples of executive overreaching motivated by fear, prejudice, partisan bias, or parochial gain find homes in our constitutional heritage today—as examples of what *not* to do. One hundred and sixty-four years after Thomas Cooper's Sedition Act conviction, the Supreme Court, in the *New York Times v. Sullivan* case, observed that "although the Sedition Act was never tested in this Court, the attack upon its validity has carried the day in the court of history."[10] Four decades after the internment of Japanese Americans, Congress and President Ronald Reagan apologized for "the fundamental injustice" and offered financial reparations.[11] Although the Japanese American detentions were never formally repudiated, the Supreme Court's opinion authorizing them has nonetheless become a byword for judicial abdication.[12]

The Cold War and the 1947 National Security Act brought a new institutionalization of intelligence powers. Until the 1940s, the United States, unlike the former Soviet Union and Great Britain, had no organized secret intelligence services. What previously was ad hoc and informal became bureaucratic, regularized, and effective—a powerful tool concentrated almost exclusively in presidents' hands. The FBI's domestic security activities burgeoned. The CIA and the National Security Agency (or NSA) were born and rapidly expanded to enormous proportions. In 2005, the federal government spent $44 billion on the intelligence community's sixteen agencies and 100,000 staff.[13]

With the swift growth of intelligence and security agencies came unprecedented secrecy. From the Alien and Sedition Acts to the Japanese American internment, executive branch overreaching largely took place in plain sight of the public. During the Cold War, secrecy justified in the name of "national security" hid governmental actions from Congress and the public, further undermining the Constitution's checks and balances.

Intelligence agencies' excesses during the Cold War came to public light most comprehensively in 1975–1976, through an investigation conducted by a Senate Select Committee known as the Church Committee after its chair, Senator Frank Church of Idaho.[14] In Part I of this book, we detail the Church Committee's investigation of the intelligence agencies, particularly the FBI, the CIA, the NSA, and other components of the Defense Department. The Church Committee found that these agencies had exceeded their authority through abusive surveillance and disruption of political activity at home (e.g., trying to provoke Martin Luther King Jr. to commit suicide) and unwise overseas covert action (e.g., hiring the Mafia to try to assassinate Cuba's Fidel Castro, and supporting the overthrow of Chile's democratically elected government). Although men and women of the intelligence agencies directly committed abuses, the most serious breaches of duty were those of presidents and other senior executive branch officials who, the Church Committee determined, had the "responsib[ility] for controlling intelligence activities and generally failed to assure compliance with the law."[15]

The Church Committee identified four key institutional flaws in government operating procedures that fostered reckless and immoral use of intelligence powers. These flaws undermined checks and balances during the Cold War, and are being repeated today to the detriment of the nation's security, compounded now by the "monarchical executive" theory.

First, national security activities were organized under ambiguous laws and fuzzy instructions. These imprecise mandates placed no effective constraint on national security agencies. When laws fail to channel or limit the executive's use of power, Congress fails in its threshold checking function.

The second institutional flaw diagnosed by the Committee was that senior executive branch officials gave implicit orders to violate the law. Sometimes these took the form of euphemism, sometimes winks and nods. Together, ambiguous laws and implicit orders allowed presidents and other senior officials to maintain "plausible deniability." A device originally designed to hide from the rest of the world America's responsibility for covert actions overseas, plausible deniability was redeployed to obscure from *Americans* responsibility for decisions inside the American government itself.[16]

The third flaw was that executive branch officials relied on an expectation of permanent secrecy to shroud the broad outlines and guiding assumptions of policy—not just operational specifics—from testing before Congress and the public. Secrecy further corroded officials' inclination to ask themselves whether their decisions would violate the law. Time and again during the Cold War, executive branch officials broke clear laws without a second thought, thinking they would never be held to account for their trespasses.

Finally, feeble congressional oversight of national security activities translated into an utter failure of accountability. Until the midseventies, Congress either did nothing to put an end to executive branch adventurism or knowingly turned a blind eye. As Supreme Court Justice Robert H. Jackson warned, ultimate power may rightly belong to Congress, "but only Congress itself can prevent power from slipping through its fingers."[17]

These institutional failings disabled the constitutional decision-making process envisaged by the Founders. They overly empowered the executive branch and yielded policies counter to our nation's elementary commitments to liberty, human dignity, and decency. The absence of initial legal restraints and subsequent oversight meant that intelligence agencies extended unwarranted powers beyond even initial targets. This entirely predictable consequence is dubbed "mission creep." During the Cold War period, those charged with protecting America thus moved, for example, from disrupting communists to disrupting civil rights leaders, antiwar protestors, and other social activists. Institutional flaws led to plainly illegal acts—sometimes purposeful, sometimes because, as one federal agent explained, "we never gave it a thought."[18]

While the Church Committee stimulated some important statutory reforms, by the mid-1980s many of the same flaws began to reappear.

Today, a new and more hazardous incarnation of executive overreaching is in evidence. Part II of this book details three of the leading ways in which the post–September 11 executive branch is misusing its intelligence and security powers: authorizing illegal torture and abuse in American-run facilities overseas; endorsing the "extraordinary rendition" system, whereby detainees are transferred for torture to other countries whose human rights records the State Department condemns; and engaging at home in illegal executive detention and spying. The growth of the intelligence bureaucracy during the Cold War means that the damage the executive branch can inflict when it oversteps the laws unchecked by other branches has increased exponentially.

With the exception of domestic spying—a conspicuous common feature of executive lawbreaking during the Cold War and again today—the specific forms of overreaching are new. But procedural failings familiar from the Cold War past are visible again. Ambiguous laws and fuzzy instructions, indirect orders, the expectation of permanent secrecy, and failures of congressional oversight all allow the White House and the intelligence and security agencies under its purview to adopt abusive tactics and drift into sweeping application of harsh tactics to innocent people.

Today, the President also deploys the monarchical executive theory to justify and shelter overreaching by intelligence and security agencies. Part III of this book explains how this theory developed, why it is wrong, and why it is significantly more dangerous than Cold War practices. It also explores how government lawyers played a pivotal role in bringing forth a monarchical executive.

The monarchical executive theory was not simply a response to 9/11. It was a realization of the vision first articulated in the Iran-Contra minority report headlined by then-congressman Dick Cheney. Within weeks of the 9/11 attacks, Vice President Cheney and his senior legal advisor David Addington, who had also been at Cheney's side in the Iran-Contra investigation, urged that the Administration ignore prohibitions on government searches contained in the Constitution's Fourth Amendment and in a host of federal prohibitions and start intercepting Americans' e-mails and telephone calls. Similar logic was also soon used to justify extraordinary rendition and indefinite detention without trial.[19]

The executive branch has many means at its disposal to put the monarchical executive theory into action. Inevitably, executive branch lawyers must interpret the laws when they apply them. This gives the Administration an opportunity to exploit ambiguities or simply sidestep legal obligations. Post-9/11, the Department of Justice crafted legal opinions that reinterpreted the laws in unreasonable, and clearly erroneous, ways. Government lawyers also argued that the presidents could ignore the law simply by invoking unspecified "national security" concerns. These legal opinions remained secret—so neither Congress nor the public knew of the laws being set aside. Dissenters within the executive branch were excluded from decision making; some were pushed out of government. And the President, when signing laws, began issuing declarations that he did not intend to follow literally hundreds of provisions of law.

But presidential unilateralism has not made the nation safer. Overreaching and the resulting abuse of elementary human rights costs us our liberties and others' support; it drives some into the arms of the enemy; and it corrodes the moral center of our nation's constitutional heritage. As General Colin L. Powell explained in September 2006, condemning an executive branch effort to water down antitorture rules, "The world is beginning to doubt the moral basis of our fight against terrorism."[20] In the current battle for hearts and minds—where success must be measured in terms of our ability to dissuade recruits to the enemy and to attract the support of allies—the resulting harm is great. Dodging the law, the President and other high officials are forced into hypocrisy or falsehoods to justify their illicit or immoral actions. Such mendacity inevitably saps both our international allies' confidence in us and our own rule of law. Five years of President George W. Bush's "war on terror" confirm a lesson drawn from 230 years of American history: when government responds to security threats by ignoring the Constitution's checks and balances, America's security, its moral luster, and its standing in the world are all diminished.

The 2006 elections showed in stark relief the centrality of checks and balances, of oversight and accountability. Few elections have so plainly been a referendum on the conduct of a presidency. Iraq, of course, was central. But more than the specifics of troop withdrawals and military strategy, it was real accountability voters emphatically demanded. Dozens of successful candidates accused their opponents of being "rubber stamps" for the Administration. The election of 2006 was thus a mandate for Congress to play its proper constitutional role. And it offers leaders of both parties a chance to remedy past errors.

This book does three things. First, it describes what went wrong. It is a Baedeker to the paths not taken, showing the consequences of oversight's absence in a constitutional system spun out of balance. Second, it explains why untrammeled executive power, power wholly out of keeping with the basic American constitutional order, is hazardous to America's safety and its values. Finally, it offers a road map for citizens and legislators of both parties who wish to reestablish the checks and balances that define our government and its place in the world.

From the nation's founding on, we have been at our strongest when policies are formulated by deliberative, open, and democratic processes, and when they embody the values underpinning the Declaration of Independence and the Constitution. Without the clarity that informed criticism brings, and without candid public debate about goals and means, our security policy all too often becomes illicit, foolish, and harmful.

The current situation demands a meaningful democratic dialogue that openly, soberly, and without recrimination wrestles with how America ought to deal with terrorism threats. What is needed now is a bipartisan commitment to real oversight, and a rejection of the executive unilateralism that brought us torture, "extraordinary rendition," and domestic surveillance. This means not just oversight, as the voters in the 2006 election sought. It also demands a reconsideration of the structures through which we achieve accountability. We must

reach solutions through well-informed public debate. This means letting go of
tools fashioned in the dark of unilateral White House deliberation. It means
letting go of policies that cause us to lose both the goodwill of mankind and
our own self-respect and integrity. And it means an informed dialogue that
avoids cheap prejudice or partisan politics. There is no "Republican" or
"Democratic" way to deal with terrorism.[21] To be critical of the current Administration is not necessarily to be partisan. Rather, these are tough questions
for all Americans. As Abraham Lincoln proposed at an earlier, far bloodier moment in American history, we must enter the debate "with malice toward
none; with charity for all . . . to bind up the nation's wounds."[22]

Part I

Cold War Lessons

1

Flawed Mandates: Early Years of the FBI and CIA

During the Cold War, as today, America faced and feared a dangerous foe.[1] The Soviet Union advanced vast and menacing armies into the heart of Europe. It blockaded Allied access to Berlin in 1948, ruthlessly repressed Hungarian freedom fighters in 1956, and put down the Prague Spring in Czechoslovakia in 1968.

Shortly after World War II, the Soviet Union also developed atomic and then hydrogen bombs, accelerating their development with espionage and information gleaned from Western traitors. Mutual nuclear destruction loomed. Americans began to fear a new, more deadly, World War III. For thirteen days in October 1962, the country sat transfixed as Soviet missiles capable of carrying nuclear bombs were discovered in Cuba within ninety miles of Florida.[2] As time passed, public concern shifted increasingly to the possibility that the Soviets and the Chinese would influence, undermine, or overthrow other governments through local wars in places such as Korea, or would ignite guerrilla insurgencies, coups, and more subtle incursions against democracies across the globe.

At home, some American officials exaggerated the threat of Communist influence. But, at the same time, that threat preoccupied many Americans, and it could not be ignored.[3]

Soviet (and Chinese) threats framed the thinking of U.S. governmental elites in foreign and domestic policy. Then, as today, some officials urged abandonment of long-standing moral norms in the face of the threat. A secret 1954 report for President Eisenhower by a commission on "Covert Actions of the Central Intelligence Agency" exemplified this approach. Chaired by General James H. Doolittle, who more than a decade earlier had led the first devastating firebomb air raid on Tokyo's civilian population, this Commission told the President:

It is now clear that we are facing an implacable enemy whose avowed objective is world domination by whatever means and at whatever cost. There are no rules in such a game. Hitherto acceptable norms of human conduct do not apply. If the U.S. is to survive, long-standing American concepts of "fair play" must be reconsidered.

The Doolittle Commission also urged that tactics "more ruthless than [those] employed by the enemy" be adopted if necessary.[4]

Today, we can examine the Cold War secure in the knowledge of America's eventual victory. Hindsight should not, however, obscure the earlier era's tangible sense of menace, or the felt necessity of vigorous response. These felt necessities, however, were used to justify "ruthless" measures—not only against foreign foes but also against Americans that the executive branch had decided were enemies, either of the nation or of individual officials holding transient political office. During the Cold War, as the Church Committee revealed most comprehensively, the executive branch engaged in widespread abuse of its security powers, operating beyond the checks and balances of constitutional government.

The institutional flaws leading to Cold War excesses can be traced back to the beginnings of the FBI's domestic intelligence gathering under President Franklin Delano Roosevelt and to the CIA's launch in 1947. In both cases, agency mandates were cast in nebulous terms with open-ended missions and inadequate boundaries. Also in both cases, executive branch officials made a conscious decision to keep the American public ignorant of the breadth and nature of the agencies' mandates. Finally, in both cases, congressional oversight was lax or nonexistent.

The FBI

In 1924, Harlan Fiske Stone, former dean of the Columbia Law School and later a Supreme Court Justice, became Attorney General for President Calvin Coolidge. Taking charge of the Justice Department, Stone concluded that many of its prior activities, particularly those of its Bureau of Investigation, the original name of the FBI,[5] were "lawless." In Stone's view, the department "maintain[ed] many activities which were without any authority in federal statutes and engage[d] in many practices which were brutal and tyrannical in the extreme." Stone had in mind incidents like the 1920 Palmer Raids, which involved "indiscriminate arrests of the innocent with the guilty, unlawful seizures by federal detectives, intimidating preliminary interrogations of aliens held incommunicado, high-handed levying of excessive bail, and denial of counsel." During the Palmer Raids, a young J. Edgar Hoover, then head of the Justice Department's General Intelligence Division, argued that to allow the detainees access to lawyers would "defeat the ends of justice," and that, lacking proof of guilt, they should nonetheless be held on the off-chance that evidence might be discovered at some future date "in other sections of the country."[6]

Shortly after the raids, a group of distinguished lawyers and legal scholars—including future Supreme Court Justice Felix Frankfurter, Harvard Law School Dean Roscoe Pound, and leading constitutional scholar Zachariah Chafee—issued a report finding that during the raids, federal agents had used torture, illegal searches and arrests, and "agents provocateurs such as have been familiar in old Russia or Spain." These agents infiltrated radical groups and, after reaching positions of power, instigated "acts which might be declared criminal." The pre-Stone Justice Department responded to these allegations by searching files, including military intelligence files, to see if Frankfurter and other responsible critics had radical associations or beliefs.[7]

Taking charge at the Justice Department, Stone issued new internal guidelines for the Bureau designed to prevent such conduct. He warned that "a secret police may become a menace to free government and free institutions, because it carries with it the possibility of abuses of power that are not always quickly appreciated or understood." He told Hoover that the Bureau ought not to be "concerned with political or other opinions of individuals. It is concerned only with their conduct and then only such conduct as is forbidden by the laws of the United States." Stone ordered that Bureau investigations "be limited strictly to investigations of violations of law,"[8] effectively prohibiting speculative government fishing expeditions into people's lives based on their political activities.

Stone cleaned house. He promoted J. Edgar Hoover to direct the bureau—with the support of the American Civil Liberties Union.[9] Eight years later, Hoover still marched to Stone's drum, telling a new attorney general, William DeWitt Mitchell, that because the Bureau was subject to "the closest scrutiny," it should not investigate matters that "from a federal standpoint, have not been declared illegal."[10]

Challenges from overseas led to changes in the Bureau's domestic role. In the run-up to World War II, President Roosevelt issued conflicting and confusing directives to the FBI describing its domestic intelligence responsibilities. Some were secret presidential orders; others were embodied only in secret memos by Hoover describing conversations with the President. Some of Roosevelt's new orders remained within the boundaries of the Stone standard. Thus, Roosevelt directed the Bureau to investigate espionage, sabotage, and violations of neutrality regulations—all examples of conduct "forbidden by the laws of the United States." In some of his instructions, however, Roosevelt dramatically broadened the Bureau's authority by tacking on what he loosely termed "subversion" to the subjects of investigation.[11] Roosevelt did not define this amorphous and imprecise term.

Roosevelt, then–Attorney General Homer Cummings, and Bureau Director Hoover explicitly rejected the idea of asking Congress for legislation to authorize expanded domestic security investigations. In a letter to Cummings, shared with Roosevelt, Hoover argued it was "believed imperative" that the expansion proceed "with the utmost degree of secrecy in order to avoid criticism or objections." Cummings added that their plans for expanded domestic investigations should, therefore, "be held in the strictest confidence," not revealed even to Congress.[12] In time, use of the word "subversive" in Roosevelt's and subsequent presidents' directives, coupled with operational secrecy, opened the door to large-scale abuses. Ambiguous instructions worked hand-in-hand with excessive secrecy to evade the checks and balances that flow from congressional and judicial involvement.

A few years later, Robert H. Jackson, another Roosevelt Attorney General and later a Supreme Court Justice and chief prosecutor at the Nuremberg war crimes trials of Nazi war criminals, warned of the uncertain breadth and inevitably subjective reach of the term "subversive":

> Activities which seem benevolent or helpful to wage earners, persons on relief, or those who are disadvantaged in the struggle for existence may be regarded as "subversive" by those whose property interests might be burdened thereby. Those who are in office are apt to regard as "subversive" the activities of any of those who would bring about a change of administration. Some of our soundest constitutional doctrines were once punished as subversive. We must not forget that it was not so long ago that both the term "Republican" and the term "Democrat" were epithets with sinister meaning to denote persons of radical tendencies that were "subversive" of the order of things then dominant.[13]

Jackson's warning concerned the fickle and unpredictable application of the term "subversive" in the context of prosecutions, not surveillance. But fourteen years later, shortly before his death and after spending thirteen years on the Supreme Court and documenting at Nuremberg the inner workings of a totalitarian regime, Jackson renewed his warning against the danger of open-ended intelligence surveillance:

> I can say with great confidence that [America] cannot become totalitarian without a centralized national police. . . . [T]he safeguard of our liberty lies in limiting any national police or investigative organization, first of all to a small number of strictly federal offenses, and second to non-political ones.[14]

Jackson proved prescient. In the Roosevelt years, the FBI generally honored the earlier Stone standards despite its expanded mandate. The Bureau's intelligence work largely consisted of investigating possible criminal conduct by Nazis or their sympathizers. Nevertheless, even during Roosevelt's watch there were inklings of the abuse and overreaching to come in the Cold War era. At the White House's request, the Bureau investigated members of the public who expressed approval of a speech by Charles Lindbergh, one of the President's leading critics.[15] The Bureau also investigated the entirely lawful conduct of groups such as the League for Fair Play, which, according to Bureau documents, was established by "two ministers and a businessman for the purpose of furthering fair play, tolerance, adherence to the Constitution, democracy . . . and good will among all creeds, races and classes." Similarly, acting at the navy's request after protests against racial discrimination by "fifteen colored mess attendants," the FBI opened a decades-long investigation of the National Association for the Advancement of Colored People, or NAACP. From this acorn sprouted multiple investigations and infiltrations of the civil rights movement during the Cold War.

The CIA

The CIA had its genesis in the Pearl Harbor attack of December 7, 1941.[16] Faced with a colossal intelligence failure that precipitated America's entry into World War II, Roosevelt turned to William ("Wild Bill") Donovan—a New York lawyer and World War I hero—appointing him to the new position of "Coordinator of Information." In 1942, Donovan formed the Office of Strategic Services, or OSS, the CIA's predecessor.[17] Its mission was to gather and analyze strategic information and to conduct covert operations. During the war, the OSS provided useful military intelligence and sabotage, including support for the Allied invasion of Normandy in 1944.[18]

In 1945, President Harry S. Truman disbanded the OSS, concerned that it could become a Gestapo-like organization in peacetime, threatening domestic civil liberties.[19] The OSS's responsibilities were transferred to the State and War Departments. The emerging Soviet threat, however, soon created a new need for centralized intelligence. Donovan called for an organization under direct presidential supervision to "procure intelligence both by overt and covert methods . . . provide intelligence guidance, determine national intelligence objectives, and correlate the intelligence material collected by all government agencies." The new agency, Donovan envisioned, would conduct "subversive operations abroad" but would be barred from "police or law enforcement functions, either at home or abroad."[20]

Donovan's idea collided with entrenched bureaucratic interests. The military, the State Department, and the FBI all saw a new central intelligence organization as a threat to their independence, funding, and influence.[21] Such interagency jealousies had broken out as early as World War II, harming U.S. intelligence efforts. For example, on hearing that OSS officers had secretly broken into the Spanish embassy in Washington to photograph documents (Franco's Spain, though "neutral," was suspected of having ties to Nazi Germany), FBI Director Hoover concluded the break-in fell within the FBI's bailiwick. Rather than protesting to the White House, the Bureau waited for a second OSS entry and had FBI cars outside the Spanish embassy turn on their sirens to frustrate their rival's operation.[22]

In 1946, President Truman established a "Central Intelligence Group," but, due to institutional pressures from existing agencies, the Group had only limited power. It was placed under the direction of a National Intelligence Authority made up of a presidential representative and the secretaries of state, war, and navy. More ambitious proposals gained traction after publication of a report by the Congressional Joint Committee on the Investigation of the Pearl Harbor Attack. Based on a multiyear investigation, this Committee recommended that the United States develop a permanent, unified intelligence effort. By 1947, Truman had arrived at the same view, and that year saw passage of the National Security Act. The main function of the Act was reorganization of the national security functions of the executive branch: unifying the military services under the new Department of Defense; creating the air force as a separate arm of the military; and establishing a National Security Council to guide the president in foreign policy matters. Of crucial importance here, the Act also transformed the Central Intelligence Group into an independent department, renaming it the Central Intelligence Agency, or CIA.[23]

Reflecting Truman's concern with preventing development of a "Gestapo," the National Security Act placed a specific limit on the CIA's powers: "The Agency shall have no police, subpoena, law enforcement powers or internal security functions."[24]

The tasks assigned to the CIA under the 1947 Act reflected Donovan's vision and the Joint Committee's recommendations. The parts of the Act dealing with the CIA outlined its roles as "advis[ing]" on intelligence activities, making "recommendations" about the "coordination" of intelligence by other government departments, and "correlat[ing] and evaluat[ing] intelligence relating to the national security." Neither covert action nor espionage—which soon became the CIA's principal activities—were mentioned. Instead, just as in President Roosevelt's orders empowering the FBI, the Act used open-ended, subjective words to describe the CIA's mission. After its other functions had been explicitly described, the Act gave the CIA catch-all authority "to perform such other functions and duties related to intelligence affecting the United States as the National Security Council may from time to time direct."[25]

A hint that this bland language might sanction more than mere ministerial labors came during testimony before Congress when the 1947 Act was under consideration. General Hoyt Vandenberg, then the Central Intelligence Group's director, referred vaguely to "certain . . . activities" that the intelligence agencies could not "expose . . . to the public gaze."[26] Thus, America's best-known and most powerful foreign intelligence agency was launched without public awareness or any congressional discussion of what a major part of its mandate meant.

Secrecy and Lack of Oversight

Within a year of the passage of the National Security Act, the President's National Security Council issued an "NSC Directive"—in effect, a law issued secretly and unilaterally by the executive—empowering the CIA to engage in "sabotage," "economic warfare," assistance to "guerrilla warfare," and "propaganda." There was no public disclosure of this transformative shift in the character and scope of CIA activities. The American people had no opportunity to debate fundamental questions about what tactics might be justified or consistent with the nation's character.

Meanwhile, for thirty years after World War II, Congress's oversight of the FBI, the CIA, and the other intelligence agencies was lax. Stated bluntly, Congress gave the FBI a free ride. This was partly out of love, partly out of fear: love because the Bureau was highly respected for its widely publicized successes in fighting crime, and fear because the Bureau's massive covert intelligence gathering reached politicians too.[27] As Justice Robert Jackson cautioned:

> All that is necessary is to have a national police competent to investigate all manner of offenses, and then, in the parlance of the streets, it will have enough on enough people, even if it does not choose to prosecute them, so that it will find no opposition to its policies. Even those who are supposed to supervise it are likely to fear it.[28]

The Church Committee's investigation brought to light a striking example of FBI Director Hoover's power to intimidate even a sitting president.[29] The Committee learned that a mistress of a Mafia don hired by the CIA to kill Fidel Castro was at the same time one of President Kennedy's mistresses. In attempting to assess the extent of the President's involvement in the Castro assassination plots, the Committee pursued the question of whether she channeled information between the President and the Mafia don. The Committee concluded that she was not a go-between and had no knowledge of the plots, but, in examining this question, the Committee discovered a letter from Hoover to the White House and Attorney General Robert Kennedy that revealed that Hoover knew about the common mistress. Given Hoover's awareness, President Kennedy and his Attorney General could hardly have replaced, or even effectively controlled, the FBI director. (Indeed, Hoover served as FBI director for almost fifty years, from 1924 until his death in 1972.)

Although the CIA had neither the FBI's reputation nor its trove of embarrassing evidence, it too escaped scrutiny. Congress found it easier, and safer, to give the CIA a free pass than to do any oversight. Senate and House committees charged with oversight made no written records, asked no tough questions, and often indicated a preference *not* to know what was done. As Clark Clifford, an aide to President Truman in 1947 and Secretary of Defense during the last years of Lyndon B. Johnson's administration, reflected in 1983, "Congress chose not to be involved and preferred to be uninformed." A longtime CIA general counsel added that the lack of congressional oversight ultimately caused problems for the CIA because "we became a little cocky about what we could do."[30]

The vacuum did not last. The Watergate scandal and other revelations of abuse in the 1970s prompted Congress to launch substantial investigations of the intelligence agencies and their use by presidents and other high executive branch officials. The most far-reaching and revealing of these investigations was that of the Church Committee. As then–Senate Majority Leader Mike Mansfield observed in 1975 when speaking in support of the resolution establishing the Church Committee:

> It used to be fashionable . . . for members of Congress to say that insofar as the intelligence agencies were concerned, the less they knew about such questions, the better. Well, in my judgment, it is about time that attitude went out of fashion. It is time for the Senate to take the trouble and, yes, the risks, of knowing more rather than less.[31]

That trouble and those risks were taken by the Church Committee, the revelations of which we turn to next.

2

Revelations of the Church Committee

In August 1963, more than 250,000 men and women, black and white, marched in the nation's capital to demand civil rights. At this March on Washington, in a speech that still echoes today, Dr. Martin Luther King Jr. told the country of his "dream" that:

> all God's children, black men and white men, Jews and Gentiles, Protestants and Catholics, will be able to join hands and sing, in the words of the old Negro spiritual, "Free at last, free at last, thank God Almighty, I'm free at last."[1]

Dr. King's speech resonates not only as a cry for civil rights but as a hymn to the American dream. In the bowels of FBI headquarters in Washington, officials of the FBI's Domestic Intelligence Division concluded that King's "powerful demagogic speech" established him as the nation's "most dangerous and effective Negro leader." The FBI therefore decided to "take him off his pedestal" and secretly to select and promote its own candidate to "assume the role of the leadership of the Negro people."[2]

In later years, using language reminiscent of George Orwell's Newspeak, the Bureau—in secret, internal documents—characterized King's organization, the Southern Christian Leadership Conference, or SCLC, as a "Black Nationalist *Hate* Group." (The SCLC was a civil rights group largely consisting of black Southern preachers.) Bureau headquarters told field agents that King had to be destroyed because he was a potential "messiah" who could "unify and electrify" the "black nationalist movement." King was a threat because he might "abandon his supposed 'obedience' to white liberal doctrines (nonviolence)."[3] Thus, an apostle of nonviolence had to be secretly attacked and destroyed as insurance against the possibility he might abandon nonviolence.

In the words of the Bureau officer in charge of the FBI's "war" against King, "no holds were barred." In April 1962, King had been secretly characterized as a "subversive" because he had signed, with 350 other citizens, a petition to abolish the House Un-American Activities Committee (HUAC), which investigated—often irresponsibly—purported communist influence in the United States. One month later, the FBI put King on a secret list of citizens to be rounded up in a national emergency. With 26,000 other targets, King was again classed a "subversive" who was in "a position to influence others against the national interest."[4]

The Bureau also sought to undermine Dr. King's organization by attempting to scare away SCLC funders. It got the Internal Revenue Service to engage in intrusive and burdensome audits. Without a judicial warrant, but with the knowledge and approval of Attorney General Robert Kennedy, the Bureau tapped the telephones of King, several of his advisors, and the SCLC office. Also, without warrants, the FBI bugged hotel rooms in which King stayed. Justifying its warrantless spying as a way of investigating possible Communist influence, the Bureau nonetheless paid only desultory attention to possible Communist links. Instead, government spying focused on King's civil rights work. FBI agents collected political intelligence for the White House about the plans of King and the broader civil rights movement. Worse, Bureau agents sought and exploited personal information about King in an effort to discredit him with, among others, the Pope, churches in America and Paris, universities, the press, funders, and public officials. (The assault on King's reputation continued even after his death.)[5]

The FBI campaign against King hit a low in November 1964. King had previously been critical of Bureau effectiveness in protecting civil rights. To explain why, he sent FBI Director J. Edgar Hoover a telegram saying that he "sincerely questioned the effectiveness of the FBI in racial incidents, particularly where bombings and brutality against Negroes are at issue." The following day, the Bureau mailed King a cassette tape of recordings—from bugs placed in hotel rooms—containing personal and intimate communications. According to Bureau records, the tape was "sterilize[d] . . . to prevent it being traced to the Bureau." With the tape came an anonymous letter, which told King, "You know you are a complete fraud . . . an evil, vicious one at that . . . your end is approaching." It concluded:

> King, there is only one thing left for you to do. You know what it is. . . .
> You are done. There is but one way out for you. You better take it before
> your filthy, fraudulent self is bared to the nation.

Dr. King and his associates interpreted the letter as an attempt to induce him to commit suicide.[6]

A Bible in one hand and the Declaration of Independence and Bill of Rights in the other, King urged America to "live out the true meaning of its creed." How could the American government come to the point of trying to destroy Dr. King? J. Edgar Hoover's personal animus against King, and his profound distaste for the social changes pressed by the civil rights movement, played important roles. But without an institutional underpinning, Hoover's bias would not have taken the form of a massive, multiyear surveillance and harassment campaign. The war against King highlights what happens when checks and balances are abandoned. The FBI, like other intelligence agencies during the Cold War, operated under a shroud of secrecy, without clear legal rules or adequate independent oversight by either Congress or the FBI's nominal chief, the attorney general. In the absence of these restraints, Hoover's particular biases could become official policy. FBI officials were not called upon to justify the lawfulness or propriety of their programs. Rather, the Bureau aggressively exploited the fuzzy boundaries of its legal mandate to justify illicit activities, such as the campaign against Dr. King.

While the King story is particularly vicious, it exemplifies the pathologies that enabled the executive branch during the Cold War to violate the law repeatedly and act in ways fundamentally inconsistent with America's best traditions. Thus, when questioned about tactics used against Dr. King, the FBI official in charge of domestic intelligence echoed the rationale of General Doolittle's 1954 presidential task force: intelligence is "a rough, tough business. . . . We have used that technique against Soviet agents. They have used it against us." Asked by Senator Walter "Fritz" Mondale at a Church Committee hearing whether anybody had objected to the tactics used against Dr. King, the FBI official testified, "As far as legality is concerned, morals or ethics, [these were] never raised by myself or anybody else."[7]

The Church Committee's multivolume reports and hearings document countless examples of abuses along the lines of those perpetrated against Martin Luther King by the major intelligence agencies, including the FBI, the CIA, and the National Security Agency, or NSA. The records of Cold War abuse show how the nation dealt with an earlier generation's crisis, and how presidents, attorneys general, and other high-ranking executive branch officials—as well as Congress—fell short of their obligations to oversee and control the intelligence agencies.[8]

The Committee found that all too often, executive branch actions—taken in the name of nebulous concepts like "national security," or "subversion," shielded by secrecy, and without the guidance of clear laws—were not "governed and controlled in accord with the fundamental principles of our constitutional system of government." As a result, the Committee's report concluded, America's secret government did far too many "illegal, improper or unethical" deeds that did not reflect "the ideals which have given the people of this country and of the world hope for a better, fuller, fairer life."[9]

Secret intelligence action was used to harass, disrupt, and even destroy law-abiding domestic groups and citizens. Too many people were spied on with excessively intrusive techniques often known to be illegal. Intelligence agencies conducted secret surveillance and infiltration of entirely lawful groups. Mail was illegally opened. Without their knowledge, Americans were dosed with dangerous drugs to test techniques being developed to combat the Soviets. Congress received incomplete or misleading intelligence on subjects of national concern, such as whether the civil rights movement or anti–Vietnam War protests were controlled from overseas. Presidents solicited intelligence agencies to spy on political opponents. The CIA attempted for years to assassinate Fidel Castro—among other assassination plots—even enlisting the Mafia in its efforts.

It is necessary not only to know the details of *what* happened, but also to understand *how* it happened, so that we can prevent it happening again. The elementary lesson still pertinent today is that in times of crisis, zealous government officials are prone to overreacting, forgetting or rejecting the Constitution's diffusion of power between the branches. Institutions go awry. An absence of checks permits abuse of intelligence powers, harming innocent Americans. During the Cold War, the agencies charged with protecting the nation slipped from legal and ethical moorings. The resulting overreaction stained the nation's reputation and made its citizens no safer.

Recently, as America begins to question how our nation should react to the new crisis caused by terrorism, references back to abuses during the Cold War period began to circulate. The public and media tended to identify abuses with the Nixon years, or even reduce them to a solitary event: Watergate. This reflexive habit hides much more than it explains. Richard Nixon and longtime FBI Director J. Edgar Hoover make convenient, larger-than-life villains. But no single man, no single party, no single administration caused the abuses and overreaching of the Cold War period. Rather, administrations from Franklin Roosevelt's through Richard Nixon's all sanctioned overly broad investigations, lawless conduct, and departures from America's ideals.[10] The abuses revealed by the Church Committee, moreover, were first and foremost long-standing institutional failings, as the governmental safeguards—like clear laws and congressional oversight—meant to constrain abuses simply collapsed.

Our Secret Police State

Charged with domestic intelligence collection, the FBI during the Cold War conducted a broad range of abusive and unjustifiable actions. Bureau officials relied on their mandate to combat "subversion," the fuzzy term Franklin Delano Roosevelt first let loose in a secret instruction. This fuzzy legal mandate, which lacked clear boundaries, permitted tactics to migrate from real suspects to entirely innocent Americans, particularly those who opposed administration policies and those who protested racial discrimination or the Vietnam War. Without clear guidelines and meaningful oversight, and with the expectation of permanent secrecy, abuse of the Bureau's powers began and steadily expanded.

In perhaps the most significant action, the Bureau developed COINTELPRO (Counterintelligence Program), an ugly program using tactics more suited to a police state than to the United States. Without the public's knowledge, COINTELPRO lasted from 1956 to April 1971. FBI Director Hoover terminated it only out of fear of public exposure. The program had nothing to do with "counterintelligence." Rather, the bureau conducted illegal investigations and meted out secret punishments. COINTELPRO "brought home" to America tactics previously used only overseas in combating the Soviets.[11]

According to FBI agents who participated in it, the first COINTELPRO program—directed against Communist Party members—was prompted by frustration with Supreme Court rulings that made criminal prosecution of party members "ineffective" or "impossible." These landmark Court rulings used the First Amendment to interpret the 1940 Smith Act, which criminalized advocacy of revolutionary violence, making it difficult to obtain convictions based on radical speech alone. Rather than comply, the FBI secretly circumvented the Court's decisions. The Bureau then expanded COINTELPRO to other dissident groups against whom, the Bureau concluded, "there were not adequate statutes" to deploy.[12] Indeed, when asked whether, during COINTELPRO's fifteen-year history, anybody at the FBI had discussed the program's constitutionality or legality, the former head of the Bureau's Racial Intelligence Section, George Moore, answered, "No, we never gave it a thought."[13]

COINTELPRO's growth exemplified the mission creep that happens when clear boundaries are lacking. The FBI moved incrementally from the Communist Party to the Socialist Workers Party, to "White Hate Groups," to "Black Nationalist Hate Groups," and on to the "New Left," a vague catch-all phrase that covered emerging protest groups, mostly of young people. Bureau agents used COINTELPRO as a way secretly to "disrupt" and "neutralize" all these groups.[14]

The FBI defined each of these targets extremely broadly. Thus the "Communist Party" program swept up not only Communist Party ranks, but also, among others, members of the National Committee to Abolish the House Un-American Activities Committee and civil rights leaders tagged as insufficiently "anti-Communist." Under the Bureau's label of "Black Nationalist

Hate Groups" fell organizations as varied as the Black Panthers, Dr. King's Southern Christian Leadership Conference, and most black student groups at universities.

COINTELPRO disruption of the "New Left" also lacked defined boundaries. Under that rubric, FBI agents targeted groups as varied as Students for a Democratic Society (or SDS), the entire student body of Antioch College, publishers of underground newspapers, and college students protesting university censorship of student publications.[15] Having secretly decided to step over the limits imposed by the First Amendment, the Bureau enjoyed few restrictions on its activities.

COINTELPRO's methods were as diverse as its targets. Its tactics ranged from promoting violence to breaking up the marriages of civil rights workers and of Ku Klux Klan members. FBI agents sabotaged political campaigns. They falsely labeled intended victims as government informers to provoke reprisals against them. Agents succeeded in stopping citizens from speaking, teaching, writing, or publishing. All of this was done secretly without authorization by statute, review by courts, or oversight from Congress. FBI headquarters approved operations so long as they would not "embarrass the Bureau"—which meant so long as the Bureau's role could be kept concealed.[16]

In a faint precursor to post-9/11 practices such as extraordinary rendition, violence against some targets during this period was outsourced. For example, the Bureau forged a letter purporting to come from the Chicago Black Panthers and sent it to the leader of the Blackstone Rangers, a "black extremist organization in Chicago." The letter falsely said the Panthers had "a hit out" on the Rangers' leader. Predicting that the letter would lead to "reprisals" against the Panthers' leadership, the internal Bureau request for approval explained that agents believed that the Rangers were prone to "violent type activity, shooting and the like."[17]

In the same vein, the San Diego FBI office boasted that it fomented violence in the "ghetto":

> Shootings, beatings, and a high degree of unrest continues to prevail in the ghetto area of southeast San Diego. Although no specific counterintelligence action can be *credited* with contributing to this overall situation, it is felt that a substantial amount of the unrest is directly attributable to [COINTELPRO].[18]

Another favored FBI method involved falsely labeling a target as a government informer, a technique known as the "snitch jacket." Asked by the Church Committee about the dangers of this technique, the chief of the Bureau's Racial Intelligence Unit told the Committee that while snitch jackets were used in his area of work, he was not aware of anyone being killed as a result. But, he added, he could not be certain whether this was due to "luck or planning": "It just happened that way, I am sure." Snitch jackets, however, continued in use after two suspected informers were killed by one of the target groups (albeit without Bureau involvement).[19]

COINTELPRO targets were not limited to famous political figures such as Dr. King or those on the fringes of law-abiding society such as members of the Klan. Among the hundreds of innocent individual citizens targeted were members of the Unitarian Society of Cleveland, who became targets because the Society's minister and some members had circulated a petition calling for the dissolution of the House Un-American Activities Committee. Similarly, the Bureau sent anonymous lodging "disinformation" to protesters traveling to Chicago for the 1968 Democratic Convention, causing them "long and useless journeys." Nonviolent citizens opposed to the Vietnam War were targeted because they gave "aid and comfort" to violent demonstrators solely by lending respectability to their cause.[20]

Without doubt, the government has a right and duty to prosecute lawless acts by, for example, the Black Panthers or the Ku Klux Klan. But this cannot justify the FBI's decision to use COINTELPRO to secretly usurp the functions of judge and jury.[21]

COINTELPRO disruption efforts often relied on the fruits of secret surveillance by wiretaps, bugs, break-ins, and mail opening targeting American citizens. The FBI justified its intrusive surveillance programs by relying on the ambiguous mandate handed down from the White House. On some occasions, intelligence agencies using these techniques knowingly and intentionally broke the law. And, as happened often during the Cold War, mission creep resulted in the net of surveillance being cast wider and wider.

For fifty years, the federal government secretly sought to preserve its power to wiretap and bug Americans without a warrant from a court.[22] After the Supreme Court began requiring warrants, presidents and attorneys general secretly ordered the FBI to continue using electronic surveillance without warrants, claiming exceptions to the Supreme Court decisions under the usual elastic terms such as "national security." It was only after the Church Committee's exposure of decades of abusive and excessive surveillance of Americans that Congress, in 1978, passed a law that finally put an end to warrantless electronic surveillance of Americans (or at least so it seemed until after 9/11).

Electronic communications, of course, did not exist at the time of the Constitution's framing. But because taps and bugs pick up everything said on the tapped phone or in the bugged room, they raise the same worries the American colonists had about so-called "writs of assistance" or "general warrants," which the British king's revenue officers used to conduct "unrestricted, indiscriminate searches of persons and homes." The colonial administrations' use of general warrants was one of the primary reasons for the Fourth Amendment's requirement of judicial warrants before most government searches. Despite Supreme Court Justice Louis D. Brandeis's warning that "writs of assistance and general warrants" are "but puny instruments of tyranny and oppression when compared with wire tapping," the Supreme Court, in 1928 in the *Olmstead* case initially resisted Brandeis's insight.[23]

Six years after *Olmstead*, Congress filled the gap in legal protection by making it a crime for "any person" to "intercept and divulge or publish" the contents of wire and radio communications.[24] But despite the new law and a Supreme Court ruling that it applied to federal agents as well as ordinary citizens,[25] the Justice Department secretly concluded it could continue to engage in warrantless wiretapping but would "comply" with the law by not distributing its intercepts outside the government. Only when Attorney General Robert Jackson took office in 1940 did the FBI cease warrantless wiretapping.[26] But President Roosevelt soon overruled Jackson. In a confidential memorandum, Roosevelt said that he was "convinced" the Supreme Court did not mean to apply its decision to "grave matters involving the defense of the nation." (Roosevelt's conviction found no justification in the opinion the Supreme Court in fact issued.) Therefore, he secretly ordered government agents to continue intercepting communications of "persons suspected of subversive activities."[27] As in his earlier order to Hoover, however, Roosevelt did not explain what "subversive" meant, or why judicial warrants could not be sought for such interceptions.

In 1954, the Supreme Court reaffirmed that a bug placed in a house during a warrantless break-in violated the Fourth Amendment. The Court seemed particularly offended by the placement of a microphone in a bedroom, and forwarded the case file to Attorney General Herbert Brownell to determine whether the federal criminal statute had been violated.[28] Even after this clear judicial signal of disapproval, however, Attorney General Brownell sent a secret memo to Hoover authorizing continued "unrestricted use" of bugs whenever the Bureau concluded it was in the "national interest."[29] As with Roosevelt's order to Jackson, Brownell's secret order, based on the open-ended term "national interest," manifested clear disregard for the law and the courts. It also opened the door to many abuses, including the bugging of Dr. King's hotel rooms.

Thirteen years later, in 1967, the Supreme Court revisited *Olmstead* and held that the Fourth Amendment barred warrantless electronic surveillance. In a footnote, however, the Court declined to extend its decision to cases "involving the national security."[30] The Court did not elaborate on that abstract caveat, seemingly unaware that those very terms had been long used by the government to circumvent earlier judicial rulings and already had underwritten years of excessive spying. In 1972, in the so-called *Keith* case, the Court further constrained government surveillance powers by holding that the president's constitutional authority did not allow for warrantless taps or bugs in cases involving claims of threats to "domestic security." The Court acknowledged that the government's position that warrants might sometimes make efforts to protect "national security" more difficult might have some "pragmatic force," but it still held that warrants were needed. Expressing concerns akin to those Attorney General Jackson had voiced thirty years earlier, Justice Lewis Powell explained:

> History abundantly documents the tendency of government—however benevolent and benign its motives—to view with suspicion those who most fervently dispute its policies. Fourth Amendment protections become the more necessary when the targets of official surveillance may be those suspected of unorthodoxy in their political beliefs.[31]

The Court cautioned, however, that it did not decide what the rules would be for warrantless electronic surveillance in cases where there was a "significant connection with a foreign power, its agents or agencies."[32]

At every opportunity during the Cold War, the executive branch secretly used vague, fuzzily worded loopholes to allow it to continue conducting warrantless searches in spite of repeated signals from Congress and the courts to desist In 1976, moreover, the Church Committee "abundantly document[ed]" a "history" that went far beyond that alluded to by Justice Powell The record, compiled by the Committee, "clearly show[ed]" that imprecise and open-ended terms like "'national security,' 'domestic security,' 'subversive activities,' and 'foreign intelligence,'" when "coupled with the absence of any outside scrutiny, has led to improper use of intrusive techniques against American citizens who posed no criminal or national security threat to the country."[33]

In some cases, the Bureau deployed even more aggressive, and clearly illegal, techniques: break-ins and mail opening. The CIA also illegally opened letters in the United States.[34] The Bureau called its warrantless break-ins and burglaries "black bag jobs." FBI officials recognized that these "techniques" "involve[d] trespassing" and were "clearly illegal." Nonetheless, the officials justified the actions to Hoover as valuable tools in their war against "subversion." The label "subversion" served, for example, to justify as many as ninety warrantless break-ins at the offices of the Socialist Workers Party between 1960 and 1966 alone. The Bureau later conceded that the party was committing no crimes, and that its overheated but constitutionally protected rhetoric fell far short of incitement to violence.[35]

Nebulous terms such as "national security" were, moreover, cynically employed after the fact to shield obviously illegal break-ins. In 1973, President Nixon and White House counsel John Dean discussed on tape a White House–ordered break-in at the office of a California psychiatrist in search of a patient's files. This patient, Daniel Ellsberg, was responsible for leaking to the *New York Times* the Pentagon Papers, an unflattering multivolume history of the Vietnam War prepared by the Defense Department itself. When the President asked what could be done if the break-in were revealed, Dean suggested, "You might put it on a national security grounds basis." Later in the conversation, the President took up Dean's suggestion, saying "the whole thing was national security." Dean replied, "I think we could get by on that."[36]

Similarly, for over twenty years the Bureau engaged in a massive illegal mail-opening program. The FBI official involved said it was his "assumption" that "what we were doing was justified by . . . the greater good, the national security."[37] In 1966, the FBI halted its own illegal mail-opening program, thereafter relying on the CIA's program. Meanwhile, at least four internal CIA memoranda recognized that the CIA's mail-opening program had "no legal basis"; that "federal statutes preclude the concoction of any legal excuse"; and that exposure could "give rise to grave charges of criminal misuse of the mails by government agencies." Instead of shutting down the program, however, the CIA's inspector general (tasked with policing legal and ethical violations within the Agency) suggested fabricating a false "cover story" given the "possibility that the operation might be blown." The deputy chief of the CIA's Counterintelligence Staff responded that it would be "relatively easy to 'hush up'" the entire affair, or to "explain" falsely that the mail opening was actually "legal mail cover activities conducted by the Post Office at the request of authorized Federal agencies." But, the deputy chief added, if these tactics didn't work, "it might be necessary, after the matter has cooled off during an extended period of investigation, to find a scapegoat to blame."[38]

At its start, the CIA's "watch list" of names of people and organizations whose mail was to be illegally opened contained fewer than twenty names. But, in another instance of mission creep, by the late 1960s the watch list had grown to approximately six hundred, including many citizens and organizations engaged in purely lawful and constitutionally protected protest against government policies. Among the domestic organizations on the CIA's list were Clergy and Laymen Concerned About Vietnam, *Ramparts* magazine, the Student Nonviolent Coordinating Committee, and the American Friends Service Committee. It was not only the mail of citizens on the watch list that was opened, however. The CIA opened the letters of many others, including Senator Frank Church and author John Steinbeck. And, during the 1968 presidential campaign, it even opened a letter passing between Richard Nixon and a speechwriter. The CIA's illegal mail-opening program ultimately generated a computerized index of nearly one and a half million names.[39]

The NSA captured even more communications of Americans. From 1945 until 1975, by agreement with the major cable companies, the NSA secured copies of every cable sent by individuals or businesses from this country to overseas locations. This far-reaching surveillance initially was justified by NSA employees as an effort to obtain encrypted messages sent by foreign embassies. But, like other programs, it soon expanded and ended up sweeping in the communications of Americans, including the leaders of demonstrations against the Vietnam War and for civil rights. Absent any legislative oversight—the NSA lacked a statutory charter—every single international cable became fair game.[40]

The NSA never even considered whether it was bound by the Fourth Amendment, court rulings, or congressional statutes. It simply assumed it was exempt from Supreme Court precedents and laws prohibiting warrantless surveillance because it labeled its spying "foreign intelligence," even when the communications covered protest activities of Americans in the United States who happened to send cables overseas.[41] The NSA thus operated without any independent restraint from another branch of government. Similarly, another Defense Department intelligence component, the Army Security Agency, was told by the Federal Communications Commission that its monitoring of radio communications to and from amateur radio operators was illegal, but it nonetheless plowed ahead with that monitoring.[42]

The Church Committee concluded that the secret decisions by the FBI, CIA, and NSA to discard or circumvent clear legal rules by relying on fuzzy, open-ended labels like "subversion," "national security," or "foreign intelligence" led to too much being collected from too many for too long:[43] millions of law-abiding Americans were spied upon by their government in secret and without the safeguard of a judicial warrant; the information collected was often wholly irrelevant to any lawful governmental purpose—indeed, sometimes, as with Dr. King, the government's principal purpose was to collect embarrassing personal information. Surveillance often continued long after it became clear no legitimate end was being served.

The Church Committee's investigation yielded many examples of wholly legitimate political and social groups subjected to illicit surveillance. Thus, FBI informers infiltrated the NAACP for twenty-five years from 1941 to 1966, even though from the outset of the surveillance the Bureau had no information to suggest that the NAACP's purposes were anything but lawful.[44] Individuals in the civil rights movement also faced seemingly endless investigations. The FBI directed three COINTELPRO actions against Bayard Rustin, a civil rights leader, principal organizer of the 1963 March on Washington, and occasional advisor to Dr. King. He was wiretapped for many years as a suspected Communist "sympathizer," even though a lengthy investigation by the Bureau's New York field office concluded that he in fact had no Communist connections. Hoover nevertheless ordered that the investigation continue because, "while there may not be any evidence that [Rustin] is a communist, neither is there substantial evidence that he is anti-communist."[45]

The FBI in the late sixties and early seventies also conducted broad investigations of what it called the "Women's Liberation Movement." Without any evidence of wrongdoing, the Bureau infiltrated women's rights activist groups around the country and generated voluminous reports detailing political and social beliefs. Once spying started, it kept going despite the clear absence of any lawful government interest. One lengthy FBI report concluded the purpose of an infiltrated women's gathering had been to "free women from the humdrum existence of being only a wife and mother." Following this report, Bureau officials instructed the field to keep on investigating. Worse, the CIA, which had no mandate to spy in the United States at all, also investigated the "Women's Liberation Movement."[46]

For about forty years, government informants infiltrated the Socialist Workers Party (SWP), even though, as Bureau officials conceded, the party had not committed any crimes and its rhetoric fell short of incitement to violence. According to the agent leading the investigation, FBI reporting covered the party's positions on the "Vietnam War," "food prices," "racial matters," "U.S. involvement in Angola," and its efforts to support a non-SWP candidate for electoral office—all speech at the core of the First Amendment's protection.[47]

These roving inquiries into the NAACP, women's rights groups, the Socialist Workers Party, and Bayard Rustin illustrate how investigations, coupled with intrusive surveillance, continued far beyond any conceivable justifiable scope in the absence of clear limits set by law and any meaningful oversight. Former Attorney General Nicholas Katzenbach told the Church Committee how such endless investigations could occur:

> The custom [had been] not to put a time limit on a tap, or any wiretap authorization. Indeed, I think the Bureau would have felt free in 1965 to put a tap on a phone authorized by Attorney General Jackson before World War II.[48]

The pervasiveness of domestic surveillance was also reflected in the sheer volume of Americans spied upon. The FBI opened more than 500,000 domestic intelligence files, each typically including several individuals' names. The army investigated more than 100,000 Americans for political reasons between the mid-1960s and 1971. (Army investigations included matters of such vital national importance as a Catholic priests' conference on birth control in Colorado and a Halloween party for Washington, D.C., schoolchildren, targeted because the army suspected a local "dissident" would be present.)[49] As part of Operation CHAOS—a domestic spying operation, begun at the request of the Johnson and Nixon White Houses, looking (unsuccessfully) for proof that antiwar protest groups were controlled by foreign interests—the CIA obtained information about hundreds of thousands of Americans that it indexed into computer records.[50] And the NSA obtained copies of millions of international cables as part of the "largest governmental interception program affecting Americans" during the Cold War.[51]

Having collected all this information—violating numerous laws in the process—intelligence agencies were hardly about to do nothing with their yield. Excess surveillance led to excess dissemination. For example, in 1970 the FBI distributed to all military intelligence agencies, two other units of the Defense Department and two units of the Secret Service, a sixteen-page report on the picketing of an Industries of the Blind plant by a group of "blind black workers." Included in the report was a copy of a handbill supporting the strike distributed at a local United Church of Christ. Similarly, the Bureau sent to army and air force intelligence and to the Secret Service a report on a "tea" sponsored by a group developing faculty-student dialogue at a junior college and on the college's plans for a course on "The History of the American Negro."[52]

An excess of such reports impeded attention to more important security issues. Flooded with reports, intelligence agencies disparaged the information they got from each other. Thus, the Secret Service destroyed more than 90 percent of the material it got from the FBI. And the FBI characterized as "junk" most of the material it got on "the domestic scene" from the CIA's illegal mail-opening program.[53]

Collecting information on legitimate speech also led the Bureau toward dangerous plans. Drawing on its surveillance files, the FBI drew up a secret list of 26,000 citizens to be rounded up and detained in a "national emergency." The list included Dr. King and author Norman Mailer, with the latter making the list thanks to his "subversive associations and ideology." The list also included "professors, teachers, and educators; labor union organizers and leaders; writers, lecturers, newsmen and others in the mass media field, scientists, doctors and lawyers," all slated for detention because of their lawful First Amendment activities.[54] In a vicious logic, an initially illicit activity—here, the surveillance of constitutionally protected activity—thus found justification in a further illicit end: plans for mass detentions on the basis of constitutionally protected opinions.

Mission creep was not limited to agencies dedicated solely to intelligence. The Internal Revenue Service also embarked on many thousands of tax investigations based upon pressure from presidents—starting with John F. Kennedy—and from intelligence agencies to investigate individuals or entities that opposed government policies. The IRS itself requested lists of targets for audits of "dissident or extremist" groups from the FBI and the Justice Department—who provided the lists in order to "deal a blow" to dissidents. People and organizations singled out for IRS investigations for ideological reasons included the Ford Foundation, the Urban League, singer Joan Baez, actor Sammy Davis Jr., actress Shirley MacLaine, columnist Jimmy Breslin, *Rolling Stone* and *Playboy* magazines, and antiwar senators Charles Goodell and Ernest Gruening.[55]

Political Uses of Intelligence Information

Unrestrained and secret use of intelligence agencies' awesome powers of surveillance and intrusion gave the executive branch a tremendous amount of information. Executive officials mined this information in ways that opened the door to political abuse of two kinds. First, inaccurate intelligence information supplied selectively to politicians influenced social policy and political action on important national issues such as civil rights and the Vietnam War, distorting democratic decision making. Second, presidents and other senior executive officials asked for and used intelligence information for naked political ends.[56] The threat, in other words, morphed from "threats to the nation" to "threats to the party."

The first problem is illustrated by FBI reporting on the civil rights movement. The Bureau never found any evidence to rebut its initial conclusion, based on secret infiltration of the NAACP, that communist efforts had not succeeded in steering the civil rights movement; nevertheless, the Bureau hinted elusively to the White House in 1956 that communist or communist-front organizations were to blame for "a marked deterioration in relationships between the races." FBI Director Hoover subsequently briefed the Eisenhower cabinet on alleged communist influence upon civil rights groups. According to one historian, this briefing "reinforced the President's . . . passivity" on civil rights legislation.[57]

In 1963, the Bureau's Domestic Intelligence Division submitted to Hoover a memo detailing Communist Party "efforts" to exploit black Americans' discontent with race relations. The memo concluded these efforts were an "obvious failure." Hoover was dissatisfied. He made it clear to the Division that "we had to change our ways or we would all be out on the street." A new memo was generated. "The Director is correct," it said; Dr. King was the "most dangerous Negro" from the "standpoint of communism . . . and national security." It was "unrealistic" to limit FBI analysis to "legalistic proofs or definitely conclusive evidence." Communist Party influence over Negroes "one day *could* become decisive." Yet even this was not quite the message Hoover promulgated outside the Bureau. Subsequently testifying to Congress, Hoover represented that communist influence among Negroes and civil rights organizations in fact *was* "vitally important."[58]

Intelligence reflecting political ideology rather than facts was not limited to domestic issues. In 1965, President Johnson told Hoover he had "no doubt" communists were behind demonstrations against the Vietnam War. Hoover agreed. Back at the FBI, Hoover told his associates he knew the Bureau might not be able to "technically state" what the President wanted, but what Hoover said he wanted—and what he got—was a "good, strong memorandum" for the President that made communist "efforts" read like communist successes.[59]

Intelligence agencies were also keenly attuned to politicians' desires. Much of the CIA's secret domestic spying, including Operation CHAOS, responded to pressure from the Johnson and Nixon White Houses for intelligence about foreign influence on anti–Vietnam War protest groups in America. CIA chief Richard Helms testified that President Johnson was "after this [kind of infor mation] all the time." CIA reports suggesting that foreign elements played "no significant role" in antiwar protests met with skeptical resistance from both White Houses. In response, the CIA expanded its intrusion on Americans' First Amendment activities, albeit without ever changing its conclusion.[60]

The force of presidential pressure is shown by Helms's compliance with requests he knew to be improper. Conscious of the law barring the CIA from "internal security functions," Helms cautioned the Johnson White House of the "peculiar sensitivity" of CIA surveillance of protest groups in America. Writing later to Henry Kissinger, then Nixon's National Security Advisor, Helms referred to the CIA's domestic spying as "extremely sensitive," and added that "[t]his is an area not within the charter of this agency." If anyone learned what the CIA was doing, Helms warned, it "would prove most embarrassing for all concerned."[61] Known illegality was cause for heightened secrecy—not for stopping illegal conduct.

Rather than furthering American intelligence efforts, the cloak of secrecy allowed the intelligence services to become politicized and lose sight of their proper mission. Although all administrations from Roosevelt to Nixon asked for and received political information from the FBI,[62] the Johnson and Nixon administrations exploited the Bureau to the greatest extent. During the closing days of the 1964 presidential election campaign, the Johnson White House sought information on all the employees of Republican candidate Barry Goldwater's Senate office. It sought information about vice presidential candidate Spiro Agnew's long distance telephone calls during the 1968 presidential campaign, and about seven senators critical of America's bombing of North Vietnam. The Bureau also supplied information on nonpoliticians, including people who signed letters to Oregon Senator Wayne Morse supporting his criticism of the Vietnam War, and many mainstream journalists, including NBC anchor David Brinkley, *Life* magazine's Washington bureau chief Richard Stolley, and authors of books critical of the Warren Commission report (about the assassination of President Kennedy).[63] The nexus between collecting intelligence and White House political interests reached its acme during the 1964 Democratic Convention in Atlantic City, New Jersey. President Johnson directed the assignment of an FBI "special squad." Originally justified by vague reference to possible civil disorders, the squad's mandate expanded to cover surveillance of political activities. The special squad thus generated many memos to the White House on the political plans of Dr. King and the Mississippi Freedom Democratic Party, a new black party challenging convention delegates from the old-line, segregationist Mississippi Democratic Party.[64]

These practices continued under the Nixon White House, which pushed for information on, for example, CBS reporter Daniel Schorr and the chairman of Americans for Democratic Action. Vice President Spiro Agnew also sought information on Ralph Abernathy, Dr. King's successor as head of the Southern Christian Leadership Conference. An internal Bureau document reporting the request explained that Agnew's purpose was "destroying Abernathy's credibility."[65] No one at the Bureau thought to protest that this was an improper goal.

Bureau reports to the Nixon White House about the fruits of warrantless wiretaps placed from 1969 to 1971 on three newsmen and fourteen executive branch employees at Henry Kissinger's request show how politicization and mission creep went hand in hand. Information obtained and disseminated concerned matters unrelated to the purported reason for the taps, which were supposed to uncover the source of leaks to the media from the White House. Instead, they yielded political information for the White House: a report on Senator Edward Kennedy's planned speech on Vietnam; the expected timing of Senator William Fulbright's hearings on Vietnam; Senator Mondale's "dilemma" about a trade bill; and what former President Johnson had said about Senator Edmund Muskie's campaign for the Democratic Party nomination for president. The taps continued on two targets even after they left the government to work on Senator Muskie's presidential campaign. Revealingly, the resulting memos began to flow to H.R. Haldeman, Nixon's political advisor, rather than to Kissinger, his national security advisor, even though it had been Kissinger who had first demanded the warrantless wiretaps for "national security reasons."[66]

The CIA: Covert Action Abroad and at Home

The National Security Act of 1947 established the CIA but did not mention covert action. Shortly after the agency's birth, however, covert action rose to dominate the CIA's portfolio. Initially a limited, ad hoc response to specific Soviet threats in Europe, covert action "soon became a routine program secretly influencing governments and covertly exercising power, involving literally hundreds of discreet actions each year." By 1953, major covert operations were ongoing in forty-eight countries. As their volume increased, they shifted purpose. For example, in the late 1940s the CIA provided concealed support to beleaguered democratic parties in France and Italy facing stiff electoral challenges from robust communist parties. But as time passed, the CIA increasingly took the offense with covert action, overthrowing governments in Iran and Guatemala, for example, as well as many other less spectacular efforts.[67]

The very existence of America's covert action programs was meant to be secret, known only to a select few within the executive branch. This secrecy became a source of power. By forestalling serious policy debate among and within branches of government, secrecy allowed presidents to circumvent the checks and balances our Constitution installs even for decision making about foreign policy. What followed were certainly not uniformly wise decisions. As the Church Committee concluded, covert actions were generally more "successful" when they were "consistent with, and in tactical support of, policies which have emerged from a national debate and the established processes of government."[68] As time passed, knowledge of some CIA covert actions became widespread. According to former Secretary of Defense Clark Clifford, this resulted in "our country [being] accused of being responsible for practically every internal difficulty that has occurred in every country in the world."[69]

Two covert actions suggest how untethered from the 1947 National Security Act's initial plan the CIA's activity became: one was the unsuccessful efforts to assassinate Fidel Castro; the other, the successful campaign to subvert democratic government in Chile.

The CIA began plotting to kill Fidel Castro in the summer of 1960; its efforts lasted through 1965. Only during the fall of 1962—the period of highest tension, when Cuba stood at the nub of a major global crisis thanks to Soviet placement of missiles on the island—were all covert actions against the Cuban regime temporarily suspended.[70] The Church Committee was surprised to find a fog of ambiguity about final responsibility for the Castro plots. Presidents Eisenhower, Kennedy, and Johnson were in office while the CIA embarked on several Castro assassination plots, although the Committee found that Johnson did not authorize the plots during his administration.[71] For Eisenhower and Kennedy, the authorization question proved more nettlesome.

By itself, the Committee's finding that the chain of authorization for such a vital decision as assassinating a foreign leader was not crystal clear was revealing. As the Committee was to discover, uncertainty was built into the national security decision-making system to ensure "plausible deniability."[72]

Determining whether Eisenhower or Kennedy had authorized or knew about assassination plots proved difficult because both men were dead, as was Allen Dulles, chief of the CIA when the plots were initiated. Nonetheless, two high-ranking CIA officials, Richard Bissell and Richard Helms, testified to their belief that the two presidents indeed authorized killing Castro. While their reasoning was inconsistent and other evidence was conflicting, Bissell and Helms both described textbook examples of plausible deniability.

Bissell was head of the CIA's Directorate of Plans—a euphemistic title for the CIA department running clandestine activities, including covert action—from before initiation of the assassination plots until mid-1961, when he was pushed out by President Kennedy in the aftermath of the failed Bay of Pigs invasion of Cuba. During the Castro plots Helms was in the Directorate of Plans. After Bissell's departure, Helms became its head.[73]

Bissell "went on the assumption" that both presidents knew about the plots. According to Bissell, Dulles would have advised the two presidents of the assassination plots in a "circumlocutious" and oblique way. Circumlocution would have been used "to shield the President . . . in the sense of intimating or making clear that something of the sort was going forward, but giving the President as little information about it as possible." Dulles thus would "leave [the President] in a position to deny knowledge of the operation if it should surface." Bissell also cautioned that neither he nor anyone else in the CIA would be told about such a conversation between the Agency's chief and a president. This would "hold to the absolute minimum the number of people who knew that the President had been consulted, had been notified and had given, perhaps only tacitly, his authorization."[74]

Helms also assumed killing Castro was authorized by the two presidents but doubted Bissell's assumption that they were told anything. It would not be appropriate, Helms explained, "to embarrass a President of the United States [by] discussing the assassination of foreign leaders in his presence." Nonetheless, Helms insisted that the Agency had authority to kill Castro even in the absence of a specific directive or authorization. Both President Kennedy and his brother Robert exerted "very intense" pressure to overthrow Castro, and "if killing him was one of the things that was to be done in this connection, that was within what was expected."[75]

In the course of Helms's testimony before the Church Committee, Senator Charles "Mac" Mathias drew an historical analogy with the twelfth century English King Henry II and Thomas Becket, archbishop of Canterbury, who was a thorn in Henry's side, and who was stabbed to death in Canterbury Cathedral by Henry's courtiers:

> SENATOR MATHIAS: Let me draw an example from history. When Thomas Becket was proving to be an annoyance, as Castro, the king said, "Who will rid me of this man?" He didn't say to somebody, "Go out and murder him." He said "Who will rid me of this man?" and let it go at that.
>
> MR. HELMS: That is a warming reference to the problem.
>
> SENATOR MATHIAS: You feel that spans the generations and the centuries?
>
> MR. HELMS: I think it does, sir.
>
> SENATOR MATHIAS: And that is typical of the kind of thing which might be said, which might be taken by the Director or by anybody else as presidential authorization to go forward?
>
> MR. HELMS: That is right. But in answer to that, I realize that one sort of grows up in [the] tradition of the time and I think that any of us would have found it very difficult to discuss assassinations with a president of the U.S. I just think we all had the feeling that we're hired to keep those things out of the Oval Office.
>
> SENATOR MATHIAS: Yet at the same time, you felt that some spark had been transmitted, that that was within the permissible limits?
>
> MR. HELMS: Yes, and if he had disappeared from the scene they would not have been unhappy.[76]

The Committee's study of the Castro (and other) assassination plots, as well as its investigation of other covert actions, revealed a foolish system that allowed, or encouraged, "the most sensitive matters to be presented to the highest levels of government with the least clarity" to maintain plausible deniability.[77]

From Chile's independence in 1818 until September 11, 1973, when the democratically elected government of Salvador Allende was overthrown in a military coup d'état, the country enjoyed a remarkable continuity of democratic rule, experiencing only three brief interruptions and none since 1932.[78] During the Cold War, the United States gave Chile more financial aid per capita than any other country in Latin America—well over a billion dollars between 1962 and 1968 alone. Besides this overt aid, the United States became deeply involved in covert action in Chile. Most was directed against Salvador Allende, who ran for Chilean president three times, starting in 1958 and finally succeeding in 1970. Allende's electoral platform involved redistribution of income, nationalization of major industries (especially copper), agrarian reform, and strengthened relations with socialist and communist countries.[79]

During the 1970 election, acting with the approval of the White House, the CIA waged secret "spoiling" operations against Allende's coalition with about one million U.S. taxpayer dollars. Despite this, Allende won a plurality. But, because he did not win a majority, under Chile's constitution the Chilean Congress had to choose the president from between the two top vote getters.[80]

Just after the Chilean election but before the Chilean Congress's action, President Nixon called CIA chief Richard Helms to the White House for a meeting with National Security Advisor Henry Kissinger and Attorney General John Mitchell. The President instructed Helms to foment a coup by the Chilean military before the Chilean Congress could select a winner. Helms's notes from the meeting included "$10,000,000 available, more if necessary" to subvert Chile's democratic election. As Helms later testified to the Church Committee, Nixon "came down very hard that he wanted something done, and he didn't care how. . . . If I ever carried a marshal's baton in my knapsack out of the Oval Office, it was that day." But Helms was also instructed not to tell the 40 Committee (the body established by the White House to review covert actions) or the Defense or State Departments about the plan for a coup.[81]

The CIA cultivated support for a coup among high-ranking Chilean military officers, with the exception of General Rene Schneider, commander in chief of the Chilean army, who insisted that the Chilean constitution be followed and presidential selection left to the Congress. Frustrated by Schneider, military leaders of the prospective coup decided to kidnap him. The CIA supplied them with weapons (including machine guns and tear gas) though they were apparently not used.[82] The initial kidnap attempt was unsuccessful, and Schneider was severely wounded resisting a second attempt. Two days later, the Chilean Congress followed their usual practice and confirmed Allende as president. Schneider died of his wounds the next day.[83]

CIA officials testified to the Church Committee that they were "told" by the White House to "continue our efforts," now aimed at Allende's ouster from the presidency. Dr. Kissinger "totally" disagreed, claiming that if "there was any further contact with military plotting, it was totally unauthorized."[84] In any event, the CIA officials explained they were "sure" that "the seeds that were laid in [the coup attempts] in 1970 had their impact in 1973" when Allende was overthrown. The system of deniability, having been temporarily abandoned during the meeting at President Nixon's office, reared its head again.

On September 11, 1973, Allende was overthrown by a military coup, committing suicide before he could be captured. The Church Committee staff report found "no hard evidence of direct U.S. assistance to the coup." At the very least, however, "the United States—by its previous actions [to foment a military coup in 1970], its existing general position of opposition to Allende, and the nature of its contacts with the Chilean military—probably gave the impression that it would not look with disfavor on a military coup."[85]

In Chile, Cuba, and elsewhere, advocates in the executive branch for a particular covert action were always "passionate" about a given short-term goal.[86] All too often, however, U.S. government officials paid insufficient attention to the long-term impact of covert actions on targeted nations—and on America's reputation. For example, many in both Chile and America were dismayed by the seventeen-year regime of General Augusto Pinochet that followed Allende's overthrow and death. In 1990, after Pinochet stepped down in the midst of popular backlash against his military regime, a "Truth and Reconciliation Commission" determined that the government killed more than three thousand people during his rule, one thousand of whom were listed as "disappeared." The 2004 report of the Chilean National Commission on Political Imprisonment and Torture catalogued 28,000 cases:

> Victims were humiliated, threatened, and beaten; exposed to extreme cold, to heat and the sun until they became dehydrated, to thirst, hunger, sleep deprivation; they were submerged in water mixed with sewage to the point of asphyxiation; electric shocks were applied to the most sensitive parts of their bodies; they were sexually humiliated, if not raped by men and animals, or forced to witness the rape and torture of their loved ones.[87]

The attendant costs to America's reputation and moral standing went unreckoned.

As with other secret tactics, there was seepage of dangerous CIA practices back into the United States. The Church Committee found that the CIA's experiments administering dangerous drugs displayed the familiar mission creep, with the Agency moving from giving them to volunteers to administering them to "unwitting" subjects. The CIA's drug experiments, facilitated by secrecy and lack of oversight, were another example of an agency knowingly violating the law.[88]

During the 1950s and 1960s, the CIA sought to understand the effects of psychotropic drugs such as LSD for both defensive and offensive reasons. The Russians might use the drugs on captured American agents, or the CIA might itself want to use them either on captured Russian agents or to disrupt and disorient targets of interest. The Agency initially gave drugs only to volunteers recruited from federal prisoners serving sentences for drug violations. The CIA, ironically (or callously), rewarded these volunteers with a dose of their own drug of choice. The Agency subsequently drifted into the secret administration of psychotropic drugs to unsuspecting civilian victims. In the Agency's sterile jargon, "unwitting . . . subjects" at "all social levels, high and low, native American and foreign" were to receive narcotics without knowing it. Recognizing that this practice was illegal and also potentially dangerous, Richard Helms, at the time a midlevel CIA executive, nonetheless secured approval for maintaining the program. He explained:

> While I share your uneasiness and distaste for any program which tends to intrude on an individual's private and legal prerogatives, I believe it is necessary that the agency maintain a central role in this activity, keep current on enemy capabilities [concerning] the manipulation of human behavior and maintain an offensive capability.[89]

One of the CIA's "unwitting" subjects was Dr. Frank Olson, a specialist in aerobiology working at the Army Biological Center at Camp Detrick, Maryland. At a 1953 conference of CIA and army scientists at a lake cabin, Dr. Sidney Gottlieb, a CIA scientist, gave Dr. Olson a dose of Cointreau laced with LSD. It killed him.[90]

Knowledge of the CIA's illegal and unethical drug experiments was kept secret for decades. The CIA's inspector general wrote in 1957:

> Precautions must be taken not only to protect operations from exposure to enemy forces, but also to conceal these activities from the American public in general. The knowledge that the Agency is engaging in unethical and illicit activities would have serious repercussions in political and diplomatic circles and would be detrimental to the accomplishment of its mission.[91]

After Olson's death, the Agency continued to experiment with "unwitting" subjects for another decade. Dr. Gottlieb and others responsible for Olson's doping received a letter from then CIA chief Allen Dulles gently criticizing them for not paying "proper consideration to the rights of the individual to whom [the drug] was being administered." But Helms was told by Dulles to inform Gottlieb and the others that the letter was "not [a] reprimand," and that no personnel file notation was being made.[92] To the contrary, Dr. Gottlieb soon received a promotion, and in 1960 he participated in a plot to assassinate the Congo's Patrice Lumumba by using a deadly toothpaste Gottlieb himself concocted.[93]

As we have seen, illicit business was often accompanied by euphemisms that fostered plausible deniability. Further hindering accountability, CIA officials themselves also used euphemisms or sterilized words to disguise, perhaps even from themselves, what they were doing. Thus, for example, when Richard Helms recommended that the CIA continue to give hallucinogens to "unwitting" subjects, he used sanitized, lifeless words such as "uneasiness," "distaste," and "tends to intrude" to describe stark risks to health and life itself.[94] Euphemisms sterilized other deadly activities as well. CIA officers who had worked on assassinations could not bring themselves, even many years later, to use honest and direct words to describe what they had plotted to do. Instead, they testified to the Church Committee about decisions to "dispose of" or "get rid of" or "eliminate" a foreign leader. Such obfuscations echoed the FBI's unbelievable classification of Martin Luther King Jr. as the leader of a black nationalist *hate* group.[95] Perhaps by using these words, some hoped deep down to feel better about what they set out to do.

And whatever the explanation for the use of euphemisms, or simple falsehoods, to describe or justify illegal acts, it seems likely that each failure to call illicit and immoral deeds by their rightful names increased the incidence of illegal acts.

Consequences and Responsibility

Underlying all the Cold War abuses and excesses at home and abroad was the assumption that the government's role would remain forever secret. Occasionally, agents developed vague plans to deal with "flap potential," such as the CIA's plan to "find a scapegoat to blame" if its decades-long illegal mail opening was exposed. Intelligence agencies did cancel a few programs out of fear of public exposure. A handful of officials resisted misuse of intelligence assets. But they were exceptions. In general, a small coterie of executive branch decision makers acted on the assumption that improper actions would remain shrouded in secrecy. Thus, they failed to consider the harm to the government, to America's reputation among other nations, and to our own self-esteem when abuses inevitably saw the light of day.

Implicit here is the question of responsibility. Indeed, the Church Committee devoted considerable attention to the roles of presidents, attorneys general, and other high-level executive officials. The evolution of the Committee's findings on responsibility demonstrates the importance of in-depth inquiry into the facts.[96]

At the inception of the Committee's investigation, the role of senior executive branch officials was not clear. In the summer of 1975, early in the assassination plots investigation, Senator Church speculated to the press that the

CIA may have acted like a "rogue elephant on a rampage," conceiving and carrying out the plots without clear authorization. Other senators, also speculating, opined that the CIA "took orders from the top."[97] When an interim report documenting the Committee's findings on assassinations was issued in November 1975, midway through the whole investigation, the Committee declined to adopt either theory. The interim report presented substantial evidence for both views, saying the conflicting evidence made it impossible to be certain whether or not Presidents Eisenhower and Kennedy authorized the assassination plots during their administrations.[98]

In April 1976, by which time the Committee had completed investigations into many other intelligence actions, it was ready in its final report, to fix responsibility at the top for abuses at home and abroad. As the Committee explained with respect to foreign intelligence:

> On occasion, intelligence agencies concealed their programs from those in higher authority; more frequently, it was the senior officials themselves who, through pressure for results, created the climate within which the abuses occurred.[99]

While intelligence agencies occasionally failed to reveal domestic programs or acts to their superiors, the Committee concluded "the most serious breaches of duty were those of senior officials who were responsible for controlling intelligence activities and generally failed to assure compliance with the law."[100] Fault at the top was shown by "demanding results" without "carefully limiting the means." Senior executive branch officials, moreover, gave de facto endorsement of wrongdoing by "failing to inquire further" after receiving indications that improper activities had been occurring, as well as by "delegating broad authority" through open-ended mandates and terms such as "national security" or "subversion" and then failing to set forth adequate guidelines or procedural checks on how their wishes were carried out. Finally, senior officials "exhibit[ed] a reluctance to know about secret details of programs."[101]

The Committee's conclusions on responsibility evolved due to the clarity produced by exposure to the whole record. Specific agency acts, examined in isolation, sometimes suggested that an agency acted on its own, even misleading political superiors. But the fuller record of many years and many agencies made clear that ultimate responsibility was properly fixed with presidents, attorneys general, and other high executive branch officials. Looking backward thirty years later, it seems there were at least three further reasons to fix ultimate responsibility on higher authorities.

First, although the FBI's power under Hoover meant attorneys general exercised only weak oversight, the attorneys general knew that was what they were doing, and so must receive a substantial measure of responsibility even for acts they did not see.

Second, however one cuts through the fog of plausible deniability to decide who was responsible for any given action, it is crystal clear that presidents, national security advisors, and other high executive branch officials knew of and exploited plausible deniability. Thus, even if they did not know about a particular action, their willful ignorance cannot absolve them of responsibility.

Finally, presidents and other high-level executive branch officials also knew that all intelligence activities, both domestic and foreign, were smothered by layers of excess secrecy. They knew Congress and the courts played no meaningful checking role. And they knew—or should have known—that excessive secrecy, the absence of checks and balances, and the use of fuzzy, open-ended authorizations were, as they are today, an invitation for excess and abuse.

To be sure, presidents and other high-ranking executive branch officials who bore responsibility for abuses and for failing to prevent improper acts also had great accomplishments. They seldom acted with bad intent. Their zeal often arose from unthinking and misplaced patriotism. Love for country, however, cannot dissolve responsibility for negligent oversight or illegality. Indeed, as Louis Brandeis warned, the "greatest dangers to liberty lurk in insidious encroachment by men of zeal, well-meaning, but without understanding."[102]

Even where there were abuses, the men and women of the agencies—which play many vital roles unrelated to abuse—deserve a measure of understanding, not solely criticism. Agents received assignments that were often almost impossible to fulfill. They were expected to predict every crisis, to supply immediately information on any issue, and to anticipate and respond to the demands of presidents. Under that kind of pressure, and acting in the shadow of the Soviet threat, it is no surprise agents interpreted their ambiguous mandates as expansively as possible.

As we have seen, assumptions of everlasting secrecy facilitated the abuses by the executive branch. Under a shroud of secrecy, the law was repeatedly ignored, flouted, and sometimes knowingly broken.[103] Secrecy masked foreign and domestic intelligence activities alike. It fostered "a temptation on the part of the Executive to resort to covert operations [overseas] in order to avoid bureaucratic, congressional and public debate."[104] The expectation of permanent secrecy and no effective oversight led many to ignore the law. William Sullivan, who headed the FBI's Domestic Intelligence Division for ten years, admitted:

Never once did I hear anybody, including myself, raise the question: "Is this course of action which we have agreed upon lawful, is it legal, is it ethical or moral." We never gave any thought to this line of reasoning, because we were just naturally pragmatic. The one thing we were concerned about, will this course of action work, will it get us what we want, will we reach the objective we desire to reach.[105]

Like the Church Committee, we do not doubt that secrecy plays an essential role in delicate intelligence work. But while the classification of proper "sources and methods" of intelligence agencies—as Congress in 1947 anticipated—has its proper place, it cannot justify submerging in shadow entire programs, sweeping policy changes, important shifts in law, or acts that subvert the ideals of America.

Most of the detailed facts needed by Congress for oversight of Cold War intelligence agencies were classified. But fair analysis of the government's security programs requires that members of Congress have access to secrets. It also requires that members of Congress assess the overuse of secrecy stamps and the harm caused by excess secrecy, sometimes determining that the nation is best served by a secret's revelation. The Committee's investigation made clear that the executive branch frequently abused its classification power, keeping secret all of the misconduct that the Committee revealed. These were not genuine secrets. Much was reflexively kept "secret" without thought, or with only the thought of avoiding embarrassment. Nevertheless, some secrets are legitimate. Oversight without heed to this is doomed, as well as irresponsible.[106]

In the first instance, it was ambiguous laws and fuzzy instructions that allowed intelligence agencies to expand their activities and adopt increasingly aggressive tactics. As the Church Committee concluded, mandates stemming from labels such as national security, domestic security, subversive activities, and foreign intelligence were both imprecise and easy to manipulate.[107]

Ambiguous and fuzzy mandates in turn led to "mission creep." Although the agencies' improprieties and overreaching behavior took root as early as Franklin Roosevelt's administration, mission creep generally meant that as time passed, the breadth of the improprieties widened, a concept colorfully captured in a comment by former White House aide Tom Charles Huston. In 1970, Huston had coordinated from the White House the abortive "Huston Plan," by which the CIA, NSA, and other intelligence agencies sought presidential sanction for ongoing illegal break-ins and mail-opening programs as well as warrantless wiretaps and bugs. Five years later, however, Huston testified to the Church Committee that intelligence activity risked unthinking expansion in the absence of a clearly defined mandate: a "move from the kid with a bomb to the kid with a picket sign, and from the kid with the picket sign to the kid with the bumper sticker of the opposing candidate. And you just keep going down the line."[108]

The question for America today as citizens once again are fearful and face a novel and deadly enemy is whether the new threat can be confronted without succumbing to the same institutional pathologies that curtailed America's freedoms and undermined its values during the Cold War. The Church Committee's comprehensive investigation provides a starting point for that inquiry.

Assuming facts can be uncovered and secrecy handled responsibly by all branches of government, genuine debate ought to be possible. Such a debate about how a nation should conduct itself in a time of crisis must be framed in terms of national values: What kind of country is America? This demands that the country address two basic questions. First, should the United States, faced with an implacable, immoral, and insidious enemy, weaken the Constitution's system of careful restraints? Should we, indeed, adopt the tactics of the enemy? In words that echo today, the Committee concluded that, even in crisis, "power must be checked and balanced, and that the preservation of liberty requires the restraint of laws, and not simply the good intentions of men."[109] The acts that the Committee exposed "did not reflect the ideals which have given the people of this country, and of the world, hope for a better, fuller, fairer life." It explained:

> The United States must not adopt the tactics of the enemy. Means are as important as ends. Crisis makes it tempting to ignore the wise restraints that make men free. But each time we do so, each time the means we use are wrong, our inner strength, the strength which makes us free, is lessened.[110]

Senator Charles Mathias, a Republican from Maryland who had been a leading advocate for creating the Committee, added a historical allusion to a subject of some relevance thirty years later:

> History also shows that men and governments have come to recognize the compelling force of ethical principles. The torturer who was once an adjunct of the courts themselves is today an international outlaw. By recognizing the sacredness of human life, mankind has sought to shed such barbarisms, barbarisms that have usually led to further violence and often to the destruction of the leaders and nations who resorted to them.[111]

Referring to the 1954 Doolittle Commission report, the Church Committee commented that "it may well be ourselves that we injure most if we adopt tactics 'more ruthless than the enemy.'"[112] For example, the Committee also found that those planning covert actions "rarely noted" the possible harms the action could cause, particularly to "this nation's ability to exercise moral and political leadership throughout the world."[113]

The second pivotal question is whether the American public should be trusted with the truth. Three decades ago, the Church Committee concluded, again in words that echo today:

> Despite our distaste for what we have seen, we have great faith in this country. The story is sad, but this country has the strength to hear the story and to learn from it. We must remain a people who confront our mistakes and resolve not to repeat them. If we do not, we will decline; but if we do, our future will be worthy of the best of our past.[114]

The Committee was unanimous that its embarrassing and unseemly findings about abuse at home should be made public. In "Additional Statements" to the final report on *Intelligence Activities and the Rights of Americans,* Democratic Senator Robert Morgan and Republican Senator Howard Baker commented in unison on the *favorable* impact of making facts, however embarrassing, public. Senator Morgan explained that "releasing this Report is a great testament to the freedom for which America stands," and expressed his "sincere hope that the Report . . . will rekindle in each of us the belief that perhaps our greatest strength lies in our ability to deal frankly, openly and honestly with the problems of our government." Senator Baker predicted the abuses being "fully aired to the American people" would have a "cathartic effect" on the FBI and the CIA. Baker supported this conclusion by quoting former CIA chief William Colby, who, in a 1976 *New York Times* opinion piece, said "this year's excitement" from the investigation could "strengthen American intelligence."[115]

Expressing agreement on values is, of course, easier when partisan motives are not ascendant. "Fundamental issues concerning the conduct and character of the nation deserve nonpartisan treatment."[116] Of course, there were some differences among Church Committee members. Senators Barry Goldwater and John Tower were most likely to dissent, although generally on the extent of proper disclosure and on remedy questions rather than on factual conclusions. But there was no partisan divide or bitterness, and large agreement on the Committee's basic task.[117] Indeed, among the Church Committee's key contributions was showing not only that intelligence oversight is a bipartisan duty, but also that intelligence excesses were not the product of any single party or presidency. Every administration, starting with Franklin Roosevelt's, turned the tools and agencies of national security to unwise or illegal use.

It remains true today that it is only through robust, open debate, grounded in a full picture of all relevant facts, that the American public can understand whether its government has erred, either out of patriotic zeal or a desire to enhance the powers of the presidency. And it is only through this debate that citizens can have confidence that our government is conducting itself in a way that merits our trust.

3

Reform and Resistance:
Consequences of the Church Committee

The Church Committee's recommendations led to reforms, some significant
and lasting, others transitory. The Committee's reports arrived as Congress,
and to some extent the nation, was repudiating what Arthur Schlesinger fa-
mously termed "The Imperial Presidency." Along with laws regulating war
powers and promoting government openness, Congress was, in the 1970s, enacting laws barring warrantless surveillance by the executive and limiting the
FBI director's tenure. Congress also established permanent oversight committees for intelligence matters.[1]

Starting in the 1980s, the executive branch and its supporters began pushing
back against legislative limits and reporting rules. Additional reforms promoted by the Church Committee foundered when supporters of broad executive power took control of the intelligence committees after 1980. Absent
comprehensive reforms, intelligence agencies, acting in secret and exploiting
new loopholes in the law, repeated familiar mistakes.[2]

The Church Committee's Reform Agenda

The Church Committee made more than 180 detailed recommendations seeking to curb abuse and increase intelligence agencies' efficiency.[3] Despite the
reform agenda's length, its unifying idea was simple: unchecked power is prone
to unwise, inefficient application, and it leads inescapably to abuse. At home,
therefore, the Committee, for example, urged elimination of the open-ended
FBI authority to investigate "subversives." "[T]he Committee's examination of
forty years of investigation into 'subversion' . . . found the term to be so vague as
to constitute a license to investigate about any activity of practically any group
that actively opposes the policies of the administration in power." Similarly,
the Committee observed, security was ill-served by instructions that could be
interpreted broadly according to officials' subjective ideas:

> The national interest would be better served if Bureau resources were
> directed at *terrorism*, hostile foreign intelligence activity, or organized

crime, all more serious and pressing threats to the nation than "subversives."[4]

(As even this list of ignored threats revealed, the Committee was in some respects ahead of its time.)

In the foreign intelligence arena, the Committee called for intelligence reorganization to realize efficiencies sought (but not achieved) by the 1947 National Security Act.[5] Similarly, it expressed concern about the danger of assuming that "technical collection systems"—i.e., spy satellites and sophisticated electronic listening devices—could replace "clandestine human collection." Used properly, human spies provide "valuable insight concerning the motivations for activities or policies of potential adversaries, as well as their future intentions," that technical collection systems cannot.[6] It was a lesson the nation had to relearn at high cost after 9/11 and again in the run-up and aftermath to the poorly planned 2003 invasion and occupation of Iraq.

Unsurprisingly, one of the Committee's main points was the need for clear laws to guide and limit intelligence agencies. In 1976, the CIA, the NSA, and the FBI all lacked detailed statutory mandates. Some bare bones statutory provisions covered the CIA and FBI, but the NSA was entirely a creature of executive branch regulations. The Committee strongly recommended that Congress enact new laws describing and limiting all intelligence agency activities.[7]

The Committee also urged formation of a permanent Senate Committee on Intelligence, recognizing that "Congressional oversight is necessary to assure that in the future our intelligence community functions effectively, within the framework of the Constitution."[8] Vigorous oversight, in the Committee's view, would both limit abuse and increase effectiveness. Former CIA chief William Colby agreed, explaining that congressional involvement would "strengthen American intelligence."[9]

The obstacles to the new Senate committee illustrate the kinds of resistance that would face all reform and oversight efforts after the Church Committee. The first barrier to reform came from powerful senior senators who ran existing committees like Armed Services, Appropriations, Foreign Affairs, and Judiciary. All those committees had previously been responsible for overseeing a piece of America's intelligence activities. But the Church Committee concluded that none saw the full picture, and that all were lax. Still, in 1976, the heads of the congressional committees worried about losing turf, and tried to stall reform by calling for a fifteen-month study of congressional oversight of the intelligence agencies. After Majority Leader Mike Mansfield killed this ploy, the barons of the Armed Services Committee forced a vote on excluding defense intelligence from the jurisdiction of the new committee. Put to a vote, the measure lost by a more than two to one margin, and defense stayed within the new committee's purview.[10] Existing committees, however, retained suffi-cient jurisdiction over military intelligence to prevent the new intelligence committee from exercising a full leadership role.

When procedural maneuvers failed to stop the new oversight committee, advocates for untrammeled executive power attacked the character of Church Committee members and staff. Senator Milton Young, the senior Republican on the Appropriations Committee and co-chair of its Subcommittee on Intel-ligence, argued that Congress could not be trusted with real oversight. Young claimed recent congressional investigations had "very adversely affected the op-eration of our intelligence system." Young insinuated that the Church Com-mittee was responsible for "disclosure" of the name of Richard Welch, the CIA's station chief in Greece, leading to Welch's "murder" in December 1975, during the Church Committee's inquiries. But Senator Fritz Mondale imme-diately corrected Young. The Committee "never had" Welch's name, and had "never asked for it." Mondale also observed that the CIA "had urged Welch not to move into [his house], because it had been known in the community that the house had been the residence of the previous head of the CIA in Greece." Young's accusation, which sought to deflect attention away from abuses and to tar advocates of reform with false accusations, was entirely baseless.[11]

Young, however, was not the first to make this spurious claim: CIA chief George H.W. Bush also tried to exploit Welch's death.[12] After Welch's death, the CIA and the Ford Administration used the mourning around Welch's death to hamper the work of the Senate and House.[13] Shortly after Bush was confirmed as CIA chief, he came before the Church Committee for an executive session. While Bush had the floor, an aide whispered in his ear. Out of the blue, Bush then blurted out the accusation that the Committee was responsible for Welch's assassination. Soon, however, Bush returned to the Committee to concede that no evidence supported the accusation that congressional inquiries into in-telligence activities had any "adverse impact on Mr. Welch's cover or any rela-tionship to his tragic death."[14]

With accusations about Welsh's murder refuted, the Senate proceeded to approve a new Senate permanent intelligence committee by a vote of 87 to 7. The new committee obtained budgetary authority over the intelligence agen-cies. The resolution also set forth the "sense of the Senate" that the executive branch would keep the committee "fully and currently informed" about in-telligence activities, including covert action, and provide the committee with all requested documents and information. Modeled on the Church Commit-tee itself, the new permanent intelligence committee was structured to reduce partisanship. The ratio of majority and minority party members was set at eight to seven—Church's had been six to five—rather than the majority's usually greater representation on regular committees. Similarly, the vice chair, who wielded real power, came from the minority party.[15]

The new Senate Intelligence Committee, and a parallel House committee created one year later, empowered Congress to perform its proper role under the Constitution's checks and balances. Mere existence of a permanent intelligence oversight committee, however, hardly guarantees effective oversight. As Frank Church explained:

> continuing congressional oversight is built into the woodwork. We did the necessary job. Political will can't be guaranteed. The most we could do was to recommend that permanent surveillance be established. We did that knowing that the Congress being a political animal will exercise its surveillance with whatever diligence the political climate of the time makes for.[16]

The resolution creating the new permanent committee fully empowered it within the Senate. As a one-house resolution, not a law, it could not *require* the executive branch to keep the committee "fully and currently informed" of intelligence activities or to provide documents or other information. In 1980, Congress filled the gap, and passed a law covering both the Senate and House committees, making disclosure obligations mandatory.[17]

After addressing congressional oversight, Congress turned to the pressing need for new laws limiting and channeling intelligence agencies' activities. Congress passed important laws reflecting the findings and recommendations of the Church Committee. But by no means did Congress respond to all the problematic practices and inefficiencies highlighted by the Committee. The most important new law was the 1978 Foreign Intelligence Surveillance Act, or FISA. Both Senate and House committee reports on FISA drew heavily from the Church Committee's extensive documentation of abuse. Presumably, reference to the Church Committee's finding that excessive surveillance occurred in every administration since Franklin Roosevelt's helped foster bipartisan consensus for the bill. FISA passed the Senate 95 to 1, and cleared the House by a narrower margin, with Vice President Mondale lobbying for passage. Signing the bill into law, President Carter explained that under FISA a "prior judicial warrant" was required for "all electronic surveillance for foreign intelligence or counterintelligence purposes in the United States in which communications of U.S. persons might be intercepted." As reflected in Carter's statement on signing the bill into law, FISA renounced all "inherent" executive power to use electronic surveillance at home in the absence of statutory authority.[18]

Besides rejecting presidential claims of "inherent authority," FISA also removed all ambiguous and open-ended words such as "subversion" and "national security" that had for decades been used to justify excessive electronic surveillance. Instead, FISA used carefully worded definitions that covered espionage and terrorism alone.

In FISA, Congress created a special federal court to hear and decide applications for foreign intelligence surveillance warrants. The law permitted only two temporary exceptions to the requirement that a judicial warrant be obtained prior to electronic surveillance involving an American. First, in emergencies, a limited period of surveillance (originally twenty-four hours, later amended to seventy-two hours) could be conducted before a warrant was obtained. Further, "following a declaration of war by Congress," warrantless searches would be lawful for up to fifteen days. Congress rejected a proposal that this exception last for a year, in the belief that fifteen days gave the president enough time to return to Congress and ask for any necessary changes in the law. Echoing Church Committee recommendations, FISA protected only United States citizens and aliens with permanent residency status.[19] The 9/11 hijackers, therefore, had no shelter from warrantless surveillance under FISA.

Although some predicted dire consequences before its passage,[20] FISA soon gained universal acceptance. In December 1981, President Ronald Reagan issued an Executive Order on United States Intelligence Activities emphasizing the need to comply with FISA.[21] Congress also amended FISA several times before and after 9/11. These changes, usually based on practical suggestions by the executive branch, preserved FISA's fundamental purpose while modifying the law based on experience and changes in technology. In many respects, FISA thus represented the checks and balances as they are supposed to work— a dialogue between branches of government.

Over time, other Church Committee recommendations found their way into law. Some new laws came quickly, such as an October 1976 law limiting the tenure of the FBI director to ten years. Never again would a director like J. Edgar Hoover dominate the Bureau for almost fifty years. Other reforms came slowly, such as the law strengthening the independence of the CIA inspector general. Some came so much later that the Church Committee's early contribution to the idea was largely forgotten. The law embodying the 9/11 Commission's proposals for reorganizing the intelligence community, for instance, echoed sentiments aired first by the Church Committee.[22]

One of the core Church proposals—enactment of comprehensive statutory charters for all the intelligence agencies—did not succeed. As a consequence, neither the FBI nor the CIA (let alone the NSA and the other Defense Department intelligence agencies) received detailed legislative guidance with clear operational mandates and specific limitations.

From its birth in 1976 through 1980, the new Senate committee struggled valiantly for this legislation. Its two first chairs, Senators Daniel Inouye and Birch Bayh, with the aid of former Church Committee member Senator Walter "Dee" Huddleston, who led a subcommittee working on charters, and intelligence committee staff director William G. Miller, produced several extensive drafts.[23] But by 1981, the very notion of comprehensive intelligence reform was a dead letter. That year, Barry Goldwater took over as chair of the Senate committee after party control of the Senate shifted in the 1980 election. Goldwater expressed skepticism about any congressional oversight of intelligence, let alone a comprehensive new statutory framework. The combination of congressional acquiescence with a new aggressive approach by the executive set the stage for a new round of executive branch overreach in the 1980s.[24]

Nevertheless, the cause for comprehensive legislation's failure cannot be boiled down to one politician alone, even one as powerful as Goldwater. The proposed bill was complex. Writing rules for intelligence agencies is always technically difficult and politically risky. Public pressure to act dwindled as memories of the Church Committee's revelations dimmed.[25] Further, the House mounted no parallel effort to prepare comprehensive legislation. Finally, Presidents Ford and Carter issued executive orders setting out rules and limits for intelligence activities, while Ford's Attorney General Edward Levi issued new, detailed guidelines for FBI investigations. These executive branch initiatives were far from identical to the new laws the Church Committee recommended and the new permanent committee sought. In many respects, they fell short of needed reform goals. But because they moved in the direction the Church Committee recommended, it became harder to press for legislation.[26]

Without doubt, the executive branch designed and issued these new guidelines in part to forestall tighter legislation. One commentator opined that Ford's executive order was a cynical effort to "prevent legislative action"; another argued that the order was "as much—and perhaps more—an attempt to maintain executive control of the reform movement as it was an attempt to accommodate reform pressures." Still another took the position that Attorney General Levi's FBI guidelines were an "attempt to delimit prospective reforms" to the "policy preferences of the executive branch."[27]

Nevertheless, it would be incorrect to dismiss these guidelines as mere gestures. Reacting to the merits of the Levi guidelines and the Ford order, which were issued shortly before publication of the Committee's final reports, the Church Committee highlighted differences in approach and shortfalls, but was generally positive. Its principal concern was prospective—that presidential executive orders and attorney general guidelines could easily be changed, and weakened, by new presidents or attorney generals acting on their own; this contrasts with laws, which require congressional involvement to alter.[28] The Committee's concerns proved prescient. Beginning in 1981, the executive branch began to slip back into old habits, sometimes secretly and sometimes by publicly rolling back restrictions contained in the executive orders or attorney general guidelines.

Rolling Back Reform

President Ronald Reagan and his Attorney General William French Smith publicly weakened the Carter executive order and the Levi guidelines to a degree.[29] But the most serious executive expansion of power and loosening of constraints, known as the Iran-Contra scandal, unspooled during the two terms of the Reagan Administration. Iran-Contra was concealed from Congress and the public, just as the abuses revealed by the Church Committee had been. In response to disclosures, Congress yet again embarked on a major after-the-fact investigation of the executive branch. In 1986, both the Senate and the House created committees that came together to hold joint hearings and then issue a joint report.[30]

Beginning in December 1981, the CIA—with President Reagan's passionate support—armed, trained, and advised the Nicaraguan Contras, a faction resisting the left-leaning Sandinista government of Nicaragua. The Contras' military campaign included attacks on undefended civilian targets, including farms, granaries, and small villages. Learning of this covert action, Representative Edward Boland of Massachusetts, the chair of the House Intelligence Committee, in 1982 proposed a budget amendment barring the CIA or the Defense Department from passing funds to the Nicaraguan rebels. Boland's amendment, which applied to fiscal year 1983, passed the House 411 to 0, and, after passing the Senate, became law. Congress and the public later learned that the CIA had used its contingency funds (which technically fell outside the Boland Amendment's scope) to circumvent the bar. And in January and February 1984, three months after the Boland Amendment expired in October 1983, the CIA mined three Nicaraguan harbors without informing Congress as the 1980 law required. Even Barry Goldwater, then the chair of the new Senate Intelligence Committee, declared himself "pissed off" that CIA chair William Casey failed to report the mining to the committee. Within months, Congress passed a second Boland Amendment barring expenditures "directly or indirectly" for "military or paramilitary operations in Nicaragua."[31]

In 1985, President Reagan also decided to override the opposition of his secretaries of state and defense and sell TOW antitank and HAWK antiaircraft missiles to Iran—a country governed by a hard-line, theocratic Shia Muslim regime—despite Reagan himself having labeled Iran a "terrorist" state. (Through student proxies, Iran had captured fifty-two American diplomats and other citizens in November 1979, holding them hostage for 444 days.) Nonetheless, Reagan hoped that providing arms to Iran would lead to the release of other American hostages in Lebanon.[32]

Missiles moved into Iranian hands via the "Enterprise," an offshore entity created by the White House's National Security Council staff, led by Lieutenant Colonel Oliver North. The Enterprise had its own airplanes, ship service, secure communications capacities, and secret Swiss bank accounts. But in 1986, the Lebanese weekly *Al-Shiraa* published details of the Enterprise's arms deals with Iran, some of which used Israel as an intermediary.[33]

The Contra funds and the Iran sales converged into the affair now known as "Iran-Contra." Pursuant to instructions from the president's National Security Council, supposedly a purely advisory body, the Enterprise secretly funneled to the Contras millions of dollars realized from the sale of missiles to Iran, allowing the executive to evade legal restrictions such as the Boland Amendment.[34]

Congress was not informed about either the sale of missiles to Iran or the use of those funds to pay the Contras. Those deliberate omissions violated a law enacted in 1980 that gave the congressional intelligence committees specific oversight responsibilities, as well as President Reagan's December 1981 executive order, which mandated executive branch cooperation with Congress under the 1980 oversight provisions.[35] As Congress's Iran-Contra Joint Committee concluded, secrecy was used "not as a shield against our adversaries, but as a weapon against our own democratic institutions."[36]

Other executive branch pathologies similar to those revealed by the Church Committee were evident in the Iran-Contra affair.[37] Admiral John Poindexter, the President's National Security Advisor, explained that he did not tell President Reagan about the diversion of proceeds from the missile sales to ensure the President had "deniability." Echoing the Church Committee, the Iran-Contra Committee concluded it was a perversion of plausible deniability to deny knowledge of covert actions to the "highest elected officials of the United States Government itself." Again echoing the earlier investigation, the Iran-Contra Committee concluded that "the common ingredients of the Iran and Contra policies were secrecy, deception and disdain for the law." Moreover, "time and again we have learned that a flawed process leads to bad" decisions about national security. As was the case at the time of the Church Committee (and as is the case again after 9/11), those defending the Administration claimed matters labeled as foreign policy should be left to the president alone. But as the Iran-Contra Committee responded, "the theory of our

Constitution is the opposite: policies formed through consultation and the democratic process are better and wiser than those formed without it."[38]

Oliver North not only masterminded the Enterprise scheme, he also lied to Congress about the Administration's aid to the Contras in a 1986 briefing. Subsequently, on the first day of the Iran-Contra Committee's hearings, the telegenic North appeared dressed in a bemedaled Marine dress uniform. He and his counsel managed to turn the tables on the investigative committee by making North's patriotism the issue rather than the Administration's wrong-doing. He assailed Congress for leaks, and condemned elected officials who opposed aid to Contra "freedom fighters."[39] Thanks to his defiant violation of the law, Oliver North became a national hero in many circles. In 1994, he ran for a United States Senate seat in Virginia—and only barely lost.[40] North may have left another lesson for the post-9/11 future: if you're going to break the law and if it is uncovered, don't apologize. Instead, proclaim it loud and long, touting your "patriotic" motives.

In response to Iran-Contra, Congress again amended the law requiring dis-closure obligations for covert actions. Henceforth, presidents themselves had to find in writing that covert actions were necessary and important. The new law flatly stated that presidents could not authorize any action "that would vi-olate the Constitution or any statute of the United States."[41]

Iran-Contra's political fallout was limited. Embarrassed by the Iran-Contra revelations, President Reagan apologized to the nation, saw his popularity drop, and changed his White House staff, bringing in former Church Com-mittee member Howard Baker as chief of staff. The President's popularity re-covered before he left office. Although Admiral Poindexter and Oliver North were both convicted of criminal offenses, their convictions were reversed on technical grounds, with the government declining to press fresh charges.[42]

Iran-Contra involved a deliberate decision by the executive branch to reject Congress's foreign policy choices and to conduct its own illegal policy. While the Church Committee documented a far greater volume of rights violations during the Cold War, these Reagan Administration foreign policy decisions evinced the same disdain for the role of Congress that past presidents had shown in letting loose intelligence agencies at home.

Central American foreign policy also spilled over the nation's borders to un-dermine the new limitations on surveillance of Americans at home. For more than two years in the early 1980s, the FBI spied on and infiltrated the Com-mittee in Solidarity with the People of El Salvador, or CISPES, along with other advocacy organizations such as the Central America Solidarity Association and the Interreligious Task Force. The FBI never found evidence of criminal activity by these groups, but in its overlong and unbounded investigation, the

Bureau intruded repeatedly on the First Amendment activities of law-abiding Americans, like the college students who largely comprised CISPES and who vocally opposed U.S. military aid to the government of El Salvador.[43]

Despite the FBI's threshold conclusion in 1981 that no evidence existed to suggest CISPES was under foreign control or implicated in any criminal activity, the Bureau in October 1983 ordered all its field offices to "determine location, leadership, and activities of CISPES." The FBI, to be sure, told agents "not to investigate the exercise of First Amendment rights." But since CISPES did little outside the shelter of the Constitution's free speech protections, FBI agents repeatedly found themselves spying on core political speech. In Wichita, agents tore down flyers posted in a public university. In Cincinnati, puzzled agents found themselves gathering information on the activities of an order of Catholic nuns. The net result was, once again, a far-ranging intrusion on the freedoms of Americans precisely because of their vocal opposition to a foreign policy decision of the federal government.[44]

In another sad retreat of earlier mistakes, the FBI expanded its investigation based on loose or nonexistent affiliations to CISPES. Churches affiliated with the sanctuary movement were placed under surveillance. Individuals who attended CISPES-sponsored films, attended CISPES conferences—even a college professor who invited a suspicious class speaker and posed a suspicious exam question—found themselves under FBI scrutiny. The FBI also compiled a list of CISPES-affiliated organizations to spy on; the list included Oxfam America, the Southern Christian Leadership Conference, and the U.S. Catholic Conference.[45] It was mission creep of a depressingly familiar flavor.

The 9/11 Commission

Lessons from the Church Committee went unheeded, setting the stage for the greatest intelligence disaster of the past half-century. The Final Report of the National Commission on Terrorist Attacks Against the United States (commonly known as the 9/11 Commission) is notable for the many parallels between its recommendations and those of its 1975–76 Senate predecessor. The 9/11 Commission's inquiry into events and government actions leading to the September 2001 attacks revealed numerous failures of coordination between intelligence agencies that recalled the institutional rivalries of the Cold War. Most important among these were "day-to-day gaps in information sharing" such as failure to translate details of an identification of one hijacker in January 2001, and an FBI analyst's refusal to share information because she "misunderstood" the rules governing the sharing of information between criminal and intelligence investigations. Highlighting these gaps in intelligence agency capacity, the 9/11 Commission argued for augmented leadership and information sharing—not increases in surveillance or disruption powers.[46] Indeed, not one of the 9/11 Commission recommendations suggested the need for new coercive or intrusive government powers. On the contrary, the 9/11 Commission cautioned that

> The burden of proof for retaining a particular governmental power should be on the executive, to explain (a) that the power actually materially enhances security, and (b) that there is adequate supervision of the executive's use of the powers to ensure protection of civil liberties. If the power is granted, there must be adequate guidelines and oversight to properly confine its use.[47]

This formulation is strikingly similar to the test suggested by the Church Committee for assessing, for example, new forms of electronic surveillance. Thirty years later, in short, the 9/11 Commission still viewed institutional checks ensuring that the executive uses intelligence powers in a responsible fashion as vital for effective, focused national security policy consistent with America's constitutional values.

Parallels between the Church Committee's recommendations and those of the 9/11 Commission run even deeper. In November 1975, Senator Frank Church gave a speech calling for a stronger CIA with better analytic capabilities.[48] In its subsequent final report on foreign intelligence, the Church Committee also called for separating the Director of Central Intelligence from the CIA, allowing the director to advise the president more efficiently and objectively and manage the intelligence community without a conflict of interest or responsibility of running a major intelligence agency.[49]

In 2001, this call for reform had yet to be heeded. At the core of the 9/11 Commission's vision was a new "National Intelligence Director" position to supersede the Director of Central Intelligence post. This new position was needed, the 9/11 Commission argued, to overcome barriers that hindered intelligence agencies' cooperation; to find ways to bridge the gap between foreign and domestic intelligence; to set firm priorities; and to allocate resources accordingly. In 2004, despite initial reservations from the Bush Administration, Congress, under heavy public pressure, passed the Intelligence Reform and Terrorism Prevention Act, creating a Director of National Intelligence with some, but not all, of the powers recommended by the 9/11 Commission.[50]

Congress too had failed to heed the Church Committee's call to action. So, unsurprisingly, the 9/11 Commission's approach to oversight again echoed the Church Committee's. As we have seen, one of the Church Committee's core recommendations was far stronger—and more focused—congressional oversight to reassert the proper balance between the executive and legislative branches and, as a consequence, to protect human liberty, reduce the risk of foolish policies, and enhance efficiency. The bipartisan 9/11 Commission came to the same conclusion. It pointed out, almost thirty years after Church, that congressional oversight of intelligence was still too fragmented, and still too often reflected age-old turf jealousies:

> Of all our recommendations, strengthening congressional oversight may be among the most difficult and important. So long as oversight is governed by current congressional rules and resolutions, we believe the American people will not get the security they want and need. The United States needs a strong, stable, and capable congressional structure to give America's national intelligence agencies oversight, support, and leadership. . . . the other reforms we have suggested—for a National Counterterrorism Center and a National Intelligence Director—will not work if congressional oversight does not change too. Unity of effort in executive management can be lost if it is fractured by divided congressional oversight.[51]

Rather than acknowledging the need for improved oversight, President George W. Bush's Administration resisted effective congressional inquiries into intelligence. It tried to politicize intelligence reform questions to dissuade criticism. And it fought tooth and nail against any effort to ensure accountability beyond the opaque walls of the executive branch itself.

Power without accountability risks unwise and abusive exercise. This is the teaching of the Church Committee and the 9/11 Commission, two bodies separated by almost thirty years. Checks to ensure that power is exercised responsibly tend to improve our security, not corrode it. But these lessons often go unheeded and instead are countered with flawed, ideologically-driven responses that paper over existing problems.

By denying the extent and scope of problems in our intelligence community, critics of the Church Committee stymied important structural changes that would have yielded more coordinated and focused responses to true threats. This problem was to persist even after 9/11. It infected intelligence agencies' analytic work in the run-up to the Iraq war, as well as the use of that intelligence.

That the lessons of the Church Committee, invoked again in the Iran-Contra and the 9/11 Commission reports, were so often and so successfully resisted thus ought to be a matter of abiding national regret. As the Iran-Contra and the CISPES spying scandals revealed, the executive branch did not reject abusive and inefficient use of spying and intelligence powers. And as 9/11 revealed, the absence of oversight contributed to the unwise and inefficient functioning of the intelligence services. Moreover, the spirit of contempt for Congress's laws animating Iran–Contra was never set aside.

Twenty-five years after its publication, the very first recommendation of the Church Committee's report on *Intelligence Activities and the Rights of Americans* remained wise counsel on September 10, 2001: "There is no inherent constitutional authority for the President or any intelligence agency to violate the law."[52]

It was wisdom that had added relevance and urgency in the years after September 11, 2001.

Part II

Adopting Tactics of the Enemy

4

Our Torture Policy

The men on the front line raised the alarm first.

Captain Ian Fishback of the 82nd Airborne Division graduated from West Point Military Academy to serve two tours of duty in Afghanistan and Iraq. In Iraq, Fishback was stationed at Forward Operating Base Mercury, ten miles east of Fallujah, then a hub of the Iraqi insurgency. There, Captain Fishback saw American soldiers routinely using violence, even torture, against Iraqi detainees: "death threats, beatings, broken bones, murder, exposure to the elements, extreme forced physical exertion, hostage-taking, stripping, sleep deprivation and degrading treatment." Other soldiers witnessed Iraqi prisoners subjected to "forced, repetitive exercise, sometimes to the point of unconsciousness, sleep deprivation for days on end, and exposure to extremes of heat and cold as part of the interrogation process." Captain Fishback also found "confusion" among his fellow soldiers about whether the long-standing laws governing the treatment of prisoners, known as the Geneva Conventions, applied in Iraq.

For seventeen months, Captain Fishback sought precise rules for interrogations from his commanders, whom he informed of abuses. But his company commander warned him not to endanger the "honor of the unit." Neither his battalion commander nor military lawyers responded to Fishback's inquiries. Military investigators showed more interest in getting names of soldiers complaining about detainee mistreatment than identifying those who endorsed or committed abuse.[1]

Frustrated, Fishback wrote to Arizona Senator John McCain, who had been a prisoner of war during the Vietnam War, and recounted the "wide range" of prisoner abuse he had seen. Then the captain posed a question:

When did Al Qaeda become any kind of standard by which we measure the morality of the United States? We are America, and our actions should be held to a higher standard, the ideals expressed in documents such as the Declaration of Independence and the Constitution.[2]

When our tactics prompt this question, something has gone terribly awry. Today, in contrast to the time of the Cold War, the military and intelligence agencies of the executive branch have clear laws against torture and abusive interrogations. Fishback's question was possible only because the current executive branch chose to discard these clear rules in favor of unchecked executive power. Torture, according to the Bush Administration, is legal because the president says it is.

The Administration's decision after 9/11 to ignore legal constraints on torture exemplifies its broader efforts to seize unfettered control of national security policy and to eliminate the checks and balances imposed by Congress and the courts. America's torture problem involves a repetition of old mistakes, familiar from the Cold War, but now compounded by a new model of executive power—the idea that the president stands above the law and can set aside the law in the name of national security.

The executive branch campaign against the torture laws also proved a testing ground for new tools to enlarge executive power, as lawyers in the Justice and Defense Departments, at the direction of their political bosses, conceived and refined legal theories to insulate executive power from congressional constraints and public oversight. As a matter of course, executive branch lawyers are always faced with the need to decide what provisions mean exactly, and how they apply to new or unexpected situations. Lawyers within the executive branch hence generate binding *interpretations* of laws for the many federal agencies within the executive branch, including the armed services and the CIA. The task of providing these binding legal interpretations falls to the Justice Department's Office of Legal Counsel, or OLC.

In the case of torture, the executive branch intentionally undermined legal checks imposed by Congress, misusing in two ways its mandate to interpret the law. First, executive branch lawyers, rather than interpreting antitorture laws fairly, found ways to interpret the laws so as to deprive them of meaning. Using faulty logic, OLC lawyers undermined the spirit and purpose of antitorture laws by promulgating an absurdly narrow definition of "torture." Moreover, the executive branch kept OLC legal interpretations secret, preventing Congress from responding. By the time Congress learned of OLC interpretations and responded, much damage had been inflicted. Such subtle corrosions of the rule of law, lost in the knots of legal analysis, are as great a hazard to the Constitution as frontal assaults.

Second, though, was the frontal assault: an outright, albeit covert, refusal to heed the law. In legal opinions on torture, the OLC pressed a theory of unlimited presidential power that gave presidents authority to set aside permanently *any* law of the United States, including laws against torture, in the name of national security. Claims to such royal presidential powers are, in effect, wholesale rejections of America's system of checks and balances. While we leave detailed examination and refutation of this dangerous idea to a subsequent chapter, we describe here how executive branch lawyers, at the direction of their political masters, invoked this notion to trump laws passed by Congress at strategic decision points.

Cold War experience demonstrated how intelligence agencies, absent clear legal limits, slip into pathological practices of mission creep and plausible deniability. When the executive branch displaced clear laws against torture in favor of nebulous standards, the result was "mission creep" of a new, more toxic, kind—and the situation Captain Fishback confronted in Iraq.[3]

Only after the threshold check of duly enacted law fails do other checks and accountability devices come into play, such as congressional oversight and judicial review. The story of torture policy also illustrates how post-hoc checks can also be stymied, leaving troubling questions about what remains today of the Constitution's checks and balances.

America's Clear Laws Against Torture

On September 10, 2001, Captain Fishback would have found an easy answer to the question of whether torture—or any lesser kind of cruel, inhuman, or degrading treatment—was allowed in wartime or moments of crisis. American law forbade all torture or degrading treatment at any time and in any place whatsoever. America had a long history as a world leader promulgating laws against torture in war and peacetime. These laws, including both domestic criminal laws and international treaties signed and ratified by the United States, were a proud capstone of the American legal system and an invaluable moral asset in American leadership against violent terrorists. They also exemplified how a government of separate branches and shared powers ought to work. Each of the three branches played a pivotal role in negotiating, drafting, enacting, and refining the laws against torture.

For fifty years and longer, America championed international treaties that put torture out of bounds during war as well as peace. Foreign torturers found no haven in America. State Department human rights reports condemned tyrannies around the world for using torture. Federal courts issued path-breaking rulings declaring that the torturer, "like the pirate and slave trader before him . . . [was] *hostis humani generis*, an enemy of all mankind." Without doubt, America's record was hardly spotless. Torture was used in some American prisons, and by Latin and Central American intelligence agencies with whom America collaborated. But the checks and balances of constitutional government broadly worked. Congress enacted clear legal standards forbidding torture; the executive branch followed them; and the federal courts punished state officials, and private citizens, who violated these laws. Derogations, in American prisons and overseas, were cause for sorrow and shame.[4]

Two bodies of international law prohibited torture and degrading treatment: the laws of war (or "international humanitarian law") and international human rights treaties. American diplomats helped draft both. Congress then incorporated both into domestic law, making them the binding law of the land.

International consensus first developed around the laws of war. Brutal and devastating European wars spurred nations to establish detailed codes for war and the treatment of captured persons in 1899 and 1907. The end of World War II saw adoption of the Universal Declaration of Human Rights. And in the 1980s, the United Nations successfully promoted a detailed treaty on torture in peacetime, typically known as the Convention Against Torture.[5]

The United States holds a strong claim to being international humanitarian law's birthplace. Despite Europe's long and bloody martial history, it was the American Civil War that prompted the first general code of wartime conduct. In April 1863, the Union army issued a general set of rules for the conduct of war, entitled General Orders No. 100. Drafted by Columbia University scholar Francis Lieber, these instructions listed soldiers' duties to civilians, captured enemy soldiers, and others "hors de combat." The code prohibited the "intentional infliction of any suffering" on captured soldiers. Lieber's code was adopted in the Franco-Prussian war of the 1870s. International diplomatic conferences at the Hague in 1899 and 1907, moreover, used Lieber's work as the basis for a new general law of war.[6]

After World War II, nations decided to replace the Hague Conventions of 1899 and 1907, which set out rules for making war. In August 1949, a group of nations, including the United States, approved four new conventions drafted in Geneva. These "Geneva Conventions" focus on the treatment of individuals caught on a battlefield, in occupied territory, or in hostile lands. Today, they are the heart of international humanitarian law—and an integral part of American law. Nothing naïve animated America's rejection of torture. Advocating for the Geneva Conventions, and later antitorture rules, American presidents acted out of hardheaded realism. They knew that a common set of rules—with no loopholes—protected captured American soldiers from torture and inhuman treatment better than ad hoc protections. Even at the dawn of the Cold War, the advantage of the moral high ground in building alliances and public diplomacy was clear.

Each Convention protects a different category of persons. Most importantly, the Third Convention covers "prisoners of war," or POWs, who are soldiers of an opposing army. POWs must be treated humanely and released at the end of the conflict. The Fourth Convention covers civilians and most others not covered by any other Convention. Like POWs, civilians benefit in the Fourth Convention from extensive protections from physical harm.[7]

The United States was deeply involved in drafting the Geneva Conventions. The Senate swiftly ratified them, making them United States law. During the 1949 drafting conference, American delegates from the State and Justice Departments vigorously advocated specific rules to outlaw the kind of violence inflicted on captured American soldiers by Japanese forces in World War II. As a result, the Geneva Conventions contain detailed regulation of food rations, barracks arrangements, and even sports. There is bitter irony in the fact that more than fifty years later, the man who was later to become attorney general, Alberto Gonzales, consigned these hard-won prescriptions to history's dustbin as "quaint" and "obsolete." Gonzales apparently did not know that many of these rules were originally proposed by America to protect American soldiers.[8]

Among its "quaint" regulations are provisions that protect both captured combatants and civilians from coercive interrogation or degrading treatment. Under the Third Convention, POWs are sheltered from any "physical or mental torture" or "any other form of coercion." Negotiators in 1949 decided not to focus only on the specific abuses inflicted by Japanese and German armies. Instead, they fashioned a broad rule against degrading treatment and torture in general. Similarly, the Fourth Convention provides that protected persons "shall at all times be humanely treated, and shall be protected especially against all acts of violence or threats thereof."[9] In short, both civilians and captured soldiers have absolute protection under Geneva from any kind of brutal or inhumane treatment, not only torture.

Most of the rules in the Third and Fourth Conventions apply only to certain conflicts, creating an ambiguity that the Bush Administration would later exploit. The Geneva rules' scope of application is defined in Article 2, also known as "Common Article 2" since it appears in each of the four Conventions. Common Article 2 reflects international law's historical roots in conflicts between nation states. Between the 1648 Peace of Westphalia, which settled Europe's sectarian Thirty Years' War, and World War II, international law has regulated the "society of states," not individuals directly. Common Article 2 states that the Geneva Conventions apply only to conflicts "between two or more of the High Contracting Parties." How does this apply to a conflict between a state and transnational terrorist groups? What happens if a "state" where a conflict takes place has collapsed? Common Article 2 thus left ambiguous questions with heightened relevance in the fragmented post-9/11 world of failed states and transnational insurgencies.[10]

Geneva's drafters, however, also included a catch-all provision in each Convention to close the loophole: Common Article 3. This provision commands

that any person no longer taking "active part of hostilities" must "in all circumstances be treated humanely." Common Article 3 then gives the vague
term "humanely" precise meaning by stating that "at any time and in any
place whatsoever," any "violence to life and person, in particular . . . cruel
treatment and torture," is absolutely "prohibited." Similarly out of bounds are
any "outrages upon personal dignity, in particular humiliating and degrading
treatment." Sweeping more broadly than Common Article 2, Common Article 3 applies to any "armed conflict not of an international character occurring in the territory of one of the High Contracting Parties."[11]

The international consensus was that Common Article 3 left no gaps in
coverage. It applied to every conflict a signatory state chose to enter, including
conflicts between a signatory state and a nonstate actor. And the United States
shared in this consensus. It also recognized Common Article 3 as "customary
international law"—that is, a binding rule for all civilized nations that could
never be disregarded.[12]

America applied this understanding of Common Article 3 in past conflicts.
As CIA station chief in Islamabad, Pakistan, in the mid 1980s, Milton Bearden managed massive flows of matériel into the Afghan anti-Soviet insurgency. Even in that uncertain environment, Bearden ensured that not only
CIA officials working in Soviet-dominated territory but also that America's
Afghan allies followed international law banning coercive interrogations. Bearden insisted that Common Article 3 be followed rigorously for fear that failure to do so would give the other side an excuse to subject his own men to
coercive treatment if captured.[13]

During the Vietnam conflict too, the United States gave Viet Cong troops
the protections of the Third Convention even though they failed to qualify as
POWs. By contrast, North Vietnam argued that the Geneva Conventions did
not apply to captured American pilots and flight crews. North Vietnam argued
it was entitled to treat captured U.S. pilots as "major [war] criminals." Its harsh
treatment of captured American soldiers such as John McCain quickly became
an international embarrassment.[14]

After the Vietnam experience, the military embedded the Geneva Conventions into American law. Military lawyers were taught to abide strictly by the
Conventions' terms. Pre-9/11 Defense Department operational regulations set
forth procedures following the Geneva Conventions' framework for battlefield
captures. Indeed, the army followed them so closely that its regulations provided that in cases of conflict between the army's regulations and the Geneva
Conventions, a soldier should follow the Geneva rule.[15]

Congress reconfirmed the American commitment to the Geneva Conventions. After the Rwandan genocide of 1994 and the mass killings in the Bos-

nian town of Srebenica in 1995, Congress passed a law criminalizing all "war crimes," or breaches of international humanitarian law such as "willful killing, torture or inhuman treatment" or any attempt to "willfully depriv[e] a prisoner of war of the rights of fair and regular trial." In Congress's eyes, America thus had an interest not only in avoiding war crimes itself, but also in ensuring that the world was free of war crimes.[16]

This pre-9/11 latticework of treaties, domestic law, and regulations embodied a commitment to a rule against torture even in the heat of battle. Congress obviously knew that captured enemy soldiers sometimes have valuable information that could even save American lives. Nevertheless, Congress, and the military itself, placed out of bounds *all* coercive interrogation, no matter what the short-term value to American military interests, by incorporating the all-encompassing Geneva regime, which left no prisoner unprotected, into American law. In the long term, America gained by knowing its soldiers could lay claim to similar protection. And the executive branch, in pre-9/11 conflicts, largely put this understanding into practice.

In addition to the rules of war, the United States also took the lead in developing clear international human rights norms against torture and lesser violence for peacetime. These rules, embodied in the 1984 Convention Against Torture and Other Cruel, Inhuman or Degrading Treatment or Punishment, provided international law's first clear definition of "torture":

> any act by which severe pain or suffering, whether physical or mental, is intentionally inflicted on a person for such purposes as obtaining from him or a third person information or a confession, punishing him for an act he or a third person has committed or is suspected of having committed, or intimidating or coercing him or a third person, or for any reason based on discrimination of any kind, when such pain or suffering is inflicted by or at the instigation of or with the consent or acquiescence of a public official or other person acting in an official capacity.

Torture is thus an official act that inflicts either pain or suffering, physical or mental, for particular reasons, including obtaining information. The Convention Against Torture also prohibits any "cruel, inhuman or degrading" treatment.[17] In 1994, Congress passed a criminal law imposing severe penalties on torture and conspiracy to torture.[18]

Even before Congress acted, federal courts routinely condemned those who committed torture. In criminal cases from the 1930s Jim Crow South, the U.S. Supreme Court drew a firm line against the use of coerced evidence. In 1980, federal courts also began to allow suits for damages based on torture in other countries. These courts, relying on a 1789 law called the Alien Tort Claims Act, permitted aliens to sue for damages based on violations of international law. American courts became a scourge of the foreign torturer, deciding cases involving human rights violations by regimes in the Philippines, Guatemala, the former Yugoslavia, and Burma. Former foreign leaders, such as the Philippine president Ferdinand Marcos, were called to account in American courts for their gross violations of basic human rights.[19]

Rejection of torture embodied more than a mere policy choice, even one shared by all three branches of government. It also found deep roots in our constitutional heritage. In America, the consensus against torture reflected the ideals of the European Enlightenment, when reformists such as Pierre Ayrault in sixteenth-century France and Cesare Beccaria in eighteenth-century Italy strived to separate the courtroom from the charnel house. The Founding Generation saw the American Revolution as "a vast exercise in the deciphering and applying of the philosophy of the age." Framers of the Constitution such as James Madison styled themselves as inheritors of Enlightenment political science. Thomas Jefferson, John Adams, and Benjamin Franklin all deeply admired Beccaria's *"Dei delitti e delle pene"* (*On Crime and Punishment*).[20]

As a consequence, the Constitution and Bill of Rights reflect the heritage of Ayrault and Beccaria. The Fifth Amendment announces that no one can be "compelled in any criminal case to be a witness against himself." The Eighth Amendment, sweeping more broadly, bars all "cruel and unusual punishments." It is difficult to imagine a constitutional government under the rule of law absent such prohibitions.

Hence, a network of laws against torture, for peace and war, applied on September 10, 2001. The three branches of federal government each played a role in developing these laws. The executive negotiated international treaties, which the Senate ratified. Congress followed up with new rules and new remedies, which in turn the courts applied. The executive branch, including the armed services, took antitorture laws seriously, incorporating them into training manuals and regulations. This ongoing dialogue between the three branches of government was the checks and balances in living operation.

It was not to last.

Assaulting the Law Against Torture

In the year after September 11, 2001, the executive branch secretly undermined or rejected almost all of these clear laws against torture and abuse. These laws formed a threshold check imposed by Congress on the executive branch. The tools in the assault on legal constraints were lawyers inside the executive branch, who developed legal interpretations of the torture laws that stripped out clear rules and prohibitions and replaced them with fuzzy standards that placed no effective restraint on executive power.

Rather than seek greater authority from Congress, and engage in public debate over the utility and morality of "enhanced" interrogation measures, the Bush Administration secretly deployed dubious legal interpretation to eliminate statutory restrictions on coercive interrogation. Although some executive department lawyers argued strenuously for the formal acceptance of Common Article 3, they were firmly beaten back by Vice President Cheney's aide David Addington. Summarizing arguments for and against the application of the Geneva Conventions in January 2002, White House Counsel Alberto Gonzales tellingly argued to President Bush that the "nature of the new war places a high premium on . . . the ability to quickly obtain information from captured terrorists and their sponsors." This need, argued Gonzales, "renders obsolete Geneva's strict limitations on questioning of enemy prisoners." Abrogating the Geneva Conventions thus was a necessary step to expanding the executive branch's power to use extreme and painful interrogation methods.[21]

This desire to break the constraints on the executive branch's use of coercive force came from the Vice President's office. Secretary of State Colin Powell's former executive assistant, Colonel Lawrence Wilkerson, explained that "the philosophical guidance and the flexibility . . . originated in the vice president of the United States' office, and his implementer in this case was Donald Rumsfeld and the Defense Department."[22]

But the hard labor fell to the Office of Legal Counsel (OLC), which provides definitive legal interpretations to all of the agencies of the executive branch. Lawyers in the OLC report to the attorney general, the head of the Justice Department, who in turn takes orders from the president. The OLC receives and responds to requests for legal opinions from the White House and other parts of the federal government, including the CIA and the Defense Department. Legal opinions from OLC are often the final word inside the executive branch. On occasion, this can mean an opinion truly is the last word, since no court generally reviews, and Congress frequently never sees, opinions issued by the OLC.[23]

In opinions requested by the White House, the CIA, and the Defense Department, the post-9/11 OLC applied deeply flawed methods of legal interpretation to undermine the legal checks Congress imposed against torture and abusive treatment.[24] The OLC first assaulted the Geneva Conventions. Then, it displaced clear legal rules prohibiting torture. The predictable consequences were mission creep and plausible deniability. The OLC deployed in these memos a dangerous concept of unchecked presidential power to dismiss the significance of the elaborate ethical tapestry of laws, treaties, and judicial precedents. This hazardous doctrine seems to recur in executive branch reasoning to authorize transfers of suspects to torture by other countries, unlimited presidential detention, and domestic spying without warrants. The immediate beneficiary of these memos, of course, was the White House that requested and endorsed them.

The OLC first took on the Geneva Conventions. The Geneva rules, mandated by Congress for more than fifty years, ought to have governed the 2001 invasion of Afghanistan, an "international" conflict involving one country's invasion by another. But in a series of secret memos, the OLC mined the Geneva Conventions creatively for ambiguities and silences to evade these laws' reach.

The OLC prepared a legal opinion for the President stating first that he had the power to "suspend" application of the Geneva Conventions in Afghanistan, and second that neither the Taliban nor al Qaeda soldiers qualified as POWs under the Third Convention and were instead "unlawful combatants," outside Geneva's ambit. (The phrase "unlawful combatant" is not mentioned in federal law, army regulations, or international law.) President Bush declined to suspend the Geneva treaties but accepted the OLC's second conclusion that neither the Taliban nor al Qaeda qualified as POWs.[25]

The basis for the President's decision was a January 9, 2002, OLC opinion, written by John Yoo and Robert Delahunty, which deployed a series of dubious legal arguments to reach this conclusion about the Taliban and al Qaeda. Initially, the opinion contended that the conflict with al Qaeda in Afghanistan was distinct from the battle against the Taliban, even though Taliban and al Qaeda forces fought side by side in Afghanistan without distinguishing uniforms or insignia. Having artificially split the Afghan conflict into two, Yoo and Delahunty then contended that al Qaeda could not benefit from the Geneva Conventions' protection. And, they argued, since Afghanistan lacked a functioning government and was not "in a position to fulfill its Convention responsibilities," Taliban troops also lost POW status. This interpretation flew in the face of past U.S. practice in Vietnam and Afghanistan; instead, it tracked reasoning deployed by Imperial Japan to deny American soldiers POW status during World War II.[26]

But Yoo and Delahunty made two critical and obvious errors. First, OLC lawyers failed to ask whether Taliban and al Qaeda members fell under the *Fourth* Geneva Convention, which protects individuals who do not qualify as POWs. Had they looked at the relevant army regulation, they would have found that the army itself initially classifies individuals as POWs (protected by the Third Geneva Convention) or civilians (protected by the Fourth): it does not have an "enemy combatant" category. The *U.S. Military Manual* further explains that a combatant not entitled to POW status is not relegated to "enemy combatant" limbo, but is a "protected person" under the Fourth Convention. That is, Yoo and Delahunty selectively read the law, focusing on one set of protections and failing to note that a different set of Geneva protections applied. Had they bothered to examine the army's own regulations and manuals, such an elementary error would have been impossible.[27]

Second, the OLC lawyers failed to ask what happens if an innocent person is accidentally swept up by the military. In a conflict where the military offered $5,000 bounties for al Qaeda and Taliban members, it was especially important to sift combatants from innocent civilians. But Yoo and Delahunty make the breathtakingly fallacious assumption that any person captured by (or handed over to) the U.S. military must necessarily be a member of the Taliban or al Qaeda. One Administration lawyer, who spoke anonymously to journalists about the OLC's reasoning, ascribed more sinister motives, explaining that the government's lawyers "wanted to make a point on executive power—that the President can designate them [the detainees] *all* enemy combatants if he wants to."[28]

The Yoo and Delahunty memo also contained a fleeting harbinger of the new legal doctrine of unlimited presidential power to resist congressional checks in matters of national security. As a historical matter, Yoo and Delahunty argued, the president had had "plenary power over the conduct of foreign relations" since the "very beginning of the Republic." Therefore, they contended, the chief executive could "suspend" America's treaty obligations under the Geneva Conventions and overrule customary international law, including Common Article 3. Further, they hinted that Congress could not criminalize war crimes committed by U.S. forces, since that "would represent a possible infringement of presidential discretion to direct the military."[29]

Secretary of State Colin Powell and the State Department Legal Advisor William Taft argued forcefully that American compliance with the Geneva Conventions should not be discarded so lightly. Neither Powell nor Taft, however, responded to the OLC's intimation of untrammeled executive power (perhaps because this idea played only a minor role in the Geneva Conventions memo). Both pointed to long-standing American practice and to principles that would protect captured American soldiers. As Secretary of State Powell explained to Gonzales, "The United States has never determined that the [Third Geneva Convention] did not apply to an armed conflict in which its forces have been engaged." As Powell well knew, during the first Gulf War, the United States held 1,196 battlefield status hearings under the Geneva Conventions.[30]

On February 7, 2002, President Bush agreed with the OLC. In his capacity "as Commander in Chief and Chief Executive of the United States," Bush declared in a formal order that "none of the provisions of Geneva apply to our conflict with al Qaeda in Afghanistan or elsewhere throughout the world." Thus, neither Taliban nor al Qaeda prisoners would be treated as prisoners of war. Nor would they be accorded the baseline benefits of Common Article 3. Instead, the President ordered:

Our values as a Nation, values that we share with many nations in the world, call for us to treat detainees humanely, including those who are not legally entitled to such treatment. Our Nation has been and will continue to be a strong supporter of Geneva and its principles. *As a matter of policy, the United States Armed Forces shall continue to treat detainees humanely and, to the extent appropriate and consistent with military necessity, in a manner consistent with the principles of Geneva.*

The President's memo bore the Orwellian title "Humane Treatment of al Qaeda and Taliban Detainees." In fact, it voided almost every existing legal guarantee of humane treatment in wartime and replaced them with a virtual invitation to engage in coercive interrogations. We would have seen no rapid deterioration in detainee treatment standards and no spread of torture without President Bush's February 2002 decision to reject the checks imposed by Congress when it adopted the Geneva Conventions into U.S. law. American troops have been deployed overseas many times in the last half-century, including in Iraq in the first Gulf War, and no comparable detainee abuse occurred. Not until June 2006, more than four years later, did the Supreme Court repudiate the President's startling claim that the minimal standards of Common Article 3 could be evaded.[31]

President Bush's February 2002 order rejected clear and unequivocal rules in favor of an ambiguous, nonbinding "policy" of "humane treatment." Like Franklin Delano Roosevelt's authorization of spying on "subversion," Bush's February 7, 2002, order invited loose interpretation and broad exceptions. The order was framed carefully to cover only the "United States Armed Forces"; other parts of the executive branch, such as the CIA, did not fall under the order. Thus, while the order demolished legal protections against coercive treatment, even torture, for *all* detainees in *all* counterterrorism operations, it established in their place a policy that was without content and restricted to only *some* of the U.S. personnel conducting interrogations.

For the armed forces too, the February 7 order removed important legal constraints on torture and violence. Neither the Geneva Conventions nor the American laws and regulations implementing it contain an open-ended exception for "military necessity"—the very phrase Attorney General Frances Biddle had decried as a "mystic cliché" used to justify the internment of Japanese-Americans in World War II. Like the exception for "national security" matters exploited by executive branch officials from J. Edgar Hoover to John Dean, this malleable exception easily swallowed the rule. The Geneva Conventions' drafters rightly recognized that in the heat of the battle, commanders frequently perceive a "necessity" to use coercive tactics in interrogations in order to extract life-saving evidence. A wartime rule against torture with an exception for "military necessity" is, practically speaking, no rule at all.

The elastic boundaries of the President's order also meant it could be extended beyond the Afghan conflict. The President's order came in the last days of the Afghan invasion. Its reference to al Qaeda as well as the Taliban suggested a broader application. Did, for example, insurgents in Iraq fall under the terms of the President's order as members of "al Qaeda" and, therefore, "unlawful combatants" ineligible for POW protection? According to Jane Mayer of the *New Yorker*, only in October 2003 did the Justice Department conclude that "Iraqi insurgents were covered by the Geneva Conventions," leaving open the question of what rules applied until then.[32]

A potent tool of executive branch self-aggrandizement has long been displacement of firm, binding rules by ambiguous, even hollow, standards. Much like Roosevelt's "subversion" standard, the "humane treatment" standard from the February 2002 presidential order turned out to place no effective constraint on the use of coercive interrogation measures, even torture. In contrast to the clear laws adopted by Congress, the term "humane treatment" quite literally meant nothing—in contrast to the detail of Common Article 3. No written guidelines on what constituted "humane treatment" existed. Even the White House could not define it.

Timothy Flanigan had been a Deputy White House Counsel in 2002, and was involved in the development of the President's legal positions on Geneva and interrogation policy. In 2005, he came up for confirmation by the Senate for a Justice Department position, which gave senators an opportunity to question him. Senator Frank Durbin of Illinois asked Flanigan to define "humane treatment." In written answers, Flanigan responded that he was "not aware of any guidance provided by the White House specifically related to the meaning of humane treatment." Flanigan added that "humane treatment" was defined in relation to "[a]ll the facts and circumstances." Later, Alberto Gonzales confirmed Flanigan's answers, conceding to senators that "the term 'humanely' has no precise legal definition."[33]

Senators' questions to Flanigan and Gonzales revealed that the "humane treatment" of the President's February 2002 order meant whatever the executive wanted it to mean. This left the executive branch with open-ended discretion to use whatever brutal tactics it saw fit. During the Cold War, the FBI misused a similar kind of discretion when it designated groups such as the nonviolent Southern Christian Leadership Conference as "hate" groups and thus domestic threats warranting surveillance and disruption. Loose language, now as then, opened the door wide to unlawful uses of intelligence powers.

Senator Durbin asked Flanigan whether water-boarding, mock execution, or physical beatings could be considered "humane." Remarkably, Flanigan refused to state categorically that these techniques (which, incidentally, would be illegal torture under federal criminal law) could *never* be classed as "humane." To the contrary, Flanigan explained, whether a particular tactic was "humane" depended on the surrounding circumstances. It is hardly surprising, therefore, that Captain Fishback would find that his superior officers in Iraq and Afghanistan "failed to set clear standards, communicate those standards and enforce those standards."[34] No such clear standard existed.

Having sidestepped the legal constraints of the Geneva Conventions that Congress codified into U.S. law, however, the White House was still not free to use any and all coercive interrogation techniques. Another legal barrier stood between the executive branch and Gonzales's desired "ability to quickly obtain information from captured terrorists and their sponsors": the 1984 Convention Against Torture and the federal antitorture statute that prohibited cruel, inhuman, and degrading treatment and criminalized torture. These laws, however, survived only a few months longer than the Geneva Conventions before being assailed by similarly flawed legal interpretations and the assertion that the president stood above the law in national security matters.

In a second series of legal memoranda, the OLC assailed the laws that prohibited torture in order to expand executive branch discretion to use painful or coercive methods of interrogation. Unlike the OLC opinions about the Geneva Conventions, however, the public does not, at the time of this writing, have access to all of the OLC's memos on torture. We know that the OLC prepared three key memos. In August 2002, the OLC prepared two memos at the request of the CIA, an agency that fell outside the President's February 2002 order and its "humane treatment" command. Two have not been released: a memo assessing specific interrogation tactics, and a March 2003 memo addressing the law that members of the armed forces must follow.[35]

The August 2002 OLC legal opinion for the CIA that *is* public concerns the scope of the federal law imposing criminal penalties for torture. The problem came into focus in March 2002, when CIA and FBI agents shot and captured al Qaeda member Abu Zubaydah in Faisalabad, in northeastern Pakistan. After treating his wounds in Pakistan, the CIA transferred Zubaydah to a secret prison outside Pakistan for questioning. But what kind of questioning? At the CIA's request, White House counsel Alberto Gonzales convened Justice and Defense Department lawyers to consider "five or six pressure techniques proposed by the CIA." (Some evidence suggests these techniques were already in use.)[36]

Although the precise timing of the decisions remains unclear, these discussions led to the August 2002 opinion, signed by the chief of the OLC, Assistant Attorney General Jay S. Bybee, but reportedly written by John Yoo with

David Addington's aid. The opinion dispenses with virtually all legal bars to official torture, first through aggressive and deeply flawed legal interpretation, and then through application of a principle of unchecked presidential power. It first refines the meaning of "torture" down to an extraordinarily narrow class of conduct (the deeply flawed legal interpretation). It then posits that the president, acting as commander in chief, can in any case override the prohibitions of criminal law, providing his subordinates with several alternative defenses to any prosecution for torture (the principle of unchecked presidential power). In practical effect, these arguments repudiated all legal constraint on coercive treatment in the course of counterterrorism operations.[37]

The federal torture statute criminalizes "any act by which severe pain or suffering, whether physical or mental, is intentionally inflicted." The OLC redefined "torture" as only such conduct that gives rise to pain "that would ordinarily be associated with a sufficiently serious physical condition or injury such as death, organ failure, or serious impediment of body functions." In other words, no organ failure (or its analog), no foul. To reach this interpretation, the OLC drew on an entirely unrelated health-benefits statute defining "emergency medical conditions" for the purpose of triggering a financial payment from the federal government.

This interpretation is implausible, since pain can be "severe" without organ failure. It exemplifies the executive's use of legal interpretation to undermine checks on executive power and authorizes coercive interrogation methods that Congress placed out of legal bounds. It also sharply conflicts with past State Department views. Consider, for example, a State Department report on the Iraqi regime of Saddam Hussein published in March 2003, which condemned:

> branding, electric shock administered to the genitals and other areas, beating, removal of fingernails, . . . suspension from rotating ceiling fans, dripping of acid on the skin, rape, breaking of limbs, denial of food and water, extended solitary confinement in dark and extremely small compartments, and threats to rape or otherwise harm family members and relatives.[38]

The OLC's opinion defined torture to exclude most of these tactics.

The most startling argument in the memo, however, concerns the scope of presidential power. The OLC concluded that the torture prohibition "would be unconstitutional if it impermissibly encroached on the president's constitutional authority to conduct a military campaign." The president, in other words, has the power "to order interrogations of enemy combatants to gain intelligence information" in whatever way he sees fit. That is, Congress, despite its constitutional power to "make rules for the government and regulation of the land and naval forces," could neither impose checks nor exercise oversight when the president acts as commander in chief. Rather, the Constitution of the United States, the OLC argued, licenses the president to ignore duly enacted law and order the torture of any citizen or noncitizen in the name of "national security."

Presidential power, according to the OLC, not only negates restraints on the president's power to order torture, it also bars other forms of interbranch oversight. Thus, the OLC argued, federal prosecutors may not pursue indictments in torture cases when torture is "authorized pursuant to one of the President's constitutional powers," thanks to the absolute presidential control over prosecutions. In addition, the OLC suggested that subordinate officers facing prosecutions for torture could also raise defenses of "necessity" and "the nation's right to self-defense" as a bar to criminal liability.[39]

Moreover, the OLC argued, the president does not even need to flex his supposed unlimited power in national security matters to loosen legal constraints on torture. Rather, the OLC invoked a principle of legal interpretation known as the principle of "constitutional avoidance" to conclude that the torture statute does not bind the president in the first instance and cannot be a basis for prosecution. In the hands of judges, the "constitutional avoidance" principle is a way of showing respect for Congress, by avoiding the conclusion that Congress would pass a law that infringed on constitutional values without careful deliberation and a clear statement of its intent. In the hands of the OLC, it became, for all practical purposes, a self-dealing way to deny congressional checks on executive power. The OLC applied the constitutional avoidance principle here to reach the remarkable conclusion that Congress did not intend to extend the criminal prohibition on state-ordered torture in the United States to impinge on the president's constitutional power to defend the national security. Relying on the flawed assumption that the president had constitutional power to order torture, the OLC contended that the torture statute simply did not reach presidentially sanctioned torture. The secrecy shrouding the August 2002 memo, moreover, ensured that the argument for a narrow reading of the statute could not be corrected by Congress.[40]

The results were predictable. In April 2002, Bush publicly announced Zubaydah's capture, labeling him "one of the top operatives plotting and planning death and destruction on the United States." But soon after, FBI agents reviewed Zubaydah's diaries. They found that Zubaydah suffered from multiple personality disorder and had three separate personas. Unsurprisingly, Zubaydah turned out to be not a top al Qaeda operative but "a logistics man, a fixer." Having declared in public that Zubaydah was something else, President Bush was not ready to back down: the new torture policy that crystallized in the August 2002 OLC opinion was rolled out. Zubaydah was tortured even though the President knew him to be a bit player suffering serious mental illness.[41]

• • •

Seeking to reassure the American public, President Bush explained: "The instructions went out to our people to adhere to the law. That ought to comfort you. . . . You might look at these laws, and that might provide comfort for you. And those were the instructions . . . from me to the government." Bush also told Bob Schieffer of CBS that he did not "think" that a president "can order torture."[42] The law on torture, as interpreted and undermined by the OLC, suggests this promise is only cold comfort. Further undermining Bush's statement, the Administration very deliberately refused to back off from its notion that the President as commander in chief can reject the application of any law.

The August 2002 memo on torture did not become public until after 2004 revelations of abuses at the Abu Ghraib prison in Iraq. Condemnation of the OLC's reasoning was quick and widespread.[43] In 2004, the White House moved publicly to repudiate the contents of the OLC's August 2002 opinion; in fact, the OLC had rejected the memo's analysis as legally untenable in late 2003.[44] Any semblance of contrition, however, was belied by the executive's actions. The Administration distanced itself from neither Jay Bybee nor John Yoo. Before the opinion's release, President Bush nominated Bybee, who had been a law professor at Louisiana State University, to the Ninth Circuit Court of Appeals, and the Senate confirmed him. The White House also pushed for Yoo to be made OLC chief. Although then–Attorney General John Ashcroft rejected the suggestion, his resistance did not hinge on concerns about the contents of Yoo's August 2002 torture memo.[45]

The OLC released an opinion in December 2004 to replace the August 2002 memo, adopting a more realistic view of the law's restrictions. But even this repudiation contained less than first met the eye. A footnote to the December 2004 memo warned that none of the "conclusions" reached in earlier OLC memos "would be different under the standards set forth in this memorandum"—that is, any interrogation tactic approved in the OLC's still-classified August 2002 legal opinion remained lawful. But there is ample evidence that tactics such as water-boarding were permitted under the August 2002 opinion. How much difference, then, did the new opinion make?[46]

There was another, more troubling, gap in the December 2004 memo. The OLC quietly but pointedly refused to repudiate the argument for unchecked presidential power. The President, in other words, kept his trump card.[47]

Metastasis of Torture

Between them, the President's February 7, 2002, order and the OLC's legal opinions on the Geneva Conventions and antitorture statutes abolished the clear legal constraints Congress had imposed on coercive interrogations by the armed forces and CIA. They left open-ended discretion in their wake. We have seen how Cold War intelligence agencies exploited such exceptions to turn surveillance and disruption techniques intended for Soviet agents against innocent Americans, and how Cold War leaders misused plausible deniability by giving indirect orders to violate the law. History thus teaches that intelligence powers wielded in secret and without checks and balances do not yield wise policy. Even if there is no guarantee of wisdom when all three branches act in unison, the chance of unwise, precipitous action is vastly higher when one branch acts without any external check—all the more so when the decision is the work of a small, highly placed coterie within the branch.

Loosening the legal fetters on executive power led directly to the spread of torture across America's global counterterrorism operations. Agencies and officers of the post-9/11 executive branch succumbed quickly to the dangers of mission creep and plausible deniability.

It was the CIA that sought the August 2002 opinion on torture. Coercive tactics authorized for the CIA quickly spread to the armed services—first in Guantánamo, and then Iraq. By 2004, *Newsweek* could point to "a mounting body of . . . evidence around the world" of abuse, torture, and deaths in U.S. custody. Even former Defense Secretary James Schlesinger conceded that prisoner abuse was "widespread and, though inflicted on only a small percentage of those detained . . . serious both in number and effect."[48] Schlesinger was talking of a "small percentage" of tens of thousands of detainees.

The spread of coercive interrogation tactics tracked widening adoption of the OLC's legal analysis for the CIA within the executive branch. In March 2003, the OLC gave the general counsel to the Defense Department a legal opinion substantially "similar" to the OLC's August 2002 memo for the CIA. This March 2003 document, entitled "Military Interrogation of Alien Unlawful Combatants Held Outside the United States," remains secret at the time of this writing. But, according to Jane Mayer of the *New Yorker*:

> The document dismissed virtually all national and internal laws regulating the treatment of prisoners, including war-crimes and assault statutes, and it was radical in its view that in wartime the President can fight enemies by whatever means he sees fit. According to the memo, Congress has no constitutional right to interfere with the President in his role as Commander-in-Chief, including making laws that limit the ways in which prisoners may be interrogated.

The OLC's memo for the military, in short, duplicated its analysis for the CIA. Standards initially designed for a limited pool of CIA agents hence migrated to the far larger pool of military interrogators.[49]

Interrogators at the Guantánamo Bay Naval Base were already straining at the leash to use coercive tactics otherwise prohibited by law. In late 2002, lawyers at Guantánamo prepared an extensive list of coercive interrogation tactics for Pentagon approval. Their request blithely ignored laws prohibiting coercive interrogation. These lawyers remarkably concluded that threats of death against a detainee or his family were "legally available" even though the Geneva Conventions unequivocally forbid such threats. Nevertheless, Secretary of Defense Donald Rumsfeld initially signed off on the use of these tactics.[50]

The Guantánamo lawyers' position provoked strong reactions, however, from more seasoned military lawyers. Navy General Counsel Alberto Mora successfully pressed Rumsfeld to rescind his initial approval. Mora then secured a place in a Defense Department working group established by Rumsfeld to design new interrogation protocols.[51]

But this working group overrode Mora and other military lawyers and adopted the analysis of the March 2003 OLC memo. Mora and other military lawyers loudly dissented. Major Jack Rives, a judge advocate general for the air force, protested to the air force general counsel that the working group relied "almost exclusively" on OLC endorsement of methods that "on their face, amount to violations of domestic criminal law" and the Uniform Code of Military Justice, which also contains criminal laws against degrading treatment. Such methods would alienate military allies, and put military commanders "at risk of criminal accusations abroad." Rives was ignored.[52]

The working group's final report, entitled "Detainee Interrogations in the Global War on Terrorism: Assessment of Legal, Historical, Policy, and Operational Considerations," repeated verbatim large portions of the August 2002 OLC opinion—including its analysis of presidential power—and listed thirty-five permissible interrogation tactics. The working group pushed the OLC's positions even further by suggesting a "superior orders" defense to criminal liability for torture. But "just following orders" has not been a defense against criminal charges for war crimes, including torture, since it was decisively rejected by the Nuremburg war crimes tribunal. So the working group endorsed an argument last seriously proffered by Nazi war criminals.[53]

The Defense Department insists that the working group report was never distributed. Interrogation tactics in Iraq, however, can be traced back to the OLC's legal analysis. Rumsfeld endorsed and adopted twenty-four of the working group's thirty-five recommendations—including "pride and ego down," "sleep adjustment," isolation, dietary manipulation, and environmental manipulation. (These anodyne terms, like nebulous authorizations used by the Cold War CIA, contained leeway for creative interpretation.) General Ricardo Sanchez, who oversaw Iraq operations, authorized working group tactics in two memos in late 2003. Sanchez's first instruction allowed the use of military dogs and up to thirty days' isolation. The second, seemingly more re-strained, instruction employed open-ended generalities such as "fear up" and "pride and ego down," and did not rule out the use of dogs. An army investi-gation concluded that Sanchez's decisions on interrogation policies "us[ed] rea-soning from the President's February 7, 2002" memo, including the notion that Sanchez "had inherent authority of the Commander in a Theater of War" to overrule the Geneva Conventions. And posters detailing interrogation poli-cies inside Abu Ghraib even tracked Rumsfeld's earlier memos.[54]

Moreover, even though the Administration disclaimed any "link between any authorized interrogation techniques and the actual abuses" at Abu Ghraib, the specific tactics used and photographed at that Iraqi prison—including hooding, stress positions, sexual humiliation, and military dogs—echoed in un-canny detail tactics authorized by the OLC and the working group report.[55]

Collaboration between military and CIA personnel in Iraq quickened the military's adoption of brutal CIA interrogation tactics. An army investigation into the Abu Ghraib incidents explained that "CIA detention and interroga-tion practices led to a loss of accountability, abuse, reduced interagency coop-eration, and an unhealthy mystique."[56]

Mission creep also occurred within the armed services. Tactics designed for one theater of operations (say, Guantánamo's more controlled quarters) "mi-grated" to other locations such as Iraq. Human Rights Watch reports that inside Iraq, military intelligence units systematized the use of abusive interrogation tactics from 2003 to 2005. Commanders at Guantánamo developed new in-terrogation techniques based on military research into behavioral psychology. Advisors from a Pentagon program known as "Survival, Evasion, Resistance, and Escape," or SERE, generated "techniques" for Guantánamo interrogators. SERE trains U.S. pilots and others at high risk of capture by enemy forces to resist interrogation by simulating coercive interrogation. SERE-tested tech-niques include water-boarding and "religious trashing" (verbal and physical assaults on religious symbols such as the Bible). Adopting SERE tactics, the military was in a very literal way following the advice of the 1954 Doolittle Commission. It was adopting the tactics of the enemy.[57]

In November 2004, Major General Geoffrey Miller, who had toughened interrogation tactics at Guantánamo, was dispatched to Iraq to create a "dynamic intelligence apparatus" and to "improve velocity and operational effectiveness of counterterrorism interrogations" at prisons such as Abu Ghraib. Miller was not alone. Members of the 519th Military Intelligence Brigade implicated in prisoner mistreatment in Bagram, Afghanistan, also transferred to Abu Ghraib, bringing with them coercive techniques.[58]

In the end, the military's own investigations found "[p]olicies approved for use on al Qaeda and Taliban detainees who were not afforded the protection of [enemy prisoner of war] status under the Geneva Conventions now applied to detainees who did fall under the Geneva Convention protections." It was a prime example of mission creep.[59]

The President's decision to reject the congressional limits on torture in the Geneva Conventions and the antitorture statutes led to another kind of mission creep. Without legal rules requiring the military to distinguish between legitimate detainees and innocent people, the innocent were imprisoned and interrogated along with the enemy. Rejecting the Geneva Conventions, the OLC concluded that the United States did not need to hold status hearings to determine whether a captured detainee indeed belonged to the Taliban or al Qaeda. Instead, the President could simply "find that all of the Taliban forces do not fall within the legal definition of POW," and there would be no "legal 'doubt' as to the prisoners' status."[60]

Yet there will always be factual as well as legal doubts about whether the right people are arrested. The predictable result of Bush's order was the lockup and coercive interrogation of uncounted hundreds, perhaps thousands, of innocent detainees.

But "evaluation was replaced by tautology," the British journalist David Rose explained in his study of the Guantánamo facility: "If you were in Guantánamo, it was because you had been 'captured on the battlefield,' and if you had been captured on the battlefield, you must have been with the Taliban or al Qaeda." In January 2002, Gonzales ordered intelligence officers to prepare a one-page form about each Afghan prisoner transferred to Guantánamo, certifying the President's "reason to believe" their involvement in terrorism. For most prisoners, intelligence personnel found they lacked enough information to fill even one page. And "as many as half"—including an "elderly and emotionally disturbed" man who was "so wizened that interrogators nicknamed him 'Al Qaeda Claus'"—had "little or no intelligence value."[61]

Plausible Deniability Once More

Mission creep was not the only Cold War pathology to appear once the Administration did away with clear laws barring torture. The Cold War intelligence community was run to maintain "plausible deniability" for political leaders. Post-9/11 torture policy was no different.

Incitement to torture came both implicitly and explicitly. From early 2002, military leaders drummed a tattoo of public messages to soldiers to "get tough" with detainees. Early on, Defense Secretary Rumsfeld dismissed other nations' complaints about prisoner mistreatment as "isolated pockets of international hyperventilation." Consistently, executive branch leaders described detainees as hard-core terrorists who did not "deserve" rights, even as internal Pentagon reports were making clear that many could not be tied to any terrorist threat. The Chairman of the Joint Chiefs of Staff, General Richard B. Myers, described the Guantánamo detainees as "people who would gnaw through the hydraulic lines at the back of a C-17 to bring it down." These statements set a clear tone, conveying the impression that all detainees were "guilty" and thus deserved abuse.[62]

According to General Sanchez, there was "intense pressure" from "different levels of the chain of command" to obtain results from Iraq detentions. The message reached the ground. An e-mail from an army captain stationed in Iraq obtained by the ACLU reported that: "Col[onel] Boltz has made it clear that we want these individuals broken. Casualties are mounting and we need to start gathering info to help protect our fellow soldiers from further attacks." Former Defense Secretary Schlesinger's investigation concluded that "pressure for additional intelligence" led to "stronger" interrogation tactics. The army's inspector general confirmed that a "do what it takes mindset," fostered by senior military and civilian leaders, "encouraged behavior at the harsher end of the acceptable range of behavior toward detainees" that "may unintentionally" have "increase[d] the likelihood of abuse." With so predictable a causal chain, the inspector general had to stretch to reach the conclusion that the incitement was not intentional.[63]

There is also evidence of more specific instructions to engage in illegal coercive treatment, albeit delivered in ways that ensured plausible deniability. Consider a briefing convened by Defense Secretary Rumsfeld about how the military should respond to the unexpected and accelerating insurgency in Iraq. Military lawyers attended the briefing, and left aghast. Soon after the Abu Ghraib scandal broke, they approached a respected New York lawyer, Scott Horton, a leader of the New York City Bar Association. Horton was given the following account by an officer who attended the briefing:

> At an intelligence briefing conducted in the summer of 2003 in the Pentagon for the benefit of Rumsfeld, and with the attendance of [Stephen] Cambone, [General William] Boykin and other senior officers, Rumsfeld complained loudly about the quality of the intelligence which was being gathered from detainees in Iraq. He contrasted it with the intelligence which was being produced from detainees at Guantánamo following the institution there of new "extreme" interrogation practices. Expressing anger and frustration over the application of Geneva Convention rules in Iraq, *Rumsfeld gave an oral order to dispatch MG Miller to Iraq to "Gitmoize" the intelligence process.*

As Horton's information shows, when General Miller took harsh tactics, including psychological tactics originally developed in the SERE program, from

Guantánamo to Iraq, he was not acting on his own initiative. It was the Secretary of Defense who wanted to "Gitmoize" tactics in Iraq, in stark violation of the Geneva Conventions.[64]

James Risen of the *New York Times* reported another example of indirect orders concerning the capture and treatment of alleged al Qaeda member Abu Zubaydah. During his March 2002 capture, Zubaydah was shot in the leg. He was treated in Pakistan before being transferred to a secret prison in Thailand. According to Risen, CIA director George Tenet met with President Bush days after Zubaydah's arrest. Risen's source told him:

> Bush asked Tenet what information the CIA was getting out of Zubaydah. Tenet responded that they weren't getting anything yet because Abu Zubaydah had been so badly wounded that he was heavily medicated. He was too groggy from painkillers to talk coherently. Bush turned to Tenet and asked: *"Who authorized putting him on pain medication?"*

(Andrea Mitchell of NBC news has suggested that the comment may have been made by Cheney, not Bush; she has not asserted that the comment was not made.)

Another journalist, Ron Suskind, explains that Bush would press CIA chief George Tenet, day in and day out, with questions about whether information was being pumped from captured al Qaeda operatives. In his book *The One-Percent Doctrine*, Suskind explains that this was "how, time and again, boundaries are stretched."[65]

Bush's comment might be interpreted as mere jocular banter. But presidents know that banter to subordinates is often perceived as orders, as the testimony of Richard Bissell and Richard Helms about the Castro assassination plots showed. In this context, it seems more likely Bush was, as Suskind suggests, giving an "order to push the CIA to get tough with Abu Zubaydah . . . indirectly, without the paper trail that would have come from a written presidential authorization." Moreover, Suskind contends that Cheney, "as far back as the Ford presidency, had experimented with the concept of keeping certain issues away from the chief executive," such as the precise details of coercive methods being used. In Cheney's eyes, adds Suskind, "the problem was that the President should [be] 'protected' from such knowledge."[66]

The Executive's Freewheeling Interpretation Power

The executive branch must interpret the laws it applies. But this obligation to interpret also furnishes opportunities to resist legal checks imposed on executive power. OLC interpretations and positions, nevertheless, bind neither

Congress nor the courts. In theory, executive misuse of its interpretive authority can be corrected by the two other branches. In practice, however, the executive branch has resources to hinder post hoc judicial and legislative constraints.

Courts have traditionally imposed scant constraint on overseas torture policies. Since the end of the nineteenth century, the Supreme Court held that not all constitutional rights apply beyond United States borders. Beyond Guantánamo, U.S. courts have not exercised jurisdiction over coercive interrogation practices. Even for Guantánamo detainees, judicial oversight has been slow and limited. Indeed, the most important practical consequence of lawsuits filed on behalf of Guantánamo detainees was not any judicial remedy but the simple fact that detainees had the chance to speak to lawyers. In any case, as it became clear that federal courts would exercise jurisdiction over Guantánamo, the executive simply shifted the focus on detainee operations further overseas, to sites in Bagram, Afghanistan, and other still-secret locations. In practical terms, therefore, direct judicial oversight proved difficult and incremental.[67]

The August 2002 OLC legal opinion also contended that the president can bar federal prosecutors from bringing criminal proceedings against individual soldiers, officers, or agents who use coercive measures on the president's orders. Because courts have long accepted that prosecutorial decisions lie almost wholly in the discretion of the executive branch, a presidential decision to decline prosecution is almost impossible to challenge. Unsurprisingly, with the exception of criminal proceedings against low-level soldiers implicated in the highly publicized Abu Ghraib proceedings, it appears most federal prosecutions for torture have been disabled. One study of the approximately hundred deaths in U.S. custody, including thirty-four confirmed homicides, found that only twelve resulted in any punishment for senior U.S. officials.[68]

As a practical matter, moreover, the Justice Department's involvement in developing legal theories to justify coercive interrogations hampered prosecutors, who risked confrontation with political superiors. One Justice Department investigation into the death of an Iraqi during CIA interrogation foundered in part because the OLC may have authorized the tactics used, a "stress position" in which the detainee assumes a crucifixion-like pose. The Supreme Court's June 2006 decision that Common Article 3 applies to all counterterrorism detention operations, however, has the effect of making it clear beyond doubt that all of the coercive interrogation policies sanctioned by the Bush Administration are "grave breaches" of the Geneva Conventions. Predictably, the Administration's response was evasive: it claimed the *military* had always followed "the overreaching requirement of Common Article 3" for "humane treatment." Of course, since the Administration viewed water-boarding as potentially humane (as Timothy Flanigan revealed), this is hardly a meaningful concession. And once again, the Administration strategically omitted all mention of the CIA.[69]

Later, responding further to the June 2006 decision, President Bush proposed legislation that tried substantially to narrow the scope of conduct criminalized by Common Article 3. In a September 6, 2006, speech, the President, surrounded by families of the 9/11 victims, pressed the case for "an alternative set of procedures" to interrogate terrorism suspects. These procedures, President Bush explained, could not be described to the public lest this "help the terrorists learn how to resist questioning." But, the President assured his audience, the procedures worked. By way of example, President Bush cited the interrogation of Abu Zubaydah, telling the nation that Zubaydah identified al Qaeda leader Ramzi bin al Shibh. Strikingly, he made no mention of al-Libi, whose tortured confession provided a false link between al Qaeda and Iraq. At the same time as he defended these "alternative procedures," the President also purported to reject torture: "The United States does not torture. . . . I have not authorized it—and I will not authorize it."[70]

But the President's argument was factually incorrect in key respects. Journalists such as Ron Suskind have cast doubt on the Zubaydah story, suggesting that Zubaydah was mentally ill and had little information. Whatever the facts of Zubaydah's sanity are, Bush's claim about al Shibh is patently false: there are more than twenty references to al Shibh's involvement in al Qaeda in the *Washington Post* alone that *predate* Zubaydah's capture. The President's claim that Zubaydah "identified" al Shibh simply does not bear scrutiny.

No less unsound is the claim that the "alternative set of procedures" cannot be revealed without tipping off the enemy. As an initial matter, these tactics are no secret. ABC News listed these "alternate" tactics, which included waterboarding and hypothermia, in a November 2005 report. It is not the case that terrorists could train to overcome such tactics. Rather, the President could not talk about the tactics without revealing his claim not to have authorized torture as manifest hypocrisy. For his claim rested on a narrow and untenable definition of "torture," a definition at odds with established law and common law. It rested, in other words, on a lawyerly obfuscation that the White House knew its audience would not pick up.[71]

The same day as Bush's speech, another less-trumpeted news conference took place across the Potomac at the Pentagon. Lieutenant-General John Kimmons unveiled a new army interrogations manual. The new manual, in accord with the Geneva Conventions, barred the army from using the "tough" interrogation tactics that Bush proposed for the CIA. Unlike Bush, Kimmons had no trouble explaining the problem with coercive interrogation techniques:

No good intelligence is going to come from abusive practices. I think history tells us that. I think the empirical evidence of the past five hard years tells us that. . . . [A]ny piece of intelligence which is obtained under duress through the use of abusive techniques would be of questionable credibility. . . .

In conclusion, Kimmons rejected "abusive practices" in no uncertain terms: "Nothing good will come of them."[72] This, of course, did not prevent the White House from pressing for authority to abuse and defending this authority by the strategic use of ambiguous and misleading language to undermine a key part of the Supreme Court's ruling that all detainees are protected by minimal standards of human decency. And it did not stop the Congress from enacting a law in September 2006, the Military Commissions Act, that left literally fatal ambiguities in antitorture rules.

Excessive secrecy has meant that legislators learn of executive legal interpretations years after the fact. Congress received no briefing when the Administration made dramatic changes in American antitorture law. And the OLC's August 2002 opinion was leaked to the press and public only after the April 2004 disclosures of prisoner mistreatment at Abu Ghraib.

There is no justification for keeping legal opinions on torture secret. Legal documents pitched at an abstract level, with no operational details, do not warrant secrecy stamps. To the contrary, when the federal government acts in our name and for our sake, the public has a heightened interest in disclosure. Examination of the documents that have been released makes it obvious that it was only fear of public revulsion and international condemnation that led to secrecy stamps.

At a minimum, there is no justification for keeping fundamental shifts in law from Congress, the body that enacted the law in the first place. Elected representatives have a powerful interest in knowing whether the laws they enact are followed or reinterpreted to the point of being unrecognizable. Indeed, in 2002, Congress even enacted a rule requiring the attorney general to report to Congress any "formal or informal policy to refrain . . . from enforcing, applying, or administering any provision of any Federal statute . . . on the ground that such provision is unconstitutional." At least with regard to antitorture laws, it appears that this law was violated. As a leading advocate of disclosure, Senator Carl Levin of Michigan explained: "There's no claim of executive privilege. There's no claim of national security—we've offered to keep it classified. . . . They just don't want us to know what they're doing, or have done."[73]

Even when Congress wants to reject a legal interpretation offered by the executive branch, it confronts considerable obstacles. Spurred by the letter from Captain Fishback, Arizona Senator John McCain proposed legislation in 2005 making abusive interrogations unlawful. Based on his own bitter POW experience, McCain argued that torture yields defective intelligence "because under torture, a detainee will tell his interrogator anything to make the pain stop." American torture also endangers captured U.S. troops by legitimizing torture, and "exact[s] on us a terrible toll in the war of ideas, because inevitably these abuses become public."[74]

The White House response, spearheaded by Vice President Cheney, deployed formidable political and legal tools. Cheney argued that clear rules on torture or lesser coercive methods "would restrict the President's ability to protect Americans effectively from terrorist attack and bring terrorists to justice." In July 2005, he briefed Senators McCain, John Warner, and Lindsey Graham. With him was Porter Goss, then the CIA chief, to present the CIA's case for coercive interrogation. Cheney's chief of staff, David Addington, a "strong and unyielding" advocate of executive power, also pressed congressional staffers to resist McCain's idea and impeded internal Defense Department efforts to issue clear antiabuse rules. This campaign culminated in the threat of the first presidential veto of the Bush presidency—of a $442 million defense appropriations bill with McCain's provision attached.[75]

When the veto threat failed, the White House found other ways to sap McCain's proposal. During the Senate-House conference, executive branch lawyers inserted last-minute exceptions, ambiguities, and riders into McCain's provision. The end result was significantly diluted. Executive branch lawyers, for example, inserted a broad defense to civil and criminal liability for coercive interrogation. This defense allows officials to justify their acts by pointing to an OLC legal opinion. Worse, the Administration hitched the McCain provision to another proviso that seemed to limit judicial remedies for Guantánamo detainees. McCain's antiabuse provision thus seemed to come with a heavy price tag: the narrowing of judicial constraints on executive conduct at Guantánamo.[76]

Finally, when President Bush signed the appropriations bill containing McCain's provision, he also issued a "signing statement." This is an official document setting forth the executive's understanding of the law. Although presidential signing statements signaling noncompliance were identified as a tool of executive power during the Reagan Administration, and defended by conservative commentator Terry Eastland, it has been President Bush who has made the most extensive use of signing statements as a means not only to interpret new laws, but also to signal his intent not to comply with Congress's directions. By April 2006, Bush signing statements had signaled the President's intent not to comply with more than 750 provisions of laws concerning national security and disclosure. Remarkably, Bush even issued a signing state-

ment indicating his intent not to comply with a federal law that mandated reports to Congress when the executive branch decides not to follow a law
because it believes it to be unconstitutional.[77]

The use of signing statements to indicate noncompliance is in sharp contrast to early presidents' practice of using their veto and refusing to sign laws
they believed unconstitutional. Unlike the presidential veto, use of a signing
statement of noncompliance is not a high-profile act (signing statements,
though, are generally available on the White House Web site), and has previously not carried heavy political costs even when the president took extraordinary measures. In the case of the McCain Amendment, Bush used his
signing statement to assert unlimited power to set anticoercion rules aside:
"The executive branch shall construe [the McCain Amendment]," Bush said,
"in a manner consistent with the constitutional authority of the President . . .
as Commander in Chief." With these words, the President rejected Congress's
authority to limit coercive interrogation tactics and claimed what Pennsylvania Senator Arlen Specter termed "authority to pick and choose what he likes
and what he doesn't like in legislation." This McCain signing statement also
demonstrates the kind of nebulous formation that the executive branch can
use to reject the application of law without revealing the legal basis or reasoning for its refusal.[78]

The McCain legislation was not the final word on abusive interrogation
tactics. In the wake of the Supreme Court's *Hamdan* ruling on Common Article 3, which cast into doubt the CIA's use of cruel and inhumane interrogation tactics, the White House pushed for new legislation that ensured "clarity"
instead of the Common Article 3 bar on cruel, humiliating, and degrading
treatment. According to the President, Common Article 3 was "very vague."
At a September 15, 2006 press conference, he complained, "What does that
mean, 'outrages upon human dignity'? That's a statement that is wide open to
interpretation. And what I'm proposing is that there be some clarity in the law
so that our professionals will have no doubt that that which they're doing is
legal."[79]

Clarity, however, was never the Administration's goal. After all, this was the
Administration that for four years had used a standard of "humane treatment"
that lacked any definition whatsoever. Rather than clarity, the Administration
sought license to torture. Its legislative proposal was a contorted text that redefined criminal violations of Common Article 3 by distinguishing between
"serious" and "severe" kinds of pain, illogically describing the former as only
pain that is "extreme." The proposal's tangled language opened up manifold
opportunities for the kind of "creative" OLC lawyering that drilled holes in
the torture statute in August 2002. Its definitions omitted "transitory" mental
harms—including, for example, death threats or threats to rape a spouse or

child, all long-recognized forms of torture that are "transitory." And a close reading of the bill suggested that none of the CIA's enhanced interrogation tactics, including water-boarding, hypothermia, and longtime standing, would be legally problematic.[80]

The ensuing public and legislative debate marked an improvement over executive unilateralism. Still, it left much to be desired. At the threshold, military lawyers were once more kept at arm's length during internal executive branch debates on the legislative process, their input confined to "mostly wording changes and procedural matters." Then, when legislation was introduced into Congress, less than a tenth of the members of Congress were told about the kind of methods the White House wanted to sanction. In a remarkable rerun of pre–Church Committee Cold War complaisance, legislators such as Senator Jeff Sessions of Alabama took the line that "I don't know what the CIA has been doing nor should I know." Few understood that the Administration's legislation would provide not "clarity" but license to abuse. And the resulting debates barely scratched the surface of the troubling issues raised by American adoption of tactics only our enemies had previously embraced.[81]

The legislation that ensued was unsurprisingly shameful. At one stroke, it gutted critical rules against torture and coercive interrogation and disabled mechanisms for ensuring that the rules that do exist are enforced. It granted the president sweeping and ill-defined new detention powers—and then dramatically cut back on the means detainees have to challenge the factual and legal bases of their detention. In so doing, it cut at the roots of one of the most important guarantees of liberty, the judicial remedy of habeas corpus. It was an assault, in other words, on the fundamental checks and balances of American governance enacted at a time of electoral fervor by a president weakened by a catastrophic foreign war and a craven Congress unwilling to meet its constitutional obligations.

Flawed Internal Investigations

Public outcry at the photographs from Abu Ghraib sparked momentary attention to the spread of torture. In response, the executive branch authorized a series of narrow investigations, largely by military officers within the chain of command, mostly focused tightly on a specific unit or incident, in part to deflect calls for a comprehensive, independent investigation by Congress.

The resulting reports shed some light, but all were limited in focus or flawed in methodology. The contrast with the Church Committee was telling. The Committee used a panoply of tools, including wide-ranging document discovery and witness testimony, to develop a full accounting of Cold War intelligence agencies' overreaching. It also included senators from both sides of the

aisle who worked in a bipartisan fashion to bring to light executive misman-
agement and misconduct.

The official investigations of torture by the Bush Administration created
the impression of oversight without the substance of accountability. Only two
of the ten or so published reports—by Vice Admiral Albert T. Church and former Defense Secretary James Schlesinger—even tried to canvas detention policy
as a whole. All the investigations shared common failings: "failures to investigate all relevant agencies and personnel; cumulative reporting (increasing the
risk that errors and omissions may be perpetuated in successive reports); con-
tradictory conclusions; questionable use of security classification to withhold
information; failure to address senior military and civilian command responsibility; and, perhaps, above all, the absence of any clear plan for corrective
action."[82] Not one report even touched on the responsibility of senior Administration officials. Compounding these inadequacies, several of the reports
have not been fully released to the public. Both the wrongs and the investigations of the wrongs thus remain obscured from proper public scrutiny.

Half the official reports focused narrowly on Iraq or Abu Ghraib alone. But
soldiers with evidence about Abu Ghraib were not contacted, or were sanctioned after coming forward, chilling other sources. And, echoing President
Bush's exclusion of the CIA from his February 2002 memo, the reports also
deliberately circumvented the problem of "ghost detainees," off-book detainees held by the CIA.[83]

The Church and Schlesinger reports, which purport to cover all Defense
Department detention operations, fall far short of comprehensiveness. The
text of Vice Admiral Church's work remains classified. Much of the text of
other reports, including that of Richard Formica, are largely blanked out.
Only an anodyne "executive summary" was released to the public. But Vice
Admiral Church's conclusion that there was "no link between approved interrogation techniques and detainee abuse" is unconvincing. It ignores the abun-
dant public information about how legal theories and specific interrogation
techniques migrated from site to site. Schlesinger's panel, handpicked by
Rumsfeld, had to complete its inquiry in forty-five days. It also omitted
"[i]ssues of personal accountability." The panel only "review[ed] Department
of Defense investigations on detention operations"; it lacked authority to conduct its own investigations. It held only three days of interviews. It was permitted to ask for Defense Department documents "unless prohibited by law."[84]

America, in short, has had no reliable and comprehensive public accounting of the consequences of its torture policy. This is a gap Congress can
quickly fill, especially given the mandate for oversight that voters demanded in
the 2006 election. With the disastrous torture legislation of 2006 difficult to

undo in the face of a likely presidential veto, rigorous and bipartisan inquiries to document interrogation and detention policy are much needed.

Reaping What We Sow

The executive branch's decision to evade checks and balances to craft its own torture policy has not made the nation safer. The gap between America's ideals and the executive's unilateral behavior has not been lost on the rest of the world. In some countries, Guantánamo has become almost as recognizable a symbol of American policy and power as the Statue of Liberty: it has become a focus for worldwide discontent. Even close American allies, such as Britain, call for its closure. The 9/11 Commission summarized the harm torture policy does to counterterrorism efforts:

> Allegations that the United States abused prisoners in its custody make it harder to build the diplomatic, political and military alliances the government will need. The United States should work with friends to develop mutually agreed-on principles for the detention and humane treatment of captured international terrorists who are not being held under a particular country's criminal laws. . . . America should be able to reconcile its views on how to balance humanity and security with our nation's commitment to these same goals.[85]

In November 2005, the former members of the 9/11 Commission, in their "9/11 Public Discourse Project," examined government progress on the recommendations in the original Commission Report. The former commissioners gave the government one of its numerous failing grades on detainee policy, noting the continued "criticism from around the globe" of U.S. interrogation policy. The former commissioners explained: "Dissension either at home or abroad on how the United States treats captured terrorists only makes it harder to build the diplomatic, political and military alliances necessary" to fight terrorism.[86]

Reputational harm from America's torture policy arises against the context of diminishing global support for American counterterrorism efforts. According to a June 2006 global public opinion survey conducted by the Pew Global Attitudes Project, "the U.S.-led war on terror draws majority support in just two countries—India and Russia"; elsewhere, "support for the war on terror is either flat or has declined."[87]

Thanks in substantive part to American torture policy, America is viewed as cynical, hypocritical, and unworthy of support. A 2006 box-office hit in

Turkey, *Valley of the Wolves*, is a telling example. It opens with an incident drawn from the Iraq war, depicting American soldiers as thugs and torturers. They are the villains.[88] In this cold light, legitimate counterterrorism efforts are condemned as naked, amoral power grabs. Needed cooperation has declined. Our security depends on other governments' willingness to aid against terrorism. Adopting tactics of the enemy comes with heavy costs, costs the Administration has ignored.

Discarding checks and balances in favor of a unilateral torture policy, in short, cannot be justified in terms of gain to the national security. By abandoning the constraints imposed by law and by circumventing the demands of public debate, the executive branch certainly increased its own power. But the open wounds inflicted by such hasty and ill-conceived executive unilateralism are ones America can ill afford to bear.

5

"Extraordinary Rendition"
and the Wages of Hypocrisy

On an unseasonably warm Veterans Day in 2005, President George W. Bush addressed a friendly crowd at the Tobyhanna Army Depot in northeastern Pennsylvania and mounted a sweeping defense of his war in Iraq. The invasion, argued President Bush, was only part of the wider offensive begun on September 11, 2001. In Bush's vision, this broader war pitted the United States against terrorism's "allies of convenience like Iran and Syria." Bush drew the crowd's attention to a United Nations investigation into the assassination of the Lebanese opposition leader, Rafik Hariri, with the possible involvement of Syrian intelligence services. He demanded that Syria, targeted already with American economic sanctions, "do what the international community has demanded" and aid the investigation. The President warned that "the government of Syria must stop exporting violence and start importing democracy."[1]

But President Bush's Administration, using devices invisible to the other two branches of the government, unilaterally decided to exploit the violent, lawless side of the Syrian government, thus aiding the enemies of democracy in that embattled nation. Within days of 9/11, President Bush signed a secret executive order authorizing a new policy of "extraordinary rendition." A "rendition" involves the transfer of an individual to another country without any judicial proceedings. Post-9/11, the phrase "extraordinary rendition" was coined to distinguish a new practice: the transfer of people suspected of having a connection to terrorism to a country that uses torture to extract information. A suspect is picked up, often outside the United States, and—without any judicial process—disappears into a global network of detention facilities run by the United States or other nations. Most of these nations, such as Syria, Egypt, or Jordan, are routinely condemned in the State Department's human rights reports as persistent torturers.[2]

This is no isolated matter. While the Bush Administration adamantly refuses to discuss candidly its transfers to torture, journalists and lawyers estimate that hundreds of individuals (perhaps more) have been swept up, detained, and subjected to brutal interrogations beyond the law.[3]

Neither Congress nor the courts have tried to constrain the executive's use of extraordinary rendition, a policy managed through unilateral presidential directives shielded from congressional and public scrutiny. Extraordinary rendition exemplifies the Administration's aggressive use of secretive unilateral directives in lieu of constitutional processes of interbranch deliberation. Just as it did during the Cold War, unchecked power, applied without restraints and shielded by secrecy, invariably leads to rights abuse. Furthermore, extraordinary rendition exemplifies how presidential unilateralism can draw the nation into hypocritical policies harmful to our broader interests in combating terrorism.

One well-documented case involving a transfer to Syria illustrates the extraordinary rendition system. Maher Arar was born in Syria and emigrated to Canada as a teenager with his family. In late 2002, Arar was vacationing with his wife and children in Tunisia when he received a call from his employer, asking him to return to Ottawa to consult with a potential client. But while in transit at New York's John F. Kennedy Airport, Arar was detained on suspicion of "being a member of a known terrorist organization" and interrogated for days. He was asked to "volunteer" to be transferred to Syria. Fearing torture, Arar refused. But federal authorities placed Arar on a plane bound for Amman, Jordan. By October 22, Arar was in Syrian custody. Syria detained Arar without charges or legal process for more than a year. That was where the nightmare began.

Arar was interrogated for eighteen hours per day and was physically and psychologically tortured. He was beaten on his palms, hips, and lower back with a two-inch-thick electric cable. His captors also used their fists to beat him on his stomach, face and back of neck. He was subjected to excruciating pain and pleaded with his captors to stop. He was placed in a room where he could hear the screams of other detainees being tortured and was told that he, too, would be placed in a spine-breaking "chair," hung upside down in a "tire" for beatings and subjected to electric shocks.[4]

To stop the torture, Arar in the end "confessed"—falsely—to having trained with terrorists in Afghanistan. Despite the confession, after 375 days' detention, Syria released Arar without explanation, allowing him to return to Montreal to be reunited with his wife and children.[5]

After Arar's release, the Syrian ambassador to Washington conceded that Syria had no evidence of Arar's complicity in terrorism. The Canadian government, facing public uproar, initiated an official investigation into Arar's kidnapping. The inquiry concluded Arar's allegations of torture were true.[6] The Canadian inquiry concluded that American authorities had made decisions both "to detain Mr. Arar and remove him to Syria," and not just to Jordan. It also found that Canadian and U.S. intelligence services had focused on Arar because of a lunch he had with another suspect in October 2001 in Ottawa. Despite the fact investigations yielded no further evidence of a connection to terrorist groups, this one lunch was sufficient to warrant his rendition to Syria, where he was tortured. Indeed, just as Arar was about to be sent to Syria, Canadian officials warned their American counterparts that while Arar had "contact with many individuals of interest," there were no indications of any "links to [a]l Qaeda."

Arar sought after-the-fact accountability, filing a lawsuit against the United States for damages. Despite its clear responsibility for Arar's transfer, the United States argued that it did not need to provide any explanation, let alone compensation, for Arar's yearlong ordeal. Indeed, it refused even to supply evidence to the Canadian inquiry. The government argued that all evidence in Arar's case was covered by a "state secrets" privilege. Originally a rule designed by courts to shield certain pieces of evidence against disclosure, this doctrine has seen service by the executive since 9/11 as a wholesale immunity from litigation—another curtailment of the Constitution's checks and balances. In practical effect, this means that the executive can commit serious or widespread violations of the law and then shield them from judicial review and from consequent liability as "state secrets."[7]

The federal district court refused to step in. Judge David Trager of the Eastern District of New York declared that "national security and foreign policy" concerns—what Attorney General Francis Biddle would have called "mystic clichés"—meant Arar merited no accounting for the year lost or for incalculable mental and physical damage. Courts, opined Judge Trager, "should not, in the absence of explicit direction by Congress, hold officials who carry out [rendition] liable . . . even if such conduct violates our treaty obligations or customary international law."[8]

The story of extraordinary rendition illustrates the tight nexus of unchecked power and unwise policy.[9] Extraordinary rendition, like abusive Cold War surveillance and disruption practices, exploits loopholes in the law. History shows that the executive branch, by acting unilaterally and using secret laws hidden from Congress and the public, ends up with foolish and harmful policies. Having done so, it resists—successfully in Arar's case—judicial oversight even after a detainee has been released. As the disparity between President Bush's Tobyhanna speech and Arar's case shows, extraordinary rendition reduces our political leaders to hypocrisy. The executive's short-circuit of the Constitution's checks and balances concentrates power in the White House in the short term, but in so doing causes lasting, tangible damage to our alliances and to our campaign against terrorism.

Rendition Before 9/11

Prior to 9/11, rendition was used to further the ends of justice by bringing a suspect back to the United States for a criminal trial. In 1886, the U.S. Supreme Court ruled that a criminal suspect who had fled to war-torn Peru and was seized there by the Pinkerton Detective Agency could be tried in the United States.[10] A century later, the Supreme Court similarly allowed the trial of a kidnapped Mexican physician for the torture and murder of a DEA agent. Even though the rendition itself was extralegal, the suspect at the end of the day had access to a judicial process, which provided a forum for challenges to wrongful detention or abusive treatment.[11]

Initially a law enforcement tool, rendition became a national security tactic in the mid-1980s, with national security agencies first using it in 1986 as a means of bringing suspects back to the United States. After Congress enacted laws criminalizing air piracy and terrorist attacks upon Americans abroad, President Ronald Reagan issued a secret covert action directive authorizing kidnapping overseas of any person wanted for terrorism, the first of several classified presidential orders that authorized various forms of rendition.

At first, rendition was deployed for defensible ends. In 1987, the FBI and CIA collaborated on "Operation Goldenrod." American agents kidnapped Jordanian terrorism suspect Fawaz Yunis, wanted in connection with the hijacking of a Jordanian airliner. He was lured into international waters off the Cypriot coast and arrested there for transfer to and trial in the United States. Prosecutors secured convictions against him for air piracy and hostage taking.[12]

The government expanded its covert rendition efforts in the mid-1990s to deal with the emerging threat of Islamist terrorism in the wake of the Afghanistan war with the Soviet Union. In 1995, the United States scored an important success through rendition. Pakistani intelligence arrested Ramzi Yousef, instigator of the 1993 World Trade Center bombing, and handed him over to members of an FBI Joint Terrorism Task Force for transport and trial in an American federal court. The Yousef case suggested we could find ways to partner with intelligence services, even unsavory ones like Pakistan's, without sacrificing fairness or justice.[13]

Nevertheless, the CIA grew worried that a U.S. court might make embarrassing inquiries about the circumstances of a terrorist suspect's capture and transfer back to the United States. The Agency thus began to explore other models of rendition. According to Michael Scheuer, a former CIA officer who headed up the Agency's bin Laden unit, the CIA in the 1990s began using rendition to transfer suspects *to* a foreign government, not just back to the United States. This allowed the agency to avoid a U.S. court's scrutiny. Scheuer later explained that Egypt became the destination of choice: "It served American purposes to get these people arrested, and Egyptian purposes to get these people back, where they could be interrogated." But he contended that "[t]he goal of arresting these people was never to interrogate [the captives]. . . . The first goal was to incarcerate these people." Scheuer insisted that rendition remained linked to a judicial process, albeit in a foreign rather than an American court.[14]

The CIA's decision to begin sending suspects to other countries, especially countries such as Egypt, nevertheless crossed an important threshold. As traditionally practiced, rendition ended in a federal court in the United States, a forum that would investigate the fairness of holding a suspect and the adequacy of his treatment. But once the CIA began sending suspects to other countries, even with the promise of a criminal trial at the other end, there was a risk that a trial might not be fair. And in countries with a weak rule of law, where courts often operate under a government thumb, rendition inevitably created a risk of ill treatment.

According to Scheuer, in every pre-9/11 rendition, "each country to which the agency delivered a detainee would have to pledge it would treat him according to the rules of its own legal game." But even Scheuer conceded that this was more façade than substance. Pressed by an Australian reporter, this former employee of the American executive branch admitted that "frankly," a suspect's treatment after handover was "not a question I'm going to look at very closely. . . . I'm not going to look very hard for something that would destroy one potential avenue of protecting American interests." And Scheuer frankly added, "You'd think I'm an ass if I said nobody would be tortured."[15]

The seeds of today's extraordinary rendition system, in short, were planted before 9/11. To be sure, when Scheuer built up the CIA's rendition system in the mid-1990s, the Agency's aim was not facilitating torture. As the Church Committee repeatedly found, however, when the executive avoided oversight to create secret, unaccountable programs, its activities had a tendency to expand beyond their original purpose. Rendition was to be no exception.

Rendition After 9/11

Renditions increased dramatically after 9/11. Governmental and nongovernmental sources estimate that renditions doubled, to at least 150 in total, in the years immediately after 9/11. Egypt's prime minister reported his country alone received "60 to 70" detainees between September 2001 and May 2005 via the American rendition system.[16]

With this change in volume came a critical shift in the purpose of renditions. Before 9/11, renditions included a criminal justice process, either in the United States or another country. In contrast, individuals "rendered" after 9/11 were never formally charged with a criminal offense or tried in a court of law. Neither Maher Arar nor others transferred to foreign custody via extralegal channels, had access to a judicial forum to assert their innocence or contest the allegations against them.[17]

Extraordinary rendition, instead, enables interrogation with coercive techniques and torture. Senior intelligence officials publicly concede that one aim of collaborating with Egyptian or Jordanian intelligence services is the circumvention of whatever rules against torture still obtain in the United States. As CIA chief George Tenet candidly explained to Congress, "It might be better sometimes for . . . suspects to remain in the hands of foreign authorities, who might be able to use more aggressive interrogation techniques." Speaking on background to the *Washington Post*, another official confirmed that Tenet's statement accurately described the Administration's purpose in expanding the use of extraordinary renditions: "Someone"—i.e., another country's intelligence agency— "might be able to get information we can't from detainees."[18]

The phrase "more aggressive interrogation techniques" is a euphemism for torture. The CIA was already pushing the envelope on coercive interrogation. Soon after 9/11, "the highest level of the CIA" authorized six "enhanced interrogation techniques," including "water boarding" (which simulates drowning) and "cold cell" (involving imprisonment in freezing conditions and dousing with cold water). Recall too that the August 2002 OLC legal opinion on torture lowered the bar considerably for the CIA. Only pain "ordinarily associated with a sufficiently serious physical condition or injury such as death, organ failure, or serious impediment of body functions" counted as torture, according to the OLC. Thus, by arguing that the CIA needed to collaborate with foreign intelligence services to take advantage of interrogation measures that were illegal under American law, Tenet implied that the Agency adopted extraordinary rendition precisely in order to transfer suspects (including innocents such as Arar) for the purpose of inflicting "death, organ failure, or serious impediment of body functions."[19]

Outsourcing interrogation to unscrupulous foreign intelligence services, however, was not the only post-9/11 change in rendition policy. In a second critical move, the CIA operated from March 2002 onward a series of secret detention facilities outside the United States at which it held terrorism suspects. These "black sites" were kept beyond the oversight of the International Committee for the Red Cross, the international agency charged with overseeing all detention operations, and beyond the effective jurisdiction of domestic U.S. and international law. These offshore facilities have been used to house at least a hundred suspects.

Black sites prompted enough unease among former and current intelligence officials that they voiced concerns about their legality and morality to journalists. The fact that intelligence personnel proved willing to approach the press hints at the considerable discomfort, even within parts of the executive branch, about following the Doolittle Commission's recommendation of using tactics of the enemy. Such leaks generated further research and revelations from other journalists and advocacy groups. Israeli and British journalists also reported on secret offshore CIA holding facilities. Human Rights Watch and others documented patterns of CIA flights that pointed to U.S. facilities in Poland and Romania as locations of "black sites." As allegations of secret facilities in Afghanistan, Thailand, Europe, and North Africa surfaced, a picture of a global U.S. network began to come into focus.[20]

Like our torture policy, our policy of extraordinary rendition developed in response to the capture of senior al Qaeda figures in 2002. On March 28, 2002, Pakistani intelligence services captured al Qaeda operative Abu Zubaydah and handed him to the CIA. The CIA first kept Zubaydah in a small, disused warehouse on an active airbase in Thailand. In June 2003, media reports of the Thai facility surfaced, and Thailand's government insisted that the site be closed, souring relations with the CIA. Abu Zubaydah was transferred to another site.[21]

After picking a suspect up, the intelligence agencies have a menu of detention options from which to choose. Since 2002, intelligence services could transfer a suspect to the Guantánamo Bay Naval Base. But when the Supreme Court decided in 2004 to allow federal courts to hear Guantánamo detainees' claims of innocence, intelligence services could no longer be certain that interrogation techniques used at Guantánamo would remain secret.[22] The two other options for avoiding judicial review of detention and interrogation decisions are extraordinary rendition and black sites.

These different detention regimes interact to create an interlinked global detention system. Suspects can be subjected to extraordinary rendition, then moved to a black site, and finally shifted to a known facility such as Guantánamo.

Consider a case documented by Amnesty International of three Yemeni men, picked up in Indonesia, Jordan, and Tanzania respectively by the governments of those countries, seemingly with the knowledge and consent of American intelligence agencies. In each case, a foreign intelligence or police service first took the men into custody. Salah Nasser Salim 'Ali was picked up by Indonesian officials while shopping in a Jakarta mall. Muhammad Faraj Ahmed Bashmilah was stopped while traveling to Jordan with his pregnant wife. Muhammad al-Assad sat down to dinner with his family at his home in Dar-es-Salaam, but was interrupted by Tanzanian immigration personnel. Each man disappeared after his arrest. For months, their wives and children knew nothing of their whereabouts, or even whether they were alive.

Bashmilah and 'Ali were transferred initially to the Jordanian intelligence service, the General Intelligence Directorate. Both were tortured. All three men then found themselves in the custody of an American intelligence agency, which flew them to an underground facility (location unknown), where other Americans questioned them. In addition to being interrogated, the men, according to Amnesty International, "were subject to extreme sensory deprivation; for over a year they did not know what country they were in, whether it was night or day, whether it was raining or sunny. . . . For the first six to eight months, they spent nearly every waking hour staring at the four blank walls of their cells, leaving only to go to interrogation, and once a week, to the showers."

In May 2005, the three men were transferred to Yemeni custody. Three months earlier, the State Department had issued a human rights practices country report describing Yemen's prisons as falling wretchedly short of international shared standards embodied in human rights treaties. Responding to inquiries by Amnesty International, the Yemeni government conceded that it lacked any legal basis to hold the three men. To the surprise of Amnesty researchers, the Yemeni government candidly explained that it was holding the men on the instructions of the American government. Just shy of a year after their transfer into Yemeni hands, the men were quietly released without charge.

Just as in the case of Maher Arar, the available evidence—not to mention the Yemeni government's own statements and acts—suggests the three men had no connections to terrorist groups. Indeed, it appears they were singled out by foreign intelligence agencies in Tanzania, Indonesia, and Jordan due to facts—such as having an "Afghanistan" visa stamp on a passport—that fell far short of justifying detention, even if they might legitimately prompt further investigation.[23]

Bashmilah, 'Ali, and al-Assad are not the only suspects to have experienced multiple forms of detention. An Australian man, Mamdouh Habib, was picked up in Pakistan in October 2001 and transferred to Egypt. He describes being hung by his arms from hooks, repeatedly shocked, nearly drowned, and brutally beaten. Habib was subsequently transferred to Guantánamo prison and later released without any charges brought against him.[24]

Arar, Bashmilah, 'Ali, al-Assad, and Habib all "disappeared." All were detained without trial. All were tortured. All were innocent. The new extraordinary rendition network dispenses with judicial restraints, and also with rules set forth by Congress and in the Geneva Conventions and the Convention Against Torture to govern the treatment and handling of individuals captured overseas. Executive branch unilateralism, in other words, here entails avoidance of judicial checks long used to sift the innocent from the guilty. Just as during the Cold War, the decision to evade checks and balances drew intelligence services into mission creep, indiscriminately pulling in both the guilty and the innocent.

The Laws We Do Not Know

The complex bureaucratic network of extraordinary rendition, disappearances, and black sites is grounded in a set of secret presidential laws and classified Justice Department legal opinions that undercut the rules enacted by Congress, enforced by the courts, and known to the people. Both this system of secret laws and the ultimate legal justifications for unchecked executive power to transfer suspects to torture are inconsistent with a government of checks and balances.

Presidential directives—or orders issued unilaterally by the chief executive, usually to subordinate executive staff—serve important functions in an increasingly complex world. Congress cannot provide the executive with complete detailed instructions on the day-to-day operation of complex bureaucratic mechanisms. Today, however, the system of presidential lawmaking combines with an excessive fondness for secrecy. And it is not only operational details that are kept from public and congressional sight. A president, using his power to issue directives and then classify them against the scrutiny of legislators and the public, can undermine constitutional protections. The complex global network of secret detentions we have described is one result of this convergence of presidential lawmaking power and secrecy.[25]

Indeed, on initial examination, it seems that any presidential lawmaking is antithetical to the Constitution. The Constitution's first words, after its preamble, explain that "*All* legislative Powers herein granted shall be vested in a *Congress*." Nevertheless, presidents have long relied on executive orders—sometimes simply to convey instructions inside the executive branch, and sometimes to make more sweeping changes. As the federal government swelled in scope and complexity after the New Deal, presidents came to rely increasingly on executive orders, issuing more than ten thousand between 1920 and 1998. Confronted with private litigants challenging executive orders, the Supreme Court, reluctant to enter headlong confrontation with the executive, dodged conflict by interpreting congressional silence as acquiescence and endorsing executive orders promulgated in the absence of legislation.[26] This judicial caution, coupled with Congress's passivity, has allowed dramatic expansion of presidential lawmaking.

Extraordinary rendition is not the first critical national security matter to be determined by presidential fiat and without constitutional debate. The Cold War, which formed the backdrop to the litany of abuse and overreaching documented by the Church Committee, was also waged largely by secret presidential directives. And since the onset of the Cold War, each White House has maintained its own system, and nomenclature, for presidential directives on foreign and domestic security policies. Among the different terms to describe these orders are "national security directives" and "presidential directives." All of these orders are kept secret as a matter of course. Hence, unlike other presidential directives, national security directives are not published in the *Federal Register* alongside all other executive orders. Congress's General Accounting Office, or GAO, concluded that not even legislative committees for intelligence and armed service matters receive copies of all directives. Indeed, the Church Committee was the first outside body to see a significant number of the directives. By the GAO's count, between 1961 and 1988, presidents issued 1,042 presidential directives on "national security" issues. Less than a quarter were published.[27]

The executive's power to enact general rules without legislation shifts the balance of constitutional power dramatically toward the presidency. The executive branch gains the initiative, and Congress and the courts are forced to react to its innovations. Extraordinary rendition, moreover, involves a form of secret lawmaking, which shifts the balance of power even further. The executive branch can change the nation's legal landscape without the knowledge or consent of either legislators or the general public. Whatever the merits of presidential lawmaking in general, *secret* executive orders describing *general* policies in derogation of known and public law cannot be justified under our constitutional order.

Extraordinary rendition is built on an edifice of secret laws. Indeed, the official responses to the September 11, 2001, attacks largely took shape through under-the-radar executive orders, despite public and congressional attention to the Patriot Act. Many of these unilateral executive orders were published in the *Federal Register*, and thus were subject to public scrutiny and challenge. But the Administration implemented other counterterrorism measures, including extraordinary rendition, via secret presidential directives. Both the Reagan and the Clinton Administrations, to be sure, used secret "presidential findings" to authorize renditions such as Operation Goldenrod. Indeed, in order to implement Michael Scheuer's reorientation of rendition to include transfers to other countries, the Clinton Administration issued two secret "Presidential Decision Directives." Administrations of both political hues, in other words, kept their rendition policies secret.[28]

Yet it is hard to see how disclosures of general policy, as reflected in legal opinions and presidential directives, could impede national security in the twenty-first century any more than it could in the 1970s. Although the executive branch clearly has an interest in concealing information about specific individuals or tactics, the metastasis in rendition policy in the absence of over-sight suggests the need for careful public scrutiny of broader policy decisions.

Today's executive rendition system began six days after 9/11. A classified presidential directive issued that day granted the CIA dramatic new powers. According to Roger Cressey, deputy counterterrorism director at the White House in 2001, the preparation of this order was "incredibly fast"; it did not go through "the usual wordsmithing exercises." Yet the presidential finding, as signed by President Bush on September 17, 2001, gave the CIA broad author-ization to kill, capture, or detain members of al Qaeda anywhere in the world. According to current and former intelligence officers, it authorized black sites, albeit in vague, general terms that lent themselves to plausible deniability. The finding did not require the CIA, when detaining and transferring suspects, to seek case-by-case approval from the White House, the State Department, or the Justice Department. The same finding released the "vast" new funds sought by Tenet to coax foreign intelligence services into new cooperation with the CIA.[29]

Congress was thus effectively excluded from debate about adopting the ex-traordinary rendition system. According to the *Washington Post*, "The CIA has decided to brief only the chairman and the ranking member of the two intel-ligence committees" about CIA activities. Even then, the Bush Administration gave legislators only skeletal details. Lawmakers complained that the briefings were too vague but felt constrained from discussing the matter in public, even in general terms. Limited briefing of congressional leaders cannot replace in-formed and robust debate involving both the Congress as a whole and the public on general contours of national security policy.[30]

Of course, congressional access to information is only a threshold require-ment for informed debate. The Church Committee benefited from a bipartisan consensus on the need for serious oversight and change. Today, consensus across the aisle is more difficult to achieve. Senators aligned politically with the White House have staunchly opposed any debate about counterterrorism policies, even those raising fundamental questions of American values, as well as the effectiveness of the strategies being used. Senator Pat Roberts of Kansas condemned legislators on both sides of the aisle who expressed concern on detention issues as showing "an almost pathological obsession with calling into question the actions of men and women who are on the front lines of the war on terror." Roberts's rhetoric was a thinly veiled effort to stifle debate.[31]

Like the September 17, 2001, presidential finding, the legal opinions pre-pared by the Bush Administration to support extraordinary rendition have not been exposed to public or congressional scrutiny. The Justice Department's Office of Legal Counsel, or OLC, reportedly with input from then–White House Counsel Alberto Gonzales, provided the President and the intelligence agencies with the justification of extraordinary rendition in an opinion dated March 13, 2002, and entitled "The President's Power as Commander in Chief to Transfer Captive Terrorists to the Control and Custody of Foreign Nations." The White House consistently resists congressional requests for this memo even though it offers no good cause for this secrecy.[32]

On September 6, 2001, President Bush announced that fourteen of the suspects held at black sites would be transferred to Guantánamo Bay Naval Base, Cuba, where he intended to have them tried before military commissions. His announcement marked the first official recognition of the secret CIA prisons.[33]

But the apparent concession was less than it seemed. Nothing in the President's speech suggested that the black site program would wholly come to end. Indeed, the *Washington Post* reported that supporters of black sites, including Vice President Cheney, received "the president's assurance, if only in theory, that the black sites program could be used again." One anonymous intelligence source told a *Washington Post* reporter, "Although there is no one in CIA custody today, it's our intent that the CIA detention program continue. . . . It's simply too valuable . . . to not allow it to move forward." Indeed, the advocacy organization Human Rights Watch cautioned that the group transferred to Guantánamo did not include at least thirteen other detainees reportedly held in black sites and whose subsequent whereabouts remained unknown.[34]

In his capacity as a law professor, John Yoo, the author of pivotal OLC opinions about post-9/11 presidential power, has revealed the likely legal justification for the program. In an article in the July 2004 issue of the *Notre Dame Law Review*, Yoo argued that the executive branch could transfer detainees wherever and in whatever fashion it chose. Referring back to British practice long before the American Revolution, Yoo drew on the practice of British monarchs during the seventeenth century. "[I]t was well-established under the British Constitution that the Crown had absolute authority to dispose as it saw fit of prisoners of war and other detainees." Yoo argued, "Parliament never sought to interfere with the executive's prerogatives regarding the disposition of prisoners of war."[35]

Extraordinary rendition thus became national policy via secretive executive lawmaking that circumvented Congress and repudiated the proper role of the federal courts. And the underlying legal justifications for extraordinary rendition, if Yoo's arguments accurately track the contents of his March 2002 OLC legal opinion, rely on monarchial prerogatives that are completely incompatible with a Constitution of separate branches, sharing power.

Rendition's Flawed Results

Unilateralism in national security policy is not merely inconsistent with the Constitution's checks and balances. Too often, the result of removing external scrutiny is foolish policy that in fact harms national security interests. Extraordinary rendition illustrates well how secretive decision making is not simply constitutionally problematic—it is also unsound national security policy.

Intelligence professionals recognize this point. As early as 1976, CIA director William Colby recommended "[i]mproved supervision" by Congress and "some public review" as a way of ensuring that "intelligence will remain within the new guidelines." Former CIA case officer Reuel Marc Gerecht, writing in the *Weekly Standard*, explained that "debate [about extraordinary rendition] could stop us from doing—or not doing—something that our collective national conscience would later regret. . . . One thing is certain: Our avoidance of this necessary debate is a disservice to the men and women of the CIA, the Pentagon, and the FBI."[36]

Has presidential unilateralism in rendition policy made the world safer? On numerous occasions, Secretary of State Condoleezza Rice claimed that current rendition policies "save[d] European lives." But Rice's claim is troublingly vague. The Administration controls the spigots of public information. Why not point to specific cases in which extraordinary rendition led to information being obtained that saved lives? Yet details to support Rice's claim have been in short supply.[37]

Rather, available evidence undermines the contention that extraordinary rendition generates useful information. Consider first the policy's intelligence-gathering goals. Extraordinary rendition is intended to channel detainees to forms of interrogation that would be unlawful when employed by American personnel. The armed forces already have an ample repertoire of interrogation tactics not involving torture (and, since the working group memo, involving torture). Experienced intelligence professionals express grave reservations about whether adding coercion works. Retired FBI agent Jack Cloonan successfully tracked down and brought to trial the al Qaeda members responsible for the 1998 bombings of U.S. embassies in Kenya and Tanzania. Cloonan argues that "torture—by hands American or foreign—is rarely ever useful or necessary." Other analysts agree, noting that much of the best pre-9/11 evidence about al Qaeda emerged through interrogations by FBI field agents who eschewed violent interrogation tactics. Former CIA officer Gerecht also explains that "a wide swath of the intelligence community" believes torture to be an "ineffective intelligence tool." This consensus has dissenters, including Gerecht himself. But there is little evidence that torture typically succeeds where other less coercive methods fail. Certainly, there is no evidence torture is worth the moral and reputational price tag that comes with the mendacity and hypocrisy that its authorization spawns.[38]

Aside from moral costs, though, does it work to send detainees to another country for coercive interrogation and torture by another intelligence service which, you hope, will tell you everything that it learns? Intelligence professionals think not. Handing a person over to another country's custody means "voluntarily diminishing, if not ending" control over the circumstances of interrogation. This in turn corrodes the reliability of the information gained. Gerecht offers a pithy example: "The mind spins thinking how agency officials would phrase the sourcing notes in intelligence collected from Syrian debriefings: Information collected by a foreign intelligence service that the United States now strongly suspects is aiding Iraqi insurgents; this intelligence service also has a long history of operationally aiding Palestinian terrorist organizations and the Lebanese Hezbollah." Collaboration with Pakistani intelligence services would suffer the same seemingly fatal internal contradictions. That is, even if extraordinary rendition yields more information by using George Tenet's "aggressive interrogation techniques," there is no way to know if the information is reliable.[39]

The most important evidence to emerge from extraordinary rendition proved false and caused real harm to America. This was evidence extracted by torture from senior al Qaeda operative Ibn al-Sheikh al-Libi, who fell into American custody in the opening months of the Afghan conflict. Al-Libi had run the Khalden training camp in Afghanistan, where he trained Richard Reid and Zacarias Moussaoui. When al-Libi was captured, veteran FBI agent Jack Cloonan, on behalf of the FBI, argued for the use of long-standing noncoercive interrogation procedures for terrorism suspects. Cloonan pointed to the successes of the 1990s during the investigation of the embassy bombing to argue that these noninvasive methods worked. According to Cloonan, he was overruled at the highest levels. The CIA's "comments about getting boots on the ground and taking the gloves off both appealed to the president and could be quickly actualized by virtue of the CIA's black budget." So, on the flimsiest of justifications, the FBI lost control of al-Libi. The CIA bound and gagged al-Libi, stuffed him into a box, and shipped him to Egypt. In Egypt, CIA sources have told reporters, al-Libi was water-boarded and subjected to the "cold cell" treatment. Even though the CIA had been authorized to use both these techniques, its boss, George Tenet, wanted to use extraordinary rendition to take advantage of unsavory allies' experience with still *more* aggressive interrogation techniques. Whatever else was done to him, al-Libi broke and told the interrogators what they wanted to hear.

What al-Libi said emerged on the world stage in September 2002, when Secretary of Defense Donald Rumsfeld alluded to "bulletproof" evidence of a connection between al Qaeda and Iraq. In February 2003, Secretary of State Colin Powell told the United Nations Security Council that a "senior terrorist operative . . . responsible for one of al Qaeda's training camps in Afghanistan" had given "credible" evidence that Saddam Hussein once offered to train al Qaeda operatives in the use of explosives and illicit weapons, including bio-chemical weapons. *Newsweek* confirmed that this "credible" source was al-Libi. President Bush, Vice President Cheney, and other senior officials all relied on al-Libi's statements about an al Qaeda–Iraq link to make their case for the Iraq war.[40]

But Administration officials knew early on that al-Libi's information was unreliable. As early as 2002, the Defense Intelligence Agency, which is part of the Defense Department, concluded that al-Libi "intentionally misled de-briefers," by "describing scenarios to the debriefers that he knows will retain their interest." Sources "with firsthand knowledge of [al-Libi's] statements" told ABC News that although al-Libi did not *deliberately* mislead his interrogators, he did tell them what *he thought they wanted to hear*. Of course, this is what anyone who wants to stop being tortured does. It reveals the general problem with coercive methods. It's not that a suspect won't talk; it's that he can't stop himself talking, even when what he says is not true. As John McCain suc-cinctly explained to the Senate, "You can get anyone to confess to anything if the torture's bad enough."[41]

Al-Libi's story also shows that publicly available information can sometimes be more reliable than the government's clandestine sources. Since the begin ning of the 1990s, Osama bin Laden said he despised the former Ba'athist regime of Saddam Hussein, as he told his biographer, the Pakistani journalist Hamid Mir.[42] Here, the information in the public domain was correct. Despite repeated and strenuous assertions by the Bush White House, no legitimate connection was ever drawn between the Iraqi regime and the perpetrators of the 9/11 attacks. The administration, however, successfully argued that its se-cret sources ought to displace public knowledge. When secret information is harvested using such dubious methods, the public and Congress are wise not to accept at face value government claims of access to privileged knowledge.

The problem of false intelligence arising from extraordinary rendition is even more pervasive than the al-Libi story suggests. In al-Libi's case, the CIA at least had a detainee who had a culpable connection to al Qaeda. But ex-traordinary rendition removes the checks and accountability mechanisms that prevent the intelligence agencies from wielding their powers in arbitrary, capri-cious, or self-interested ways. Taking away these checks has a predictable result. Increasing evidence suggests post-9/11 extraordinary rendition yields an intolerably high proportion of "false positives"—innocent people detained by mistake.

In late 2005, the rendition system comprised about one hundred detainees, with two ranks of prisoners. About thirty were "major terrorism suspects," such as al-Libi or Khalid Sheikh Mohammed, who professed public allegiance to al Qaeda. In these cases, the risk that beyond-the-law detention is factually erroneous is low (whether it is wise is another matter). But another seventy or so detainees have "less direct involvement in terrorism" and "limited intelligence value." Among these individuals, there are also "a growing number" of what the CIA's inspector general calls "erroneous renditions." Numbers between ten and three dozen erroneous detentions have been reported—an extraordinarily high error rate.[43]

There are several reasons for this unacceptable error rate. Most important, extraordinary rendition is distinguished from the traditional law enforcement and criminal justice system by the absence of checks, such as courts and congressional oversight, to identify errors and correct the zeal of field-based operatives. A case that came to light in 2005 involving a German citizen, Khaled El-Masri, illustrates how this absence can allow the self-interested motives of intelligence personnel to overtake a critical view of a suspect's intelligence value.

Just before the end of 2003, El-Masri was on his way to a holiday in Macedonia after quarreling with his wife. At the Tabonovce border crossing, Macedonian border police hauled him off a bus and detained him because his name was similar to that of a known associate of one of the 9/11 hijackers. Macedonian police then contacted the Skopje station of the CIA. They reached its deputy chief, a junior officer, because the station chief was on vacation. Instead of carefully considering the evidence for and against the conclusion that El-Masri was indeed the 9/11 hijackers' former associate, the deputy station chief let petty bureaucratic imperatives take over. He used El-Masri as a chance to get ahead. According to one CIA officer, the deputy chief "really wanted a scalp because everyone wanted a part of the game."[44]

The deputy station chief was not the only one searching for scalps. In the CIA's Counterterrorism Center in Langley, Virginia, the director of the al Qaeda unit, an aggressive former Soviet analyst, when told of El-Masri's capture, "insisted that [El-Masri] was probably a terrorist, and should be imprisoned and interrogated immediately," even though the evidence against him was slim. On this basis, El-Masri was taken to a black site, an abandoned brick factory used as a prison in northern Kabul, in Afghanistan, where he was told: "You are here in a country where no one knows about you, in a country where there is no law. If you die, we will bury you, and no one will know." Like Arar and Habib and the three Yemeni men, El-Masri was innocent. And, three months later, analysis of his passport demonstrated that he was not the suspected terrorist but someone else entirely. Rather than redress its error, the CIA kept El-Masri detained for a further two months. Indeed, the CIA released El-Masri only as a consequence of pressure from the State Department.[45]

The current absence of any judicial check on executive discretion compounds the problem. Like Arar, El-Masri sought judicial relief and was rebuffed. A federal district court in Alexandria, Virginia, rejected his claim on the basis of the "state secrets privilege," which is "an evidentiary privilege derived from the President's constitutional authority over the conduct of this country's diplomatic and military affairs." The court accepted the dubious proposition offered by the executive branch's lawyers that any official admission or denial of rendition practices would harm government security. To the contrary, it is courts' facile and thinly reasoned acceptance of a de facto lawless zone that poses the risk to constitutional order and individual liberties.[46]

The facts of El-Masri's case are, moreover, not unique. An extraordinary rendition conducted in Milan in 2003 was also the product of local CIA initiative. According to former intelligence officials who spoke to the *Washington Post*, "the kidnapping was the inspiration of the CIA station chief in Rome, who, like the Skopje deputy chief, wanted to play a more active role in taking suspected terrorists off the street" and had his officers come up with a list of people to seize.[47]

The intelligence services responsible for extraordinary rendition have every incentive to generate information to justify their practices, even if this information is false. But they have almost no incentive to make sure their decisions are correct. After all, once a person has been "disappeared," shipped off to a decrepit and forgotten jail in the Egyptian hinterland, who will say the agency was wrong? And if someone does complain, who would believe them? And even if they were believed, who would do anything? How many other false positives are there among the hundred-plus people detained in black sites? How many El-Masris were never let go?

We have seen this before. The absence of checks on executive power inevitably ends in a spiral of increasingly harmful and indiscriminate use of intelligence powers against innocent people.

Bureaucratic pressures are not the only dynamics pushing extraordinary rendition toward error, bad intelligence, and ruined lives. Torture also generates false evidence that can justify a decision to detain an innocent. If this sounds improbable, recall that Maher Arar "confessed," despite being innocent of any connection to terrorism, and was thereby detained for a whole year. It is impossible to know how many detainees "confess." Consider too what happened to one of the three Yemenis whose cases were documented by Amnesty International. He recounted being shown photographs of men and asked whether he knew any of them. One of the photographs depicted the Al-Jazeera correspondent Taysir Alluni. The Yemeni detainee was "told that if he said he knew him, his situation would improve." Such interrogations are simply not going to provide worthwhile evidence. On the contrary, they will lead to detention of more innocents.[48]

Extraordinary rendition thus is a vicious circle. A decision to channel a suspect into the extraordinary rendition system instead of the traditional criminal justice system means evidence from that person, gathered by torture, cannot be used in American criminal prosecutions, where courts reject evidence gained by torture. The executive branch must therefore transfer the person named by the original suspect to detention facilities that do not adhere to adequate procedural protections. The more the intelligence agencies use extraordinary rendition, the more they *have to* use it.

Extraordinary rendition also jeopardizes the government's ability to convict in federal court those who are indeed guilty. Mistreatment, even outside rendition, imperils criminal prosecution. Consider how the prosecution of American citizen John Walker Lindh, who joined the Taliban and was captured in Afghanistan, suffered because of the FBI's decision (over Justice Department advice) to interrogate Lindh without a lawyer. Lindh asked for counsel but instead was held "blindfolded, naked, and bound to a stretcher with duct tape." Rough treatment and disregard of Lindh's request for counsel rendered his confession worthless, needlessly jeopardizing a worthwhile prosecution.

The same problem arises with evidence gathered through extraordinary rendition. Consider the case of American citizen Jose Padilla, who was first arrested in Chicago in early 2002. In May 2002, President Bush designated Padilla as an "enemy combatant" to be detained indefinitely as a result of evidence gathered in black site interrogations of Abu Zubaydah and Khalid Sheikh Mohammed. The government initially cited Padilla's involvement in a plot to use a radiological weapon, a "dirty bomb," in the United States. But the government never charged Padilla with this crime. After more than three years' detention without charge or legal process, Padilla was transferred from military custody and brought before a civilian court for criminal trial. Although the government did not retract its initial allegations, Padilla was not charged with the dirty bomb plot. Rather, the eventual charges focused on Padilla's alleged minor role in a separate conspiracy to provide aid to fighters outside the United States. The Justice Department could not charge Padilla with a dirty bomb plot because the evidence gathered from Zubaydah and Khalid Sheikh Mohammed could not be used in a federal court. That evidence would, by dint of its source, be considered wholly unreliable. The Justice Department's inability to charge Padilla, in short, emanated directly from decisions about how to treat Zubaydah and Khalid Sheikh Mohammed.[49]

The government did, however, charge one of Padilla's alleged co-conspirators for his involvement in the dirty bomb plot—but it did so before a military commission at Guantánamo. Ethiopian student and British resident Binyam Mohammed was arrested in Pakistan, transferred first to Morocco, and then taken to Guantánamo, where he was charged with a conspiracy to explode a dirty bomb. Evidence that a federal court would not consider, however, may be admissible in a military tribunal. Extraordinary rendition, in short, provides one of the motives for derogating from the basic standards of American criminal justice.[50]

Extraordinary rendition thus tends toward the production of flawed evidence. It tends to foster new erroneous detentions. The results of extraordinary rendition show that structures of accountability endorsed by Congress and the federal courts are not mere sops to fainthearted idealists. They are essential to the legitimacy and effective functioning of any intelligence gathering system, especially one grounded in interrogation practices. Accountability, which is what checks and balances create, is a necessary part of effective counterterrorism, not a barrier to success.[51]

The Wages of Hypocrisy

Presidential unilateralism means turning the law aside. But executive branch officials are typically reluctant to admit this, pushing them to unavoidable hypocrisy, and even mendacity. Efforts by senior American officials, including President Bush and Secretary of State Condoleezza Rice, to defend their unchecked decision making only amplify the damage to counterterrorism policy by fostering distrust among allies and reducing our moral capital in a world already leery of a superpower.

Before leaving in December 2005 on a whistlestop European trip aimed at securing cooperation in counterterrorism efforts, Secretary of State Rice gave a speech on the tarmac at Andrews Air Force Base seeking to preempt mounting European concerns about extraordinary rendition. Rice's statements appeared unequivocal: "The United States does not permit, tolerate, or condone torture under any circumstances," she said. It is the "policy" of the administration, moreover, that: "The United States does not transport, and has not transported, detainees from one country to another for the purpose of interrogation using torture. . . . The United States has not transported anyone, and will not transport anyone, to a country when we believe he will be tortured." She added: "Where appropriate, the United States seeks assurances that transferred persons will not be tortured."[52]

Rice's comments echoed similar statements by the Attorney General and the President. Nine months previously, President Bush explained that extraordinary rendition's goal is "to arrest people and send them back to their country of origin with the promise that they won't be tortured. That's the promise we receive." A few days earlier, Attorney General Alberto Gonzales underscored that United States policy is not to send suspects "to countries where we believe or we know that they're going to be tortured." But, unlike Rice and the President, Gonzales acknowledged that the United States "can't fully control" what happens on a suspect's receipt.[53]

Such justifications reek of hypocrisy. Take first the Administration's claim to be following the law. Both Rice and Gonzales carefully referred to a "policy," and avoided talking of the "law." A policy is a nonbinding preference that may be overridden. Their choice of words trades on a loophole in federal law. When the United States ratified the Convention Against Torture and Other Cruel, Inhuman or Degrading Treatment or Punishment in 1994, it also adopted a series of "declarations," "reservations," and "understandings" that limit American responsibilities under the Convention. One of these caveats states that ratification alone did not endow the Convention's rules with legal force under U.S. law. A law would need to be enacted by both houses of Congress and signed by the president for legal consequences to flow under U.S. law.[54]

Only one of the laws enacted to implement the Convention, however, addresses *overseas* transfers and renditions. This law, the 1998 Foreign Affairs Reform and Restructuring Act, or FARRA, states that: "It shall be the *policy* of the United States not to expel, extradite, or otherwise effect the involuntary return of any person to a country in which there are substantial grounds for believing the person would be in danger of being subjected to torture, regardless of whether the person is physically present in the United States." Rice's and Gonzales's statements rely on FARRA's policy statement but do not acknowledge its nonbinding quality.[55]

More troubling is Secretary Rice's reference to diplomatic "assurances," echoing the President's reference to a country's "promise" not to torture. Diplomatic assurances, or formal representations from one government to another, are today's version of plausible deniability—except today they are not even plausible. The form assurances take is unclear. The *Washington Post* reports that the CIA's general counsel demands a "verbal assurance from each nation that detainees will be treated humanely."[56] Given State Department human rights reports, and all the other evidence about torture in nations that collaborate with the United States in extraordinary rendition, there is no reason to believe the promises contained in any assurance. Further, assurances lack the force of law. Nor is there reason to accept that the assurances, including those received from Syria in Maher Arar's case, were believed by the President or Dr. Rice: countries that routinely violate their own laws against torture and trash their own citizens' human rights are asked, with a wink and a nod, to "promise" not to do what they generally do—just in this one case.

Unsurprisingly, there is no evidence to suggest the United States ever protested to Syria, Egypt, or any of its other extraordinary rendition partners about torture after a transfer. In February 2005, the new CIA chief Porter Goss told Congress that the CIA had an "accountability program" to monitor posttransfer conduct, but tellingly conceded that once a prisoner was out of the CIA's control, "there's only so much we can do."[57] In Arar's case, the State Department received "appropriate assurances from Syrian officials" prior to the transfer. But these assurances were clearly not respected; they simply gave cover for the Administration's assertion that it was not violating its obligations under the Convention Against Torture.[58]

Relying on diplomatic assurances is a clear violation of the Convention Against Torture. The Convention, which is the law of the land, bars a signatory state from expelling, returning, or extraditing a person to another country "where there are substantial grounds for believing he would be in danger of being subjected to torture." Explaining its scope, the treaty directs signatories to "take into account all relevant considerations including, where applicable, the existence in the country concerned of a consistent pattern of gross, flagrant, or mass violations of human rights." Hence, the treaty focuses attention on the *actual* risk to a person—not whatever antitorture laws a country might have signed, and still less, a convenient, ad hoc "assurance" or "promise."[59]

Diplomatic assurances are simply a convenient "check the box" way of evading the Convention's prohibition on returns to torture, an empty gesture at compliance when the U.S. government knows it is violating the law. Indeed, as the advocacy group Human Rights Watch has noted, there is no known instance in which "assurances have been sought from a county in which torture and ill-treatment were not acknowledged human rights problems."[60]

There is no doubt that the Administration knows it is rendering people to countries that regularly torture. The State Department's report on Egypt in 2005 painted a grim picture of "a systematic pattern of torture by the security forces," including "stripping and blindfolding victims; suspending victims from a ceiling or doorframe with feet just touching the floor; beating victims with fists, whips, metal rods, or other objects; using electric shocks; and dousing victims with cold water." Sexual abuse was not uncommon. The State Department's human rights report on Syria that same year described how Syria's prisons and justice system suffer from "[c]ontinuing serious abuses including the use of torture in detention, which at times, results in death; poor prison conditions; arbitrary arrest and detention; [and] prolonged detention without trial."[61]

The Administration's statements are the epitome of hypocrisy. We condemn countries at the same time that we collaborate with them in the very practices we claim to abhor. Diplomatic assurances are simply the grossest evidence of that hypocrisy. They stretch the credulity of America's citizens and its allies, to say nothing of nations and people who already view the United States with skepticism.

Unsurprisingly, European audiences received Secretary Rice's defense of the extraordinary rendition system with skepticism as well. European politicians and journalists roundly condemned extraordinary rendition. A Conservative Party member of Britain's parliament described Rice's comments as "surgically precise language to obfuscate and distract" that had been "drafted by lawyers with the intention of misleading an audience." Journalists in Britain and elsewhere seized on the ambiguities in Rice's speech around the term "policy" and the use of diplomatic assurances as evidence that the Bush Administration was engaged in manifest hypocrisy, as well as acts in gross violation of long-established international law.[62]

Public uproar led several countries, including Canada, Sweden, Italy, and Germany, and the European Union overall to establish judicial or parliamentary investigations of specific extraordinary renditions concerning their citizens or the use of their territory. During Rice's visit, Germany's foreign minister and prime minister pressed for clarification of the American position. Rice's evasive responses only sparked more outrage. The conservative German newspaper *Die Welt* bluntly stated that "no one believes these [diplomatic] assurances." With less restraint, the leftist *Tageszeitung* ran a fake CIA recruiting advertisement proclaiming, "Torturers Wanted: U.S. Citizens May Not Apply." Secretary Rice's visit, rather than answering concerns, served to crystallize the view, held across the European political spectrum, that the American government was engaged in morally reprehensible policies with which European states should have no truck.[63]

Rice's justification also prompted a sharply worded judicial rebuke. In December 2005, Britain's House of Lords, the nation's highest court, issued an opinion barring the use of evidence gained by torture in immigration proceedings. Uniformly praised across the political spectrum in the United Kingdom, the Lords' judgment condemned the extraordinary rendition system in no uncertain terms. "The use of torture is dishonorable," wrote Lord Goff. "It corrupts and degrades the state which uses it and the legal system which accepts it. . . . In our own century, many people in the United States, heirs to [the] common-law tradition, have felt their country dishonored by its use of torture outside the jurisdiction and its practice of extra-legal 'rendition' of suspects to countries where they would be tortured."[64]

Some "realists" argue that the violation of international legal norms, and consequent popular, press, and judicial opprobrium, have little strategic consequence. A distinguished proponent of the realism thesis in international relations (although not of rendition policy), Professor John Mearsheimer argues that international legal norms "have minimal influence on state behavior and thus hold little promise for promoting stability in the post Cold-War world." According to Mearsheimer and other realists, mere moral indignation, sound, and fury in European cafés and courts has scant relevance to decisions about national security.[65] In the "world of stark and harsh competition" depicted by Mearsheimer and his fellow realists, nation-states are red in tooth and claw. They have little time to pause and ruminate on the morality of counterterrorism cooperation, let alone sanction their allies for overreaching. "[A]ll states are forced to seek the same goal: maximum relative power," goes Mearsheimer's teaching.[66]

Might then the executive branch's decision to step above the law, setting rights and values aside, be defensible in pragmatic terms? Experience with rendition policy suggests not. The unavoidable hypocrisy of claiming to stand above the law does real harm to the nation's interests.

As an initial matter, extraordinary rendition led to diplomatic setbacks for the United States. In 2005, Dutch foreign minister Ben Bot suggested that the Netherlands' contribution to NATO deployments in Afghanistan would be jeopardized if American officials "continue[d] to beat around the bush" on the question of "black sites" in Europe. Bot's statement gives concrete form to the public pressure on European governments on extraordinary rendition.[67]

European governments may see pragmatic advantages in yielding to public protests about the immorality of extraordinary rendition. Their objections to extraordinary rendition are a way of seizing moral high ground. Further, moral condemnation has strategic uses. As Robert Kagan observes, "Europe's assaults on the legitimacy of U.S. dominance may also become an effective way of constraining and controlling the superpower."[68]

In addition, extraordinary rendition creates roadblocks to police and intelligence cooperation. In Sweden, for instance, public outcry was triggered by a report in the television program *Kalla Facta* that Swedish police handed over two Egyptian asylum seekers to CIA custody at one of Stockholm's airports for them to be rendered into Egyptian custody. After transport, one was allegedly tortured and sentenced to twenty-five years' imprisonment. As a consequence, Swedish police drafted new regulations for deportations, requiring Swedish, not foreign, control of such operations.[69]

Resistance to intelligence and law enforcement cooperation comes from official sources too. The British House of Lords in December 2005 prohibited use of possibly coerced evidence in immigration decisions, rejecting the argument of Eliza Manningham-Buller, head of Britain's Security Service, that intelligence services needed to rely on foreign intelligence services for information, and could not be in the business of querying what methods were used to extract vital information.[70]

German courts also balked at acquiescence to the extraordinary rendition system and the use of black sites, with serious consequences for counterterrorism efforts in Germany. In early 2004, German courts acquitted two Moroccan men accused of direct involvement in the planning of the 9/11 attacks. Mounir el-Motassadeq and Abdelghani Mzoudi were released because the United States declined to provide testimony sought from detainees at black sites, including Ramzi bin al-Shibh. Although no explanation was forthcoming, it seems reasonable to suppose that al-Shibh had been subjected to coercive interrogation techniques that the Administration had no wish to see examined and condemned in a German courtroom. Faced with the acquittals, the Justice Department produced a summary of al-Shibh's statements. A German court then convicted el-Motassadeq on a lesser count of belonging to al Qaeda but acquitted him of the more serious charge of complicity in the attacks. The court criticized the United States for continuing to withhold evidence centrally relevant to the complicity count.[71]

Worse, extraordinary rendition led to criminal charges against CIA agents in Italy. On February 17, 2003, CIA agents snatched in broad daylight from the streets of Milan an Egyptian cleric, Osama Moustafa Hassan Nasr. As a university student, Nasr joined Jamaat al Islamiya, a violent jihadist faction in Egypt. With Jamaat itself facing violent repression by the state, Nasr fled to Albania, then Germany, and finally Italy. On February 17, 2003, CIA agents bundled him into a van. His wife and two children had no word of him until April 2005, when they received a letter from him, mailed from Alexandria, Egypt.

Nasr's kidnapping—"the inspiration of the CIA station chief in Rome, who wanted to play a more active role in taking suspected terrorists off the street"—occurred without full Italian cooperation. But as a former member of the Egyptian Brotherhood, Nasr had been under regular surveillance by the Italian police.[72] In June 2005, Milan prosecutor Armando Spataro issued Europe-wide arrest warrants for twenty-two alleged CIA operatives. In July 2006, Italian police arrested two Italian intelligence agents, Marco Mancini and Gustavo Pignero, alleging that both had been involved in the planning and execution of Nasr's kidnapping. Spataro explained that Nasr had been the subject of ongoing Italian investigation, and that the CIA's kidnapping had "seriously damaged counterterrorism efforts in Italy and Europe. . . . In fact, if Nasr had not been kidnapped, he would now be in prison, subject to a regular trial, and we would have probably identified his other accomplices." Revelations that the CIA operatives involved in the kidnapping stayed in luxury hotels in Milan, Florence, and Venice before and after the kidnapping, racking up more than $100,000 in bills, only added to the impression that the operation had been conceived in a reckless and foolish manner, more James Bond than George Smiley.[73]

Finally, extraordinary rendition weakens international judicial and prosecutorial cooperation by providing a low-cost means of circumventing formal legal channels, undercutting countries' incentives to improve methods of cooperation. Long-term counterterrorism strategy depends on the United States' ability both to eliminate lawless pockets in which al Qaeda can thrive and to strengthen the democracies of countries in which al Qaeda seeks recruits. Extraordinary rendition, however, strengthens abusive intelligence services in nondemocratic states, such as Egypt, Jordan, and Syria, against forces of liberal and democratic reform.

Since the overthrow of the Egyptian monarchy in 1952, Egypt has labored under "total executive domination," in which democratic and parliamentary resistance is subdued through a host of constitutional and extralegal methods. The parliamentary elections of 2005 thus were "hardly free and fair," but were accompanied by violent repression by security forces. In December 2005, an Egyptian court sentenced Ayman Nour, a leading opposition figure, to five years' hard labor in a case widely seen as retribution for running against President Hosni Mubarak. The Egyptian prime minister has admitted to receiving, even by mid-2005, "60 to 70" terrorist suspects, whether through rendition or by extradition, since 9/11. In the same period, Egypt received approximately $50 billion annually in U.S. aid, with a significant amount flowing to security agencies who work with the CIA. Egyptian-American cooperation in extraordinary rendition strengthens the least law-abiding elements of the Egyptian state, its internal security forces, and thus corrodes prospects for Egyptian democracy.[74] Certainly, we may never be able to avoid all cooperation with such security agencies, but it surely does not behoove us to work with them in a way that undermines our strategic goals in the region and limits our ability to bring international pressure to bear against lawless and undemocratic practices.

In Jordan, which has been a "hub" for extraordinary renditions, CIA personnel work hand in hand with the Jordanian intelligence service, the General Intelligence Directive. As a consequence, the Jordanian government received what one analyst calls "a free pass on human rights." In Syria, intelligence services were responsible for the undermining of democratic governance in their own country. They also played a pivotal role in destabilizing Lebanon, efforts that reached a peak with the murders of Lebanese politicians Rafik Hariri and Gibran Tueni in late 2005. Indeed, the German newsweekly *Der Spiegel* has reported that a Syrian general who figured in the U.N. investigation of the Lebanese leader Rafik Hariri's murder was also a liaison with Germany in the extraordinary rendition of a German citizen named Muhammed Haydar Zammar. As long as the brutal intelligence services of countries such as Egypt and Syria have behind-the-scenes support from the CIA, efforts to promote stable, predictable governance—the sine qua non of the international rule of law—will founder.[75]

The Costs of Presidential Unilateralism

Hypocrisy is the price tag of unilateral executive action in violation of settled American law. America's actions are scrutinized by the rest of the world—and, as Colin Powell has learned, other nations will "doubt the moral basis of our fight against terrorism." American values and standards used to be high moral benchmarks for many across the world; thus American misconduct takes on a meaning that transcends borders, with consequences for the rule of law in countries around the world. Egypt's president Hosni Mubarak declared that U.S. policy proved "that we were right from the beginning in using all means, including military tribunals, to combat terrorism." Sudan and Zimbabwe, too, justified "disappearances" of political foes on the ground that America does the same. American efforts to reform the United Nations' Human Rights Commission were stymied in part because the United States was no longer viewed as a credible advocate for human rights. Thus, the Zimbabwean representative to the body swatted away American criticisms, proclaiming that "those who live in glass houses should not throw stones." Pointing to American offshore detention policies, the representative asserted that the United States had "a lot of dirt on its hands." Indeed, in May 2006 the UN Committee Against Torture, a treaty body that monitors compliance with antitorture norms, issued a damning condemnation of American torture and extraordinary rendition policy.[76]

Hypocrisy's consequences pinch close to home too. The 9/11 Commission explained that the United States must "offer an example of moral leadership in the world, commit to treat people humanely, abide by the rule of law, and be generous and caring to our neighbors." The 9/11 Commission echoed the findings of the Church Committee on the careful choice of allies:

> When Muslim governments, even those who are friends, do not respect these principles, the United States must stand for a better future. One of the lessons of the long Cold War was that short-term gains in cooperating with the most repressive and brutal governments were too often outweighed by long-term setbacks for America's stature and interests.

By flouting the checks and balances of limited government under law, extraordinary rendition undermines American support for democracy and pluralism. Although President Bush says "any comparison" of America to its enemies is "unacceptable to think," this comparison is inevitably made by millions overseas when they hear of American torture and extraordinary rendition.[77] To millions of Arabs and Muslims, stories of extraordinary rendition and black sites speak louder than words about American values. America, of course, has not fallen to al Qaeda's level. But, as Captain Fishback said, "our actions should be held to a higher standard." And extraordinary rendition's persistence gives al Qaeda a potent recruiting tool.

Executive branch unilateralism is no mere abstract legalistic concern. It ought to concern all those with a stake in the nation's security. Extraordinary rendition undermines counterterrorism efforts and blights our reputation. In the end, it is but the latest harmful, foolish policy to emerge from the failure to respect the Constitution's carefully calibrated government of separate branches, sharing powers.

6

Bringing War Back Home

The checks and balances of constitutional government are commonly thought to bind tighter at home than overseas. Yet the Bush Administration's flawed legal theories of unlimited executive powers, which underpin overseas torture policy and extraordinary rendition, did not remain outside America's borders. Wielding those same legal tools, the executive branch issued secret laws after 9/11 supported by secret Justice Department legal opinions to make striking incursions on *Americans'* privacy and liberties. Devices and doctrines of the battlefield came home to justify unchecked surveillance and detention of American citizens and residents.

In 9/11's wake, military intelligence agencies harnessed the White House's sweeping view of executive power to classify the entire homeland as a field of ongoing battle. The Defense Department's National Security Agency began spying on Americans without warrants within days of September 11, 2001. Another Defense Department agency, the "Counter-Intelligence Field Activity," or CIFA, initiated direct surveillance of ordinary Americans—targeting opponents of the Bush Administration's decision to go to war against Iraq as well as those who advocated change to the military's policy on homosexuals. More troublingly, the military subjected American citizens to unilateral presidential detention—including one picked up on U.S. soil. The Justice Department took the position that such citizens had no right to a meaningful opportunity to defend themselves.

Because prevailing laws on torture and extraordinary rendition predated 9/11, the Administration could contend (even if wrongly) that events had superseded such rules. But Congress enacted new legislation *after 9/11* on electronic surveillance at home. It passed new criminal penalties for supporting terrorist groups. And it authorized limited preventive detention of noncitizens within the United States. Instead of working within new laws, the executive branch mined the laws' ambiguities to grab powers Congress never intended to grant. The Administration secretly sidestepped checks Congress inserted into law. And once more, the exercise of unchecked presidential power led to abusive mission creep and to inefficient, abusive use of intelligence powers.

Blame for these unwise policies does not lie entirely at the President's door. Congress too fell far short of its constitutional obligations. As in the Cold War, it failed to resolve statutory ambiguities that the executive exploited to its own advantage (although the federal wiretapping statute is a notable paradigm of clarity). Courts have largely placed only a marginal check on the executive branch. Worse, Congress failed to conduct proper oversight even after the President's illegal use of war powers became known. To date, legislators have shown little appetite for getting the factual details, let alone for acting decisively.

America: A Surveillance State Again

Congress acknowledged the need for new surveillance powers after 9/11 by making changes to the 1978 Foreign Intelligence Surveillance Act, or FISA, in October 2001. It returned to the same statute in 2002, 2004, 2005, and 2006 to expand government spying authority. All these changes remained within a framework of checks and balances. Congress preserved the rule that no surveillance could proceed without a judicial warrant, and left unchanged the requirement that the attorney general report to Congress about FISA's use on a semiannual basis.[1]

The White House chose to disregard the legislature's efforts. Almost from the first days after 9/11, the Administration has spied on Americans without judicial warrants and without reporting to Congress. To this end, the executive branch invented an ambiguity in an entirely unrelated law that Congress passed to authorize the 2001 Afghanistan invasion and claimed to find a hidden reserve of unlimited presidential power in the Constitution. While we do not know the full extent of domestic spying, we can be reasonably sure such spying continues unabated in the absence of firm congressional or judicial intervention.

The first public changes to FISA came in the USA Patriot Act. Drafted during the week after 9/11 and then introduced to the House on September 19, 2001, the Patriot Act covered sixteen complex topics, including new electronic surveillance powers, in 161 separate sections spread across 350 densely packed pages. It expanded the government's tools for obtaining information, and made it easier to share information gained by FISA warrants between intelligence agencies and law enforcement officers. House Judiciary chairman James Sensenbrenner proclaimed it "the most dramatic modernization of prosecutorial and police powers that Congress has ever passed."[2]

Three years later, Congress responded to the 9/11 Commission's findings by amending FISA to make surveillance easier. Congress recognized and acted to fix the so-called "Moussaoui problem," adding language to FISA to make it simpler to obtain a search warrant for a suspect seemingly acting alone and without known assistance from a foreign government or terrorist group.[3]

Outward appearances suggested that FISA's flexibility accommodated the changed circumstances since 9/11. Congress did not resist additional surveillance powers, eventually reauthorizing in 2006 many of the powers first granted in the Patriot Act.[4] For the first four years after 9/11, on the surface, there was a suggestion that Congress and the executive branch might be able to forge the sort of cooperative relationship the Constitution envisages between legislators and the White House.

The White House did nothing to suggest that its new statutory surveillance powers were inadequate. On the contrary, senior officials repeatedly voiced their respect for law, and for the checks and balances of constitutional government under law. In the midst of the 2004 presidential campaign, for example, President George W. Bush stopped in Buffalo, New York, and promised that his Administration would vigorously use the surveillance powers granted by FISA and other laws against terrorism suspects, but would nonetheless remain within the bounds of law:

> [T]here are such things as roving wiretaps. Now, by the way, any time you hear the United States government talking about wiretaps, it re-quires—a wiretap requires a court order. Nothing has changed, by the way. When we're talking about chasing down terrorists, we're talking about getting a court order before we do so. It's important for our fellow citizens to understand, when you think Patriot Act, constitutional guarantees are in place when it comes to doing what is necessary to protect our homeland, because we value the Constitution.[5]

A little more than a year later in Columbus, Ohio, President Bush again promised domestic surveillance would remain within the rule of law:

> The Patriot Act was written with clear safeguards to ensure the law is ap-plied fairly. The judicial branch has a strong oversight role. Law enforce-ment officers need a federal judge's permission to wiretap a foreign terrorist's phone, a federal judge's permission to track his calls, or a fed-eral judge's permission to search his property. Officers must meet strict standards to use any of these tools. And these standards are fully consis-tent with the Constitution.[6]

Along with the President, key officials responsible for surveillance echoed the message that FISA provided the necessary tools to deal with terrorism. In 2002, then-head of the National Security Agency (and subsequently chief of the CIA) General Michael V. Hayden told Congress that the NSA "would have no authorit[y]" inside the United States, and that he did not "want to be perceived as focusing NSA capabilities against U.S. persons in the United States." (Since the Church Committee's revelations of indiscriminate NSA spying during the Cold War, the NSA scrupulously insisted it engaged in no domestic spying.) In 2005, Hayden wrote that NSA "[i]ntelligence collection must not be undertaken to acquire information concerning the domestic activities of U.S. persons," and affirmed that the NSA operated in accord with FISA.[7]

Both Hayden and the President knew, however, that their statements were—to put it charitably—misleading. They suggested that all government wiretap surveillance was being carried out pursuant to the FISA rules for warrants. The truth was that since at least 2002 the NSA engaged in sweeping electronic surveillance of Americans in the absence of judicial warrants with the full knowledge and active assent of both the President and General Hayden.[8] While the Administration adamantly resists disclosing information about the scope of its warrantless spying or the internal procedures supposed to ensure that the government's awesome powers are not abused, or to release the OLC's relevant legal opinions, the facts we have give ample cause for concern that mistakes documented by the Church Committee are being repeated and deepened.

Created by President Harry Truman by secret directive in October 1952 to marshal the nation's electronic surveillance resources, the NSA worked until 1992 without a legislative charter. The agency quickly grew. Intelligence scholar Loch Johnson reports that the NSA soon had "the largest floor space, the longest corridors, the most electrical wiring, and the biggest computers of any agency within the intelligence community." It was "a vast mechanical octopus, reaching sensitive tentacles into every continent in search of information on the intentions and capacities of other nations."

The NSA collects signals intelligence from telegrams, telephones, faxes, e-mails, and other electronic communications, and then disseminates this information among other agencies of the executive branch. The Church Committee found that, while an extremely valuable national resource, the NSA had not exercised its vast power with restraint or due regard for the Constitution. On the contrary, during the Cold War, it collected every international telegram sent from America, and kept watch lists of Americans involved in protest activities—all without even minimal supervision from the courts, Congress, or even the agency's political superiors.[9]

Immediately after 9/11, after almost three decades' hiatus, the NSA again started spying on the contents of Americans' electronic communications without warrants.[10] The NSA pursues at least two significant domestic intelligence gathering operations without statutory authority. According to *New York Times*

reporters James Risen and Eric Lichtblau, one part of the NSA's domestic surveillance program really took clearer shape after the capture of al Qaeda members such as Abu Zubaydah in early 2002, when the NSA began tracing
telephone numbers in the United States and monitoring calls from those numbers. At first, the NSA exploited intelligence embedded in captured computers and cell phones belonging to al Qaeda members. This important
intelligence work, however, led to another far more ambitious approach,
which built tenuous links outward from each terrorist suspect into the broader
world. Risen explains:

> The CIA turned those names, addresses, and numbers over to the NSA,
> which then began monitoring those numbers, as well as the numbers of
> anyone in communication with them, and so on outward in an expand-
> ing network of phone numbers and Internet addresses, both in the
> United States and overseas. . . . [T]he NSA is using the Program to con-
> duct surveillance on the telephone and e-mail correspondence of about
> seven thousand people overseas. . . . NSA is targeting the communica-
> tions of about five hundred people inside the United States.[11]

It thus seems that the NSA has been spying—and may still be spying—both on
calls between the United States and overseas, and also on many wholly domestic calls. The latter are squarely protected from government intrusion by
both the First Amendment's speech protection and the Fourth Amendment's
shelter against warrantless searches.

High-volume data collection is feasible thanks to changes in telecommunications technology. Now, the NSA can collect and sift enormous volumes of
data with ease. Billions of bytes of digital and nondigital communications traffic flow via transoceanic fiber-optic cables, bounced from satellite to satellite,
to be channeled through enormous data routing switches in the United States.
These switches handle both entirely domestic and entirely international communications. With access to the switches, author James Bamford explains,
"Somebody [at the NSA] pushes a button in an office thousands of miles away
and [a civilian's] cell phone, their e-mail, their BlackBerry, their fax, everything goes into it."[12]

High-volume data collection and the application of vast computing resources
to analyze this data enabled a second set of NSA activities. While Risen and
Lichtblau revealed a program of clandestine spying on the *contents* of people's
calls, Leslie Cauley of *USA Today* reported a different kind of secret monitoring program involving dragnet collection of information about calls that did
not pick up content data. Neither FISA nor the Fourth Amendment bar this
kind of data collection. Another federal statute, the Stored Communications

Act, does, however, prohibit telecom companies from handing such data to the government in the absence of lawful authority. Mere days after Director of National Intelligence John Negroponte stated that the government was "absolutely not" monitoring domestic calls without warrants, Cauley reported that some telecommunications providers provided the NSA with detailed calling records that revealed source, destination, and timing information, but not content. This data allowed the NSA to reconstruct and analyze calling patterns. And by matching telephone numbers with other databases, moreover, the Agency could learn who was making calls. In the wake of Cauley's story, executive branch officials maintained that they acted within the law's bounds, but carefully avoided confirming or denying the facts Cauley reported.[13]

In acquiescing to NSA requests, the telecom giants followed their Cold War predecessors, which gave the NSA unrestricted access to overseas telegram traffic without asking any questions. Documents filed in a lawsuit brought by the Electronic Frontier Foundation cast important light on how today's telecom companies facilitate the NSA's warrantless surveillance. At AT&T's San Francisco Internet and telephone hub, the documents revealed, the government installed millions of dollars worth of equipment that permits messages to be filtered out and stored as they pass through the hub. The equipment allows the government to select only international communications—but it could easily catch domestic communications too. Similar filters existed, the documents suggest, in Atlanta, San Jose, Los Angeles, San Diego, and Seattle. Although noncontent data (such as source, destination, and timing data) is unprotected by the Fourth Amendment, the companies apparently violated federal law that bars handover of such information to the government absent a subpoena or court order.[14]

The government has two main ways of studying such enormous volumes of data: link analysis and pattern analysis (which is also known as "data mining"). It seems that the NSA uses both. Both provoke troubling questions. Link analysis involves the "join-the-dots" method described by James Risen and Eric Lichtblau. Most of us, however, are connected to thousands of people by two degrees of separation, and to hundreds of thousands by three degrees of separation. The overwhelming number of leads generated by link analysis inevitably contains countless false positives—innocents who have no substantial connection to and no knowledge of terrorist activities.[15]

Pattern analysis, or data mining, uses technologies such as statistical analysis and modeling to identify hidden patterns and subtle characteristics in large data sets. In 2004, the General Accounting Office found that the federal government had 199 data-mining operations, fourteen of which were related to counterterrorism.[16]

Data mining and link analysis no doubt have legitimate uses in detecting suspicious activities. Before 9/11, the military's "Able Danger" project used data mining to search for terrorist threats, and some say it may have identified Mohammad Atta as a suspect (although it was far from putting the pieces of the 9/11 plot together). As a result, legal commentators of divergent political views, such as Phillip Bobbitt and Judge Richard Posner, endorse data mining as a useful counterterrorism tool. But, as with any other surveillance technology, the question is not whether data mining ought be used at all; rather, we must ask what checks and accountability mechanisms are needed to guard against its abuse. Identifying suspects through patterns in communication data is not foolproof science. Open questions remain about how often the NSA managed to target a person correctly.[17]

There are other collateral risks in data mining, especially since the source, destination, and timing information may be connected to more intimate or personal data. According to intelligence historian Timothy Naftali, the NSA is engaged in "fishing expedition[s]." And there is no guarantee the agency uses "privacy appliances"—that is, digital devices to strip personal information from electronic communication, so as to minimize privacy violations. The net result is that the NSA captures a lot of information but does not necessarily filter out clearly irrelevant, personal data.[18]

Information gathered on innocent Americans, moreover, is easily misused. In the Cold War, the FBI often funneled the intelligence it gathered through surveillance to political appointees in the government, distorting government policy on the civil rights movement. This concern has resonance today. The NSA's catch does not stay in the agency's Fort Meade headquarters. Other intelligence agencies ask for information—and get it. The Defense Intelligence Agency (part of the Defense Department) allegedly used NSA intercepts as a basis for direct surveillance of people and vehicles in the United States who are "suspected of posing a threat." Worse, political appointees with no intelligence responsibilities can access NSA intercepts. In confirmation hearings for John Bolton's appointment as U.S. ambassador to the United Nations, Bolton admitted to senators that while at the State Department he circumvented privacy protections that shield innocent Americans. Bolton had asked the NSA for communications between Americans and foreigners. Usually the names of Americans are expunged when NSA intercepts are shared, but Bolton asked for—and got—the names put back in. He was not alone. *Newsweek* revealed that between January 2004 and May 2005, the NSA supplied executive branch policymakers with the names of about ten thousand American citizens.[19]

NSA intercepts also may be misused in criminal investigations. According to James Risen, evidence gathered by warrantless eavesdropping is used to obtain warrants in the Foreign Intelligence Surveillance Court. If true, this would mean that evidence obtained illegally by the NSA was "laundered" through the FISA process for potential use in a criminal trial in an end run around Fourth Amendment protections. Concerns about abuse of the FISA process prompted the FISA court to seek a special briefing from the Administration about NSA's activities, and precipitated the resignation of one judge from the FISA court.[20]

Sensitive to these risks, Congress blocked funding in 2003 for a Defense Department data mining program called "Total Information Awareness," or TIA, out of privacy concerns. TIA was run by Iran-Contra veteran John Poindexter. Rather than follow Congress's direction, however, the executive branch took a leaf from the Iran-Contra book: it simply moved TIA to a different part of the Defense Department, the "Advanced Research and Development Activity" unit of the NSA at Fort Meade in Maryland. According to the *National Journal*, government contractors with contracts to build TIA found "their funding remained intact, often under the same contracts." The privacy concerns that drove Congress to terminate TIA, however, are not dissolved by a mere name change. But Congress did not pursue this initial response, and instead did nothing as the executive branch circumvented its clear command.[21]

Privacy abuses are not the sole kind of risk attendant on the NSA's sweeping surveillance. Like other executive branch efforts that circumvent the constraints imposed by other branches of government, unchecked intelligence gathering can hinder as much as help counterterrorism efforts. Months before 9/11, a congressional report concluded that "[i]ntelligence agencies are faced with profound 'needle-in-a-haystack' challenges" sorting useful leads from an ocean of worldwide communications. Indeed, before 9/11, several al Qaeda communications were intercepted without their significance being registered.[22]

But a bigger haystack does not help the search for needles. After 9/11, the NSA inundated the FBI with a deluge of unverified leads and unfiltered surveillance intercepts. Agents followed up "thousands of tips a month," a task that "diverted agents from counterterrorism work they viewed as more productive." According to intelligence sources, fewer than ten U.S. citizens or residents out of thousands so targeted generated enough suspicion even to justify a FISA warrant, which demands an exceedingly low threshold of information and is only the threshold step in any investigation. That so few FISA warrants were obtained, therefore, is a sign that the search process was deeply flawed.[23]

As evidence that the NSA's warrantless surveillance generated results, the Administration pointed to the cases of Iyman Faris, an Ohio truck driver allegedly associated with Khalid Sheikh Mohammed, and a 2004 conspiracy of British citizens to manufacture fertilizer explosives. But former counterterrorism officials familiar with both cases rejected the notion that signals intelligence from the NSA played any significant role in either case.[24]

Well aware that the public would likely perceive sweeping warrantless electronic surveillance as invasive or counterproductive, the Bush Administration argued that the NSA's warrantless searches were "limited" and "very conservative."[25] At the same time, it refused to disclose all the facts to the public or to the whole of Congress. Legal opinions on which the NSA's program was justified, moreover, were kept secret, and remain so at the time of this writing. Just like the Administration's rationalizations for extraordinary rendition, official justifications for domestic surveillance were full of silences and ambiguities.

In a press briefing, Attorney General Alberto Gonzales described the NSA program as:

> intercepts of contents of communications where . . . one party to the communication is outside the United States. And this is a very important point. . . . Another very important point to remember is that we have to have a reasonable basis to conclude that one party to the communication is a member of al Qaeda, affiliated with al Qaeda, or a member of an organization affiliated with al Qaeda, or working in support of al Qaeda.[26]

Even this disclaimer is full of startling admissions. Gonzales suggested that the NSA used a low threshold to trigger surveillance—a "reasonable basis to conclude" standard—that seemed easier to meet than the "probable cause" standard of FISA (and, of course, much easier to meet when no case for the warrant needs to be made before a court). Former NSA director Michael Hayden also explained that the NSA bypassed FISA because it wanted "a subtly softer trigger" than FISA allowed—which is a nice way of saying that the NSA could spy on the basis of thinner evidence than the law demands. Gonzales, moreover, revealed that the NSA was not just targeting terrorists but anyone deemed "affiliated" with or "working in support" of terrorists. But he did not explain what these murky terms mean in practice. Harvard Law School professor Laurence Tribe cautioned that "the breadth and elasticity of the notions of 'affiliation' and 'support,' coupled with the loosely-knit network of groups Al Qaeda is thought to have become," together mean that the "definition casts so wide a net that no one can feel certain of escaping its grasp."[27]

Gonzales, moreover, refused to rule out the possibility that NSA surveillance extended beyond what he described and also included purely domestic communications. Testifying before the Senate Judiciary Committee in February 2006, Gonzales stated that the surveillance documented by the *New York Times* was "all that [the president] has authorized." But in a follow-up letter, Gonzales clarified that he "did not and could not address . . . any other classified intelligence activities." Indeed, some months later, Congress and the public learned that the executive branch had been scooping up financial data on

Americans from foreign and domestic financial institutions, using subpoenas and simply buying data.[28]

Electronic spying by the NSA is not the only way in which intrusive surveillance practices crept back to the American homeland. Gonzales's disclaimer left open the possibility that the Defense Department's intelligence agencies, or other government agencies, used other intrusive surveillance techniques such as informants and physical searches in the absence of statutory license. In one curious case, the office of an Oregon lawyer representing a defendant in a terrorism case was twice broken into under circumstances that suggest that legal documents were being sought. In response to the lawyer's request for information, the NSA's director of policy wrote that "the existence or nonexistence of responsive records is a currently and properly classified matter." The possibility of physical searches and other intrusive measures being used in the United States against American citizens raises the specter of the internal police service feared by earlier attorneys general Harlan Fiske Stone and Robert Jackson—except this time it is not the FBI (the focus of Stone's and Jackson's concerns) but the military that is the danger.[29]

The NSA is merely one of several military agencies, all under the aegis of the executive branch, that engage in domestic spying. Indeed, the scale of other domestic military counterterrorism operations, and the concomitant "militarization of counterterrorism," would surprise many Americans.[30] The armed forces' new Northern Command, established in Colorado Springs after 9/11, houses more security analysts than either the State Department's Bureau of Intelligence and Research or the Department of Homeland Security. In February 2002, the Defense Department established the Counter-Intelligence Field Activity (CIFA), at the Northern Command to conduct data-collection, surveillance, and "offensive and defensive counterintelligence efforts" inside the United States. An opaque executive order—there is no authorizing statute—describes CIFA's goals as to "detect and neutralize espionage against the Defense Department." Despite initially being a policy coordination body, CIFA swelled in its first three years into "an analytic and operational organization with nine directorates and ever-widening authority." At least according to the Pentagon, "There is no absolute ban on intelligence components collecting U.S. person information."[31]

CIFA thus has a sweeping mandate (not even demarcated by statute) and is not constrained by limits on intelligence collection that apply to the CIA and FBI. Vague instructions and the absence of checks, as we have seen, are a recipe for mission creep. What ensued was entirely predictable. As a former senior Defense Department official summarized, "[The military] started with force protection from terrorists, but when you go down that road, you soon are into everything . . . where terrorists get their money, who they see, who they deal with." The parallel with Cold War intelligence gathering is all too clear.[32]

The best example of military mission creep is the "Talon" database. Talon stands for "Threat and Local Observation Notice." The database includes "raw, unverified information" on "suspicious activities." According to a 2003 memo by then–Deputy Defense Secretary Paul Wolfowitz, Talon tracks "deliberately targeted or collateral" threats, including people "taking photographs, annotating maps or drawings of facilities"; using binoculars "or other vision-enhancing devices"; and engaging in other "attempts to obtain security-related or military specific information."[33]

In December 2005, NBC News acquired a sample of about 1,500 reports of suspicious activity logged by CIFA in the Talon database. These reports made clear that CIFA understood its "offensive and defensive counterintelligence" role very broadly. The Talon database included a substantial amount of information on activities that most people would classify as legitimate political speech at the core of the First Amendment. In a troubling rerun of Cold War practices, CIFA seemed to focus especially closely on speech disagreeing with the military's policies—just as during the Vietnam War, antiwar groups found themselves under scrutiny. CIFA collected information on a Quaker meeting house in Lake Worth, Florida, that planned to protest military recruiting at local high schools, and targeted dozens of other antiwar protests. CIFA personnel gathered data on the vehicles used by peace protestors and intercepted e-mail communication between such groups. According to a March 2004 *Wall Street Journal* article, military personnel also attended academic conferences and tracked participants' public statements. The *Journal* pointed to a February 2004 incident in which an army intelligence officer attended an academic conference at the University of Texas law school, and later demanded videotapes of the event so the agents could confirm the identities of "three Middle Eastern men" who had made "suspicious" remarks about the military.[34]

CIFA also directed its surveillance resources against individuals who disputed the military's recruiting policy. A Freedom of Information Act request revealed in 2006 that CIFA had a post-9/11 "surveillance program monitoring [lesbian, gay, and bisexual] groups" at New York University, the University of California at Berkeley, and the University of California at Santa Cruz. Although the Defense Department conceded this surveillance had been inappropriate, it did not indicate what measures, if any, it would take to prevent similar mission creep.[35]

CIFA's conduct was far from unique. The FBI, returning to its old habits, was also spying on antiwar activists. Between November 2002 and March 2005, the FBI's Pittsburgh office kept the interfaith Thomas Merton Center under surveillance. Whether this is the sole instance of FBI spying on antiwar activists, and whether all such activities ended in March 2005, remain open questions.[36]

Absent a thorough investigation, the scope of NSA, CIFA, and FBI surveillance through electronic wiretapping, physical searches, informants, and simple eavesdropping will remain unknown. Nevertheless, it is disturbingly clear that mistakes of the past are being repeated once more. Rather than focusing on the *nation's* enemies, intelligence services are trained on American dissenters from the government's policies.

Lies and Whispers: How Checks and Balances Failed

Congress has two main tools to guard against executive overreaching: clear laws and vigorous oversight. Both mechanisms have failed. Consider first the clear restraint on domestic spying absent a judicial warrant imposed in FISA. It was again the Justice Department's Office of Legal Counsel, or OLC, that provided legal tools to circumvent FISA. In 2002, President Bush signed a secret presidential order authorizing NSA surveillance in the homeland, akin to the order used to set the extraordinary rendition program in motion. He relied on a classified OLC opinion by John Yoo. As previously mentioned, at the time of this writing, this opinion remains secret. In January 2006, nevertheless, the Justice Department issued an unsigned forty-two-page legal defense of the NSA's activities. (By contrast, no legal defense of CIFA's activities was forthcoming; that agency so far has largely escaped public scrutiny.) This January 2006 document does not, however, likely reflect the classified 2002 OLC legal opinion; rather, it relies heavily on Supreme Court cases from 2004 that obviously were not available in 2002. Nevertheless, it throws some light on the administration's reasoning in circumventing FISA.[37]

Yoo and his OLC colleagues confronted daunting obstacles in the shape of FISA. Congress in 1978 made it clear that FISA extinguished all claims to unilateral presidential surveillance authority. Moreover, FISA includes no vague terminology like President Roosevelt's loose term "subversive," which proved so open to abuse. FISA has a bright-line criminal prohibition of *all* warrantless surveillance unless "authorized by statute." To obtain a warrant, a government agent needs to show probable cause that a person is either an agent of a foreign power or preparing to engage in terrorism.[38]

FISA carves out three exceptions to its warrant requirement, none broad enough to justify the NSA program. First, no warrant is required to spy on a foreign government. Congress, however, chose not to apply this exception to terrorist groups (a category that is far more malleable than "foreign government"). Second, FISA contains an exception to the warrant rule for the fifteen days after a congressional declaration of war (neither the Afghanistan nor the Iraq war was preceded by such a declaration). The 1978 act's legislative history also explained that this waiver was a way of allowing "consideration of any amendment to this act that may be appropriate during a wartime emergency." Congress expected the executive to seek new authorization within fifteen days, even if the country was at war. Finally, FISA has an exception for emergencies that allows an agent to begin surveillance with a seventy-two hour window in which to obtain a warrant. When it drafted FISA, in short, Congress anticipated the need to adapt to unexpected contingencies.[39]

Faced with a clear congressional prohibition on surveillance outside the judicial framework established by FISA, the Justice Department relied on two arguments to get around it, one supposedly based on the Constitution and the other on Congress's September 14, 2001, Authorization for the Use of Military Force, or AUMF, which authorized the war in Afghanistan. According to former NSA chief General Michael Hayden, however, it was the first argument—based on the President's alleged power to override the law passed by Congress—that was crucial for getting the program off the ground. As in the development of the Administration's torture policy, the approval of seasoned career lawyers with expertise in a field was not sought. The Pentagon counsel with responsibility for supervising the NSA, Richard Shiffrin, only learned of the warrantless domestic spying in December 2005, when he read about it in the *New York Times*. The Vice President and his counsel had simply bypassed Shiffrin and gone straight to Hayden.[40]

Thus, the Justice Department argued that the president has power to do whatever he thinks is necessary to counter terrorism, even if such measures violate laws enacted by Congress. According to the Justice Department, the president has "primary responsibility and necessary authority," as commander in chief and the chief executive, "to protect the Nation and to conduct the Nation's foreign affairs." In these capacities, the Justice Department stated, a president has certain "powers and duties with which Congress cannot interfere." The Justice Department quoted President Roosevelt's 1940 authorization of domestic warrantless wiretapping of "persons suspected of subversive activities against the Government." Ironically, it was Roosevelt's authorization that first opened the door to generations of abusive and unnecessary spying. Moreover, Roosevelt's authorization came long before Congress had spoken definitively on the subject. Like the Administration's justification for bypassing the torture statute, this claim of unfettered presidential power suggests that neither Congress nor the courts has any authority to check the executive in matters of purported national security.[41]

Questions linger about what the Bush White House sought to justify under this sweeping theory of executive powers. According to the *New York Times*,

Vice President Cheney and his aide David Addington sought to set aside all statutory and constitutional privacy protections after 9/11 and simply start spying on people. At the time of this writing, it is impossible to know whether there are other domestic spying programs of which we are unaware. Indeed, the chair of the House Intelligence Committee Peter Hoekstra criticized the Administration in July 2006 for failing to brief Congress on yet another surveillance program that had been kept secret. A week after Hoekstra's complaint, the Justice Department formally declined a request by the Senate Judiciary Committee to disclose any other warrantless electronic surveillance programs in existence.[42]

The Justice Department's second claim relied on a different statute, the September 2001 AUMF (although Hayden's account of the program's authorization made no mention of this argument being developed in 2001–2). Congress enacted the AUMF to permit the use of force against al Qaeda redoubts in Afghanistan. The Justice Department pointed to a phrase in FISA that suggested that warrantless surveillance would be legal if it was "authorized" by another statute. The AUMF, claimed the Justice Department, was also a statute that "authorized" warrantless wiretapping in the United States. That is, the executive branch took the AUMF—intended as a mandate for the use of overseas force—as license to treat the whole of the United States as a battlefield in which the president could deploy the same measures he could use on the Afghan battlefield. To support this line of reasoning, the Justice Department pointed to a 2004 Supreme Court decision in which the AUMF had been treated as statutory authorization to hold U.S. citizens captured on the battlefield in Afghanistan who had been caught while fighting against U.S. forces.[43]

This argument is wrong in fact and deeply troubling in principle. It is wrong in fact because both Congress and the Supreme Court understood the AUMF to apply to conflict *overseas*, and not to bring the war, with its looser latticework of legal protections, back home. It is wrong in principle because the argument's practical consequence is to sweep away almost all constitutional rights and statutory protection of liberties within the United States.

Enacting the AUMF, Congress specifically considered and decided not to grant the President the extraordinary power to treat the United States as a battlefield. Two days before the AUMF was enacted, the White House asked for authority to "deter and preempt any future acts of terrorism or aggression against the United States." Rejecting this open-ended authority, Congress chose instead wording that permitted force against Osama bin Laden and al Qaeda, and those who harbored them. Just before the Senate went to vote on the AUMF, the White House pressed for addition of the phrase "in the United States" to the resolution's text. Congress refused to make this change. It thus refused to grant the executive open-ended license to use war powers in the

United States. Notably, Congress did not authorize the use of force against persons or groups "affiliated with" or "working in support of" al Qaeda, contrary to Gonzales's claim about the NSA's program.[44]

Recognizing the limited scope of the AUMF, the Supreme Court in 2004 interpreted it narrowly in a case involving the executive branch's detention power. The AUMF, explained a plurality of four justices, applied to individuals who were "part of the supporting forces hostile to the United States or coalition partners *in Afghanistan and who engaged in an armed conflict against the United States there.*" The Supreme Court, like Congress, clearly constrained the military force authorization's scope.[45]

Yet the Justice Department disregarded all this to conclude that "what the laws of war permit" is allowed in the United States. This is an extraordinary and dangerous principle. The Justice Department would have us believe that in passing the AUMF, Congress silently stripped away a multitude of laws, including all the procedural protections associated with the criminal process and laws restricting the involvement of the military in law enforcement, not to mention the constitutional protections of life and liberty. If the Justice Department were correct, the executive branch could use in the United States tactics ranging from surveillance to indefinite presidential detention (and why not even murder?) against anyone the president judged to be involved in terrorism. The entire world, from Kabul to Kansas City, would become a battlefield. And our freedom and privacy would exist only at the whim of the White House.

But Congress clearly did *not* intend to vest the president in the homeland with the awesome powers wielded by a battlefield commander. Had it done so, FISA would have been irrelevant for terrorism cases. Yet Congress returned to FISA multiple times after 9/11, in large part to make counterterrorism investigations easier. Similarly, in the Patriot Act, Congress facilitated cooperation between intelligence analysts and law enforcement personnel. Foreign intelligence, Congress said, could be simply "a significant purpose," and not necessarily "*the* purpose" of a FISA search. Three years later, Congress added the "lone wolf" provision, allowing surveillance of suspected terrorists who lacked known links to designated terrorist groups or foreign powers. None of this tinkering would have been necessary, or even legally relevant, had Congress really meant to issue a blank check when it passed the AUMF.[46] After 9/11, the Justice Department considered a proposal (which was never floated before Congress) that would have relaxed FISA's warrant requirement, arguably permitting some of the NSA spying that occurred after 9/11. This suggests the Justice Department itself believed that the AUMF did not grant open-ended permission to spy.[47]

In 2002, moreover, Senator Mike DeWine of Ohio proposed an amendment to FISA that would have permitted the issuing of warrants whenever an agency had a "reasonable basis to believe" that a person, whether citizen or foreign national, had ties to al Qaeda or related groups. When Senator DeWine proposed his legislation, the Administration opposed it as unnecessary and *likely unconstitutional*. In July 2002, a Justice Department lawyer argued to the Senate Select Intelligence Committee that lowering the proof standard for FISA warrants might not pass constitutional muster, and might not be necessary. He added that the Justice Department had not yet found evidence that the probable cause standard "caused any difficulties."[48]

Finally, the Bush Administration looked into amending FISA to authorize the NSA's warrantless surveillance by quietly approaching friendly legislators on Capitol Hill. But, as Attorney General Gonzales explained:

> We have had discussions with Congress in the past—certain members of Congress—as to whether or not FISA could be amended to allow us to adequately deal with this kind of threat, and we were told that that would be difficult if not impossible. . . . [W]e were advised that [this] was not something we could likely get, certainly not without jeopardizing the existence of the program, and therefore, killing the program.[49]

Although Gonzales later tried to back away from this statement, what he meant is clear: the White House approached some in Congress after the executive branch started spying illegally without warrants. Told it could not get such a statute passed, the Administration kept on doing what it had been doing regardless of the lack of statutory authority.

The Administration's contempt for Congress reflected more than a momentary lapse, as indicated by an incident in the run-up to the 2003 Iraq war. In 2003, the White House carefully resisted any intimation that it needed congressional approval for the invasion. "We don't want to be in the legal position of asking Congress to authorize the use of force when the president already has that full authority," explained a senior administration official. "We don't want, in getting a resolution, to have conceded that one was constitutionally necessary." Thus, one important reason the executive wants to bypass Congress is to avoid any impression that it depends on Congress for its power.[50]

Once clear laws failed, post hoc constraints also fell short. Congressional oversight faltered even after broad outlines (but not details) of NSA domestic surveillance became known. The National Security Act requires the executive branch to provide congressional intelligence committees with briefings on "intelligence activities," which includes signals collection such as the NSA's spying efforts. But the disclosure law is poorly phrased. It begins by stating that Congress's intelligence committees must be kept "fully and currently informed." But then it adds a vague and open-ended caveat that allows the executive branch to abbreviate disclosures "[t]o the extent consistent with due regard for the protection from unauthorized disclosure of classified information relating to sensitive intelligence sources and methods or other exceptionally sensitive matters." This means that intelligence agencies could present briefings that deliberately omitted information vital to legislators' understanding of a program.[51]

As usual, the executive branch exploited the statute's ambiguity to the hilt. The White House provided "more than a dozen" congressional briefings, but only to a select group of legislators known as the "gang of eight." This includes the chairs and ranking minority members of both House and Senate intelligence committees, and also the House and Senate majority and minority leaders.[52] But a "gang of eight" briefing is far from sufficient to enable members of Congress to conduct real oversight. As a former CIA lawyer explains:

> The eight are prohibited from saying anything about the briefings to anyone, including other intelligence panel members. . . . It is virtually impossible for individual members of Congress, particularly members of the minority party, to take effective action if they have concerns about what they have heard in one of these briefings. It is not realistic to expect them, working alone, to sort through complex legal issues, conduct the kind of factual investigation required for true oversight and develop an appropriate legislative response.[53]

By exploiting the vagueness of intelligence oversight legislation, the Administration opted for a kind of "consultation" that gutted the possibility of effective oversight.

Not all the gang of eight accepted the legality of the NSA's activities. Both Representative Jane Harmon of California and Senator Jay Rockefeller of West Virginia protested the briefings' "lack of specific details," which obstructed the legislators' ability to make a judgment about the process. But to no avail. The Administration declined to proffer new legislation, and ignored protests from the Hill.[54] In any case, informing select members of Congress is not the same as obtaining a law passed by both houses and signed by the president.

Debate on the NSA domestic surveillance also polarized along partisan lines, further hindering oversight. Republicans, with a handful of beleaguered exceptions, reflexively supported the President. President Bush accused the press and his Democratic critics of "helping the enemy" by even discussing the NSA program. CIA chief Porter Goss claimed his agency suffered "severe damage" from the *New York Times* revelation, insinuating that anything other than passive acceptance of the executive branch's position equaled dangerous dissent. Summarizing the Administration's attitude toward democratic debate, presidential advisor Dan Bartlett insisted, "It would be our choice to not have to talk about this at all."[55]

White House strategists pushed the Oliver North "best defense is a vigorous offense" strategy one step further. Shortly after President Bush admitted to ignoring FISA, his chief political advisor Karl Rove gave a rare public speech to the Republican National Committee: "President Bush believes if al Qaeda is calling somebody in America, it is in our national interest to know who they're calling and why." Rove thundered, "Some important Democrats disagree." Rove was lying. No Democrat said that wiretaps ought not to be used against terrorist suspects. Rather, some Democrats, with a handful of Republicans, insisted that the President needed to remain within the rule of law. Nevertheless, Vice President Cheney also charged the Administration's critics with "yielding to the temptation to downplay the threat and to back away from the business at hand." The President and his political allies invoked variations on Rove's argument some forty-eight times in the subsequent week. Doing so, they sought to transform a question of checks and balances and the separation of powers into a fight about who was "weaker" on national security.[56]

In this heated context, effective congressional hearings became a distant prospect. The Senate Judiciary Committee held public hearings that skirted key questions of fact about what the NSA was doing. The Senate Intelligence Committee, headed by Kansas Republican Pat Roberts, failed to hold any proper oversight hearing. Even confirmation hearings for Michael Hayden's nomination as CIA chief failed to yield a meaningful debate. Echoing the Iran-Contra minority report, Senator Roberts leapt to neuter Congress even before the executive branch had a chance to do so. Roberts wrote to Judiciary Committee leaders Arlen Specter and Patrick Leahy warning them that the president had "constitutional authority to collect intelligence information incident to actual or potential attack," and that Congress should steer clear of oversight because it "cannot assert complete dominion" over these issues. Roberts was not alone. Shamelessly, Senate Majority Leader Bill Frist threatened advocates of oversight with a restructuring of the Senate's intelligence committee to make it *even more* partisan if they persisted in calling for an inquiry into whether innocent Americans had been spied on.[57]

Nor is the claimed legal basis of NSA spying efforts clear. At the time of this writing, Congress has not secured copies of the original OLC memos justifying NSA spying. Nor has it investigated CIFA's activities. Moreover, a Justice Department ethics investigation into the authorization of NSA's spying foundered when the ethics investigators were denied security clearances to review material concerning the NSA. Ironically, conservative thinkers who first advocated for a strong executive also argued that the president "must address allegations of malfeasance." The notion that the president can break the law and then stymie all investigation into why laws were broken is a hazardous combination indeed.[58]

And yet, after failing to act in the face of widespread spying on Americans, Congress had a veritable temper tantrum when the FBI searched the office of a congressman accused of fraud. Despite the fact the search was conducted pursuant to a valid warrant and in pursuit of evidence that a criminal law had been violated (and was sanctioned subsequently by Chief Judge Thomas Hogan of the District of Columbia federal district court), House majority and minority leaders Dennis Hastert and Nancy Pelosi assailed the FBI's actions.[59] Their protests, which reflect legislators' narrow concerns about their own or colleagues' (possibly criminal) dealings, are in stark contrast to their failure to protect the rest of the nation's rights. Congress, without doubt, is capable of confronting executive overreaching. The Congress of 2006 has an electoral mandate for aggressive oversight. The question is whether it will step up to the plate.

The President's Lock-Up Power

Beyond surveillance, the executive branch brought other wartime tools to bear against people in the United States. The Administration also invoked the September 2001 AUMF and its claimed constitutional powers to hold citizens and noncitizens indefinitely without access to an independent tribunal to assess the evidence alleged to justify holding them.

Freedom from bodily restraint lies at the root of all other liberties. It is "the essence of a free society," as Supreme Court Justice John Paul Stevens eloquently wrote in a stirring dissent; it is also a freedom that receives vigorous protection in the U.S. Constitution. American law inherited the English law's procedural device of habeas corpus—known grandly as the Great Writ of *"habeas corpus ad subjiciendum."* By seeking the habeas remedy, a detainee could ask a court to inquire into the legality and the factual basis for his detention. This judicial remedy against arbitrary executive branch imprisonment was as old as Magna Carta. The English parliament enshrined it in the 1679 Habeas Corpus Act, which was hailed by the jurist William Blackstone as "a second Magna Carta and stable bulwark of our liberties." The American Founders embedded the habeas remedy in the Constitution, guaranteeing a means to test executive detention in all but the most exceptional circumstances.[60]

But the Bush Administration contended that the president could designate anyone, U.S. citizen or foreigner, anywhere in the world as an "enemy combatant," and detain that person indefinitely without any independent review of the president's determination. The term "enemy combatant," however, lacks any clear historical precedent. Certainly, it is no license for a virtually unlimited and unreviewable presidential detention power.

How wide the President's purported detention power reached became clear during legal proceedings concerning the Guantánamo detentions held in a Washington, D.C., federal court. Guantánamo detainees were picked up all over the world, shipped to Guantánamo, and summarily labeled "enemy combatants." Under questioning from federal District Court Judge Joyce Hens Green, government lawyers revealed that the executive branch believed it had power to detain indefinitely "enemy combatants," including:

> a little old lady in Switzerland who writes checks to what she thinks is a charity in Afghanistan but [what] is really a front to finance al Qaeda activities, . . . a person who teaches English to the son of an al Qaeda member, . . . and a journalist who knows the location of Osama bin Laden but refuses to disclose it to protect her source.[61]

The idea of executive detention without authorization from Congress is foreign to the American legal tradition. During the Republic's early years, Congress enacted statutes empowering the executive to hold aliens. The Alien Enemy Act of 1798, and the Safe Keeping and Accommodation of Prisoners of War Act of 1812, are early examples. But even during these early conflicts, federal courts still exercised supervisory jurisdiction, even over the detention of "enemy aliens." In 1813, for example, Chief Justice John Marshall issued a habeas writ to a British citizen named Thomas Williams, who had been confined as an enemy alien. Finding that the government's own regulations did not authorize the detention, Marshall and his fellow Justice St. George Tucker discharged Williams from his imprisonment. In short, even in wartime both Congress and the courts still had authorizing and supervising roles in detention decisions.[62]

In the early days of the Civil War, with supply lines to the north threatened, President Abraham Lincoln broke with historic precedent and declared the habeas remedy unavailable. He confined many Confederate enemies without any process and initially without an authorizing statute. But Lincoln's actions, as we shall see in a later chapter, taken as the country stood on the precipice of collapse, were extraordinary and almost unique in American history. The terrorist threat creates the risk of heavy casualties, but it does not threaten to displace our whole system of constitutional governance as the Confederacy's secession did.[63]

During the Cold War, in a deviation from historical patterns, Congress enacted the Emergency Detention Act of 1950 over President Harry S. Truman's veto, to allow mass detentions during "emergencies." And as late as 1970, government still had fiscal and administrative provision for camps like the ones used to detain Japanese Americans during World War II. This shameful law remained on the books until Congressman Abner Mikva warned of these arrangements and forced through the Non-Detention Act of 1971, which barred *any* detention without clear statutory authorization.[64]

To overcome this long tradition, the Bush Administration created a category it called "enemy combatants," who could be detained indefinitely at the President's discretion via exercise of his war powers. The term "enemy combatant" might sound as if it comes from the laws of war, but the term has no historical grounding or fixed meaning. Hence the government can invoke it to justify a sweeping power to detain civilians indefinitely without any possible test of whether their claimed connections to terrorism are real. Once more, creative legal maneuvering yielded new, effectively unchecked, powers to the executive.

No law or treaty initially defined the term "enemy combatant." A 1942 Supreme Court opinion used the term in passing to define a different category of "unlawful combatants." *Quirin*, as this Supreme Court case is called, ratified after-the-fact trials and executions of Nazi saboteurs who were captured after entering the United States. Supreme Court Justice Antonin Scalia described the *Quirin* decision as "not th[e] Court's finest hour." But in *Quirin*, the Court at least correctly applied international law, and distinguished between "lawful combatants," who had to be treated as POWs, and "unlawful combatants," who could be tried "for acts which render their belligerency unlawful." In describing "unlawful combatants," the Court spoke of the spy and the "enemy combatant who without uniform comes secretly through the lines for the purpose of waging war by destruction of life or property." *Quirin* used the term "enemy combatant" solely to refer to a person who could be tried for violations of the law of war, unlike a POW. It said nothing about indefinite presidential detention.[65]

As the Supreme Court expressly confirmed in June 2006, the Geneva Conventions, especially Common Article 3, today protect even alleged spies and saboteurs who cross enemy lines in civilian dress from unfair trials and mistreatment. The idea of an "enemy combatant" without rights or access to judicial review is alien to the laws of war.[66]

Thus the category of "enemy combatants" emerged piecemeal. The executive first applied it to noncitizen detainees captured in combat operations in Afghanistan.[67] The President's November 13, 2001, "military order" creating military tribunals for war crimes applied to any noncitizen who had "as their aim to cause injury to or adverse effects on the United States, its citizens, national security, foreign policy, or economy." The President, moreover, claimed power to detain anyone who "aided or abetted" such conduct. These categories later took on formal shape as the "enemy combatant" classification. This military order suffered from circular logic. To be eligible for trial by military commission, a person must already be designated as, in effect, an enemy of the United States. Only the guilty, in other words, would come before military commissions. But the order provided no way for a person to challenge this threshold executive determination of culpability. It simply presumed the fact of guilt. And this presumption purported to justify indefinite detention.[68]

Further, the order exercised a free-floating war power untethered from the terrorism threat. Law professors Neal Katyal and Laurence Tribe warned that "a future president might unilaterally declare that America is engaged in a 'War on Drugs,'" and designate alleged crack dealers as "enemy combatants" subject to indefinite detention without trial. The White House Counsel at the time, Alberto Gonzales, however, promised the order would "cove[r] only foreign war criminals," and not "United States citizens."[69]

This promise first came undone when two American citizens, Yaser Hamdi and John Walker Lindh, were found among those captured on the Afghan battlefield. Lindh was threatened with "enemy combatant" designation but then was transferred to the criminal justice system. Hamdi was designated an enemy combatant and, after a brief confinement in Guantánamo, was transferred to a military brig in South Carolina. The threat made against Lindh and Hamdi's designation made it clear that American citizens too could be designated as "enemy combatants," in addition to the noncitizens to whom the November 2001 military order applied.[70]

Until mid-2002, the "enemy combatant" designation was at least confined to situations of actual conflict. Lindh and Hamdi, for example, were picked up in Afghanistan. The Administration's claim that it was exercising the traditional prerogatives of war make some sense, even if its interpretation of the law of war was deeply flawed. But the Administration's initial limitation of the term "enemy combatant" to the battlefield also proved hollow.

Eight months after the military order, American citizen Jose Padilla was yanked from the criminal justice system (where he was in the process of being indicted) and thrust into military detention on the basis of President Bush's decision that he was an "enemy combatant." Padilla was first detained as a "material witness" to a criminal investigation on his arrival at Chicago's O'Hare International Airport on May 8, 2002. More than a month later—after Padilla had been moved to New York to appear before a grand jury and after he had been provided with appointed counsel in the criminal justice system—he was flipped into military custody. The President's order declared Padilla "a continuing, present and grave danger to the national security of the United States," without explaining how a person in ongoing criminal detention could pose such a threat. Then–Attorney General John Ashcroft interrupted a trip to Moscow to announce breathlessly that Padilla had been about to explode a "radiological dirty bomb"—again without explaining how Padilla could have managed this while manacled inside a federal jail. Later, the government conceded that its own proof suggested Padilla had only suggested the idea of a dirty bomb to a collaborator. Nevertheless, Padilla spent forty-two months in detention as an "enemy combatant" without receiving an opportunity to challenge the factual bases of this designation before an independent magistrate.[71]

A year later, in June 2003, the executive branch picked up a second person in the United States and designated him an "enemy combatant." Ali Saleh al-Marri was a Qatari national who arrived in the United States with his wife and five children on a student visa to study at Bradley University in Peoria, Illinois. He was first arrested on fraud-related charges. Like Padilla, al-Marri was in the custody of the criminal justice system when he was designated an "enemy combatant."[72]

The Padilla and al-Marri detentions suggested that the term "enemy combatant" has sweeping, perhaps unlimited, scope. And it was not until two years after Padilla's detention that the Administration even got around to defining the term for Congress and the public. In 2004, Deputy Defense Secretary Paul Wolfowitz issued an order defining "enemy combatant" for the purpose of the Guantánamo detentions as "an individual who was part of or supporting Taliban or al Qaeda forces, or associated forces" or "who has committed a belligerent act or has directly supported hostilities in aid of enemy combatants." Under this definition, the Administration claimed power to detain even the little old lady in Switzerland who gave money to the wrong charity—a detention power unchecked by any substantive limits.[73]

In September 2006, Congress enacted a definition of "unlawful enemy combatant" as part of the Military Commissions Act of 2006, although it did not explicitly tether a detention power to that provision. It is unclear at the time of this writing whether the Administration will invoke that provision as a basis for detention. Drafted by Administration lawyers, and inserted into the legislation two days before the House voted on the bill, the definition is staggeringly broad. Congress never adequately or meaningfully discussed the definition. No legislator can credibly say he or she understands its full consequences. For the definition does not distinguish between citizens and noncitizens. It applies in Boise and in Basra. It applies not only to those who "engage in hostilities" but also to those who "purposefully and materially supported hostilities"—a phrase that admits no clear or predictable meaning. And, even worse, it allows the President or Secretary of Defense to establish a "competent tribunal" to designate enemy combatants—without providing any limits on the composition or conduct of that body or the standards it would apply. Applied with maximum vigor, this provision could contain a literally unchecked detention power that could apply to anyone, anywhere, anytime. At the time of this writing, it remains to be seen how this "loaded gun," inserted into American law in a fit of reckless partisan fever, will be in fact used.

Even before this legislation, though, the term "enemy combatant" had seeped into the legal system by virtue of the government's use of the "enemy combatant" designation as a threat in criminal plea bargaining to force individuals to agree to lengthy sentences without the benefit of a criminal trial.[74] The designation hence spread from individuals who were carrying a gun and engaged in armed hostilities against U.S. forces, to individuals already in federal lockup. And whereas detentions on a battlefield may carry a relatively small risk of error (although the use of bounties to round up "Taliban members" in Afghanistan renders even this assumption debatable), the same cannot be said for people picked up off the streets of Peoria or Baltimore, who do not come labeled "innocent," "guilty," or "enemy combatant."

The Justice Department again justified the President's sweeping detention power as part of his constitutional authority as head of the armed forces and in terms of the powers Congress granted when it passed the AUMF: "The President has authority as commander in chief and pursuant to Congress' authorization for use of military force to order [a U.S. citizen's] detention as an enemy combatant." The Justice Department described the detention power as "an essential aspect of warfare" and a "core aspect of the President's constitutional powers as Commander in Chief" in gathering intelligence and preventing new attacks.[75]

Like the executive's claims of surveillance power, the use of this power depended on the characterization of the entire United States as a battlefield. In one of the judicial proceedings in the Padilla case, Paul Clement, the Solicitor General of the United States, indeed argued that "the United States unfortunately was made a battlefield on September 11," and that those suspected of being enemies even within the United States ought to be treated no differently from those swept up off an Afghan or Iraqi battlefield.[76]

Even as the executive branch sought to extend the geographic scope of the "war" in a way that augmented its own power, it also was systematically paring away, through secret legal opinions, the legal protections that applied specifically in wartime. Rather than follow the Geneva rules, which would have required a hearing to determine any captive's status even in wartime, the Justice Department argued than an "enemy combatant" deserved *no* independent judicial review of the basis of their detention. Of course, according to Administration briefs filed to the Supreme Court, the Office of Legal Counsel, the CIA, the Defense Department, and the Attorney General all would work strenuously and carefully to ensure that only the correct citizens would be labeled "enemy combatants." When it lost on this extreme position in the courts, the Administration tried to minimize the scope of review that a court would exercise.[77]

When pressed, the Administration has proved reluctant to allow its factual claims that a person is an "enemy combatant" to be tested in a court of law. For more than two years, the Administration insisted that Hamdi was so dangerous he had to be held incommunicado, denied even access to counsel. When the Supreme Court finally heard Hamdi's case, and declared he was entitled to a hearing in court, the Administration decided to release Hamdi to Saudi Arabia without giving him a hearing and without charging him with any offense, terrorism-related or otherwise, but stripping him of U.S. citizenship and making him promise he would not leave Saudi Arabia for five years.[78]

The government also evaded judicial review in the case of Jose Padilla. In November 2005, two business days before filing a brief in the Supreme Court, and with a real prospect of a ruling on presidential detention power at home, the government abruptly ended Padilla's three-and-a-half years' military detention. Padilla was charged in a criminal proceeding in Miami with offenses entirely unrelated to Ashcroft's "dirty bomb" allegation, and transferred out of military custody. (As explained earlier, the evidence against Padilla derived from prisoners in "black sites," and thus could not be used without triggering questions about the way in which those prisoners had been treated.) The government then asked the federal Fourth Circuit Court of Appeals that had last heard Padilla's case to dismiss the matter as moot before the Supreme Court could exercise review. The Fourth Circuit refused. As well-known conservative Judge J. Michael Luttig wrote, reviewing the government's sudden maneuver:

> [The government's] actions have left not only the impression that Padilla may have been held for these years, even if justifiably, by mistake—an impression we would have thought the government could ill afford to leave extant. They have left the impression that the government may even have come to the belief that the principle in reliance upon which it has detained Padilla for this time, that the President possesses the authority to detain enemy combatants who enter into this country for the purpose of attacking America and its citizens from within, can, in the end, yield to expediency with little or no cost to its conduct of the war against terror—an impression we would have thought the government likewise could ill afford to leave extant.[79]

On April 3, 2006, the Supreme Court declined to hear Padilla's challenge to his indefinite detention. Dissenting from that decision, Justice Ruth Bader

Ginsburg cogently argued, "Although the Government has recently lodged charges against Padilla in a civilian court, nothing prevents the Executive from returning to the road it earlier constructed and defended." With the threat of enemy combatant redesignation hanging over Padilla, in other words, the case was hardly moot or undeserving of review.[80]

As Judge Luttig explained, the government's decision to evade judicial review in the Hamdi and Padilla cases casts serious doubt on the claims made against both men. It raises the substantial possibility of the government's using war powers when it lacks the evidence to indict a person through the normal criminal justice system. With Padilla's discharge into civilian custody, al-Marri is at the time of this writing the only (known) person in the United States detained as an enemy combatant. Perhaps because he is not a citizen, his case has received less attention. This is a mistake. As Georgetown law professor David Cole incisively argues, "What we do to foreign nationals today often paves the way for what will be done to American citizens tomorrow."[81] And Padilla's case shows that this is no hypothetical concern.

"Enemy combatant" detention is another example of vaguely defined powers, fashioned by the executive branch for its own use, metastasizing beyond any legitimate initial use to encompass a broad range of unreasonable and dangerous ends. Like domestic surveillance, presidential lockup has elicited scant reaction from Congress. With only a handful of individuals behind bars, legislators are hard-pressed to see the dangerous logic deployed by the President as a real risk to American freedoms. The Administration's decision to circumvent the criminal justice system—for both surveillance and detention and to exercise unchecked war powers, however, challenges the fundamental premises of the constitutional order. If the President's claims to war powers at home are accepted, Congress and the courts are left on the margins. Checks and balances no longer operate.

Time and again, however, America has learned that an executive branch left to its own devices makes poor choices, a wisdom that President Bush's new homeland surveillance and detention powers do not dispel. As Supreme Court Justice David Souter perceptively observed, the executive will always err in this way:

> For reasons of inescapable human nature, the branch of government asked to counter a serious threat is not the branch on which to rest the Nation's entire reliance in striking the balance between the will to win and the cost in liberty on the way to victory; the responsibility for security will naturally amplify the claim that security legitimately raises. A reasonable balance is more likely to be reached by a different branch. . . .[82]

Legal theories that justify unchecked presidential powers thus pose serious threats to the constitutional order. One such argument rests on misreading laws, such as the AUMF, to grant "monarchical" powers to the President.[83] The other is the constitutional claim to unlimited presidential authority in matters of national security

And it is that dangerous legal theory to which we now turn.

Part III

The Constitution Turned Upside Down

7

Kings and Presidents

Familiar failings from the Cold War era and earlier history returned to haunt the nation in the wake of 9/11. But this time abuses were compounded by a new and dangerous idea. To justify illicit invasions of liberty and privacy, the executive branch's lawyers argued that the president has unlimited power to violate federal statutes. President Bush agreed. Specifically, he asserted under the Constitution a novel authority in the name of "national security" or "military necessity" to disregard *permanently* any law enacted by Congress. The Administration used this power to justify set-asides of long-standing federal statutes barring torture, indefinite detention, and warrantless spying. In the Cold War, the FBI and the CIA violated the law but hid or denied their actions. After 9/11, government overreaching claimed a *legal* basis through theories about "executive power." Abuse became official policy and practice of the United States.

No sitting president before President Bush asserted or used power under the Constitution to set aside laws wholesale. Such power means a president can ignore statutes passed by Congress whenever he claims that "national security" or "military necessity" is at issue. This claim finds precedent in the seventeenth-century British kings' royal "prerogative" power to "suspend" or "dispense" with laws enacted by Parliament.[1] But that power, grounded in ideas about the "divine" right of kings, did not survive the English Civil War and the Glorious Revolution of 1688, which ended the Stuart dynasty. Certainly, it did not find its way into our founding documents, the 1776 Declaration of Independence and the Constitution of 1787.

To the contrary, the Founders had a healthy skepticism of power, and designed the Constitution to check its concentration in any one branch of government. This is evident not only from the text of the Constitution but also from the eloquently expressed sentiments in the 1787 Philadelphia Convention and in the subsequent debates in the states about the Constitution's ratification. History decisively repudiates the power President Bush asserts to suspend the laws. Whatever residual unilateral power the executive branch has simply does not stretch as far as the Bush Administration claims.[2]

The scope of "executive power" under the Constitution is a complex and much argued one. There is ongoing debate in the academic literature, for example, on the exact scope of executive power in the foreign affairs field and the question whether Congress can limit the president's power to remove subordinate executive officials.[3] We are not here concerned with those fine-grained debates. Rather, we focus on the Bush Administration's purported "suspension power" in the name of national security.

Contemporary ideas of unchecked presidential power arose in reaction to reforms that followed from the Church Committee's revelations, as well as other limits on executive power crafted in the 1970s.[4] Former President Richard Nixon first advanced a claim to unchecked executive authority over national security matters, claiming imperiously that "when the President does it, that means it's not illegal."[5] Nixon's view of presidential powers unchecked by law was taken up and advanced in the decades after Watergate by opponents of the reforms of the 1970s. These reforms met stiff resistance from the executive branch and seeded an intellectual backlash against checks and balances in favor of presidential power. While the backlash gained ground in the 1980s, it was the national crisis of 9/11 that created room for aggressive claims of presidential authority.

Seeds of Counter-Revolution

In the days after the nation learned about the NSA's domestic spying program in violation of the federal law banning warrantless surveillance enacted in 1978, the White House was unrepentant and unapologetic. Traveling to Muscat, Oman, in December 2005, Vice President Dick Cheney gave reporters his historical perspective on President Bush's decision to bypass FISA without informing Congress fully or the public at all. His explanation reached back to the reaction during the 1970s to executive overreaching:

> [O]ver the years there had been an erosion of presidential power and authority. . . . [A] lot of the things around Watergate and Vietnam, both, in the '70s served to erode the authority, I think, the President needs to be effective especially in a national security area. If you want reference to an obscure text, go look at the minority views that were filed with the Iran-Contra Committee; the Iran Contra Report in about 1987. . . . [T]hey were actually authored by a guy working for me, for my staff, that I think are very good in laying out a robust view of the President's prerogatives with respect to the conduct of especially foreign policy and national security matters. . . . I do believe that, especially in the day and age we live in, the nature of the threats we face—it was true during the Cold War,

as well as I think what is true now—the President of the United States needs to have his constitutional powers unimpaired, if you will, in terms of the conduct of national security policy. That's my personal view.[6]

Some years earlier, in January 2002, Cheney cited the "erosion of the powers and the ability of the president of the United States to do his job" as the source of his felt "obligation" to "pass on [the] offices in better shape than we found them."[7] As Cheney's comments make clear, the Administration's vision of unchecked presidential power over "national security" matters preceded 9/11. It was rooted instead in a visceral counterrevolution against post-Watergate and post–Church Committee reforms designed to give Congress a meaningful checking function in national security policy making.

During the Cold War, the FBI and CIA frequently violated the law but never claimed the law did not apply to them. Only one person believed that a president indeed stood above the law: former President Richard Nixon. In written answers to questions from the Church Committee delivered in March 1976, Nixon asserted an unlimited constitutional power to set aside statutes in the name of "national security." Nixon argued that "any action a president might authorize in the interest of national security would be lawful." By way of example, Nixon cited President Franklin Delano Roosevelt's internment of Japanese Americans during World War II. (Less than a month before Nixon developed this response, however, then–President Gerald Ford issued a proclamation denouncing the injustice of those wartime internments.) Nixon also justified warrantless mail openings, arguing that it "results in preventing the disclosure of sensitive military and state secrets to the enemies of this country."[8] The warrantless surveillance of the Cold War, the disruption of the civil rights movement, the testing of narcotics on "unwitting" Americans all could be justified under this power. In his cynical conversation with White House Counsel John Dean that was caught on tape, Nixon envisaged the open-ended use of intelligence powers against political enemies—in that instance the burglary of the office of Daniel Ellsberg's psychiatrist—hidden under the rubric of "national security." It is imprecise labels of this ilk, the Church Committee concluded on a review of thirty years' conduct, that the executive branch too often manipulated to authorize intrusive techniques against Americans.[9]

Nixon proclaimed this belief after his resignation from office. In an interview with talk-show host David Frost, Nixon reiterated his position on unchecked executive power:

FROST: So what, in a sense, you're saying is that there are certain situations . . . where the president can decide that it's in the best interests of the nation or something, and do something illegal.

NIXON: Well, when the president does it, that means that it is not illegal.

FROST: By definition.

NIXON: Exactly. Exactly. If the president determines that a specified action is necessary to protect national security, then the action is lawful,
even if it is prohibited by a federal statute.[10]

Few, if any, of even Nixon's most ardent supporters echoed the former president's claim. But a seed was planted.

How did this monarchical view of the executive branch reemerge after being so soundly discredited by Nixon's misconduct? The Church Committee's
findings led to FISA, and in both the Senate and the House, to new permanent intelligence committees. In the same era, Congress also enacted legislation
to promote government openness, to limit the use of military force overseas,
and to check the president's foreign affairs powers. Predictably, new checks and
balances provoked resentment in the executive branch. Dick Cheney was, at
the time of the Church Committee, President Gerald Ford's staff coordinator
(working for, and then taking over from, Donald Rumsfeld), at the front line
of battles over executive power. Cheney emerged from his Ford White House
experience a committed foe of oversight of or limits on the executive branch.[11]

The counterrevolution against checks and balances took off in the 1980s.
After President Reagan's victory in the 1980 presidential election, voices inside and outside the Administration began pressing for expanded presidential
power. Edwin Meese III, one of Reagan's attorneys general, saw increased
presidential power across the board as one of the core missions of the Department of Justice. To that end, the Meese Justice Department offered a defense of
what they called a "unitary executive"—a reading of the Constitution that supported expansive and exclusive executive authority. Indeed, it was first under
Meese, two hundred years after the Constitution's drafting, that the phrase "unitary executive" became "a commonplace around the Justice Department."[12]

Unitary executive advocates in the 1980s made a simple claim with complex, far-reaching consequences. Their central argument was that the Constitution created a government of three wholly separate powers: the lawmaking
power, a judicial power, and an executive power. Each of these three powers
was "distributed to identified organs of government." Unitary executive advocates found in the Constitution an *absolute* separation of powers between
the three branches of government. Thus, any attempt by one branch to impinge on the powers of another was per se unconstitutional.[13]

With this stark view of separation between branches, unitary executive
advocates claimed that any law infringing on an "executive" power was unconstitutional. They emphasized the "degree of seriousness" with which the
Constitution's "trifurcation of power" must be taken. According to unitary

executive advocates, if a government power could be characterized as "executive," Congress could not exercise *any* control, direct or indirect, over the use of that power by the executive branch.[14]

To explain this rigid view of the Constitution's division of power, unitary executive advocates pointed to the "impetuous vortex" of congressional power "which tended to strangle government through preoccupation with trivia." The executive branch, they explained, had to have powerful defenses because of Congress's inevitable tendency to overwhelm it.[15] (To make this argument, unitary executive advocates had to ignore recent history, particularly in the national security field. Through the Cold War, Congress in fact *failed* to provide meaningful oversight of intelligence activities, contributing to the litany of abuse exposed by the Church Committee. And in response to Iran-Contra, Congress was hamstrung by partisan division and mustered only lukewarm responses.) The advocates of the unitary executive highlighted historical arguments for "energy" in the executive branch, plucking language out of its historical context to license what in practical consequence amounted to executive branch hegemony.[16]

This Reagan-era vision of a unitary executive is distinct and different from the much more sweeping claims of unchecked presidential power after 9/11. Unlike the monarchical vision put forward after September 2001, the "unitary executive" thesis rested on at least defensible readings of the Constitution. Nevertheless, the history of ideas is replete with notions that migrate from their original home, detach from their original historical moorings, and have unexpected, untoward consequences. And indeed the "unitary executive" and the "monarchical executive" are linked in three ways—by common history, shared methodology, and common intellectual commitment.

First, both find shared roots in the conscious reaction to the constraints placed on executive power in the 1970s. According to Charles Fried, solicitor general of the United States under President Reagan, unitary executive theory was a response to the "tremendous increase in congressional ascendancy as a response to the Watergate and Vietnam-era troubles." Terry Eastland, a conservative commentator and author of one of the first books about unitary executive theory, agreed, adding that "a great deal of it was a response to the fact that Congress was in Democratic hands."[17]

Second, advocates of augmented executive power in the 1980s and after 2001 both relied and rely almost exclusively on "originalist" claims to establish the pedigree of their Constitution readings. Meese and his colleagues grounded their claims on their view of the "original intent" of the Founding Generation. One advocate of the unitary executive theory, Justice Antonin Scalia of the Supreme Court, thus highlighted the first Massachusetts constitution's rigid specification of different branches of powers. Solicitor General

Fried pointed to a theory described by the late seventeenth-century English philosopher John Locke of "prerogative powers." But, tellingly, Fried himself never developed this point while he was solicitor general. And in fact, the Founding Generation never took up Locke's theory.[18]

Finally, both the "unitary executive" theory of the 1980s and the "monarchist executive" theory of the post-9/11 era stressed the idea of exclusive control by the executive branch over certain areas of law. The critical difference between them is the scope of powers viewed as "executive," and therefore outside legislative or judicial control. In the 1980s, the OLC's arguments focused on the question of whether the president controlled administrative agencies through firing and discipline procedures. It is at least arguable that those who framed and ratified the Constitution intended the chief executive to have such control. In the post-9/11 era, however, the Administration's lawyers argued that the president could exercise plenary power over all matters touching on national security—a much broader and far less plausible claim.

During the 1980s, the Justice Department opposed limits to the removal of executive officers and to disclosure rules covering advice given to the president. With the exception of Justice Scalia, the Supreme Court never wholeheartedly endorsed even these more limited claims. Unitary executive theorists won an important victory when the Court invalidated the "legislative veto," which allowed Congress to oversee federal administrative agencies through "vetoes" of agency decisions by congressional resolution. But the Justice Department lost a challenge to the office of "independent counsel." This position was created to conduct criminal investigations inside the executive branch. It was a thorn in the flank of unitary executive advocates, who believed presidents must have unfettered control of all federal prosecutions. Further, the Court declined to endorse cleanly the Justice Department's suggestion that the president had broad constitutional authority to refuse to disclose information to Congress about judicial nominees. The Court thus steered a pragmatic course, generally taking realistic stock of the multiple values at stake when two branches of government clash.[19]

As far as we can tell, no unitary executive advocate of the 1980s argued that the president had power to set aside laws of the kind that barred torture or warrantless wiretapping—or indeed any laws except some concerning internal workings of the executive branch. Nevertheless, the defensible, if debatable, claims of unitary executive advocates of the 1980s set the stage, in theoretical and political terms, for a return to expansive presidential powers, including today's indefensible claims of unchecked presidential power.[20]

Unitary executive advocates also took their arguments directly to the public. Attorney General Meese argued in public speeches that the president had a power of "nonacquiescence" in Supreme Court decisions. Even if the Supreme Court announced a general constitutional principle in one case, Meese argued, the president had no obligation to follow that rule except in the case at hand. Under Meese's nonacquiescence theory, for example, a women's rights group could have won a ruling that gender discrimination in social security benefits was unconstitutional, but if the same discriminatory framework was used in many other federal statues, the executive branch would have authority under the "nonacquiescence doctrine" to ignore the judicial ruling as it applied to those other statutes. The women's rights group would have to litigate every statute's constitutionality in turn. Not surprisingly, Meese's idea met heavy criticism. He soon backed off.[21]

It was the Iran–Contra scandal that crystallized the most aggressive version of unitary executive theory in national security and foreign affairs. Ironically, the most vigorous arguments on behalf of broad executive power came from Capitol Hill, not the White House.

Iran–Contra led to a congressional investigation and a voluminous committee report about the illegal and deceptive acts of Oliver North and his colleagues. Unlike the Church Committee, however, the Iran–Contra Committee split sharply on partisan grounds, and issued both a majority and a minority report, with the minority report endorsed by all six House Republicans on the Committee. Leading the charge for the minority report was a Wyoming representative by the name of Dick Cheney. In 1978, Cheney had won a seat in the Wyoming delegation to the House of Representatives. His move along Pennsylvania Avenue, however, did not alter the views he had developed in the Ford White House.

The Iran–Contra minority report proved a pivotal point in the development of unchecked executive power. It was both a reaction to the Church Committee and a harbinger of the post-9/11 world. The link to the past is evident from the report's opening pages. It began by conjuring up and condemning an "all but unlimited Congressional power" that "began to take hold in the 1970s in the wake of the Vietnam War." The minority report cited the Church Committee as a prime offender. Elaborating these themes, Cheney in 1989 condemned the "congressional aggrandizement" of the 1970s, and warned that the "legislative branch is ill-equipped to handle the foreign policy tasks it has taken upon itself."[22] When Cheney spoke in December 2005 of "the president's prerogatives with respect to the conduct of especially foreign policy and national security matters," he was indeed reiterating a long-held vision already fully formed and articulated in 1986. In addition to Cheney, the minority committee also had on staff a young lawyer named David Addington who later became legal counsel and chief of staff to Vice President Cheney. A "hard-edged and bureaucratic infighter," Addington, who had worked in the office of the CIA general counsel and the Defense Department, went on to help Vice President Cheney wield influence "throughout the government in his bid to expand executive power."[23] Twenty years later, 1986's minority was in charge.

The minority report's analysis rejected the lessons of the Church Committee and ignored the decades of documented misconduct by intelligence agencies to press an expansive version of unitary executive theory in the national security context. According to the minority report, the White House was victim of an overreaching and power-hungry Congress. Discussing Iran-Contra, the minority report overlooked clear evidence that officials serially violated the law and then lied to Congress. The minority report downplayed these criminal acts as "mistakes" to be overlooked since no one acted "out of corrupt motives."[24] When the executive branch violates the law, it seems, its good faith redeems the act. But when Congress exercises oversight, the White House is victimized. This reversal of reality, building on the rhetoric of victimization in conservative political culture,[25] deflected attention from the harms inflicted by the absence of oversight.

The minority report rejected congressional checks when the executive claims to act in the name of "national security," describing the long-accepted notion that the Constitution's structure was intended to check government power as a "fallacy." Instead, it argued that the "principles underlying separation had to do with increasing the Government's power as much as with checking it." Hence, the minority report reasoned that the Constitution allocated the powers of "deployment and use of force," as well as "negotiations, intelligence gathering, and other diplomatic communications" to the president alone. The report thus reasoned that "the President's inherent powers" historically had allowed the executive to act "when Congress was silent, *and even, in some cases, where Congress had prohibited an action.*" Even the lies of Oliver North and his colleagues were lawful, explained the minority report, thanks to the president's "constitutionally protected power of withholding information from Congress." Rather, the minority report argued, the constitutional problem lay in President Reagan's "less-than-robust defense of his office's constitutional powers."[26]

Cheney persevered in this vision of presidential power after leaving Congress. Back in the White House as President George H.W. Bush's Secretary of Defense, Cheney argued that in light of the president's "inherent power to initiate covert actions," the White House had constitutional authority to refuse to give notice of covert actions to Congress. Cheney hence rejected *any* legislative limits on executive power in national security matters, and could find no "justification for further restrictions on the power and flexibility of future presidents." Another participant in the Iran-Contra minority report, staff member Bruce Fein, echoed Cheney: "Congress cannot interfere with the President's choice of how to use intelligence agencies in furtherance of legitimate constitutional objectives," such as "deterring aggression" by other countries.[27]

President Bill Clinton's stint in the Oval Office proved that executive branch aggrandizement was not a simple partisan issue. Under Clinton, the OLC also issued guidelines for the use of military force in the absence of congressional approval that, in the words of one commentator, "suffered mightily from circularity and from abdication of all power to the president." In his use of war powers, Clinton was as aggressively unilateralist as previous occupants of the White House. In March 1999, Clinton approved the application of aerial military force against the Yugoslav Republic without clear congressional authorization, arguing it was necessary to prevent gross human rights violations in Kosovo. Clinton also applied a gamut of unilateral policy-making tools to circumvent a hostile Congress. While Clinton never took the absolutist position of Cheney and the minority report, his presidency did not step back from executive unilateralism.[28]

On September 10, 2001, leading figures in the executive branch supported an aggressive vision of unchecked executive power. This power, however, remained for the most part untested.

The next day, everything changed.

The Counterrevolution Ascendant

Unitary executive theory returned, reinvigorated and in a new form, after 9/11 to justify the executive branch's use of torture, detention, and spying in violation of federal law. Executive branch lawyers asserted a novel "suspension" theory. The president, they argued, has the same power as the old English kings to "suspend" laws. The lawyers were not describing just an emergency power that could be used only in the interval between a crisis and Congress's subsequent meeting. Rather, executive branch lawyers described an ongoing authority to set aside legal checks imposed by Congress.

Glimpses of the Bush Administration's vision of unchecked executive power are discerned first in opinions on overseas detention operations from late 2001 and early 2002. The Administration's lawyers in the OLC issued opinions on the Geneva Conventions, upholding the Defense Department's blanket treatment of terrorism suspects captured outside the United States as "enemy combatants," and authorizing the use of Guantánamo Bay Naval Base as a long-term detention center beyond the law for detainees. Both opinions focused on the interpretation of statutes or treaty provisions. In both cases, though, the OLC hinted that whatever statutes and treaties might say, the president had power to set them aside. In a third September 2001 legal opinion on the president's war powers, the OLC gave further intimation of its vision of vast presidential powers.

Consider first the OLC's views on detainee treatment. The law, the OLC opined, gave the president broad latitude. But the OLC also contended that even if treaties or laws *did* constrain the president, he nonetheless could override them. One OLC opinion concluded that no federal court had power to hear pleas from detainees in Guantánamo. The OLC argued that courts ought to be "reluctant to . . . interfere with matters solely within the discretion of the political branches of government." The Supreme Court later rejected this assertion in 2004.[29]

Another OLC opinion concluded that the Geneva Conventions could be read to deny detainees hearings to determine whether they were in fact Taliban or al Qaeda. In a coda, the OLC argued that, in any event, the president had authority as "a constitutional matter" to "consider performance of some or all of the obligations of the United States under the [Geneva] Conventions suspended" based on Afghanistan's failure to follow the Conventions. The president needed this power to suspend the Geneva Conventions, the OLC contended, since the United States would otherwise be "effectively remediless" in the face of breaches of the Conventions by an adversary.[30] At first, this sounds plausible. But on closer examination, the logic is strained. Why use remedies against the *citizens* of a country, not the government that commits a breach? International law, in any case, does not allow suspension of treaties "of a humanitarian character" such as the Geneva Conventions, a position the State Department has long shared. At bottom, the OLC simply assumed that it made "little sense" to limit presidential power.[31]

These early memos shed light on the asserted roots of the president's suspension power. Like Meese and Fried, the OLC claimed the views of the Founding Generation were on its side. Dissecting the Geneva Conventions, the OLC invoked the president's "plenary control over the conduct of foreign relations," and pointed to a speech by John Marshall, before he became Chief Justice, calling the president "the sole organ of the nation in its external relations." (Revealingly, the OLC omitted the context of the speech, which made clear that Marshall was talking about the president's power to communicate with other nations, not a general foreign affairs power, much less a power to ignore laws.) More revealingly, the OLC looked behind America's founding to the powers of the English monarchs. Designing the Constitution, the OLC contended, the Framers had "unbundled some plenary powers that had traditionally been regarded as executive," such as "the King's traditional power to declare war," and assigned them to Congress. But the OLC posited that other "plenary powers of the king," were simply "conveyed to the President." The presidency, in short, was meant to be a republican form of monarchy.[32]

The same argument runs through the academic work of John Yoo, before, during, and after his dominant role in the OLC. In 1997, Yoo argued that British political history ought to guide interpretation of the Constitution's war-related powers today. In a 2002 article, written while he was in the OLC, Yoo claimed that the president possessed the "plenary powers of the King" except where *explicitly* abrogated by the Constitution.[33]

Yoo elaborated these positions in later writings. Citing John Locke, he contended that presidents alone respond properly to wartime exigencies, while cumbersome legislatures "should not interfere in the executive branch's war decisions." He argued that "the founders intended that wrongheaded or obsolete legislation and judicial decisions would be checked by presidential action." In Yoo's opinion, that is, presidential disagreement with the substance of a law or Supreme Court opinion is sufficient to permit the President—presumably even in secret—to "sidestep laws that invade his executive authority."[34]

In a 2004 article, Yoo defended the legality of extraordinary renditions. His defense again rested on British practice:

> [U]nderstanding of the Constitution's allocation of powers between Congress and the President is informed by the unwritten British Constitution's allocation of powers between Parliament and Crown. The Framers lived under the British Constitution as colonists, and in drafting their own Constitution they borrowed heavily from the legal and political concepts that formed the foundation principles of British constitutional government. Significant departures from the framework of the British government were explicitly spelled out in the Constitution's text. . . .[35]

Yoo conjured the Crown's "absolute authority to dispose as it saw fit of prisoners of war" to vindicate "the executive's prerogatives regarding the disposition of prisoners of war." Including, that is, sending them to torture. For Yoo, the "original understanding" of the Constitution is not Madison's. It is King James I's. And it was accepted not in 1787 in America, but in Britain, and there only before the Glorious Revolution of 1688.

The August 2002 torture opinion for the CIA provides the clearest perspective on the OLC's understanding of presidential power. (According to Jane Mayer of the *New Yorker*, there is also a still-secret September 25, 2001, OLC opinion that sets forth in detail the monarchical executive theory.) The August 2002 torture opinion argued that the federal statute criminalizing torture covered only a narrow band of conduct. The antitorture law, the OLC also contended, "would be unconstitutional if it impermissibly encroached on the President's constitutional power to conduct a military campaign." From this premise, the memo jumped to the conclusion that prosecutors could not bring criminal charges against official torturers, and that officials had a defense to criminal liability based on "the nation's right to self-defense." The military then incorporated and expanded this position in the Defense Department working group in early 2003 over the objections of senior military lawyers such as Navy General Counsel Alberto J. Mora, who had consistently opposed the adoption of harsh tactics.[36]

The OLC began from the premise that the president must "protect the security of the United States and the lives and safety of its people," and has power "requisite to the complete execution of its trust." Like the earlier opinions on the Geneva Conventions, the August 2002 opinion looked back before the Constitution for support. "The framers," contended authors Yoo and Bybee, understood the Constitution's clause naming the president the "commander in chief," as "investing the President with the fullest range of power understood at the time of the ratification of the Constitution as belonging to the military commander." They referred to a practice "as old as war itself" of capturing, detaining, and interrogating prisoners. Because military commanders through the ages have used torture to extract information from enemy soldiers, the OLC reasoned, the president of the United States has inherent constitutional power to do so too. Again, according to the Administration's lawyers, the Constitutional text is infused with pre-Independence practices—practices, in other words, associated with European monarchies, and with the torturers of pre-Enlightenment time that the Founding Generation had so abhorred.[37]

The Bush Administration has never stepped back from its broadest claims to presidential suspension power. The OLC's December 2004 opinion, which replaced the August 2002 opinion, simply said it was "unnecessary" to describe the outer edges of presidential power in light of what it called "the President's unequivocal directive" to refrain from torture. Therefore, it neither withdrew the August 2002 analysis of presidential power nor finessed it. Moreover, Attorney General Alberto Gonzales in Senate and public appearances artfully avoided any retreat from the aggressive vision of presidential power contained in the August 2002 opinion.[38]

Consistent with the OLC's breathtaking conception of presidential power, the executive branch resisted any congressional and judicial efforts to check President Bush. Justifying the policy of presidential detention, the Justice Department argued that the President's role as commander in chief "traditionally" included power to determine who ought to be detained, or "engage[d] . . .

with deadly force," as a member of the enemy, even in the United States. Justice Department lawyers claimed that "long-standing historical practice and applicable rules of engagements" vindicated the president's power to make these decisions without oversight from either Congress or the courts. In legal briefs to the Supreme Court, the Justice Department argued that Congress had no power to limit the president from detaining citizens and noncitizens alike within the United States. Wielding his "core" presidential authority, executive branch lawyers argued, the president had unfettered power to decide on "military measures." This vision of presidential power leaves Congress as well as the courts on the sidelines once the president claims national security is at issue.[39]

Justifications of presidential spying without warrants were even bolder. Recall that the NSA spying program involved the interception of American citizens' communications, implicating in some instances privacy interests protected by the Fourth Amendment of the Constitution. Faced with a federal statute regulating *all* electronic surveillance of American citizens and residents within the United States, the Justice Department simply asserted "constitutional limits on Congress's ability to interfere with the President's power to conduct foreign intelligence searches." The Justice Department invoked the President's role in foreign affairs and his "authority to direct the Armed Forces in conducting a military campaign." Since the NSA was part of a "military campaign," the Justice Department concluded, any law that curtailed the President's discretion to spy on American citizens or residents in the American homeland was unconstitutional.[40]

The President and Emergencies

Before addressing the Administration's claims, it is worth making one important clarification. Throughout American history, presidents have been understood to have a power of first response to emergencies in the limited period before Congress can meet and decide on further responses. We do not dispute that the executive has this "protective" power. Hence, while the draft Constitution initially vested Congress with power to "make war," the Constitutional Convention altered this to "declare war" in order to make clear that the executive branch retained power, without congressional authorization, "to repel sudden attacks" or to defend federal property or officials against unexpected threats.[41]

There is no question that presidents have power to respond to a sudden crisis before Congress can act. President Abraham Lincoln's response to the start of the Civil War provides the archetypal example. On April 15, 1861, Lincoln responded by calling forth the state militia, and, four days later, proclaiming a blockade of Southern ports. In the ensuing weeks, Lincoln faced an immediate crisis in Maryland, where an angry Baltimore mob attacked Union troops from Massachusetts who were marching south. Sixteen soldiers were killed. Baltimore's mayor ordered the destruction of railroad bridges connecting the city to the north, seeking to prevent the movement of more Union troops heading south to protect Washington from Confederate forces in Virginia. The possibility of the capital's isolation suddenly loomed. Lincoln issued additional executive proclamations enlarging the army and requisitioning funds. On April 27, he even suspended judicial remedies against unilateral executive detention in Maryland. Lincoln then ignored an order issued by the Chief Justice of the United States, Roger Taney, in his capacity as an individual Justice that had declared that only Congress had power to order detention without judicial oversight. When a U.S. marshall arrived at Fort McHenry bearing Taney's order compelling a prisoner's release, the marshall was refused entry.[42]

In the eleven weeks between his first emergency proclamation and the convening of Congress, Lincoln thus violated the Constitution and told a Supreme Court Justice that his order was worthless. Does Lincoln's action license the sweeping abrogation of laws on torture and surveillance that we have seen since 9/11? Isn't the parallel between the threat to the nation on the eve of the Civil War and the external threat from al Qaeda compelling? Indeed, isn't it surely the *obligation* of a president, in Lincoln's stirring words, to refuse to allow "all the laws but one to go unexecuted, and the Government itself go to pieces lest that one be violated"?[43]

The short answer is no, as Lincoln's own subsequent actions demonstrated. Lincoln's conduct is neither precedent nor license for the decisions to set aside the laws against torture and warrantless eavesdropping after 9/11. There are two critical differences between what Lincoln did in 1861 and what the Bush administration has been doing since September 2001. First, Lincoln acted in the immediate interval between a crisis and Congress's first meeting. Lincoln, to be sure, stretched this emergency power by setting Congress's convening for the symbolic date of July 4, allowing him some leeway to set war policies. But there was never a pretense that Congress could be permanently cut out of the picture.[44]

Second, Lincoln did not act in secret, hiding his decisions from Congress and the public. In contrast, Lincoln sought and obtained congressional ratification for his actions. When Congress met, Lincoln presented an elaborate defense of his emergency measures in a special July 4 message. "These measures, whether strictly legal or not," Lincoln contended, "were ventured upon, under what appeared to be a popular demand, and a public necessity; trusting, then as now, that Congress would readily ratify them." After lengthy debate, in which several senators made clear they believed Lincoln's actions unlawful absent congressional approval, Congress enacted on August 6, 1861, a law providing that "all the acts, proclamations, and orders" issued by Lincoln in the emergency were "approved and in all respects legalized and made valid, to the same intent and with the same effect as if they had been issued and done under the previous express authority and direction of the Congress of the United States."[45]

Neither Lincoln nor the Congress of his day believed in open-ended "national security" powers for the president. No one endorsed an executive "national security" power that allowed a president to trump Congress's solemnly formalized choices. Lincoln's emergency measures exemplified a limited "protective" power to respond to immediate crisis before Congress can act. Exercising emergency powers, Lincoln knew he acted at the risk of congressional disapproval, and that only Congress could authorize his illegal deeds. Congress's role in setting forth binding rules, even for emergencies and war, never fell into doubt.[46]

The Revolution Betrayed

The Bush Administration's argument for unlimited presidential power is simple—and also simply wrong. The Constitution's text, the historical context, contemporary comments of the Revolutionary generation, and the background presumptions of American and British law all undermine the case for presidential power unbound by laws.

The Bush Administration points to the president's possession of the "executive power" and his role as "Commander in Chief of the Army and Navy of the United States," in order to argue that Congress lacks *any* power to regulate the president when he acts in defense of the nation's security. The Administration does not refer to this unfettered authority as a "suspension power," the term used by the seventeenth-century English monarchs. Nevertheless, it is quite clear that President Bush has claimed exactly that wide-ranging power to *suspend* application of the law. Recall, for example, the OLC's warning that "Any effort by Congress to regulate the interrogation of battlefield combatants would violate the Constitution's sole vesting of the Commander-in-Chief authority in the President." This is a claim that the president has exclusive power over martial and national security matters, and need not follow statutory checks in those areas. This echoes the Iran-Contra minority report's view of separation of powers as a device to *increase* executive power. But that should be no cause for concern, the Bush administration's lawyers claimed, since the executive is always "deliberate, conscientious, and humane."[47] The Founding Generation, rather more credibly, assumed that men and women who took government office would be just as susceptible to error and hubris as the rest of humanity. The Administration's conduct since 2001 has hardly disproved this enduring wisdom.

The notion that there are *some* authorities assigned exclusively to one branch of government is not entirely without foundation. Thus, the Supreme Court in past cases warned that no one branch of government can impinge on the "central prerogatives" of another consistent with the Constitution, albeit without adequately explaining how we know what a "central prerogative" is. The Court has applied this reasoning only infrequently, however, to executive branch powers. More important, it never said that "national security" is a "central prerogative" of the executive where neither the Congress nor the courts may tread.[48]

The Administration's claims rest on an interpretation of the Constitution's grant of power to the executive branch. Scholars and judges contest the "proper" method of interpreting the Constitution. Administration lawyers often purport to be "originalists," though their actual claims are anything but faithful to the original text or meaning. They argue that the Constitutional text and the understanding of the Founding Generation alone determine the Constitution's meaning. This "original" historical meaning is putatively located by looking at the text of the Constitution, and the meaning attributed to that text in the 1780s and 1790s in contemporary writing and political debates. Originalists use the historical and theoretical backdrop to the Constitution's adoption, in addition to the debates surrounding ratification, to fill in constitutional meaning.[49] We are skeptical of relying on "original meaning" in practice and in theory. Nonetheless, we focus here on the Administration's flawed originalist claims for the presidential suspension power. This means turning first to the Constitution's text, and then examining the ideas on which the Founding Generation drew and the debates over ratification.[50]

The Constitution is a brief text of seven articles drafted in 1787 at the Philadelphia Constitutional Convention, and twenty-seven later-enacted amendments. In the document's first three articles, the Framers crafted a government of legislative, executive, and judicial powers. But a review of the document's text unambiguously reveals that the Framers did not design a government of three entirely separate powers but one of "separated institutions sharing powers" (to use political scientist Richard Neustadt's celebrated maxim). As James Madison approvingly said of early state constitutions in the *Federalist Papers* in 1788, "There is not a single instance in which the several departments of power have been kept absolutely separate and distinct." The Administration's present claim to unchecked power is fundamentally inconsistent with this vision of shared and overlapping powers, or checks and balances.[51]

Not only is the Administration's claim in tension with the Constitution's infrastructure, it also runs into further difficulties when one examines the textual allocation of powers between Congress and the executive branch. For it is Congress that comes first in the Constitution's ordering of branches, in Article I of the document. It is Congress that receives the lion's share of detailed, textually specified powers in the Constitution's opening movement. And it is "the legislative authority," according to James Madison, that "necessarily predominates" in a republican government. The Administration's assertion of exclusive authority over "national security" or "foreign affairs" does not survive exposure to the Constitution's text.[52]

Yale scholar Charles Black succinctly expressed this point in 1975:

> With some changes in detail—changes mainly or entirely made necessary by the fact that a few provisions in Article I refer forward to other articles—a complete, ongoing government, with all the necessary organs, could have been formed, and could have functioned down to now, if the Constitution had ended at the end of Article I.[53]

Of course, the question whether Congress exercises its tremendous constitutional powers is not solely a legal question. It is, more centrally, a question of political will.[54]

Start with the powers allocated to the executive branch, and both the paucity of exclusively executive powers and the predominant role of Congress become clear. The bulk of Article II is devoted to the process of selecting a chief executive. The president's powers, listed in the second section of the article, are sparse and largely depend on Congress for their exercise. The occupant of the White House can demand opinions of the heads of government departments, make treaties (but only with the agreement of two-thirds of the Senate), appoint officers and judges (again only with the advice and consent of the Senate), and receive ambassadors. The ability to *receive* ambassadors is thus the only "foreign affairs" power that is textually committed to the executive branch alone. These carefully limited powers, most exercised only with another branch's collaboration, hardly bespeak freewheeling executive power.

The arguments for unchecked presidential power rest on two phrases in Article II: the so-called "Vesting Clause" and the "Commander in Chief" clause. Neither one justifies an unchecked executive power to suspend the laws in the name of national security.

The Article II Vesting Clause states that "The executive Power shall be vested in a President of the United States." Advocates of presidential power set aside the specific powers granted in Article II and contend that these thirteen words concentrate in the president a host of implied, unspoken powers held by kings and queens of the past. Thus, the OLC argued in the August 2002 torture memo that this "sweeping grant vests in the President an unenumerated 'executive power.'" Among these unspoken powers, the OLC contended, "the Founders entrusted the President with the primary responsibility, and therefore the power, to ensure the security of the United States in situations of grave and unforeseen emergencies."[55] Taken as endorsement of Lincoln's overt acts in the face of immediate crisis, this is unobjectionable. But the Bush Administration, exploiting the fuzziness in the word "emergencies," extends this power far beyond the immediate crisis, eclipsing in the process the roles of its coordinate branches.

Simply put, this text alone cannot sustain a sweeping power to suspend the laws. Not only is the Vesting Clause entirely silent on the question of the president's power to suspend the laws, the other powers assigned to the president would be rendered entirely superfluous by such a broad reading of the Vesting Clause. Hence, if the Framers believed that the Vesting Clause alone was enough to entrust the president with all powers associated with the kings of the seventeenth century, they would not have needed to include in Article II a pardon power or a recess appointment clause. Unsurprisingly, scholars and judges tend to view readings of the Constitution that leave part of its text without meaning as plainly incorrect. Moreover, the Bush Administration's reading of the Vesting Clause is incongruent with the Constitution's general infrastructure of separate institutions *sharing* power, evident in the multibranch appointment and treaty-formation processes among other places.

This leaves the Commander in Chief Clause. This states simply that the president "shall be Commander in Chief of the Army and Navy." This is the first practical presidential power to be listed in Article II, and is pivotal to the Administration's arguments. It is, moreover, the most plausible source of presidential power in the national security field. The OLC, however, took a step further and contended that "the President enjoys *complete discretion* in the exercise of his Commander-in-Chief authority and in conducting operations against hostile forces." It argued, in other words, that Congress has *no* role in regard to "operations against hostile forces."[56]

Without doubt, the OLC is correct that the president has important responsibilities as leader of the military. But does the Constitution's text support the OLC's assertion of *exclusive* power? The text decisively answers no.

Set against the frugal provisions of Article II, Article I's list of legislative powers is an embarrassment of riches, even regarding matters military. Critically, the powers assigned to Congress include several important powers directly related not only to *when* a president can exercise military power but also *how* he may use that power. Moreover, Congress has numerous powers concerning external relations more generally. The text of the Constitution thus assigns to Congress considerable power to determine when the nation goes to war, and also the power to determine the rules for those wars' conduct. The initiation of hostilities is largely committed to Congress. The legislature must "declare" war. It can also license small-scale conflicts by granting "Letters of Marque and Reprisal" (enabling private parties to conduct hostilities) or call up militias "to execute the Laws of the Union, suppress Insurrections and repel Invasions." Congress, that is, plays a large role in determining when force is appropriate.[57]

More important, Congress has significant power to regulate the *conduct* of war. Hence, Congress can issue rules for "Captures on Land and Water." And, most relevant to whether the President can override Congress's law on coercive interrogations or warrantless spying, Congress can "make Rules for the Government and Regulation of the land and naval Forces." There is no reason to exclude from such rules matters of detention, interrogation, or spying.

While claiming to have an "originalist" view of the Constitution, the acolytes of exclusive presidential power in fact ignore all those parts of the Constitution that are inconvenient for their views of the text. Military matters are simply not an area in which presidents, even when they act as commander in chief, have a wholly free hand. On the contrary, the "Commander in Chief" clause reflects nothing more than the Founding Generation's commitment to insuring that the military would never again be "independent of and superior to the Civil power," as it had been under British rule. As Justice Robert H. Jackson said in rejecting sweeping war powers claims by President Harry Truman, "the Constitution did not contemplate that the title Commander-in-Chief of the Army and Navy" would make a president "also Commander-in-Chief of the country, its industries, and its inhabitants." Jackson added that a president "has no monopoly of 'war powers,' whatever they are."[58] But it is precisely this monopoly that the supposedly originalist post-9/11 Administration, in reckless disregard of the Constitution's text, asserts.

A secondary claim, found in OLC opinions from early 2002, is that the president has "plenary control over the conduct of foreign relations," a notion that draws on a poorly reasoned Supreme Court decision from 1936. As in the military matters, however, Congress has extensive powers concerning foreign affairs: it can regulate foreign commerce, establish a "uniform" rule of immigration, and define "Offenses against the Law of Nations," which today would clearly include torture. Contrary to OLC's assertion, there is no "secret reservoir of unaccountable power" presidents can tap simply by labeling a policy question as "foreign affairs."[59]

Other provisions of the Constitution further undercut the Administration's assertion of unlimited national security authority. Most important, Article II obliges the president to "take Care that the Laws be faithfully executed." He thus has an affirmative objective to *fulfill*, not to break, the law. And an executive power to set aside laws would leave the limited presidential veto (which can be overcome by two-thirds majorities in both houses of Congress) in effect without function, at least for laws such as FISA that are primarily directed at the executive branch alone. Why would the Framers of the Constitution have bothered to include a presidential veto if the chief executive can simply ignore a law?[60]

Further, the Constitution already contains a limited power to suspend legal rights in times of crisis—but assigns it to Congress. Article I contains what has become known as "the suspension clause," which states that habeas corpus, the judicial remedy against unlawful imprisonment, cannot be "suspended, unless when in Cases of Rebellion or Invasion the public Safety may require it." Embedded in Article I, the suspension power has long been understood to lodge suspension decisions in Congress.[61]

The omissions from Article II of the Constitution, which describes the executive branch, also speak against the Administration's claim to unchecked powers. Had the Framers wished to incorporate in the executive branch exclusive authority over national security matters, at the expense of laws enacted by Congress, they had at least two ways of doing so, neither of which is reflected in the constitutional text. First, the Constitution's relatively sparse articles do not use the phrase "separation of powers." This is important because the Framers could have used this phrase to signal the absolute division of power suggested by the present Administration. Indeed, several of the thirteen original state constitutions had such clauses, so the device was not unfamiliar in 1787. In a government of generally shared powers, that phrase could have been deployed to carve out an area of exclusive executive branch authority, but it was not. Second, Charles Fried, President Reagan's solicitor general, suggested that the Framers "looked to Locke." In his 1689 publication *Second Treatise on Government*, English political philosopher John Locke endorsed a monarchial "prerogative" power to suspend the laws, to deal with unanticipated circumstances. But the Constitution does not mention a "prerogative power." Neither Fried nor his successors in President George W. Bush's White House explain how this theoretical grafting can be anchored in the Constitution's text.[62]

Finding little comfort in the Constitution's text, the Administration fell back to the historical context of the Constitution to ground its claim of unchecked presidential national security authority. In the August 2002 memo on torture, for example, the OLC argued that "any power traditionally understood as pertaining to the executive—which includes the conduct of warfare and the defense of the nation—unless expressly assigned in the Constitution to Congress, is vested in the President." In particular, we have seen that the OLC focused on pre-Revolutionary British practices. According to the OLC, the distinctive historical meaning of the term "executive power" supports the President's present claims to reject congressional control of interrogation, detention, and spying decisions.[63]

The OLC is correct that the historical understanding of constitutional terms such as "executive power" can properly shed light on the meaning of the Constitution today. But the OLC has its history woefully wrong. First, it is wrong to suggest that there was some fixed meaning of the term "executive power" that slipped silently into the Constitution. There simply was no consensus definition of "executive power" to incorporate into Article II. Neither does history support the assertion that the term "executive power" includes the power to set aside wholesale a law enacted by Congress. Indeed, American constitutional traditions stand four-square against the idea of an executive power to "suspend" the laws based on loose claims of "national security."

Historians teach that the Framers of the Constitution drew from numerous sources. First, having grown up British subjects, the former colonists naturally enough looked to British experiences of government, sometimes with approval and sometimes with revulsion. Second, they had a reserve of experience based on more than a decade of their own experience after the Declaration of Independence under the Articles of Confederation and thirteen new state constitutions. Those who prepared and ratified the federal Constitution indeed had intimate familiarity with state constitutions from drafting and using these documents. Third, they looked to contemporary political philosophy. Just as today, numerous currents of political theory attracted support at the end of the eighteenth century. The English theorist John Locke, the French essayist Baron de Montesquieu, and the English jurist William Blackstone all provided insights into the proper scope of executive power. And, in stark contrast to the assertions of advocates of unchecked presidential power, these sources uniformly confirm that the Founding Generation had little truck with the idea of unchecked presidential power, even in times of war or crisis. The debates within the Constitutional Convention and during ratification, moreover, confirm this impression.[64]

The men who prepared and ratified the Constitution lived most of their lives as subjects to a British king and were steeped in British constitutional history. This history, however, provided a powerful warning *against* vesting the executive branch with an open-ended power to set aside statutory provisions. Moreover, even if the OLC were correct that the Constitution somehow silently absorbed British practices, the latter do not support an executive suspension power.

First of all, the British constitution did not even have a clear "separation" of powers. Rather than three branches, Britain had three "estates"—the monarchy, the aristocracy, and the commons—that came together when the king sat in Britain's bicameral Parliament. Lacking a monarch or an aristocracy (let alone the "lords spiritual" who sit in Britain's upper house), the new Americans could hardly copy the British constitution in every jot and tittle.[65]

Long before American independence, moreover, the British tried and rejected the idea of an executive with power to set aside laws passed by the legislative branch. For centuries, English kings had both lawmaking and a "suspension" prerogative. The latter allowed kings to "dispense" others from having to obey a law, and "suspend" that law entirely. Both the early seventeenth-century King James I, who wrote *The True Law of Free Monarchies* in defense of kings' divine right, and his son Charles I claimed an absolute prerogative right to take any action outside the law they believed necessary for the nation's security. Addressing Parliament about his "Prerogative or mystery of State," King James once ordered the speaker of the House of Commons "to acquaint that house with our pleasure that none therein shall presume to meddle with anything concerning our government or mysteries of State." As James later explained, to dispute the king's use of prerogative powers was "Atheisme and blasphemie."[66]

But this suspension power was long gone before the Constitution's adoption. It did not survive the Glorious Revolution of 1688, which cast out James II, in part as a consequence of James's exercise of the prerogative power in early 1687. The English 1689 Bill of Rights repudiated all suspension powers: "The pretended power of suspending of laws, or the execution of laws, by regal authority, without consent of Parliament, is illegal." Thus, the monarch's prerogative power to bypass the law had been a stranger to English law for almost a century at the time of the American Revolution. But none of *this* history figures in the analysis of the present Administration.[67]

On our side of the Atlantic, the Founding Generation was acutely aware of the hazards of British kings' prerogative power to suspend the laws. In an influential essay called "Thoughts on Government," future president John Adams argued that American executives ought to be "stripped of most of those badges of domination called prerogatives." Thomas Jefferson's Proposed 1776 Constitution for Virginia stated starkly that executive power did not include those "powers exercised under our former government by the crown as of its prerogative." During the 1787 Philadelphia Convention, James Wilson announced that the royal prerogatives did not provide "a proper guide in defining Executive powers." And in 1806, Supreme Court Justice William Paterson, writing in his capacity as a circuit judge, rejected an executive officer's claim to a dispensing power such as that claimed by King James I. Twenty-two years later, the full Supreme Court echoed Paterson, noting that a "dispensing power . . . has no countenance for its support in any part of the constitution." There is, in short, a pervasive historical record showing the nation's original and unequivocal rejection of any executive power to suspend laws passed by the legislature. Again, none of this figures in the Administration's rhetoric.[68]

Early American experience also undermines the Administration's broad view of executive power. America was born in 1776 with the Declaration of Independence, a document that squarely rejected unchecked executive rule with a military cast. The Declaration, drafted initially by Thomas Jefferson, has a long list of wrongs by King George III. It condemns the king's attempts to "render the Military independent of and superior to the Civil power," and to hinder the colonial legislatures, and for "abolishing our most valuable laws." The concern with military oppression reflected the clear and manifest danger of the day. In the months that Jefferson and the Continental Congress were drafting and revising, General George Washington and his troops faced British forces at Boston, and again in Long Island, New York. Washington's success was by no means certain. Yet, casting monarchy aside, Jefferson began from the "self-evident" truth that "all men are created equal," and that the People can alter or abolish any government that "becomes destructive" of human "Life, Liberty, and the Pursuit of Happiness." And the British monarchy, even stripped of its prerogative powers, failed this test. As Justice Robert Jackson suggested, "the prerogative exercised by George III, and the description of its evils in the Declaration of Independence" left "no doubt" that the model of the British king was decisively rejected by Americans in designing the Constitution's new executive branch.[69] Once again, the Administration ignores all this.

In the wake of the Declaration, the former colonists showed scant affection for strong executives. The Articles of Confederation, the first federal constitution, did not even create an executive branch. The thirteen states, on the other hand, adopted a variety of forms, with one state eliminating its governor and most of the others creating some kind of multiple executive, or privy council, that would be selected by the legislature. Remaining governors lost their veto powers and retained only greatly narrowed powers of appointment. Celebrating the first Virginia constitution, Thomas Jefferson proudly spoke of having destroyed the "kingly office" entirely, and "absolutely divested [it] of all its rights, powers and prerogatives." Hence, some states, such as Virginia and South Carolina, specifically demanded that executive powers be exercised in accord with the "laws" of the state. In light of these trends, historian Gordon Wood concluded that "separation of power" in the early Republic primarily meant "insulating the judiciary and particularly the legislature from executive manipulation."[70]

The variety in the states' first constitutions also proves that there was no clear definition of the "executive power" to be incorporated by reference into the federal Constitution. As James Madison explained, the separation of powers was a fluid and pragmatic concept:

> Experience has instructed us that no skill in the science of government has yet been able to discriminate and define with sufficient certainty, its three great provinces—the legislative, executive, and judiciary. . . . Questions daily occur in the course of practice which prove the obscurity which reigns in these subjects, and which puzzle the greatest adepts in political science.[71]

Political theory proved no surer guide to the meaning of the term "executive power." For the theorists disagreed about what the term meant. And the one theory most in line with the Bush Administration's position actually received scorn from the country's founders.

To begin with the theorists' conflicting views on executive power, John Locke, for instance, did not distinguish the judicial branch from the executive. He did draw a distinction between what he called the "federative power" over foreign affairs and the "executive" power; but this is simply not the principal line the U.S. Constitution follows. The preeminent expert on British common law, William Blackstone, used the mixed government framework of the British constitution. Only the Baron de Montesquieu invoked a theory of strict separation of powers, and he set his face squarely against excessively powerful government.[72]

Yet it was Locke who furnished the closest model for the power the Administration seeks today. Locke's 1689 *Second Treatise on Government*, which Charles Fried quoted, described a "prerogative power" for a prince to act for the common good, sometimes in contradiction to the law. But even Locke emphasized his prerogative power as an interim device, to be used "in the infancy of governments" and discarded as legislation covered specific questions with new laws. Even Locke insisted that the executive was "both ministerial and subordinate to the legislative." In any case, by the time of the American Revolution, the Founders viewed Locke's prerogative as "so odious in its very name . . . but nobody ever thought of it but to hate it, and to thank God it was utterly exterminated." Madison made this sole reference to Locke's prerogative theory in one of his letters, noting that it "shows how much the reason of the philosopher was clouded by the royalism of the Englishman." Hardly an endorsement.[73]

The Framers wove these varied strands of history, revolutionary theory, and practice together in Philadelphia in the summer of 1787, and in the debates in state ratification conventions. The discussions both in Philadelphia and around the young country confirm that while no clear formulation of "executive power" was available during the founding period, there was general agreement that Congress, rather than the president, ought to hold the lion's share of constitutional powers.

The members of the Constitutional Convention largely agreed that there should be *some* kind of stronger executive which would be separate from the legislature, thereby breaking from the Articles of Confederation and most of the existing state constitutions. Recall that soon after the Convention's opening, James Wilson, an influential Pennsylvania delegate, objected that "the Prerogatives of the British Monarch" were not a "proper guide in defining the Executive powers." Almost all subsequent debate about the executive branch in the Constitutional Convention focused on whether it would be composed of one or several positions—that is, whether the federal government would follow the model of states with a governor, or the states with an executive council. But historian Forrest McDonald notes that "no one made any extensive comments as to just what [the executive power] would include." No one invoked the Vesting Clause as a source of undefined and amorphous power. Indeed, discussion of executive power beyond issues of tenure and election never advanced far at all. Instead, the task of hammering out specific executive powers was left to a separate committee of detail, which eschewed clear formulations drawn from Locke, Montesquieu, or Blackstone. The exact formulation of the Vesting Clause, indeed, was never discussed, but was the result of last minute stylistic rewrites. As McDonald tartly concludes, in describing the terse and narrowly focused debates around the presidency's creation, "so much for the doctrine of the separation of powers."[74]

The state ratifying conventions brought divergent views on "executive power" to the ratification debates about the Constitution. These debates also do not support the broad reading of "executive power" that the Bush Administration has put forward. Hence, James Wilson gave a long speech on October 6, 1787, in the Pennsylvania statehouse defending the new draft constitution. A soaring and eloquent peroration, Wilson's speech became a focal point in the ratification debates. Repeating his condemnation of sweeping executive power at the Convention, Wilson promptly rejected the equation of president with king, underscoring how even the president's textual powers of appointment and treaty making required congressional acquiescence. Wilson's response, moreover, illuminates the concerns that opponents of the Constitution's ratification, the Anti-Federalists, expressed in trying to defeat the Constitution. These Anti-Federalists were worried that the presidency would be dependent on the Senate. They feared the president's collaboration with the Senate would re-create a de facto alliance of a new aristocracy and a new monarchy. Although their fears proved groundless, the focus on the president and the Senate acting together shows that the Founding Generation feared the *combination* of monarchy (president) and aristocracy (the Senate) that had long concerned English political theorists.[75]

Less widely read during the ratification debates but deeply respected today are the *Federalist Papers* by James Madison, Alexander Hamilton, and John Jay. These set out a definitive vision of the new Constitution. In the *Federalist Papers*, the "executive power" is described as constrained and in practice subordinate to Congress. James Madison explained that the "executive magistracy"—that is, the president—"is carefully limited, both in the extent and the duration of his powers." Alexander Hamilton, one of the most ardent defenders of executive power, also starkly rejected the comparison between the English monarchy and the office of president. Describing the new presidency in the famous *Federalist 69*—a pivotal text on executive power that is absent from the OLC memos—Hamilton listed each power of the president described in the Constitution's text, and compared it to one in the British constitution. He thus described the Commander in Chief Clause as giving the president "nothing more than the supreme command and direction of the military and naval forces, as first general and admiral." He also pointed to the president's "*qualified* negative" of proposed laws, as opposed to the "*absolute*" negative of the English monarchy. All this does not read like open-ended license to set aside laws. And defending his vision of "Energy in the executive," Hamilton did not point to some extratextual "executive power." To be sure, he argued at length the virtue of a single president instead of a multiperson council, but this question does not bear on the scope of executive power, but on whether the executive branch would culminate in "one man" or a council of "greater number." Tellingly, the unitary executive advocates of the 1980s took Hamilton's argument about the *structure* of the executive branch and transformed it into an argument about the *scope* of executive power.[76]

Later, as George Washington's Treasury secretary, Hamilton defended a broader conception of presidential power in public debates about the president's power to issue a proclamation of neutrality without congressional assent. Hamilton's broadside, which asserted a sweeping claim that the executive power is "subject only to the exceptions and qualifications which are expressed" in the Constitution, reflects not only the views of one who lauded the monarchy early in the 1787 Constitutional Convention, but a federal officer with a substantial and immediate stake in aggrandizing presidential power. Leaving aside the trenchant response this sparked from James Madison, Hamilton's argument, which advocates of presidential power frequently refer to, is entirely circular since it only returns the analysis to the question of how powers are, in fact, allocated by the Constitution.[77]

It is not Hamilton the executive official, but Hamilton the Constitution's advocate, who speaks with still persuasive voice today. In *Federalist 69*, Hamilton compared a monarch and the new president, asking, "What answer shall we give to those who persuade us that things so unlike [a monarch and a president] resemble each other?" The same answer one would give, explained

Hamilton, to one who would take the U.S. Constitution to establish "an aristocracy, a monarchy, and a despotism." It is an answer that is still good today.[78]

The Supreme Court and Presidential Lawbreaking

The understanding of separate institutions, sharing powers finds confirmation in a long string of Supreme Court cases. Dating back to the beginning of the nineteenth century, the Supreme Court has repeatedly rejected presidential claims of power to set aside the laws in times of crisis and even war. In an 1804 case concerning the seizure of foreign vessels, Chief Justice John Marshall led a united Supreme Court in decisively rejecting an executive claim to be able to act in excess of legal authority even in wartime. He concluded that the seizure of a ship by one of President Thomas Jefferson's officers had contradicted the terms of a statute, and was thus illegal. The president, that is, has no power to act outside the law. This case, and others like it, fatally undercut claims by the Administration's supporters that judicial involvement in wartime decisions is "entirely new in American history."[79]

This understanding took canonical form in 1952, when Justice Robert Jackson published an opinion in a dispute that has become known as the Youngstown Steel Seizure case. Jackson's opinion concerned the legality of President Harry S. Truman's seizure of steel mills around the country during the Korean War. Truman wanted to prevent a national strike that he believed would imperil the war effort. Lacking statutory power, Truman invoked "inherent authority" to act when the "well-being and safety of the Nation" were in peril. He relied on a memo from former Attorney General Tom Clark, who by then was on the Supreme Court, and on secret oral assurances from then–Chief Justice Fred Vinson, that the Court would approve his decision. Vinson proved a poor oracle. The Court rejected Truman's claim to inherent wartime power by six votes to three. Of the resulting opinions, the most famous is Jackson's concurrence.[80]

Central to Jackson's concurrence was his identification of three categories of executive action, dependent on the degree of congressional support or opposition, for the purposes of assessing constitutionality. In the first category were executive acts with "an express or implied authorization of Congress," which received the greatest deference from the federal courts. In the second category fell executive acts without "either a congressional grant or denial of authority." This Jackson described as a "zone of twilight" in which "any actual test of power is likely to depend on the imperatives of events and contemporary imponderables rather than on abstract theories of law." And finally, the third category included those instances in which an executive act was "incompatible with the expressed or implied will of Congress." In this realm, a

president's power fell to its lowest ebb, with courts viewing the executive's acts
with great skepticism.[81]

Jackson's opinion is a monument of American law. Jackson penned an opinion that plunged directly into the political realities of executive-legislative relations. The opinion grapples with hard realities of power in a way that few
other Supreme Court opinions past or present have. But Jackson had scant pa-
tience for claims of "inherent" presidential power even in wartime:

> Loose and irresponsible use of adjectives colors all non-legal and much
> legal discussion of presidential powers. "Inherent" powers, "implied"
> powers, "incidental" power, "plenary" powers, "war" powers and
> "emergency" powers are used, often interchangeably and without fixed
> or ascertainable meaning. . . .

Jackson resisted such "self-serving" arguments from government lawyers. He
rejected Truman's claims to prerogative power, warning of its alarming consequences. Truman's claim, if accepted, would "vastly enlarge" presidential power
at home and overseas.[82] The task of responding to crises rather falls to Congress, Jackson explained:

> The essence of our free Government is "leave to live by no man's leave,
> underneath the law"—to be governed by those impersonal forces we call
> law. Our Government is fashioned to fulfill this concept so far as hu-
> manly possible. The Executive, except for recommendation and veto, has
> no legislative power. . . . With all its defects, delays and inconveniences,
> men have discovered no technique for long preserving free government
> except that the law be made by parliamentary deliberations.[83]

But Congress can, and Congress does, all to often fail. As we have seen during
the Cold War and more so in the post-9/11 era, Congress is often too divided
by partisanship, too subservient to the White House, too scared—or simply
too apathetic or too ill-informed—to exercise its powers at all, let alone exercise them wisely.

In another wartime opinion, Jackson warned against judicial endorsement,
in times of crisis, of emergency powers. In the *Korematsu* case, Jackson issued
a dissenting opinion that has become more respected than Justice Hugo Black's
reviled majority opinion upholding the Japanese American internment:

> Once a judicial opinion rationalizes such an order to show that it con-
> forms to the Constitution, or rather rationalizes the Constitution to

show that the Constitution sanctions such an order, the Court for all time has validated the principle. . . . The principle then lies about like a loaded weapon ready for the hand of any authority that can bring forward a plausible claim of an urgent need. Every repetition imbeds that principle more deeply in our law and thinking and expands it to new purposes.[84]

James Madison insisted that the world's first republican constitution would remedy "the defect of better motives" by dividing power between three branches of government and by including devices that allowed ambition to counteract ambition. The Constitution, therefore, did not have "loaded weapons" hidden in the expansive generalities of vague phrases such as "executive power." And, certainly, it did not grant the president expansive power to set aside the law whenever an ill-defined "national security" interest could be called into play.[85]

Changing Times, Changing Threats

The Constitution was drafted more than two hundred years ago, before skyscrapers, before jet planes, before Islamist terrorism. Does it remain relevant?

Of course, the framers intentionally did not provide a detailed legal code with answers to every imaginable problem. As James Madison explained in *Federalist 37*,

> All new laws, though penned with the greatest technical skill and passed on the fullest and most mature deliberation, are considered as more or less obscure and equivocal, until their meaning be liquidated and ascertained through by a series of particular discussions and adjudications.[86]

Madison thus knew that much depended on the paths chosen by the generations that would first build practices based on the Constitution. These generations' motives, behavior, and idiosyncrasies would shape and resolve the ambiguities and gaps of the founding document. Much of what we today consider "constitutional law" is, in fact, a compound of custom, practical necessity, and happenstance—and certainly not the inevitable result of the Constitution's text. This compound seeped into gaps in the text as America's constitutive document was "liquidated and ascertained," and today has solidified alongside the words themselves.[87]

Furthermore, successors to the Founding Generation faced unexpected political developments and new problems. Necessarily, the America of 1887 (let alone 2007) differed radically from the littoral sliver of the North American continent colonized by Europeans in 1787. By and large, the Constitution's text proved a resourceful toolkit as a tumultuous nation engaged in breakneck territorial and fiscal expansion in its first hundred years. But in some instances— the American Civil War, most clearly—the right constitutional fix was wanting. Americans deployed their Constitution innovatively in response to the day's felt necessities. After the Civil War, the Thirteenth, Fourteenth, and Fifteenth Amendments embodied new terms of the national settlement. Eventually— but after much too long and with too much blood and misery—these new terms reformed entirely the American legacy of individual rights. In the Depression too, the bounds of the federal government enlarged dramatically in response to national economic crisis, despite the absence of constitutional amendment. According to legal scholar Bruce Ackerman, the consequent birth of the federal administrative state was a landmark reconfiguration of American government, and what he calls a transformative "constitutional moment."[88]

Thus, *some* constitutional change is necessary, even salutary, for the Constitution to further the ideals of the original text under changing circumstances. Indeed, while the Bush Administration's principal defense of unchecked presidential power rested on its extraordinarily flawed rendition of "original meaning," Administration lawyers also used the present to frame that history. They in effect contended that their vision was simply another necessary constitutional change impelled by the present necessities of a post-9/11 era.

In the August 2002 OLC torture opinion, Yoo and Bybee began their discussion of presidential power in the present day, looking at "the threat presently posed to the nation . . . in the context of the current war against the al Qaeda terrorist network."[89] The Justice Department's defense of domestic NSA spying begins the same way, waving the bloody flag of 9/11. Administration lawyers again argued that new threats demand new responses, which included the President's domestic surveillance program. According to executive branch officials, a new era demanded more "speed and agility," which the 1978 FISA law supposedly hampered. (The Justice Department, to be sure, did not explain why FISA's exception for emergencies, which allows the government to seek an after-the-fact warrant, could not accommodate new needs.) Congressional interference even risked "a subsequent terrorist attack" by al Qaeda in the United States.[90]

The present threat is thus used as a cudgel to attack political opponents of unlimited presidential power. Consider John Yoo's assault on another law professor, Michael Ramsey, for supposedly abetting terrorists by arguing that Congress has a role in national security matters. "One can only imagine," wrote Yoo, "the advantage that terrorists or rogue nations would draw from public congressional deliberations, which might give them the advance notice of a possible attack necessary to conceal their forces or disperse their weapons facilities." (This kind of critique, incidentally, simply does not apply to the legal memos Yoo himself prepared about torture, detention, and spying while he was at the OLC. The Administration was not hiding its use of torture from terrorists, but from the American public.) This is a half-step from the assertion that challenges to presidential authority *aid* the enemy; it is, in short, a veiled effort to silence criticism and debate by equating the former with something tantamount to treason.[91]

Yoo's argument recalls nothing so much as the argument made by federal prosecutors at the 1800 trial of the Pennsylvania newspaper editor Thomas Cooper, who published a handbill critical of President John Adams. It was not proper or legal for Cooper, explained the prosecutor, "to raise surmises and suspicions of the wisdom and design of measures of this kind, which he cannot explain, or the people understand."[92] Today, just as in 1800 under the discredited Sedition Act, the arguments for silence and stifling debate would ensure that the people cannot explain or understand, let alone judge, drastic measures taken in their name. Now, as at the Founding, this is a denial of democracy.

While constitutional change involves shifting strategies to reach the goals of the original text under changing circumstances, it does not permit wholesale abandonment of the Constitution's original architecture. Unlimited presidential power over national security is not only unnecessary, even counterproductive, for today's counterterrorism efforts, it is plainly incompatible with the Constitution's basic architecture, and the preservation of democratic governance under law.

Most telling, the theory of unchecked presidential power is not a response to 9/11. Seeded in the Ford White House in 1976, it took on full form fourteen years before the September 11 attacks in the Iran-Contra minority report. September 11 was simply the opportunity to realize a long-treasured ideology, an ideology squarely at odds with the constitutional design.

Today is also not the first time the executive branch has urged abrogation of long-standing constitutional protections in the face of a new external threat. And it is not the first time supporters of the executive branch tried to bully their interlocutors into silence. More than sixty years ago, Justice Department lawyers raised similar arguments to defend the application of martial law to Hawaii during World War II. Supporting the Supreme Court's rejection of the government push to replace civilian courts with military tribunals, Justice Frank Murphy explained:

The argument is made that however adequate the "open court" rule may have been in 1628 or 1864 it is distinctly unsuited to modern warfare conditions where all of the territories of a warring nation may be in combat zones or imminently threatened with long-range attack even while civil courts are operating. Hence if a military commander, on the basis of his conception of military necessity, requires all civilians accused of crime to be tried summarily before martial law tribunals, the Bill of Rights must bow humbly to his judgment despite the unquestioned ability of the civil courts to exercise their criminal jurisdiction. . . . The argument thus advanced is as untenable today as it was when cast in the language of the Plantagenets, the Tudors and the Stuarts. It is a rank appeal to abandon the fate of all our liberties to the reasonableness of the judgment of those who are trained primarily for war. It seeks to justify military usurpation of civilian authority to punish crime without regard to the potency of the Bill of Rights. It deserves repudiation.[93]

Justice Murphy's logic applies with equal force to today's attempt by the Administration and its allies to scare opponents into silence by raising the specter of further terrorist attacks. Irresponsible scare-mongering plays no constructive role in today's debates.

The argument—implicit in the writings of Yoo and others—that accountability is incompatible with security does not survive the mildest scrutiny. The framers and ratifiers of the Constitution rightly rejected the idea that unchecked power would necessarily be wisely used. They understood human nature too well to make this error, or to assume that leaders would make cost-effective decisions and refrain from political abuses in the absence of external monitoring and correction. The plain fact, learned through hard lessons time and again, is unsupervised power is abused and misdirected. Resources are wasted. Real threats go unaddressed. This was the lesson of COINTELPRO and Operation CHAOS. Nothing in today's torture, rendition, spying, and indefinite detention policies suggests human nature has evolved since Madison's day, or since the Church Committee some three decades ago. Wise restraint—not unchecked and unbounded license—still makes us safe and keeps us free.

In 2004 and again in 2006, the Supreme Court returned to the question of the president's war powers and reaffirmed these foundational principles. In a trilogy of 2004 cases concerning the detention of citizens and aliens designated as "enemy combatants" in the United States and at Guantánamo Bay, the Court flatly rejected the executive branch's request for a free hand when it came to national security. With unmistakable firmness, Justice Sandra Day O'Connor, writing for a plurality of the Court and expressing views echoed by eight of its members, explained, "A state of war is not a blank check for the President when it comes to the rights of the Nation's citizens. . . . Whatever power the United States Constitution envisages for the Executive in its exchanges with other nations or with enemy organizations in time of conflict, it most assuredly envisions a role for all branches when individual liberties are at stake." Two years and a day later, the Supreme Court returned to the theme of separate branches, sharing powers. In a striking repudiation of the Bush Administration's claims to unilateral power, Justice John Paul Stevens flatly declared that "the Executive is bound to comply with the Rule of Law that prevails in this jurisdiction." Reciting the text of Articles I and II, Stevens underscored the need for congressional endorsement for executive action, even if a claim of "national security" was made. As Justice Stephen Breyer's concurring opinion explained:

> Where, as here, no emergency prevents consultation with Congress, judicial insistence upon that consultation does not weaken our Nation's ability to deal with danger. To the contrary, that insistence strengthens the Nation's ability to determine—through democratic means—how best to do so. The Constitution places its faith in those democratic means. Our Court today simply does the same.[94]

The Framers' Enduring Wisdom

The Constitution's structure of separated branches that share powers built on sound insights into human psychology. It demanded the involvement of multiple branches in nettlesome national decisions. And the Constitution was not written in or for quiet times. The drafters of the federal Constitution, and those who endorsed it through ratification, saw war, invasion, and rebellion before they arrived at Philadelphia. After overcoming monarchical tyranny, they debated the Constitution in the shadow of a continuing threat from Britain, with jealous neighbors infringing from north and south, and foreign war, and domestic unrest not far from mind. Nor is our Constitution one that presumes the beneficence and wisdom of leaders who, by dint of lineage or election, find themselves in political power. Born in struggle, built to persist through coming trials, our Constitution is no mere fair-weather friend to liberty. Its protections are intended to endure through war and crisis.[95]

Under such circumstances, the Founders hoped, the Constitution would shelter political and human liberties through the "auxiliary precautions" of separated institutions sharing powers, where the overlap of powers means no one branch of government can overtake and supersede the others. The

Founders intuited the concern raised by their French contemporary the Marquis de Condorcet, that "One is more sure of subjugating people's minds by frightening them, for fear is an imperious passion." They thus designed a Constitution based on insight that men are not angels, and are not more inclined to be so in times of emergency.[96]

8

The King's Counsel

How did we stray so far?

Government lawyers have become instruments by which fundamental constitutional principles are eroded. Particular responsibility falls at the feet of the Justice Department's Office of Legal Counsel. Tasked with providing legal opinions for the whole executive branch, the OLC issued a series of rulings from September 2001 onward retrogressing to a monarchical vision of government, with a correlative neutering of the Constitution's checks and balances. During the Cold War, plausible deniability was expanded to hide the internal decision-making of the American government, enabling presidents to evade responsibility for covert actions by denying knowledge of them. Now, presidents can evade responsibility a new way: they just say their lawyer said it was legal.

Lawyers have special obligations in a nation, such as the United States, founded on a shared commitment to the rule of law. And government lawyers have even greater obligations. Government lawyers serve not only the political leader of the moment but also must preserve and protect the enduring values of the Constitution. A handful of OLC lawyers under the Bush Administration failed to live up to these obligations. Seizing on a divisive vision of unchecked executive power that has hovered in the wings since the Iran-Contra scandal, they lost their moral and constitutional bearings. Courageously, other government lawyers resisted pressures to support the Administration's wishes. But their persuasive views went unheeded; and most ended up frozen out from decision making.

While we believe their legal analysis to be clearly wrong, the OLC lawyers picked by the Administration presumably genuinely believed the Constitution awards presidents a crown. However genuine their beliefs, they breached clear professional obligations in the way they voiced them. They failed even to mention key Supreme Court cases. They failed to identify, let alone respond to, weaknesses in their legal arguments. They failed to consider the expertise of other parts of the federal government such as the military and the State Department. They failed to consider harms to the nation that would flow from following their cramped legal advice. And they failed to note that their legal analysis would handicap America's leadership in the worldwide battle for human rights. These lawyers knew, or at least should have known, their advice could not exist in a vacuum; it must be informed by the predictable, practical consequences it will likely have.

Failing to honor the law or to provide balanced advice, OLC lawyers after 9/11 became instruments of grave harm to the Constitution. The political vision of an unchecked presidency, however, predated 9/11. It was the product of a generation of politicians and bureaucrats who cut their teeth in post-Watergate Washington, and who have since then striven to reassert executive-branch dominance. Harshest criticism ought to be reserved for these politicians, not their legal counsel. Indeed, the most likely explanation for the glaring shortcomings in the OLC memos is simple. The OLC lawyers were simply giving cover to their clients in the White House at the expense of their true clients, the American people and the U.S. Constitution.

American Lawyers in Public Life and Government

In America, no prince, no religious creed, no normative ideology, no caste or clan dictates our lawful conduct, although many of them play a role.[1] Unlike most nations historically, and unlike many nations today, law is part of our shared sense of the American story.

As supreme law of the land, our written Constitution plays a crucial role. Nevertheless, the Constitution often provides only general principles of government. It stands in contrast to the Napoleonic Code of 1804 and its continental European successors which sought to provide precise answers to every question. Similarly, the structure of the Constitution derives from broad, loosely defined concepts like checks and balances and "equal protection of the law." Because the Constitution is a *written* document that is expressed broadly in words and concepts that are not self-defining, it leaves many questions open to debate and legal argument. Many, perhaps most, of the government functions that vitally affect our nation and its people are debated, and ultimately allocated, on the basis of legal analysis, which itself is often grounded in history and experience. The quality of the government's legal analysis thus matters a great deal.[2]

One hundred and seventy years ago, in his thoughtful survey of democracy in America, Alexis de Tocqueville referred to lawyers as the sole enlightened class that the people do not generally distrust adding that "the American aristocracy is at the attorney's bar and the judge's bench." Lawyers in the twenty-first century are hardly viewed so favorably. Too often, legal counsel do not seem to serve the public interest. Nonetheless, de Tocqueville's observation about lawyers' pivotal role in America's public life likely will remain true for the foreseeable future—at least as long as we are guided by a Constitution that demands skilled interpretation. Critically, lawyers have a responsibility to keep faith with the values underpinning our Constitution.[3]

Whether in public service or private practice, lawyers have two distinct roles where this obligation comes into play. First, lawyers provide clients with legal advice to help them make decisions. Second, they litigate in defense of clients' interests in court. In the federal government, the OLC takes the lead in the first role, and the office of the solicitor general in the second, at least for cases before the Supreme Court. So while the OLC refined legal arguments in favor of wide-ranging executive power in legal opinions for the White House and CIA, the solicitor general deployed these arguments in the courts. Whether acting as litigator or advisor, however, a lawyer has clear ethical obligations. Litigating lawyers of course must defend their clients' position unless it is simply not possible to make a plausible argument. But even during litigation, good lawyers ought to alert their client to weaknesses in the client's position and the risks in continuing to press it.

Compared to private counsel, government lawyers have greater obligations in litigation to serve the broad public interest as well as their clients' narrow interest. Government lawyers have unique disclosure obligations in the criminal context, and must follow open government laws that do not bind private practitioners. The solicitor general, the sole federal official required by statute to be "learned in the law," has dual responsibilities of representing the United States as a litigator in the Supreme Court and also informing the Court of any judicial decision's broader consequences for the law of the land. Reflecting this dual loyalty, the solicitor general is often called the "Tenth Justice." Francis Biddle, a wartime solicitor general under Franklin Roosevelt, summarized the role with a rhetorical flourish: "The Solicitor General has no master to serve except his country." Biddle elaborated that a solicitor general "is responsible neither to the man who appointed him nor to his immediate superior in the hierarchy of administration. The total responsibility is his, and his guide is only the ethic of his profession framed in the ambience of his experience and judgment."[4] Biddle's rhetoric may have overstated the case. The solicitor general is bound to put forward the best professionally defensible arguments on behalf of the client, while at the same time remaining fair and attentive to broader consequences beyond the questions of the day.

The duty of the government's chief legal advisor, the OLC, is less complex. It is to state the best view of the law—and not solely to state the best case for the client's position. Created in 1950, the OLC bears responsibility for preparing legal opinions for the president, a duty originally conferred in 1789 on the attorney general. Today, the OLC reports to the attorney general.[5] Like the solicitor general, the post of assistant attorney general for the OLC is sufficiently important to require Senate confirmation. The OLC has specific obligations to give advice that reflects not merely the immediate interests of the office's political client but also fidelity to the law and the Constitution.

All legal advisors, in government or not, have obligations to consider all sides of a legal question. And as Elihu Root, a lawyer who served with distinction in both government and private practice, once wrote, "Half the practice of a decent lawyer consists in telling would-be clients that they are damned fools and should stop." Even where he or she believes a client's position to be correct, the "decent lawyer" (in both senses of that phrase) alerts the client to counter-arguments, weaknesses, and risks.[6] As Stephen Gillers, a legal ethics scholar at the New York University School of Law, observes, in private practice "even the most aggressive corporate lawyer will include significant qualifying language . . . simply as a matter of self-protection and self-respect, anticipating that new corporate managers, a regulator, or a plaintiff, may later question the failure adequately to explore risks and contrary arguments."[7] To a greater degree than a litigator, therefore, a lawyer who acts as counselor or advisor has an obligation to give unalloyed perspectives on both the advantages and the risks of recommended courses of action.

Owing to its unique position within the federal government, the OLC must take heightened care fulfilling this role. Unlike the solicitor general, who steps in *after* a government action has been challenged, the OLC gives advice about actions that have *yet* to take place. Thus, the OLC influences what the government does in the future, rather than merely defending past actions. When the state stands poised to deploy its awesome resources against the liberty of a lone individual, the need for careful anticipatory legal scrutiny becomes even sharper. Furthermore, the OLC issues legal rulings that are the *binding final word* for agencies within the federal government on contested issues of federal law; its opinions for the White House are not binding on the OLC's superiors, but have persuasive force.

For several reasons, moreover, the OLC in effect often has the "last word" in terms of what the Constitution or federal law demands. In many instances, there is no external review of governmental action governed by an OLC decision. Federal courts have long treated many issues as "political questions" not amenable to judicial resolution. And in many instances, there will simply be no private plaintiffs in a position to challenge (or perhaps even know about) a particular government action. As a Reagan-era OLC alumnus observed, this means the OLC needs to maintain its reputation and credibility within the executive branch for "principled legal interpretation." And that entails an obligation to pay close attention to the public interest, as well as a government client's narrower concerns. In short, an OLC lawyer giving advice has even greater responsibility than a private attorney to do justice to all sides of a question.[8]

This is not a duty to "get it right." Legal issues often present tricky and uncertain issues. Reasonable minds can and often do differ on how to answer strictly legal questions. Even a quick glance at the frequency with which the Justices of the Supreme Court divide on narrow questions of statutory interpretation with no political dimension ought to dispel the notion that legal questions necessarily have clear answers.[9] But while it can be debated exactly how OLC lawyers should balance their commitment to the "best" view of the law, as opposed to the delivery of a plausible view of the law that achieves their client's objectives, what is clear is that OLC lawyers cannot perform their professional duties properly unless they point out weaknesses in their conclusions, and the risks and harms that might flow from accepting these conclusions.

This conception of the OLC's role predates the office's formation. Indeed, it runs back to the origins of the Republic. President George Washington reportedly told the first attorney general, Edmund Randolph, that in matters of advice he wanted "a skilled neutral expounder of the law rather than a political advisor." In the years before the Civil War, Attorney General Caleb Cushing wrote that in discharging his duty to prepare for the president written opinions on contested matters of law, the attorney general acted in a "quasi judicial" capacity as a "public officer, acting judicially, under all the solemn responsibilities of conscience and of legal obligation."[10]

This tradition was largely maintained by the OLC during twentieth-century presidencies. Thus, during the Nixon Administration, an issue arose about whether the President could impound funds that Congress had ordered spent. William Rehnquist, who then was head of OLC, and who later went on to be an Associate and then Chief Justice of the Supreme Court, flatly rejected Nixon's claim to an "inherent" impoundment power. "It may be argued that the spending of money is inherently an executive function," wrote Rehnquist, but "it seems an anomalous proposition that because the Executive branch is bound to execute the laws, it is free to decline to execute them." Clearly, Rehnquist understood the hazards of presidential claims to disregard the law. Even more starkly, Rehnquist understood that OLC's job was not to sign off on whatever its boss of the day happened to want.[11]

Under Presidents Ronald Reagan, George H.W. Bush, and Bill Clinton, the OLC continued to set generally high standards of ethics and integrity. Thus, Reagan's chief of OLC, Theodore Olsen, explained the office's function as drafting opinions that "provide as objective a view as possible" of the law, not "to prepare an advocate's brief or simply to find support for what we, and our clients, might like the law to be." The head of OLC during the first

George H.W. Bush Administration, Douglas Kmiec, referred to the OLC as having a "quasi judicial" stance, one of "remarkable independence" from political pressures. And Randolph Moss, who headed the office toward the end of the Clinton years, explained that the OLC "should take the obligation neutrally to interpret the law as seriously as a court." While there are academic theorists who have contended that a president's lawyers have broad discretion in pandering to an office-holder's narrow, particular interests, such views are alien to the best traditions of the OLC under Republican and Democratic administrations.[12]

The OLC Today

The Justice Department's post-9/11 opinions on torture, presidential detention, and spying authority are at odds with this long tradition of fidelity to the rule of law. As even former staffer and defender of the Iran-Contra minority report Bruce Fein has argued, the present Justice Department's arguments "oscillate between the risible and the chilling." Commenting on NSA's domestic spying, Fein observed that Justice's "unprecedented and invidious" arguments risk destruction of "the nation's constitutional dispensation and bulwarks against tyranny." While hardly the first time government lawyers strayed from the ideals that ought to animate their work, the OLC opinions that the public has seen are nevertheless serious derogations from the obligations of government lawyers.[13]

How could this have happened? One possible explanation is grounded in history. When, in the past, the executive branch overstepped its constitutional bounds in times of crisis, the behavior of lawyers was seldom praiseworthy, and sometimes blameworthy. After passage of the 1798 Sedition Act, government lawyers argued that it was a crime for ordinary citizens to "raise surmises and suspicions of the wisdom" of the president's "measures." During World War II, government lawyers once more elevated the "mystic cliché" of "military necessity" above ethical and legal responsibilities with consequences the nation came later deeply to regret. Thus, when the internment of Japanese Americans on the West Coast was challenged all the way up to the Supreme Court, government lawyers filed a brief arguing that the internment infringed no constitutional rule. But in that brief, government lawyers knowingly and intentionally succumbed to pressure from officials supervising the military by failing to disclose to the Court specific facts inconsistent with the army report claiming "military necessity" for evacuating Japanese Americans from the West Coast.[14] And, of course, during the decades of the Cold War, not one general counsel or other lawyer in the intelligence agencies called the improper conduct documented by the Church Committee into question. Lawyers, in short, are not immune to losing their judgment, even though it is lawyers above all who must guard the wise restraints that keep the nation free.

After 9/11, lawyers in the OLC veered once more from the office's best tradition of fair-minded impartiality. A familiar crisis mentality, to be sure, played a role. In interviews, OLC and White House lawyers stress their perception that "[s]omething fundamental had changed" on 9/11. But the felt necessities of a crisis moment do not explain everything. The OLC's vigorous assertion of presidential prerogative was not limited to the immediate days after 9/11. It endured for the months and years that followed. The OLC's responses, moreover, reflected the sweeping vision of executive supremacy described by Dick Cheney in the Iran-Contra minority report in 1987. And not all lawyers in the OLC or the executive branch agreed with this vision. Some expressed their discomfort and disagreement, and found themselves edged out of decision-making roles. Lawyers with a long history of advocating expansive visions of presidential power occupied the driver's seat.[15]

The crisis mentality, in short, does not entirely explain why OLC lawyers failed to live up to their own office's high standards. It certainly cannot account for their failure to mention contrary authority or to consult with diplomatic or military experts. In light of the known facts, a more probable additional explanation is that the OLC lawyers were well aware of what their client wanted. And just gave it. No shades of gray. No possible counterarguments. No explanations of the risks if the advice is followed.[16]

The flaws in the OLC's reasoning are most clearly on display in the August 2002 torture memo written by John Yoo and signed by Jay Bybee, which watered down the federal criminal bar against torture and asserted presidential power to set aside the laws banning torture that Congress had enacted. Yoo has since defended the torture memo, arguing that "the lawyer's job is to say, 'this is what the law says and this is what you can't do'" While claiming not to answer "moral and policy concerns," Yoo framed his analysis in terms of the possibility of "surprise attacks on innocent civilians, with WMDS." That is, Yoo presents his *legal* analysis in a way that sweeps away any *moral* objections to torture.[17] But the August 2002 memo does not even accurately say what the law is. And it certainly does not raise, let alone adequately address, what the Constitution and its Bill of Rights prohibit the president from doing. Rather, the legal analysis of the Yoo/Bybee memo ignores relevant laws bearing directly on the question at hand, omits case law and executive branch practice clearly implicated by the issues discussed, and makes legal arguments that are extraordinarily weak.

It is not just that Yoo and Bybee reached implausible conclusions in interpreting the federal torture statute and in vesting unchecked power in the President. Reading the torture statute, Yoo and Bybee looked for a definition of "severe pain" in a health benefits statute that defined "emergency medical conditions." In doing so, they bypassed authorities directly concerned with torture, and ignored voluminous court decisions interpreting the meaning of "torture" in the context of claims for political asylum. And while mentioning some of these authorities in passing, they incorporated none in their final analysis. As OLC later conceded, the health-benefits statutes refer to pain in a "very different context" from torture and for very different reasons. Further, the health-benefit statutes do not even define "severe pain." Indeed, "organ failure" (the operative term in the health benefits statute) is not even necessarily associated with pain at all. In other words, Yoo and Bybee ignored the directly relevant law, reached out to an unrelated statute, and wrenched out of context one phrase they could use to bypass the obvious broad meaning of the torture bar.[18]

The Yoo and Bybee analysis was also distorted by omission of clearly relevant statutes and cases. For example, Yoo and Bybee concluded that executive branch agents would have a "necessity defense" against any criminal charge of torture. But they failed to mention that, mere months before the torture memo, the Supreme Court had stated unequivocally that defendants could not argue in mitigation of criminal liability that their acts had been "necessary" unless Congress provided for such a defense explicitly in the statute. No such defense is in the torture statute. Moreover, the Yoo/Bybee memo omitted all mention of other federal statutes—including the War Crimes Act, the assault statute, and the Geneva Conventions—that contain prohibitions on physical coercion. It thus left the false impression that the torture statute was the only prohibition that bound CIA personnel.[19]

These other statutes did receive attention in a separate March 2003 OLC memo not yet in the public domain, described as "breathtaking" by one lawyer who saw it. This memo, explained Jane Mayer of the *New Yorker*, "dismissed virtually all national and international laws regulating the treatment of prisoners, including war-crimes and assault statutes, and it was radical in its view that in wartime the President can fight enemies by whatever means he sees fit."[20]

A fair, balanced, and professionally responsible opinion would have noted and described the extreme breadth of the OLC's final definition of "torture" to any client that wanted a full and fair analysis of the relevant law. It would also have noted the potential consequences if Congress, the courts, and the public disagreed with the extraordinary reading of the law. Lawyers cannot seal themselves off from all responsibility for the obvious consequences of their advice. With OLC's 2002 opinion characterizing torture as inflicting physical pain "equivalent in intensity to the pain accompanying serious physical injury, such as organ failure, impairment of bodily function, or even death," observers read the opinion to permit the pulling out of fingernails, "burning detainees with cigarettes, administering electric shocks to their genitals, hanging them by their wrists, submerging them in water to simulate drowning . . . and sexually humiliating them."[21] And while the OLC referenced past executive branch comments seemingly ruling out such practices, its final conclusions draw only selectively from the comments, and its ultimate rule would permit some, if not all, of these acts. Indeed, some of these practices were in fact used by the CIA and armed forces against detainees.[22] The OLC, secretly and abandoning caution, opened the door to adopting tactics of our enemies.

A balanced opinion would also have raised the interaction between the Administration's view of the Geneva Conventions and its view on torture. An inevitable implication of the OLC's conclusion was that the Geneva Conventions' requirement of a battlefield status hearing could be omitted, and, as a consequence, innocent bystanders detained along with combatants.[23] In tandem with the August 2002 memo on torture, this meant that it would be inevitable that innocent people would be tortured. It is difficult to know whether such an egregious and harmful legal judgment would have been made if the State Department, responsible for ensuring compliance with the Convention Against Torture had had a chance to see the opinion. In any case, a lawyer, particularly one in the service of the federal government, ought not to turn a blind eye to obvious facts.[24]

The Yoo/Bybee analysis of the president's constitutional powers as commander in chief suffered, however, from an even more significant omission. The OLC's central claim, to recap, was that Congress lacked power to regulate acts of a president claiming to act as commander in chief. Thus, they claimed, despite the law unequivocally banning torture, President Bush had unlimited power to order that captured detainees be tortured. The OLC failed to mention the historical and textual evidence piled up against this claim, including the Supreme Court's early precedent.[25] It also failed even to mention the most recent and authoritative opinion on presidential power in wartime: the *Youngstown* case.

Justice Robert Jackson's opinion in *Youngstown*, striking down President Truman's seizure of the nation's steel mills, has become the canonical statement of presidential wartime powers. A clever lawyer, no doubt, could try to distinguish the general principles announced in *Youngstown* by arguing that they apply only to actions within the United States; this would still, though, be a weak argument, given that the same principles have been applied overseas since 1804, and that President Bush has asserted counterterrorism power within the United States, such as the warrantless NSA spying on Americans. But a clever lawyer, and even a barely competent lawyer, would have cited

Youngstown and confronted it head-on. In a startling omission, Yoo and Bybee simply ignored the most important case on the matter at hand.[26]

There was, explained Georgetown Law School professor David Luban, "near consensus [in the legal academy] that the legal analysis in the torture memo was bizarre." A group of former OLC lawyers issued a "statement of principles" reminding the present OLC of its duty to provide "an accurate and honest assessment of applicable law, even if that advice will constrain the administration's pursuit of desired policies." Distinguished legal philosopher Jeremy Waldron termed the memo "dispiriting and shameful," and explained how the memo evinced a "bewildering refusal" to follow usual legal methods of textual analysis. Harold Hongju Koh, Dean of the Yale Law School and a former OLC lawyer, described the memo as the "most clearly erroneous legal opinion" he had ever read.[27]

The Yoo/Bybee legal opinion was not the result of two OLC lawyers going on a frolic of their own. On the contrary, the memo "was vetted by a larger number of officials, including lawyers at the National Security Council, the White House Counsel's office, and Vice President Cheney's office." News reporters have unearthed evidence that the torture memos were the product of a process directed by ideologues led by Iran-Contra minority committee veteran David Addington, who "generally excluded dissenters" and used the post-9/11 environment as an opportunity to put into practice his and Cheney's cherished ideals of executive branch unilateralism. Addington's "main man at Justice," and author of almost all the key OLC opinions on national security issues and presidential power, was his protégé John Yoo. According to one news report, "Bybee, Yoo, and Addington saw the torture statute . . . as an unwarranted infringement on executive-branch power."[28]

The OLC August 2002 legal opinion on torture and others that followed were the product of "a small group of conservative legal officials at the White House, the Justice Department, and the Defense Department" rather than a reflection of the OLC's best institutional tradition. According to military lawyers, the internal debate on the applicability of the Geneva Conventions to the Taliban and al Qaeda was "not an open and honest discussion." The insular and uncritical nature of debate since 9/11 leads some Washington journalists to suggest that President Bush may have become "the most isolated president in modern history, at least since the late-stage Richard Nixon," given how constricted his immediate policy circle has become. For example, the office of then–White House counsel Alberto Gonzales ignored the concerns raised by both the State Department and the military's own lawyers about stripping some combatants of Geneva's protections. It appears that the State Department—which deals with issues of torture in totalitarian states on a regular basis—simply did not get a look-in during the drafting of the OLC's torture memos.

Likewise, with the backing of the President and Vice-President, Addington pressed forward to create a system of military tribunals allowing any nonciti-zen captured anywhere in the world to be subject to military trial with wholly inadequate procedures (which the Supreme Court invalidated in the 2006 *Hamdan* decision). Once more, vital legal opinions were sought, and seemingly obtained, from John Yoo. Yet again, the process was secretive and stripped of consultation, even within the executive branch.[29]

Policy makers also fought to ensure that internal dissenters, who did not toe the preferred line of unlimited presidential power, were simply cut out of the decision-making process. Tellingly, Addington worked hard to "scale back the authority of lawyers in the uniformed services," replacing seasoned legal pro-fessionals with hardened ideologues, for the vision of unchecked executive power found staunch opponents in many military lawyers. Men and women who valued the honor and reputation of the armed services, military lawyers often proved unwilling to just go along with Cheney, Addington, and Yoo's wholesale abandonment of American traditions. Several military lawyers, in particular Alberto J. Mora, the navy's general counsel, argued strenuously against the effort to bypass the Geneva Conventions and water down protec-tions against torture. But these military lawyers were simply shut off, some-times bluntly told that they were not allowed access to new policies as they developed. Mora learned of abusive interrogation techniques at Guantánamo in October 2002, and pressed Secretary Rumsfeld for stricter controls; he suc-ceeded, but only temporarily. When it came to establishing formal rules for the armed services, Mora's attempts to ensure that the rules barred coercive treatment failed when the Defense Department "outflanked" him by obtain-ing "a separate, overarching opinion from the Office of Legal Counsel" on coercive interrogations by the military, written by John Yoo—an opinion that, in effect, gutted all protections against torture. After learning of Yoo's opinion, Mora sought to resist the incorporation of Yoo's views into military practice. But Mora was overruled by his boss, William Haynes, the Pentagon's general counsel. Haynes too was one of the anointed inner circle; he had been Addington's special assistant while at the Pentagon in the late 1980s.[30]

The President and his lawyers assert that their extravagant claims to power flow from new military exigencies in a time of terror. But this claim is hard to sustain in light of the concerted opposition of career military personnel such as Mora. The post-9/11 vision of unchecked executive power, in other words, did not follow from military exigencies of the post-9/11 world. It was not even endorsed by the men and women within the executive most familiar with modern warfare. On the contrary, establishing unchecked executive power meant that military lawyers and their concerns had to be silenced.

Even within the Justice Department, legal justifications for controversial torture, detention, and spying policies were ringed around with "remarkable" secrecy, with dissenters carefully excluded. The lawyer to succeed Jay Bybee as the head of OLC, law professor Jack Goldsmith, was isolated by Addington for challenging the August 2002 torture memo. When Deputy Attorney General James Comey, a well-respected former U.S. attorney from New York, balked at the Administration's request for sign-off on the warrantless NSA's domestic spying, the White House simply went around him too. To bypass Comey, White House Chief of Staff Andrew Card and White House Counsel Alberto Gonzales made a dramatic bedside visit to Attorney General John Ashcroft, who was in the hospital with a rare and painful pancreatic disease, seeking the Justice Department's continued approval of spying without warrants in the United States. Thanks to Comey's resistance to unchecked surveillance, however, the White House was forced to reform procedural components of the surveillance program in 2004. But since public information about the initial program, and the procedural reforms Comey pushed, has not been forthcoming, it is impossible to assess the significance of this effort.[31]

Comey resigned in 2005, commending those "committed to getting it right" at the Justice Department, and noting that, "some of them did pay a price for their commitment to right, but they wouldn't have it any other way." After his resignation, Comey spoke at the University of Richmond Law School. He concluded his speech by urging law students "to participate and demand the details" in debates on security issues. "Understand them and then take a position. If we do that, [we] will be in a great place. When we look back thirty years from now, whether people agree or disagree, I hope they will say, 'We looked into it; we thought about it; we chewed on it, and we did the best we could.'"[32] The full and vigorous debate Comey urged is, of course, precisely what Addington and his allies tried to stifle even within the executive branch. They succeeded in shifting the debate in Congress and in public regarding rules for CIA interrogation policy, indefinite detention, and military commissions.

Secrecy smothered signs of dramatic changes in the law; they rose to public attention only when leaks and intrepid investigative reporting discovered them. Attorney General Gonzales, with circular opaqueness, explained the Administration's refusal to disclose OLC memos (such as the March 2003 memo on torture rules for the military) by saying that "non–public OLC opinions are not disclosed outside the executive branch."[33] But the fact that the Administration backed off its definition of torture as soon as it became publicly known, and has declined to assert to the public its most aggressive theories of executive power suggests that these memos were not disclosed simply because they were indefensible. And senior officials knew it.

No secrets worthy of protection are found in the OLC opinions on torture.[34] On the contrary, as in the Cold War, excessive secrecy is today a handmaiden of abuse. In a democracy that rests upon checks and balances, and with a "government of laws and not of men," Congress and the public without doubt are entitled to know if and when a president believes he can ignore the law. Every citizen is entitled, at the least, to know what the law of the land is, and what powers are delegated to or seized by America's leaders. Excessive secrecy served in the Cold War, and serves now, the executive branch's interest in accumulating power and avoiding embarrassment. The question for today is how Congress and the public can and will respond.

Conclusion:
A Republic, If You Can Keep It

A lady asked Dr. Franklin [as he left the Philadelphia Constitutional Convention] Well Doctor what have we got a republic or a monarchy. A republic replied the Doctor if you can keep it.
   —Papers of Dr. James McHenry on the Federal Convention of 1787[1]

The Constitution endures so long as the American people preserve it.

Since 1787, each new generation of Americans has asked itself whether it would take up the "unfinished work" begun by Franklin and his fellow delegates. Will, today, the form of government established in the Constitution of 1787 persevere? Or, by fear or inadvertence, will it slip away?[2]

In the name of national security, the Administration of President George W. Bush claims that the Constitution's structure of separated branches sharing powers is inadequate. It claims we must place unfettered, absolute trust in the executive branch. Our nation's history—from the Sedition Act to the illicit domestic spying and disruption and the harmful foreign covert actions exposed by the Church Committee—teaches that such claims are dangerous, as well as unfounded. As the Church Committee wrote, imprecise and open-ended authorizations, "coupled with the absence of any outside scrutiny," invariably have led "to improper use of intrusive techniques against American citizens who posed no criminal or national security threat to the country."[3] And the actions of the Bush Administration since 9/11 prove once again that power cannot be safely entrusted to one person alone.

With an arrogance born of historical amnesia, the Bush Administration invoked 9/11 to claim a power unprecedented on this side of the North Atlantic to suspend or wholly circumvent laws passed by Congress barring torture, detention without judicial review, and wiretapping without warrants. Its claims were *not* simply responses to the threat manifested on 9/11. Rather, fifteen years earlier, Dick Cheney and David Addington had made the very same claims for sweeping executive power in their Iran-Contra minority report. September 11 gave them the opportunity to implement this long-cherished vision, and a chance to slander and scare opponents with the smear of disloyalty.

Why should we be concerned about the monarchist claims of executive power? We have shown that these claims contravene the Founding Generation's understanding of human nature, the language of the Constitution, the history of its adoption, and judicial precedent. But the case against the monarchical vision of presidential power is not just that it is wrong. It is also that it is harmful to American interests. Said to make us safer, it in fact makes us less secure.

Because all human beings are flawed, and none are "angels," and because power corrupts, our Constitution sought to increase the chance of wise—and reduce the chance of foolish—decisions by involving all three branches in important decisions. The Bush Administration believes only the executive, or a small coterie within the executive, should determine key policies, acting largely in secret. As they reject a role for the other branches at home, so they act internationally without genuine consultations with our allies overseas.

The Administration insists that its plunge into torture, its lawless spying, and its lock-up of innocents have made the country safer. Beyond mere posturing, they provide little evidence to back up their claims. Executive unilateralism not only undermines the delicate balance of our Constitution, but also lessens our human liberties and hurts vital counterterrorism campaigns. How? Our reputation has always mattered. In 1607, Massachusetts governor John Winthrop warned his fellow colonists that because they were a "City on a Hill," "the eyes of all people are upon us."[4] Thomas Jefferson began the Declaration of Independence by invoking the need for a "decent respect to the opinions of mankind." In today's battle against stateless terrorists, who are undeterred by law, morality, or the mightiest military power on earth, our reputation matters greatly.

Despite its military edge, the United States cannot force needed aid and cooperation from allies. Indeed, our status as lone superpower means that only by persuading other nations—and their citizens—that our values and interests align with theirs, and so merit support, can America maintain its influence in the world. Military might, even extended to the globe's corners, is not a sufficient condition for achieving America's safety or its democratic ideals at home. To be "dictatress of the world," warned John Quincy Adams in 1821, America "would be no longer the ruler of her own spirit." A national security policy loosed from the bounds of law, and conducted at the executive's discretion, will unfailingly lapse into hypocrisy and mendacity that alienate our allies and corrode the vitality of the world's oldest democracy.[5]

The 9/11 Commission concluded that success against the terrorists themselves is not simply a matter of killing or capturing people. It means neutralizing their ideology. It means stopping their ideas from spreading, viruslike, seeding new recruits, new threats. Thus, French scholar Giles Kepel explains that "the Bush Administration's war on terror . . . succeeded in stirring up unprecedented hatred for America around the world." Kepel accordingly ranks America's decision to adopt its enemies' tactics as bin Laden's most important post-9/11 victory. By undermining America's moral credibility, the administration's hypocrisies lent unwarranted credence to the apocalyptic, confrontational ideologies of bin Laden and his fellow travelers, ideologies that seek to depict America and Europe as implacably hostile to Islam in an effort to garner wider support in the Muslim world.[6]

Making the executive supreme makes the nation no safer—either from its enemies or its own worse impulses. Indeed, the abiding genius of the Founding Generation was its rejection of the idea that unchecked unilateral power is ever properly vested in any one branch of government. Our government was framed "to control itself," as James Madison wrote in the *Federalist Papers*. "Ambition must be made to counteract ambition." Dividing powers between three branches, the Founders harnessed human passions in the cause of limited government. Madison, again writing in the *Federalist Papers*, provided the enduring explanation for this division of government: "The accumulation of all powers, legislative, executive, and judiciary, in the same hands, whether of one, a few, or many, and whether hereditary, self-appointed, or elective, may justly be pronounced the very definition of tyranny." For this reason, the framers and ratifiers of the Constitution entrenched "the essential precaution in favor of liberty" by fashioning a Constitution of separate branches that shared powers so that "the *whole* power of one department" would never be exercised "by the same hands which possess the *whole* power of another department."[7]

Under our Constitution, the people therefore elect a "*body* of citizens" in Congress with "enlightened views and virtuous sentiments."[8] These representatives have the lion's share of national power—unless they surrender their independent power. Many of those powers concern war making and foreign affairs, and the latter are often inextricable from questions of war and peace. But a monarchical vision of presidential power neuters these congressional powers. It renders hollow the elaborate process of representative democracy if a single person can alter in secret the laws that protect human liberty and bodily integrity, and then cloud from public sight the consequences of these acts.

The threat of terrorism will not end soon. To the contrary, accelerating technological change makes it easier to unleash destructive force against innocents. This time of terror will last well into the twenty-first century.[9] Al Qaeda and its terrorist allies act without moral qualms. Without question, our responses must be resolute, resourceful, and determined. But in their zeal to help defend the nation, the President and his subordinates have lost sight of the Constitution's guidance without clear gains to the nation's safety. Reaction to the errors and excesses of the Bush Administration, however, cannot mean a retreat into fortress America. As former Church Committee member Gary Hart warned, "Insecurity has shredded national boundaries, leapfrogged great armies, and is all around us."[10] A retreat from the world would not make us safer.

Recognizing therefore that the battles will be long and hard, the Republic must nonetheless endure. Staying the course charted by the original Constitution means resisting the lures of unchecked power, which cannot be a long-term solution and which, in any case, works poorly even in the short-term. Constitutional government under law, the kind crafted in the Constitution and left to succeeding generations' care, demands the division and dispersion of power between the three branches.

So, what can we do? First and foremost, to rebuild the Constitution's checks and balances, the Congress must act—as the Supreme Court began to do in its 2006 decision on military commissions—by enacting meaningful limiting legislation and by holding effective oversight hearings. This process began in fall 2006, as legislators considered a gamut of legislation on military commissions, coercive interrogations, and indefinite lockup. But this debate has been hindered by a lack of information and a surfeit of partisanship. Instead of measured debate and meaningful responses, Congress reduced accountability, most importantly by cutting back on the protection of habeas corpus. For the gain of a few sound bites in a midterm election, legislators of both parties shamefully sold a heritage of historical liberty dating back to the Magna Carta. All too often indeed, we have seen, "the text of the Constitution places all the power in Congress, but the structure of the presidency is such, and the structure of Congress is such, that the power tends to flow from Congress to the presidency and that leadership tends to be looked for in the President." Congress's unwillingness to take responsibility for difficult security decisions shows predictable human weakness. As Yale law scholar Charles Black noted in 1975, "Pretending not to have power is a way of passing the buck; and Congress has abundantly passed the buck."[11]

Torture policy, extraordinary rendition, warrantless domestic spying, indefinite presidential lockup: the executive branch developed all of these tactics without Congress's knowledge and with total disregard for statutory prohibitions. Even after the 2006 election, government lawyers continued to press the monarchical executive theory in a challenge to the NSA's warrantless domestic spying presented in Michigan federal court. And in Washington, D.C., other Justice Department lawyers argued that one Guantánamo detainee should not be permitted to speak to his lawyer lest he reveal what coercive tactics (or torture) were used in his interrogation. But Congress can make a difference here. Sixty years ago, Senator Harry Truman knew that to monitor the activities of the Roosevelt Administration was not to seek revenge or to obstruct the government—it was the only way to assure that taxpayer interests would be protected and that the war would be waged effectively. Oversight alone, to be sure, rarely will be enough to steer policy. But does anybody truly believe that we would have seen the explosion of illegal activity, unjustifiable torture, and legal end runs had the Administration been required to defend its actions before empowered and diligent congressional overseers?

Congress will change its ways when voters start demanding that it fulfill its Constitutional mandate. We need a new "contract" between representatives and their electors, one in which all recognize that neither security nor liberty are partisan issues, and that a Congress that leaves too much to the White House is a Congress that falls far short of its duties. Voters, both Democratic and Republican, must ask their candidates whether they are willing to fulfill their constitutional responsibilities.

Yet, to do so means overcoming long-standing structural and partisan difficulties. The Bush Administration has parlayed national security into a partisan issue, stifling and polarizing debate, echoing the days of the Alien and Sedition Acts.[12] Control of the White House and Congress by one party inevitably dampens oversight even more. According to Harvard Law School professor Daryl Levinson, political party affiliation is now "a much more important variable in predicting the behavior of members of Congress vis-à-vis the President than the fact that these members work in the legislative branch." From the start of national politics, the theory of separate branches with distinct institutional interests foundered against the reality of national political parties. Since the election of 1800, moreover, chief executives have claimed a special popular mandate in election victories, and asserted a transcendent claim to national leadership that allowed legislators to ride a president's coat tails. This mythic mandate, political scientist Robert Dahl argues, "not only impairs deliberation but also other means to a more enlightened understanding on the part of citizens and the Congress" of the common good.[13]

Congress today is also brutally fissured. In the House, most seats are blatantly gerrymandered to reduce democratic competition and push winners away from the center. Legislators stagger under a flood of federal campaign monies. Democracy is compromised in this fractious, dollars-soaked milieu. But the stakes today are too high, both for political parties and the American people, for corrosive partisan games to persist.[14]

There are, moreover, 535 members of Congress, speaking in a Babel of voices; there is but one president. The executive branch benefits from "unity" and "duration," making decision-making quicker, although not wiser. Today, the executive also draws on intelligence resources backed by at least forty-four billion dollars spread across sixteen intelligence agencies that employ one hundred thousand agents and analysts. It controls what information the Congress and the people get from the intelligence community, and thus can contort public understanding of the value of intelligence activities.[15]

Overcoming partisanship, the myth of the presidential mandate, and the structural disadvantages of being a multimember body, demand more than a one-time fix. As an initial matter, the Church Committee demonstrated that nonpartisan investigations and oversight are feasible even in the face of presidential intransigence. And the Church Committee cannot be written off as an isolated incident. The 9/11 Commission similarly strived to overcome party bias, even arranging its seating to break up clusters of Republicans and Democrats. Similarly, three decades before the Church Committee, Harry Truman, as a senator, conducted a vast investigation that effectively exposed military waste and inefficiency during World War II, even while his own party held the White House.[16]

Beyond reducing partisanship, Congress needs to find enduring statutory mechanisms to ensure that it has the information and the corrective devices to identify and stop mission creep, plausible deniability, and outright flouting of the law. It still needs, in other words, to heed the calls for comprehensive statutory organization of intelligence agencies that came from both the Church Committee and the 9/11 Commission. Pivotal to both the Church Committee and 9/11 Commission reform agendas was the need for new framework statutes for intelligence agencies, laws that laid down clear responsibilities and, by implication, imposed clear limits on intelligence work. Yet this need, acknowledged by various Congresses and White Houses, has never been met.[17]

Congress has failed to match the rapid growth of intelligence agencies with a legal infrastructure for supervising and restraining those agencies. More than fifty years after the National Security Act, the CIA still operates with skeletal statutory guidance. The NSA only recently obtained a statutory mandate—but one that is still far too ambiguous. "Sunshine" laws, designed to promote openness in government, make too many exceptions for the national security state. By contrast, the New Deal led to tremendous growth in the federal bureaucratic apparatus for conducting domestic policy. Congress, the executive branch, and the courts nevertheless developed new tools to preserve the checks and balances of constitutional governance. Congress, for example, enacted the Administrative Procedure Act, which elaborated procedural frameworks for agency rule-making and adjudications. Courts developed judicial doctrines that ensured that agencies took their rule-making and adjudication roles seriously. And agencies developed internal versions of separated powers (for example, firewalls between agency enforcement and agency adjudication staff) to improve the quality of governance.[18]

Carefully designated framework statutes are needed to delineate clear missions. Recognizing the fickleness of partisan tides, Congress also needs to entrench oversight structures that ensure a continuous flow of accurate information about the functioning (and malfunctioning) of the executive branch. New statutes, for example, would contain stronger internal checking mechanisms, such as inspectors general and special counsel. Whistleblowers would receive protection from retaliatory action. As Georgetown law professor Neal Katyal suggests, Congress might want to create dedicated channels for anonymous dissent from the field, such as the Foreign Service currently has. At present even internal dissent is stifled. In one telling incident in mid-2006, a CIA contractor who posted on an internal blog a criticism of the Administration's decision to use coercive interrogation measures had her job terminated and was subsequently threatened with criminal prosecution for her comments.[19]

Effective national security policy also demands far more openness. Unregulated secrecy hides error and bureaucratic failure from public sight. As political theorist Sissela Bok explains in her book on the topic, it allows bureaucrats "to correct mistakes and to reverse direction . . . often without embarrassing explanation." Secrecy is necessary on occasion. But it often makes us less safe. Legislators (and the public) are disabled from meaningful debate when the executive branch conceals vital changes in law and policy. Misrepresentations also abound in Administration speechifying on national security. Secretary of State Condoleezza Rice promised that prisoner transfers would not end in torture. President Bush implied that spying would not be conducted without warrants. And he said simply that "we don't sanction torture," trading on our natural disbelief that America could or would stealthily turn into a nation that uses the rack and the screw. In each case, these were outright deceptions, or, at a minimum, blatant misrepresentations.[20]

Secrecy and misrepresentation have a place in the bag of national security policy makers—but only when used to shelter the national interest.[21] Secrecy ought not be used to obscure excesses, embarrassments, and failures of the executive branch—or to prevent much needed course corrections. But the executive branch rarely will make honest differentiations between these two categories; it will, more often than not, read the evidence in its own favor. Moreover, the executive branch's interest in keeping secrets can compound its failure to respond to real security problems when the problem of retaining secrets overtakes the need to deal with real risks. Indeed, the 9/11 Commission's members properly condemned the Defense Department and the Federal Aviation Authority for hiding details of the failures in military responses to the attacks from the Commission and the public. Such failures are better identified and fixed than glossed over.[22]

External checks on executive branch classification decisions are therefore essential. Today, the Administration has carefully managed the press's access to classified information. Six months after the *New York Times* first broke the story of NSA warrantless spying, the Justice Department convened a grand jury in Alexandria, Virginia, to pursue indictments under the Espionage Act, a criminal statute long considered in tension with the First Amendment.

In Congress, it made sure that "[i]nformed questions [were] cut off at the source." This is an unconscionable failure of congressional will that renders the nation far less safe. The Church Committee proved that congressional bodies can handle national security "secrets" with care. It further proved that many secrecy claims were little more than makeweight efforts to block the public from learning of an agency's mistakes and misdeeds. This remains true today. Questions about what can properly be kept from the public are entirely in the hands of presidents, leaving them free to declassify selectively for narrow partisan or protective ends. Again, Congress has the tools to address excessive secrecy, both by investigations and by laws, should it decide to use them.[23]

Secrecy also fosters public hypocrisy. Presumably, the Secretary of State and the President made their misleading statements because, while willing to benefit from torture, they understood the revulsion the rest of the world and most Americans would have to such methods. But their hypocrisy, once exposed, causes even greater harm. We believe Americans still would say, as the Church Committee concluded, that while "crisis makes it tempting to ignore the wise restraints that make [us] free . . . each time we do so, each time the means we use are wrong, our inner strength, the strength that makes us free is lessened."[24]

At the beginning of the chain of democratic responsibility stand the people. It is the people who are entitled to decide the course of the Republic based on a clear view of the facts. They alone can call their legislators and presidents to account and keep the Constitution alive. To meet Franklin's challenge in times of terror is their collective work of conscience. For, as Judge Learned Hand eloquently argued, democracy lives or dies in the hearts and minds of its citizens, and "when it dies there, no constitution, no law, no court can save it."[25]

What was wrought with human hands in Philadelphia in 1787 can today by human hands be undone. Benjamin Franklin, of course, did not see his successors' task as an easy one; nor was it. And yet it is our task, the "great task remaining before" us, a task that demands what Lincoln at Gettysburg termed "the last full measure of devotion," to carry on, to persist another step into the future, for another generation, bearing unceasingly forward against the tide "the unfinished work" of America's Constitution.

Acknowledgments

We should first acknowledge the pleasure each of us had in working with the other in conceiving, drafting, and editing this book. The Brennan Center for Justice at NYU School of Law—where we both work—has been, and continues to be, an exciting and welcoming place for those interested in transformative ideas coupled with effective acts.

Without the help of Antrina Richardson, the book would never have been produced. Each of us claims the other's handwriting was worse, but Antrina had to struggle with more of the handwriting of the elder writer, who does all first drafts by hand.

Ross M. Benjamin and Ana Muñoz, two first-rate young writers and thinkers, supplied valuable, thoughtful, and substantive research, editing, and mechanical support. We further benefited from thoughtful reading and comments on portions of the book from Edward Burlingame, Stephen Gillers, David Greenwald, Loch Johnson, Eric Lane, Ronan McCrea, Henry Monaghan, Christopher Muller, Burt Neuborne, E. Joshua Rosenkranz, Zoe A. Salzman, Seema Shah, Stephen J. Schulhofer, Serrin Turner, and Michael Waldman. What we say should not be mistaken for their views. All errors, of course, remain ours. Thanks are also owed to our editor at The New Press, Diane Wachtell—whose edits and comments improved the text immensely—and her assistants Joel Ariaratnam and Melissa Leviste.

Finally, we are deeply grateful for the love, support, and wise advice we get from our wonderful wives Ricky and Margaret.

Notes

Introduction

1. For Nixon's statements to the Church Committee, see "Appendix: Select Committee Interrogations for Former President Richard M. Nixon," in *Final Report of the Select Committee to Study Governmental Operations with Respect to Intelligence Activities, United States Senate, Book IV: Supplemental Detailed Staff Reports on Foreign and Military Intelligence* (1976), 157–58. Nixon quoted in Derek Jinks and David Sloss, "Is the President Bound by the Geneva Conventions?" *Cornell Law Review* 90 (2004), 97, 149. For the minority report, see Report of the Congressional Committees Investigating the Iran-Contra Affair, with Supplemental, Minority, and Additional Views, S. Rep. No. 100-216, H. Rep. No. 100-433 (1987), 465.
2. See Benjamin F. Wright, "The Federalist on the Nature of Political Man," *Ethics* 59 (1949), 1.
3. *The Federalist*, No. 51, Clinton Rossiter, ed. (New York: Mentor Books, 1961), 322 (emphasis added).
4. This is also called the "separation of powers." Because that term has complex, multiple meanings, we do not use it. See Garry Wills, *Explaining America: The Federalist* (New York: Penguin Books, 2001), 97–161; William B. Gwyn, "The Indeterminacy of the Separation of Powers and the Federal Courts," *George Washington Law Review* 47 (1989), 474.
5. See Geoffrey R. Stone, *Perilous Times: Free Speech in Wartime, From the Sedition Act of 1798 to the War on Terrorism* (New York: W.W. Norton, 2004); Arthur M. Schlesinger Jr., *The Imperial Presidency* (New York: Mariner Books, 2004).
6. For the Alien and Sedition Acts, see John Chester Miller, *Crisis in Freedom: The Alien and Sedition Acts* (Boston: Little, Brown, 1951); Stone, 16–78. For "served primarily," Cooper, and convictions, see Stone, 56, 63, 67.
7. For Palmer Raids, see Stone, 135–233; Edwin Palmer Hoyt, *The Palmer Raids* (New York: Seabury Press, 1969); William Preston, *Aliens and Dissenters: Federal Suppression of Radicals, 1903–1933* (Cambridge: Harvard University Press, 1963). For Palmer quote, see Stone, 224 (Attorney General A. Mitchell Palmer on Charges Made against Department of Justice by Louis F. Post and Others, Hearings before the House Committee on Rules, 66th Cong, 2d Sess 27 [1920]).
8. For Japanese American internment, see Peter Irons, *Justice at War: The Story of the Japanese American Internment Cases* (New York: Oxford University Press, 1983); Roger Daniels, *Prisoners Without Trial: Japanese-Americans in World War II* (New York: Hill and Wang, 1993). For Jackson and FBI quotes, see Stone, 284, 288, 298.

9. For criticism of DeWitt, see Stone, 295, and Irons, 212–18, 278–310. For "a Jap is a Jap," see Stone, 292 (quoting testimony before the House Naval Affairs Subcommittee, April 13, 1943). For "white man's country," see Stone, 294. As to electoral politics, 1942 was an election year. Roosevelt preferred to emphasize the war in Europe first; incarcerating the Japanese Americans helped to "pacify" those who wanted to focus first on Asia, and to quell West Coast hysteria. Stone, 296.

10. See 376 U.S. 254, 276 (1964). The Palmer Raids were soundly condemned by legal groups when they occurred. In 1924 a new Attorney General, Harlan Fiske Stone, described the Justice Department under his predecessor as "lawless," engaging in "many practices which were brutal and tyrannical in the extreme." See Alpheus Thomas Mason, *Harlan Fiske Stone: Pillar of the Law* (New York: Viking, 1956), 149.

11. Civil Liberties Act of 1988, Pub. L. No. 100-383, 102 Stat. 903, 1988. At the Constitution's bicentennial in 1976, President Gerald Ford issued Presidential Proclamation No. 4417, acknowledging that the evacuation and internment of Japanese citizens was "wrong" and calling "upon the American people to affirm with me this American Promise—that we have learned from the tragedy of that long-ago experience" and "resolve that this kind of action shall never again be repeated." Stone, 305 (quoting 3 C.F.R. Proc 4417 [February 19, 1976]).

12. The Supreme Court upheld the detentions in *Korematsu v. United States,* 323 U.S. 214 (1944), in which the majority stated: "We cannot reject as unfounded the judgment of the military authorities . . . that there were disloyal members of the [Japanese American] population, whose number and strength could not be precisely and quickly ascertained. . . . To cast this case into outlines of racial prejudice . . . confuses the issue." Later, many justices expressed shame and regret at their decision. Stone, 304–5.

13. See Mark Mazzetti, "Spymaster Tells Size of Secret Spy Force," *New York Times,* April 21, 2006, A21; see also Mark M. Lowenthal, *Intelligence: From Secrets to Policy* (Washington, DC: CQ Press, 2000), 24–39.

14. The Committee's full name was the "United States Senate Select Committee to Study Governmental Operations With Respect to Intelligence Activities." The Church Committee reports we cite most extensively are: *Final Report of the Select Committee to Study Governmental Operations With Respect to Intelligence Activities, United States Senate, Book I: Foreign and Military Intelligence* (1976), hereafter *Bk. I; Book II: Intelligence Activities and the Rights of Americans* (1976), hereafter *Bk. II; Book III: Supplementary Detailed Staff Reports on Intelligence Activities and the Rights of Americans* (1976), hereafter *Bk. III; Interim Report: Alleged Assassination Plots Involving Foreign Leaders* (1975), hereafter *Assassinations.* For the Church Committee hearings, see *Hearings Before the Select Committee to Study Government Operations With Respect to Intelligence Activities of the United States Senate, Vol. 1: Unauthorized Storage of Toxic Agents* (1975); *Vol. 2: Huston Plan* (1975); *Vol. 3: Internal Revenue Service* (1975); *Vol. 4: Mail Opening* (1975); *Vol. 5: The National Security Agency and Fourth Amendment Rights* (1975); *Vol. 6: Federal Bureau of Investigation* (1975); and *Vol. 7: Covert Action* (1975). For electronic versions, see http://www.aarclibrary .org/publib/church/reports/contents.html. Books on the Church Committee include Loch Johnson, *A Season of Inquiry: The Senate Intelligence Investigation* (Lex-

ington: University Press of Kentucky, 1985); Frank John Smist, *Congress Oversees the United States Intelligence Community, 1947–1994* (Knoxville: University of Tennessee Press, 1994), 25–81; LeRoy Ashby and Rod Gramer, *Fighting the Odds: The Life of Senator Frank Church* (Pullman: Washington State University Press, 1994), 453, 468–92.

15. *Bk. II*, 137.
16. *Assassinations*, 11–12, 277–78.
17. *Youngstown Sheet and Tube v. Sawyer,* 343 U.S. 579, 654 (1952).
18. For "never gave it a thought," see *Bk. II*, 140 (quoting George C. Moore's testimony of November 3, 1975, 83).
19. Scott Shane and Eric Lichtblau, "Cheney Pushed U.S. to Widen Eavesdropping," *New York Times*, May 14, 2006, A1; Siobhan Gorman, "Wiretapping Preoccupied Hayden at NSA," *Baltimore Sun*, May 14, 2006.
20. See letter from General Colin S. Powell to Senator John McCain, September 13, 2006 (on file with authors); Lieutenant General (Ret.) David W. Barno, "Challenges in Fighting a Global Insurgency," *Parameters: U.S. Army War College Quarterly* 36 (2006), 15.
21. Hence some of the fiercest criticism of executive overreaching has come from the Right. See, e.g., Bob Barr, "NSA Kabuki Theater," *Findlaw,* February 9, 2006, available at www.findlaw.com.
22. Second Inaugural Address, March 4, 1865, available at http://www.yale.edu/lawweb/avalon/presiden/inaug/lincoln2.htm.

Chapter 1: Flawed Mandates

1. *Bk. I*, 109. For Cold War documents, see http://www.wilsoncenter.org/index.cfm?fuseaction=topics.home&topic_id=1409.
2. For first-hand account of the Cuban Missile Crisis, see Robert Kennedy, *Thirteen Days: A Memoir of the Cuban Missile Crisis* (New York: W.W. Norton, 1969).
3. For exaggeration of the domestic Communist threat, see Haynes Johnson, *The Age of Anxiety: McCarthyism to Terrorism* (Orlando: Harcourt, 2005); Richard H. Rovere, *Senator Joe McCarthy* (New York: Harcourt, 1959).
4. See *Bk. 1*, 50, and *Assassinations*, 259, n. 1 (quoting James Doolittle et al, *The Report on the Covert Activities of the Central Intelligence Agency*, September 30, 1954). For Doolittle Raid, see Carroll V. Glines, *Doolittle's Tokyo Raiders* (Princeton: Van Nostrand, 1964).
5. For FBI history, see *Bk. II*, 21–136, and *Bk. III*, 373–558. For the FBI's antecedents, see *Bk. II*, 23–28, and *Bk. III*, 378–406. For additional perspectives on FBI history, see Richard Gid Powers, *Broken: The Troubled Past and Uncertain Future of the FBI* (New York: Free Press, 2004); Curt Gentry, *J. Edgar Hoover: The Man and His Secrets* (New York: W.W. Norton, 1991); John Elliff, *The Reform of FBI Intelligence Operations* (Princeton: Princeton University Press, 1979).
6. For Stone's views on the Bureau of Investigation, see *Bk. II*, 23 (quoting letter from Harlan Fiske Stone to Jack Alexander, September 21, 1937), 149. For Hoover quotes, see *Bk. III*, 384.
7. For the Palmer Raids report and the reaction of the Justice Department, see *Bk. III*, 385 (quoting the National Popular Government League, *Report Upon the Ille-*

gal Practices of the United States Department of Justice, May 1920; memoranda from J. Edgar Hoover to General Churchill, January 23, 1920, and May 13, 1920).

8. For Stone's warning, see *Bk. II*, 23 (quoting *New York Times*, May 10, 1924). For Stone's order, see *Bk. II*, 24 (quoting Stone letter to Hoover, May 13, 1924).

9. For Hoover's appointment and the ACLU's support, see *Bk. III*, 388–89.

10. See *Bk. III*, 391 (quoting memo from Hoover to Attorney General, January 2, 1932).

11. For Roosevelt-Hoover conversations, see *Bk. II*, 24–27; *Bk. III*, 391–406. When Roosevelt authorized FBI investigations of "subversives" in 1940, he instructed that they be limited "insofar as possible to aliens." *Bk. II*, 36 (quoting confidential memorandum from President Roosevelt to Attorney General Jackson, May 21, 1940). But see *Bk. III*, 463 (quoting statement of President Truman, July 24, 1950); ibid., 464 (quoting letter from Hoover to Sherman Adams, Assistant to the President, January 28, 1953; attached memorandum on "FBI Liaison Activities," January 26, 1953, and statement of President Eisenhower, December 15, 1953).

12. For "believed imperative," see *Bk. III*, 398 (quoting memo from Hoover, enclosed with a letter from Cummings to the President, October 20, 1938). For "the strictest confidence," see *Bk. II*, 28 (quoting letter from Cummings to the President, October 20, 1938).

13. *Bk. III*, 411 (quoting Robert H. Jackson, "The Federal Prosecutor," *Journal of the American Judicature Society* [June 1940], 18); *Bk. II*, 30.

14. *Bk. III*, 411–12 (quoting Robert H. Jackson, *The Supreme Court in the American System of Government* [New York: Harper Torchbook, 1963], 70–71). For Jackson at Nuremberg, see *Trial of the Major War Criminals Before the International Military Tribunal* (Nuremberg: IMT, 1947), 98–155; Robert H. Jackson, *The Nürnberg Case* (New York: Alfred A. Knopf, 1947).

15. For early domestic intelligence generally, see *Bk. II,* 30–34, and *Bk. III*, 412–17. For Lindbergh, see *Bk. II*, 33 (citing memorandum from Stephen Early, Secretary to the President, to J. Edgar Hoover, June 17, 1940). For League for Fair Play, see *Bk. II*, 32, and *Bk. III*, 415 (quoting report of New York City field office, October 22, 1941, summarized in Justice Department memorandum from S. Brodie to Assistant Attorney General Quinn, October 10, 1947). For the NAACP, see *Bk. III*, 416 (quoting report of Washington, D.C., Field Office, March 11, 1941).

16. For CIA's history, see *Bk. I*, 21, 97–125; Thomas Powers, *Intelligence Wars: American Secret History from Hitler to Al-Qaeda* (New York: New York Review Books, 2002).

17. For Donovan and the formation of the OSS, see Powers, 3–20.

18. Powers, 13.

19. Rhodri Jeffreys-Jones, *American Espionage: From Secret Service to CIA* (New York: Free Press, 1977), 189.

20. See "Central Intelligence Agency" at http://www.fas.org/irp/cia/ciahist.htm.

21. Melissa Boyle Mahle, *Denial and Deception* (New York: Nation Books, 2004), 9.

22. *Bk. III*, 425–26 (quoting Donald C. Downes, *The Scarlet Thread: Adventures in Wartime Espionage* [New York: British Book Centre, 1953], 87–97, and R. Harris Smith, *OSS: The Secret History of America's First Central Intelligence Agency* [Berkeley: University of California Press, 1972], 20).

23. Sec. 102 (A), 50 USC § 403-1 (2006); *Bk. I*, 104–5.

24. See 50 USC § 403-3 (2006).

25. See 50 USC § 403-1 (2006).

26. For Vandenberg's testimony, see *Bk. I*, 129 (quoting Vandenberg, Senate Armed Services Committee hearings, April 29, 1947, 492).

27. According to Congressman Hale Boggs, "Our apathy in this Congress, our silence in this house, our very fear of speaking out in other forums, has watered the roots and hastened the growth of a vine of tyranny which is ensnaring that Constitution and Bill of Rights which we are each sworn to uphold. Our society can survive many challenges and many threats. It cannot survive a planned and programmed fear of its own government bureaus and agencies." *Bk. II*, 240 (quoting *Congressional Record*, April 22, 1971, 11562).

28. *Bk. III*, 412 (quoting Robert H. Jackson, *The Supreme Court in the American System of Government* [New York: Harper & Row, 1963], 70–77).

29. *Assassinations*, 129–30.

30. For quotes, see Frank J. Smist Jr., *Congress Oversees the United States Intelligence Community, 1947–1989* (Knoxville: University of Tennessee Press, 1990), 5, 9.

31. For Mansfield, see Smist, 50.

Chapter 2: Revelations of the Church Committee

1. See *Martin Luther King Jr., I Have a Dream: Writings and Speeches that Changed the World* (New York: HarperCollins, 1992), 105–106.

2. For "most dangerous and effective Negro leader," see *Bk. II*, 11, and *Bk. III*, 107–109 (quoting memorandum from William Sullivan to Alan Belmont, August 30, 1963). For "take him off his pedestal," see *Bk. II*, 11, and *Bk. III*, 136–33 (quoting memorandum from Sullivan to Belmont, January 8, 1964). For the FBI's treatment of King, see *Bk. II*, 11–12, 219–23, and *Bk. III*, 79–184.

3. For "Hate Group," see *Bk. III*, 179–180 (emphasis added), quoting memorandum from FBI director Hoover to Special Agents in Charge (SACs), August 25, 1967. For "messiah," see *Bk. II*, 11–12, and *Bk. III*, 180, quoting memorandum from Hoover to all SACs, March 4, 1968.

4. For "no holds were barred," see *Bk. II*, 11, and *Bk. III*, 81 (quoting William C. Sullivan's testimony of November 1, 1975, 49). For secret list, see *Bk. III*, 87–88. For characterization of King as "subversive," see *Bk. III*, 88, n. 27 (quoting FBI report, New York, April 13, 1962). For the House Un-American Activities Committee, see Victor Navasky, *Naming Names* (New York: Viking Press, 1980).

5. For FBI efforts to discredit King, see *Bk. II*, 221–23, and *Bk. III*, 140–46, 172–79.

6. For King's criticism of the FBI, see *Bk. III*, 158, quoting *New York Times*, November 20, 1964, 18. For the facts on the tape and letter, see *Bk. II*, 11, 220–21 and *Bk. III*, 158–61. Andrew Young, then King's assistant, is one source for King's interpretation of the intent of the letter: "[T]hat is the way we discussed it, to commit suicide, or that he was going to be publicly humiliated." William C. Sullivan, the FBI official in whose files a draft of the letter was found, conceded the letter could be so interpreted. Carl Rowan, who had been a high-ranking federal official in the Kennedy and Johnson administrations, revealed that he was later told by an FBI source that Hoover had been present at a meeting where the letter and suicide were discussed. In the meeting, according to Rowan's source, specific allusions were made to recent news reports of an alleged youthful suicide

attempt by King. See *Bk. III*, 160–61; Taylor Branch, *Pillar of Fire: America in the King Years: 1963–1965* (New York: Simon & Schuster, 1998), 528–29, 556–57; David Garrow, *Bearing the Cross: Martin Luther King Jr. and the Southern Christian Leadership Conference* (New York: William Morrow, 1986), 373–75.

7. *Bk. II*, 141 (quoting William C. Sullivan's testimony of November 1, 1975, 92–93). Mondale chaired the Domestic Intelligence Subcommittee of the Church Committee. See also Walter F. Mondale, *The Accountability of Power: Toward a Responsible Presidency* (New York: D. McKay, 1975), and "Democracy's Challenge: Balancing Personal Liberty and National Security," lecture, April 27, 2000, Minneapolis, Minnesota (on file with authors).

8. For the Church Committee's comprehensiveness, see Frank J. Smist, *Congress Oversees the United States Intelligence Community, 1947–1989* (Knoxville: University of Tennessee Press, 1990), 10.

9. *Bk. II*, v; S. Res. 21, January 27, 1975, § 1. For "the ideals," see *Assassinations*, 285.

10. This specific conclusion is at *Bk. II*, viii.

11. For COINTELPRO, see *Bk. II*, 10–12, 65–94, 211–23; *Bk. III*, 1–79. For "brought home," see *Bk. II*, 212, n. 7 (quoting Former Assistant Director William C. Sullivan's testimony of November 1, 1975, 97–98); *Bk. III*, 7. For termination of COINTELPRO, see *Bk. III*, 3 (citing memorandum from C.D. Brennan to W.C. Sullivan, April 27, 1971, and letter from FBI headquarters to all SACs, April 28, 1971). For "ugly program," see Frederick A.O. Schwarz Jr., "Intelligence Activities and the Rights of Americans," *The Record of the Association of the Bar of the City of New York*, January/February 1977, 43, 46.

12. See *Bk. II*, 211, and *Bk. III*, 10–11.

13. For "we never gave it a thought," see *Bk. II*, 140 (quoting George Moore's testimony of November 3, 1975, 83).

14. For mission creep and description of the five targets, see *Bk. II*, 213; *Bk. III*, 4. For "disrupt" and "neutralize," see *Bk. III*, 20 (quoting memorandum from FBI headquarters to all SACs, August 25, 1967).

15. For the Communist Party of the USA (CPUSA) and the New Left program of COINTELPRO, see *Bk. II*, 88–89, 213–14; *Bk. III*, 4–5, 16–27.

16. For examples of COINTELPRO methods, see *Bk. II*, 216–19; *Bk. III*, 7–8. For "embarrass the Bureau," see *Bk. II*, 156 (quoting FBI manual).

17. *Bk. II*, 271–72, n. 20 (quoting memo from Chicago field office to FBI headquarters, January 18, 1969).

18. *Bk. II*, 218 (quoting memorandum from San Diego field office to FBI headquarters, September 15, 1969) (emphasis added).

19. For the "snitch jacket," see *Bk. II*, 218–19; *Bk. III*, 9, 46–49. For chief of the FBI's Racial Intelligence Unit, see *Bk. II*, 219 (quoting George Moore's testimony of November 3, 1975, 62, 64). For continued use of the technique after the killing of two suspected informers, see *Bk. II*, 218, n. 50.

20. For the Unitarian Society, see *Bk. II*, 214, n. 14 (citing memo from FBI headquarters to Cleveland field office, November 6, 1964). For "disinformation" and "long and useless journeys," see *Bk. II*, 216, n. 34 (quoting memo from Chicago field office to FBI headquarters, September 9, 1968). For "aid and comfort," see *Bk. II*, 213 (quoting testimony of the supervisor of the FBI's "New Left" pro-

gram, October 28, 1975, 69); *Bk. II*, 214, n. 19 (quoting memo from Detroit field office to FBI headquarters, October 11, 1966, and memo from FBI headquarters to Detroit field office, October 26, 1966).

21. *Bk. II*, 212.

22. For wiretaps and bugs, see *Bk. II*, 105–7, 198–201; *Bk. III*, 271–351.

23. For the notion that taps and bugs raise the same worries as "general warrants," see *United States v. Ehrlichman*, 376 F. Supp. 29, 32 (D.D.C. 1974). For Brandeis comment, see *Olmstead v. United States*, 277 U.S. 438, 476 (1928).

24. See 47 U.S.C. §§ 605 *et seq.* (2006).

25. See *Nardone v. United States*, 302 U.S. 379 (1937); 308 U.S. 338 (1939).

26. See *Bk. III*, 278–79. Jackson reversed the Justice Department's policy concerning wiretapping in Order No. 3343, issued March 15, 1940, prohibiting all FBI wiretapping.

27. *Bk. III*, 279 (quoting memorandum from Roosevelt to Jackson, May 21, 1940).

28. *Irvine v. California*, 347 U.S. 128 (1954).

29. *Bk. II*, 190 (quoting memorandum from Brownell to Hoover, May 20, 1954).

30. *Katz v. United States*, 389 U.S. 347, 358, n. 23 (1967). The Omnibus Crime Control Act of 1968 established warrant procedures in criminal cases, but did not limit the "Constitutional power of the President," although without any definition of that term, Public Law, June 19, 1968, 82 Stat. 197, 42 U.S.C. 3711; *Bk. II*, 106; *Bk. III*, 275.

31. *United States v. United States District Court*, 407 U.S. 297, 319–320 (1972); *Bk. II*, 107; *Bk. III*, 275.

32. 407 U.S. at 309, n. 8.

33. *Bk. II*, 205, 208. Franklin Roosevelt's Attorney General Francis Biddle strongly but unsuccessfully opposed Japanese American internments without individual hearings as "ill-advised, unnecessary and unnecessarily cruel." Later, Biddle observed with regret "the power of suggestion which a *mystic cliché* like 'military necessity' can exercise on human beings." See Geoffrey R. Stone, *Perilous Times: Free Speech in Wartime, From the Sedition Act of 1798 to the War on Terrorism* (New York: W.W. Norton, 2004), 293, 304; Francis Biddle, *In Brief Authority* (New York: Doubleday, 1961), 226 (emphasis added by authors). Justice Robert H. Jackson also condemned the "loose and irresponsible" use of "adjectives . . . without fixed or ascertainable meanings" like "inherent" or "war" presidential powers. *Youngstown Sheet and Tube v. Sawyer*, 343 U.S. 579, 646–47 (1952).

34. For break-ins, see *Bk. II*, 61–62, 190–92, 204–5; *Bk. III*, 353–71. For mail openings, see *Bk. II*, 58–59, 190–92, 203; *Bk. III*, 559–677.

35. For "involves trespassing" and "clearly illegal," see *Bk. III*, 358 (quoting memorandum from W.C. Sullivan to C.D. DeLoach [Subject: "Black Bag" Jobs], July 19, 1966). For break-ins to Socialist Workers Party offices, see *Bk. II*, 204, n. 102. For the FBI's concession, see *Bk. II*, 180 (quoting Robert Shackelford's testimony of February 2, 1976, 89–90).

36. See *Bk. II*, 208, n. 126; David Rudenstine, *The Day the Presses Stopped: A History of the Pentagon Papers* (Berkeley: University of California Press, 1996).

37. For the existence of FBI mail-opening programs for over twenty years, see *Bk. III*, 561–62. For "justified by the greater good," see *Bk. II*, 14 (quoting Branigan's testimony of October 9, 1975, 41).

38. For cancellation of the FBI's mail-opening program in 1966, see *Bk. II*, 12. For the quotes and citations of four internal CIA memoranda recognizing illegality, see *Bk. II*, 142. "No legal basis" is from a memorandum from Chief, CI Project, to Chief, Division, September 26, 1963. "Federal statutes preclude" and "give rise to grave charges" are from memorandum from the deputy chief of the Counterintelligence Staff to the director of the Office of Security on February 1, 1962. For quotes from inspector general and deputy chief of the Counterintelligence Staff, see *Bk. II*, 147–48.

39. For growth in the CIA's watch list and the people and organizations covered, see *Bk. II*, 208–9 and *Bk. III*, 573–74. For the letter to Nixon, see *Bk. II*, 8. For nearly 1.5 million, see *Bk. II*, 6.

40. *Bk. III*, 739–40. For NSA, see *Bk. III*, 733–83; *Hearings, Vol. 5: The National Security Agency and Fourth Amendment Rights*, passim; James Bamford, *The Puzzle Palace: Inside America's Most Secret Intelligence Organization* (New York: Penguin, 1983); James Bamford, *Body of Secrets: Anatomy of the Ultra-Secret National Security Agency* (New York: Anchor Books, 2002); L. Britt Snider, "Recollections from the Church Committee's Investigation of NSA," *Studies in Intelligence* (Winter 1999–2000), 43–51.

41. See *Hearings, Vol. 5: The National Security Agency and Fourth Amendment Rights*, 45 (questioning by Mondale). The prevalence of this attitude is also supported by Schwarz's recollection of his discussions with the NSA's general counsel.

42. *Bk. III*, 790; *Bk. II*, 285, n.75.

43. For discussion of too much information being collected, see *Bk. II*, 6–10, 165–82.

44. For NAACP, see *Bk. II*, 8, 179–180.

45. *Bk. II*, 181, and *Bk. III*, 5, n. 7.

46. For the FBI reports on the "Women's Liberation Movement," see *Bk. II*, 7. The quote is from a memorandum from Baltimore field office to FBI headquarters, May 11, 1970, 2. For the CIA's investigation, see *Bk. II*, 102.

47. *Bk. II*, 180.

48. *Bk. II*, 188, n. 21, and *Bk. III*, 285, n. 47 (quoting testimony of Nicholas Katzenbach, November 12, 1975, 87).

49. For numbers, see *Bk. II*, 6. For the birth control conference and Halloween party, see *Bk. II*, 8 (quoting Military Report: Sec. II, "The Collection of Information About the Political Activities of Private Citizens and Private Organizations"). For army investigations, see *Bk. II*, 77, 167, 174, and *Bk. III*, 785–834.

50. See *Bk. II*, 167–68, and *Bk. III*, 682. For Operation CHAOS, see *Bk. II*, 174–75; *Bk. III*, 679–732.

51. See *Bk. II*, 108, and *Bk. III*, 740–41. For "largest governmental interception program," see *Bk. III*, 740; Loch Johnson, *A Season of Inquiry: The Senate Intelligence Investigation* (Lexington: University Press of Kentucky, 1985), 104–8.

52. For dissemination, see *Bk. II*, 253–64. For "blind black workers," the "tea," and "The History of the American Negro," see *Bk. II*, 256 (quoting memorandum from Charlotte field office to FBI headquarters, December 10, 1976, and memorandum from Tampa field office to FBI headquarters, May 29, 1969).

53. *Bk. II*, 254. For the argument that the volume of material from the FBI hindered law enforcement, see *Bk. II*, 19 (quoting New Haven police chief James Ahern's testimony of January 20, 1976, 7–8).

54. For the FBI's detention lists, see *Bk. II*, 54–56, and *Bk. III*, 436–47, 510–16,

542–48. For categories of detention and "subversive associations," see *Bk. II*, 55. For Mailer, see *Bk. II*, 56. For King, see *Bk. III*, 87–88.

55. For IRS intelligence gathering, see *Bk. II*, 168; *Bk. III*, 835–920; *Hearings, Vol. 3: Internal Revenue Service*, passim. For President Kennedy's pressure on the IRS, see *Bk. III*, 843. For "dissident or extremist" groups and "deal a blow," see *Bk. II*, 256, and *Bk. III*, 884. For people and organizations singled out, see *Bk. III*, 842; Johnson, *Season of Inquiry*, 91.

56. For political uses, see *Bk. II*, 225–52.

57. See *Bk. II*, 232–33. For "marked deterioration," see *Bk. II*, 233, n. 40. For Hoover's subsequent briefing, see *Bk. II*, 250–51, n. 151a. For "reinforced the President's passivity," see ibid. (quoting J.W. Anderson, *Eisenhower, Brownell, and the Congress: The Tangled Origins of the Civil Rights Bill of 1956–57* [Tuscaloosa: University of Alabama Press, 1964], 34).

58. *Bk. II*, 250. "Obvious failure" is from a memorandum from Baumgardner to William Sullivan, August 23, 1963, 1. "We had to change our ways" is from William Sullivan's testimony of November 1, 1975, 20. "The Director is correct," "most dangerous Negro," "standpoint of communism," "unrealistic," "legalistic proofs," and "one day could become decisive" are from a memorandum from Sullivan to the FBI director Hoover, August 30, 1963. "Vitally important" is from hearings before the House Appropriations Subcommittee, 88th Congress, 2nd Session (1964), 309. (emphasis added.)

59. *Bk. II*, 251 (quoting Hoover memorandum, April 28, 1965).

60. For "after this all the time," see *Bk. II*, 181, n. 85, and *Bk. III*, 689 (quoting Richard Helms's testimony before the Rockefeller Commission on January 13, 1975, 163–64). For "no significant role" and expansion of CIA coverage of Americans, see *Bk. III*, 681.

61. *Bk. III*, 697 (quoting a memorandum from Richard Helms to President Johnson, September 4, 1968, and a letter from Richard Helms to Henry Kissinger, February 18, 1969).

62. For examples of the successive administrations' uses of the FBI to obtain political information, see *Bk. II*, 227, 237–38.

63. *Bk. II*, 228–30.

64. *Bk. II*, 117–19, 234–35.

65. *Bk. II*, 230–31. Agnew denied that he made such a request but agreed he received the information (*Bk. II*, 231, citing staff summary of Agnew interview on October 15, 1975).

66. *Bk. II*, 235–36.

67. For covert action, see *Assassinations*, passim; *Bk. I*, 141–61; Gregory F. Treverton, *Covert Action: The Limits of Intervention in the Postwar World* (New York: Basic Books, 1987). For covert actions in Chile, see *Covert Action in Chile, 1963–1973, Staff Report of the Select Committee to Study Governmental Operations With Respect to Intelligence Activities, United States Senate* (Washington: U.S. Government Printing Office, 1975), hereafter *Chile Staff Report*, passim. Other reports on particular covert actions were submitted to the Senate, but not made public. For early history of covert action and "soon became a routine program," see *Bk. I*, 153.

68. *Bk. I*, 154.

69. *Bk. I*, 141 (quoting Clark Clifford's testimony of December 5, 1975, *Hearings, Vol. 7: Covert Action*, 51).

70. For Castro and Cuba, see *Assassinations*, 71–180, 255, 257, 263–70, 274–77. For Castro assassination plots from 1960–1965, see *Assassinations*, 71. For halt in covert actions against the Cuban regime in fall 1962, see *Assassinations*, 148 (quoting Theodore Sorensen's testimony of July 21, 1975, 11).

71. *Assassinations*, 264.

72. For plausible deniability, see *Assassinations*, 11–12, 277–78.

73. For Helms and Bissell, see Richard Helms and William Hood, *A Look Over My Shoulder: A Life in the Central Intelligence Agency* (New York: Random House, 2003); Richard M. Bissell, with Jonathan E. Lewis and Frances T. Pudlo, *Reflections of a Cold Warrior: From Yalta to the Bay of Pigs* (New Haven: Yale University Press, 1996); see Thomas Powers, *The Man Who Kept the Secrets: Richard Helms and the CIA* (New York: Knopf, 1979).

74. For "went on the assumption" and "shield the president," see *Assassinations*, 111 (quoting Bissell testimony, June 9, 1975, 26 and 61 respectively). For "circumlocutious," "leave [the President] in a position to deny," and "hold to the absolute minimum," see *Assassinations*, 118 (quoting Bissell testimony, June 11, 1975, 5–6).

75. For Helms's testimony on presidential authorization, see *Assassinations*, 148–51. For "embarrass a President of the United States," see *Assassinations*, 151 (quoting Helms's testimony on June 13, 1975, 29). For "very intense" and "killing him," see *Assassinations*, 149 (quoting Helms's testimony, June 13, 1975, 26 and 137 respectively). Bissell testified that the President and the Attorney General had told him, "Get off your ass about Cuba," but that he had not considered that to be authorization to attempt to assassinate Castro. Rather, "formal and explicit approval" would be required for assassination activity. See *Assassinations*, 141 (quoting Bissell's testimony of July 25, 1975, 37–38 and 38–39 respectively).

76. *Assassinations*, 139 (quoting Helms's testimony on June 13, 1975, 72–73).

77. *Assassinations*, 277.

78. For Church Committee sources on covert action in Chile, see *Assassinations*, "Schneider," 225–54, 256, 262, 272, and *Chile Staff Report*; for continuity, see *Chile Staff Report*, 3.

79. *Chile Staff Report*, 4–5.

80. *Chile Staff Report*, 19–20, and *Assassinations*, 225.

81. *Assassinations*, 227–28, quoting Helms testimony on July 15, 1975, 6, 10, 18.

82. *Assassinations*, 225, 240–46.

83. *Assassinations*, 246.

84. *Assassinations*, 254, quoting testimony of CIA official Thomas Karamessines on August 6, 1975, 128–29 and 26, and Kissinger's testimony of August 12, 1975, 75–77.

85. *Chile Staff Report*, 28; see also Peter Kornbluh, ed., *The Pinochet File: A Declassified Dossier on Atrocity and Accountability* (New York: The New Press, 2003); cf. Scott Sherman, "Kissinger's Shadow Over the Council on Foreign Relations," *The Nation*, December 27, 2004.

86. *Bk. I*, 160.

87. See James Reynolds, "Finding Chile's Disappeared," BBC News Online, January 10, 2001; Tom Burgis, "Chile's torture victims to get life pensions," *The Guardian*, November 30, 2004. For the quote from the report, see Peter Kornbluh, "Letter from Chile," *The Nation*, January 31, 2005.

88. For drug experiments, see *Bk. I*, "CIA Drug Testing Programs," 392–411.

89. For a description of the initial experiments and "unwitting subjects," see *Bk. I*, 391. For the Helms quote, see *Bk. I*, 394 (quoting memorandum from the Deputy Director for Plans to the Deputy Director of Central Intelligence, December 17, 1963, 2–3).

90. For the Olson story, see *Bk. I*, 394–99. Olson committed suicide by jumping out a window at a New York hotel.

91. *Bk. I*, 394 (quoting inspector general memorandum, 1957, 217).

92. For the continuation of the drug experimentation program until 1963, see *Bk. I*, 403. For quotes, see *Bk. I*, 398–99. "Proper consideration" is from a memorandum from Director of Central Intelligence to Sidney Gottlieb, February 12, 1954. "Not a reprimand" is from a note from deputy director of Central Intelligence to Richard Helms, February 13, 1954.

93. For assassination attempt on Lumumba, see *Assassinations*, 19–70. In *Assassinations*, Gottlieb is referred to by the code name Joseph Scheider.

94. *Bk. II*, 142; see also *Bk. I*, 394.

95. *Bk. II*, 177; *Bk. III*, 179–80 (quoting memo from Hoover to FBI Special Agents in Charge, August 25, 1967).

96. For an eloquent and moving statement of the importance of detailed facts, see the remarks of Senator Phillip Hart on the final day of the Committee's public hearings on the FBI, *Hearings, Vol. 6, FBI*, 41. Contemporaneous documents and access to actual witnesses are both necessary to master the intricacies of intelligence and security institutions and to learn the truth about their conduct. The White House and the agencies initially resisted the Committee's demands for detailed documents. But continued pressure from the Committee eventually led to compliance. See, e.g., Loch Johnson, *A Season of Inquiry*, 27–44. (When CIA chief William Colby first appeared to testify before the Committee in 1975, Schwarz got him to commit to producing the key documents. During counsel's first visit to FBI headquarters, FBI officials attempted to divert attention from a real investigation by showing pictures of severed heads on an urban street, but the Bureau also soon cooperated by providing their secret and highly embarrassing documents.) With respect to witnesses, the CIA initially proposed that a "monitor" from the agency accompany any current or former intelligence official called for questioning, including preliminary questioning by staff members. In addition to observing, the monitors would give witnesses "advice." The Committee refused after Republican Senator Richard Schweiker said it would make the Committee "the laughing stock of the Hill." Witnesses thereafter always appeared without monitors. Johnson, *A Season of Inquiry*, 43; *New York Times*, May 10, 1975. For an example of the inadequacy (indeed, gross inaccuracy) of internal agency reports about the facts, see *Bk. II*, 271 (describing an FBI report on COINTELPRO action designed to provoke a killing as an effort to "drive a wedge between" two black groups in Chicago).

97. Johnson, 57.

98. For authorization evidence and conclusions, see *Assassinations*, 6–7, 148–61, 260–67.

99. *Bk. I*, 11.

100. *Bk. II*, 137.

101. For "demanding results," see *Bk. II*, 139. For "failing to inquire further," "dele-

gating broad authority," failing to establish adequate guidelines, and "exhibiting a reluctance to know," see *Bk. II*, 265.

102. For "greatest dangers," see *Olmstead v. United States*, 277 U.S. 438, 479 (1928). (Brandeis, J.)

103. For examples of intelligence programs breaking and ignoring the law, see *Bk. II*, 137–63.

104. *Bk. I*, 156.

105. *Bk. II*, 14, 141 (quoting William Sullivan's testimony of November 1, 1975, 92–93).

106. In contrast to the parallel 1975–76 House Committee on Intelligence (often known as the Pike Committee, after its chair, Otis Pike), which floundered at the outset and foundered at the end on issues of secrecy, the Church Committee benefited from a record of avoiding leaks. There were only two leaks stemming from the Church Committee and neither affected security. See Smist, 38, 48–49.

107. *Bk. II*, 205.

108. For Huston, see *Bk. II*, 4 (quoting Tom Charles Huston's testimony of September 23, 1975, *Hearings, Vol. 2: Huston Plan*, 45). For the Huston Plan, see *Bk. II*, 111–16; *Bk. III*, 921–83; *Hearings, Vol. 2: Huston Plan*, passim. Johnson, *Season of Inquiry*, 78–88.

109. *Bk. II*, v.

110. *Assassinations*, 285.

111. *Assassinations*, 345–46.

112. *Bk. I*, 50 (quoting James Doolittle et al, *Report on the Covert Activities of the Central Intelligence Agency*, September 30, 1954, 6–7); *Assassinations*, 259.

113. *Bk. I*, 156.

114. *Assassinations*, 285.

115. For Morgan, see *Bk. II*, 363–65. For Baker, see *Bk. II*, 373–75. For Colby, see William Colby, "After Investigating U.S. Intelligence," *New York Times*, February 26, 1976, A30.

116. *Bk. II*, viii.

117. Smist describes the Church Committee's "unity and bipartisanship" as key to its success. Among his references is Howard Liebengood, a close aide to Republican Senator Howard Baker: "The Senate Watergate Committee was brutally partisan . . . by way of contrast, on the Church Committee, Republicans and Democrats worked hand in hand on projects together." Smist, 41.

Chapter 3: Reform and Resistance

1. Arthur M. Schlesinger Jr., *The Imperial Presidency* (Boston: Houghlin Mifflin, 1973); Arthur S. Schlesinger Jr., *The Cycles of American History* (Boston: Houghton Mifflin, 1986).

2. For a history of the resurgence of executive power, see Andrew Rudalevige, *The New Imperial Presidency: Renewing Presidential Power after Watergate* (Ann Arbor: University of Michigan Press, 2005).

3. For the Committee's recommendations, see *Bk. I*, 423–74 and *Bk. II*, 289–341.

4. *Bk. II*, 319 (emphasis added). The Committee also stated that vital national interests were served by "properly controlled and lawful intelligence," e.g., "to mon-

itor potential military threats from the Soviet Union and its allies, to verify compliance with international agreements such as SALT, and to combat espionage and international terrorism." *Bk. II* (v). On terrorism, the *Report of the U.S. Commission on National Security/21st Century*, chaired by former Senators Gary Hart (a member of the Church Committee) and Warren Rudman, available at http://www.fas.org/man/docs/nwc/, reached the same conclusions. The bipartisan commission spent two and a half years studying the potential problem of domestic terrorism and issued its recommendations in early 2001. Bush Administration officials told Hart and Rudman that they preferred to put aside the recommendations, turn over the task of assessing terrorism threats to Vice President Dick Cheney, and assign the coordination of responses to the Federal Emergency Management Agency (FEMA). The Hart-Rudman Commission had concluded that terrorism comprised a threat that demanded far more than FEMA's attention. After September 11, Gary Hart noted: "We predicted it. We said Americans will likely die on American soil, possibly in large numbers—that's a quote [from the commission's Phase One report] from the fall of 1999." Jack Tapper, "Commission Warned Bush," *Salon.com*, September 12, 2001.

5. *Bk. I*, 426, 449–51.
6. For quote, see *Bk. I*, 437.
7. For statutory charters, see *Bk. I*, 425–27, 435–36 (CIA), 464 (NSA); *Bk. II*, 298 (CIA), 308–9 (NSA), 318–20 (FBI).
8. For "congressional oversight is necessary," see *Bk. I*, 2. For Church Committee recommendation of a permanent intelligence oversight committee, see *Bk. I*, 424; *Bk. II*, 339; Loch Johnson, *A Season of Inquiry: The Senate Intelligence Investigation* (Lexington: University Press of Kentucky, 1985), 227–51; Frank J. Smist, *Congress Oversees the United States Intelligence Community, 1947–1989* (Knoxville: University of Tennessee Press, 1990), 82–83; see House Permanent Select Committee on Intelligence, *Compilation of Intelligence Laws and Related Laws and Executive Orders of Interest to the National Intelligence Community* (April 1983), 343–51; Johnson, 283. See also *Congressional Record*, May 19, 1976, 14673–75. For debate on S. Res. 400, see *Congressional Record*, May 12, 1976, 13656, 13678–95; May 13, 1976, 13973–90; May 17, 1976, 14149–73; May 18, 1976, 14259–66; May 19, 1976, 14643–79.
9. See William E. Colby, "After Investigating U.S. Intelligence," *New York Times*, February 26, 1976, A30. This comment came immediately after Colby said that the investigations had "made clear that the rule of law applies to all parts of the American Government, including intelligence."
10. Johnson, *Season of Inquiry*, 227–30, 241–47.
11. See Johnson, *Season of Inquiry*, 242–43; Smist, 83. See also *Congressional Record*, May 19, 1976, 14645. Church made points similar to Mondale's in a subsequent interview. Smist, 64.
12. President Ford selected Bush to replace William Colby, who was regarded by the White House, particularly Henry Kissinger, as too cooperative with the investigation. At the same time, he chose Donald Rumsfeld, who had been serving as a member of his White House staff, to replace James Schlesinger as Secretary of Defense.

Church opposed Bush's appointment as CIA chief. Senator Church's speech was primarily about the need to strengthen the CIA's ability to provide the "best possible understanding of foreign capabilities, leaders and developing events." To do this, it was "imperative that we preserve the professional stature of the Central Intelligence Agency by keeping it free from the eroding forces of politics and partisanship." Bush, prior to the appointment, had been serving as ambassador to China. However, as Church pointed out, his "principal political role had been that of chairman of the Republican National Committee." Upon the appointment, Bush and Ford had each referred to Bush's continued ambition for a vice presidential nomination, and Church believed that Bush was too much a partisan to assert the necessary CIA independence from the judgment of the president. Thus, he argued, while George Bush was "a likeable man," "a capable man," and there were "many political offices that he could hold with distinction," he was "not the man to head up the CIA." See *Congressional Record*, November 11, 1975, 35788.

13. In so doing, the Administration seemed to "dance on [Welch's] grave." Smist, 64 (quoting Schwarz).

14. For George H.W. Bush's concession, see *Bk. I*, 458, quoting page 41 of his testimony of April 8, 1976. The aide whispering in Bush's ear is from Schwarz's recollection of the executive session.

15. For budgetary authority, see S. Res. 400, Sec. 3 (a) (4) at *Congressional Record*, May 19, 1976, 14673. For "sense of the Senate" and "fully and currently informed," see S. Res. 400, Sec. 11 (a) at *Congressional Record*, May 19, 1976, 14675. For the ratio of majority and minority party members, see S. Res. 400, Sec. 2 (a) at *Congressional Record*, May 19, 1976, 14673. For the vice chair, see S. Res. 400, Sec. 2 (c) at *Congressional Record*, May 19, 1976, 14673.

16. Smist, 81 (quoting interview with Frank Church, April 25, 1983).

17. See the Accountability for Intelligence Activities Act (also known as the 1980 Intelligence Oversight Act), 50 U.S.C. 413.

18. See Foreign Intelligence Surveillance Act of 1978, Pub. L. No. 95-511, 92 Stat. 1738 (codified at 50 U.S.C.§ 1801–1811). For the Senate committee report, see S. Rep. 95-701, 1978 U.S.C.C.A.N. 3973. For the House committee report, see H.R. Conf. Rep. 95-1720, 1978 U.S.C.C.A.N. 4048. For Carter's signing statement, see Statement of Signing S. 1566 into Law, October 25, 1978, available electronically at http://www.cnss.org/Carter.pdf. Foreign Intelligence Surveillance Act, Statement on Signing S. 1566 into Law, October 25, 1978, available at http://www.cnss.org/fisa.html. See also George Lardner Jr., "Carter Signs Bill Limiting Foreign Intelligence Surveillance," *Washington Post*, October 26, 1978, A2. For further early material on FISA, see editorial, "National Security Wiretaps," *Washington Post*, September 6, 1978, A14.

19. For FISA's coverage, see 50 U.S.C. § 1802 (h) (i). For exceptions, see 50 U.S.C. § 1802 (a) (1) (foreign powers); § 1805 (f) (emergencies); § 1811(declarations of war). For the Church Committee's definition of "Americans," see its Recommendations section at *Bk. II*, 95, n. 6.

20. Former Deputy Attorney General Laurence Silberman, for example, argued that courts would systematically "overweight the instances of individual privacy claims because it is, after all, the protection of those claims on which judicial authority is based." See Arthur Lowry, "Who's Listening: Proposals for Amending the Foreign Intelligence Surveillance Act," *Virginia Law Review* 70 (1984), 297, 321–22.

21. Executive Order 12333, United States Intelligence Activities, December 4, 1981, Part 2, Sec. 2.5. See 46 FR 59941, 3 CFR, 1981 Comp., 200.

22. For the tenure of the FBI director, see Crime Control Act of 1976, Pub. L. No. 94-503, § 203, 1976 U.S.C.C.A.N. (90 Stat. 2427) (codified at 28 U.S.C. § 532 note). For covert action reporting, see the Accountability for Intelligence Activities Act (also known as the 1980 Intelligence Oversight Act), 50 U.S.C. 413. For strengthening the CIA inspector general, see 50 U.S.C. § 403 (q), as added September 29, 1988 in Public Law 100-453, Title V, § 504. For the law resulting from the 9/11 Commission's recommendations, see Intelligence Reform and Terrorism Prevention Act of 2004, S. 2845.

23. Miller had been the Church Committee's Staff Director, and had principal staff responsibility for the Committee's Final Report on *Foreign and Military Intelligence (Bk. I)*. He later became an ambassador to Ukraine. Several other Church Committee staffers, including John Elliff, a leading scholar on the FBI, worked with Miller on the staff of the Senate's new permanent Intelligence Committee.

24. See Smist, 97–99. For Goldwater's hostility, see Loch Johnson, "Legislative Reform of Intelligence Policy," *Polity* 17 (Spring 1985), 567.

25. David Aaron, a task force leader on the Church Committee staff, and deputy director for national security affairs under Carter, attributed the failure to pass a charter to "legislative insistence on prior notification to Congress of intelligence activities even in times of emergency." Johnson, *Season of Inquiry* 300, n. 14 (referencing testimony in House Permanent Select Committee on Intelligence, Hearings on Congressional Oversight of Covert Activities, September 22, 1983, 98).

26. For Ford's executive order, see Executive Order 11905, February 18, 1976, 41 FR 7703. For Carter's executive order, see Executive Order 12036, January 24, 1978, 43 FR 3674. Carter's Administration included many veterans of the Church Committee, including Vice President Mondale, National Security Council Deputy Director David Aaron, and Frederick Baron, who worked on intelligence issues for Attorney General Griffin Bell. For Levi guidelines, see FBI Statutory Charter, Hearings Before the Committee on the Judiciary, 95th Congress, Second Session on FBI Statutory Charter, Part 1, April 20 and 25, 1978 (Washington, DC: U.S. Government Printing Office, 1978), 18–26.

27. For "prevent legislative action" and "an attempt to maintain executive control," see Smist, 79–80; John. M. Oseth, *Regulating U.S. Intelligence Operations* (Lexington: University of Kentucky Press, 1985), 97. For "attempt to delimit prospective reforms," see Athan Theoharis, *Spying on Americans: Political Surveillance from Hoover to the Huston Plan* (Philadelphia: Temple University Press, 1978), 235.

28. For the Committee's reactions, see *Bk. II*, 318–20 ("The Committee's approach to FBI domestic security investigations is basically the same as that adopted by the Attorney General's guidelines. . . . Both are cautious about any departures from former Attorney General Stone's maxim that the FBI should only conduct criminal investigations. . . . However, the Committee views its recommendations as a somewhat more limited departure. . . . The Attorney General's guidelines have been read by FBI officials as authorizing intelligence investigations of 'subversives.' . . . While the Justice Department, under its current leadership, might not adopt such an interpretation, a different Attorney General might").

29. For Smith guidelines, see FBI Domestic Security Guidelines, Oversight Hearing Before the Subcommittee on Civil and Constitutional Rights of the Committee

on the Judiciary, House of Representatives, 98th Congress, First Session on FBI Domestic Security Guidelines, April 27, 1983 (Washington, DC: U.S. Government Printing Office, 1987). For Reagan's executive order, see Executive Order 12333, United States Intelligence Activities, December 4, 1981 at 46 FR 59941, 3 CFR, 1981 Comp., 200.

30. For Iran-Contra, see *Report of the Congressional Committees Investigating the Iran-Contra Affair*, H.R. Rep. No. 433, S. Rep. No. 216, 100th Cong., 1st Sess. (1987); Harold Hongju Koh, *The National Security Constitution: Sharing Power after the Iran-Contra Affair* (New Haven: Yale University Press, 1990); Smist, 258–67; Hannah Bentley, "Keeping Secrets: The Church Committee, Covert Action, and Nicaragua," *Columbia Journal of Transnational Law* 25 (1986–87), 601.

31. For the Contras' campaign, see Eric Alterman, *When Presidents Lie: A History of Official Deception and its Consequences* (New York: Viking, 2004), 265–66. For another account and Goldwater quote, see Andrew Rudalevige, *The New Imperial Presidency: Renewing Presidential Power after Watergate* (Ann Arbor: University of Michigan Press, 2005), 200–205. For the first Boland Amendment, see Further Continuing Appropriations, 1983, Pub. L. No. 97-377, § 793, 96 Stat. 1830, 1965 (1982). The second Boland Amendment is quoted at Bentley, 631.

32. For the decision to sell TOW and HAWK missiles to Iran, see *Report of the Congressional Committees Investigating the Iran-Contra Affair*, Part 1, Executive Summary, 7. For Reagan's designation of Iran as "terrorist," see Ronald Reagan, Remarks at the Annual Convention of the American Bar Association, July 8, 1985, available at http://www.reagan.utexas.edu/archives/speeches/1985/70885a.htm. For the fifty-two captured American diplomats, see United States Congress House Committee on Foreign Affairs, Library of Congress, Foreign Affairs and National Defense Division, *The Iran Hostage Crisis: A Chronology of Daily Developments, January 1–25, 1981*, (Washington, DC: U.S. Government Printing Office, 1981). For Lebanon hostages, see *Report of the Congressional Committees Investigating the Iran-Contra Affair*, Part 1, Executive Summary, 6.

33. For the Enterprise, see *Report*, Executive Summary, 4. For its arms deals with Iran, including some via Israel, see *Report*, Executive Summary, 6–9. For *Al-Shiraa*, see *Report*, Executive Summary, xv.

34. See *Report*, Executive Summary, 9.

35. Executive Order 12333, Sec. 3.1

36. *Report*, Executive Summary, 17.

37. For a suggestion of some of these before the Iran-Contra committee report, see F.A.O. Schwarz Jr., "Recalling Major Lessons of the Church Committee," *New York Times*, July 30, 1987, 25.

38. For "highest elected officials," see *Report*, Executive Summary, 16. For "the common ingredients" and "time and again," see *Report*, Executive Summary, 11. For "the theory of our constitution," see *Report*, Executive Summary, 20.

39. For North's testimony, see Smist, 260–61. For a contemporary reaction, see Tom Shales, "What a Difference a Day Makes," *Washington Post*, July 11, 1987, G1.

40. "In Brutal Race, Robb Beats North," *New York Times*, November 9, 1994, A1. North had gained enormous national popularity thanks to his congressional testimony.

41. See Intelligence Authorization Act for Fiscal Year 1991, PL 102-88, 1991 HR 1455, 105 Stat. 429 (codified at 50 USCA 413b), § 503 (a) and § 503 (a) (5).
42. Reagan's apology speech of March 4, 1987, is available at www.presidentreagan .info/speeches/iran_contra.cfm. For the convictions of Poindexter and North and their reversals, see the Independent Counsel's report, Lawrence E. Walsh, *Iran-Contra: The Final Report* (New York: Times Books, 1994), available electronically at http://www.fas.org/irp/offdocs/walsh/chap_02.htm; *United States v. Poindexter*, 951 F.2d 369 (D.C. Cir. 1991); *United States v. North*, 910 F.2d 843 (D.C. Cir. 1990), amended by 920 F.2d 940 (D.C. Cir. 1990).
43. Rudalevige, 180.
44. For the Wichita and Cincinnati incidents, see David Cole and James X. Dempsey, *Terrorism and the Constitution: Sacrificing Civil Liberties in the Name of National Security* (New York: The New Press, 2002), 27.
45. Ibid., 21–33.
46. For accounts of these errors, see *The 9/11 Commission Report* (New York: W.W. Norton, 2004), 266–67, 271, 339–52. Beginning the evening of the 9/11 attacks, some critics blamed the Church Committee for 9/11. Thus former White House Chief of Staff and Secretary of State James Baker offered his opinion that the Committee had "in effect, unilaterally disarm[ed] our intelligence capacities." Intelligence agencies, Baker said, subsequently shied away from the "down and dirty" business of penetrating terrorist cells. The editorial page of the *Wall Street Journal* proclaimed the intelligence services had been "reeling" ever since Church. Both the *Journal* and thriller writer Tom Clancy announced that the Church Committee "gutted" the CIA's human intelligence capacities. And L. Paul Bremer, who went on to try to manage Iraq's occupation and reconstruction, also offered his view that the Church Committee "did a lot of damage to our intelligence services." For Baker, see ABC News Special Report, "America Under Attack," September 11, 2001, Nexis. For the *Journal* editorial, see "Unspooking Spooks," *Wall Street Journal*, September 18, 2001. For Clancy, see transcript of *The O'Reilly Factor*, with Tom Clancy, September 20, 2001, Nexis. For Bremer, see James Ridgeway, "The Bush Family Coup," *Village Voice*, December 30, 2005.

These critics, quick to exploit the fear and dismay prompted by 9/11, ignored the record of the Church Committee's work, including its urging the FBI to focus on terrorism, not political dissent; its argument that investigation of "international terrorism" was one reason why intelligence was a "vital national interest"; its emphasis on the importance of human spies rather than technology; and its push for strengthened CIA analytical capabilities. The critics also glossed over the absurdities of their own argument. How could the CIA, after more than a quarter-century and the administrations of five presidents (plus the first nine months of a sixth, George W. Bush), still be "reeling" from a blow by one Senate committee, many of whose recommendations had been successfully resisted? Ironically, during those years, James Baker had served as Chief of Staff for President Reagan for four years and for the first President Bush for a few months; he also served as secretary of the Treasury under Reagan and Secretary of State under Bush. If any agencies were "disarmed," was Baker seriously claiming that he and his bosses, Presidents Reagan and Bush (himself a former CIA director), did not know? Or that they lacked power to rehabilitate supposedly neutered agencies? Or that responsibility for the agencies' flaws bypassed Baker and the two presidents he served to land somehow at the Church Committee's feet?

47. *9/11 Commission Report*, 394–95.
48. See *Congressional Record*, November 11, 1975, 35786–35788.
49. *Bk. I*, 432–35, 449–50.
50. For the 9/11 Commission call for a new "National Intelligence Director," see *9/11 Commission Report*, 411–15. For the new Act, see Intelligence Reform and Terrorism Prevention Act of 2004, S. 2845.
51. *9/11 Commission Report*, 419–20.
52. *Bk. II*, 297.

Chapter 4: Our Torture Policy

1. For death threats, see "A Matter of Honor," *Washington Post*, September 28, 2005, A2. For other soldiers and "confusion," see Human Rights Watch, "Leadership Failure: Firsthand Accounts of Torture of Iraqi Detainees by the U.S. Army's 82nd Airborne Division" (September 2005).
2. Ian Fishback, "A Matter of Honor," *Washington Post*, September 28, 2005, A2.
3. For example, "Policies approved for use on al Qaeda and Taliban detainees, who were not afforded the protection of the Geneva Conventions, now applied to detainees who fall under the Geneva Convention protections." Independent Panel to Review Department of Defense Detention Operations (August 2004), 14.
4. *Filártiga v. Pena Irela*, 630 F. 2d 876 (2d Cir. 1980). For torture in U.S. prisons, see Judith Green, "From Abu Ghraib to America: Examining Our Harsh Prison Culture," *Ideas for an Open Society*, October 2004, 2; Alan Eisner, "Terror Cells: Abuse of Iraqi Detainees Is an Echo of the Cruelties Inflicted on U.S. Inmates," *Washington Post*, May 9, 2004, D1.
5. International Covenant on Civil and Political Rights, Art. 7, adopted December 16, 1966, S. Exec. Doc. No. E, 95-2 (1978), 999 U.N.T.S. 171; Convention Against Torture and Other Cruel, Inhuman or Degrading Treatment or Punishment, adopted December 10, 1984, S. Treaty Doc. No. 100-20 (1988), 1465 U.N.T.S. 85.
6. Louis Fisher, *American Military Tribunals & Presidential Power: American Revolution to the War on Terrorism* (Lawrence: University of Kansas Press, 2005), 71–82.
7. For Geneva Conventions, see Michael Byers, *War Law: Understanding International Law and Armed Conflict* (New York: Grove Press, 2006), 115–35; Ingrid Detter, *The Law of War* (Cambridge: Cambridge University Press, 2000), 158–59; Derek Jinks and David Sloss, "Is the President Bound by the Geneva Conventions?" *Cornell Law Review* 90 (November 2004), 97, 108–9. The full Conventions are reproduced at 6 U.S.T.S. 3316.
8. For the American perspective on the Conventions' drafting, see Raymond T. Yingling and Robert W. Ginnane, "The Geneva Conventions of 1949," *American Journal of International Law*, Vol. 45 (1951), 407. Yingling and Ginnane were the American negotiators in Geneva in 1949. For Gonzales's comment, see memorandum for the president from Alberto R. Gonzales re: "Application of the Geneva Conventions on Prisoners of War to the Conflict with al Qaeda and the Taliban," January 25, 2002, 2.
9. Third Convention, Arts. 3 and 13; Fourth Convention, Arts. 3 and 27.

10. Common Article 2. For Westphalia, see Philip Bobbit, *The Shield of Achilles: War, Peace and the Course of History* (London: Penguin Books, 2002), 501–19.

11. For Common Article 3, see Byers, 69–90, 132–33; Detter, 185–87; Jean S. Pictet, "The New Geneva Conventions for the Protection of War Victims," *American Journal of International Law* 45 (1951), 462, 471.

12. For customary international law and Common Article 3, see Ian Browlie, *Principles of Public International Law* (New York: Oxford University Press, 2003), 488–90; Jordan Paust, "Executive Plans and Authorizations to Violate International Law Concerning Treatment and Interrogation of Detainees," *Columbia Journal of Transnational Law* (2005), 811, 831–32 and n. 19.

13. Milt Bearden, "When the C.I.A. Played by the Rules," *New York Times*, November 4, 2005, A27.

14. For Vietnam, see Howard S. Levie, "Maltreatment of Prisoners of War in Vietnam," in Richard Falk, ed., *The Vietnam War and International Law*, Vol. 2 (Princeton: Princeton University Press, 1969), 361.

15. For military lawyers' training, see CDR Brian J. Bill et al, *Law of War Workshop Deskbook* (June 2000), 82. For military regulations, see Army Regulation 190–8 § 1–1.

16. For War Crimes Act, see 18 U.S.C. §§ 2441 et seq. (2006). The Third Convention in Article 130 and the Fourth Convention in Article 147 list "grave breaches."

17. International Covenant on Civil and Political Rights, Arts. 1 and 7, adopted December 16, 1966, S. Exec. Doc. No. E, 95-2 (1978) (emphasis added), 999 U.N.T.S. 171; Convention Against Torture and Other Cruel, Inhuman or Degrading Treatment or Punishment, adopted December 10, 1984, S. Treaty Doc. No. 100-20 (1988), 1465 U.N.T.S. 85. Torture is defined in Article 1(1), and CID in Article 16.

18. See 18 U.S.C. § 2340 et seq.

19. For Supreme Court's cases, see *Chambers v. Florida*, 309 U.S. 227 (1940); *Brown v. Mississippi*, 297 U.S. 278 (1936). For ATCS, see *Filártiga v. Pena Irela*, 630 F. 2d 876 (2d Cir. 1980).

20. Gordon S. Wood, *The Creation of the American Republic, 1776–1787* (New York: W.W. Norton, 1969), 5. For framers and ratifiers of the Constitution, see Jack N. Rakove, *Original Meanings: Politics and Ideas in the Making of the Constitution* (New York: Vintage, 1996), 46–56; Gordon S. Wood, *The Radicalism of the American Revolution* (New York: Vintage, 1991), 95–109. For Beccarias reputation, see Christopher Hitchens, *Thomas Jefferson: Author of America* (New York: Harper Collins, 2005), 39–40. For torture's roots, see Sadakat Kadri, *The Trial: A History from Socrates to O.J. Simpson* (New York: Random House, 2005), 3–69; Edward Peters, *Torture* (Philadelphia: University of Pennsylvania Press, 1996).

21. Memo from Alberto R. Gonzales to the President, "Decision re Application of the Geneva Convention on Prisoners of War to the Conflict with al Qaeda and the Taliban," January 25, 2002, 2. For Addington and Common Article 3, see Tim Golden and Eric Schmitt, "Detainee Policy Sharply Divides Bush Officials," *New York Times*, November 2, 2005, 1.

22. For Wilkerson, see transcript of *CNN Live*, Sunday, November 20, 2005; Mark Follman, "Colonel of Truth," *Salon*, February 27, 2006.

23. For OLC's role, see Cornelia T.L. Pillard, "The Unfulfilled Promise of the Consti-

tution in Executive Hands," *Michigan Law Review* 103 (2005), 676; Randolph D. Moss, "Executive Branch Legal Interpretation: A Perspective from the Office of Legal Counsel," *Administrative Law Review* 52 (2000), 1303, 1309–10; cf. "Principles to Guide the Office of Legal Counsel," December 21, 2004 (on file with authors).

24. Most these memos are in Mark Danner, *Torture and Truth: America, Abu Ghraib, and the War on Terror* (New York: New York Review Books, 2004).

25. Memorandum from John Yoo and Robert J. Delahunty for William J. Haynes II, "Application of Treaties and Laws to al Qaeda and Taliban Detainees," January 9, 2002; Memorandum from President George W. Bush, "Humane Treatment of al Qaeda and Taliban Detainees," February 7, 2002, in Danner, 105–6.

26. During World War II, Japan classed its American captives not as POWs but as "belligerents," and tortured them at the secret Ofuma interrogation center. See Jess Bravin, "What War Captives Faced in Japanese Prison Camps, and How U.S. Responded," *Wall Street Journal*, April 7, 2005.

27. See army regulation 190-8, § 1-1 (b) (4) ("In the event of conflicts or discrepancies between this regulation and the Geneva Conventions, the provisions of the Geneva Conventions take precedence".) For U.S. army manual and Fourth Geneva Convention, see Knut Dörmann, "The legal situation of 'unlawful/unprivileged combatants,'" *International Review of the Red Cross* 85, no. 849 (March 2007), 45.

28. Jane Mayer, "The Hidden Power," *New Yorker*, July 3, 2006, 44.

29. Memorandum from Yoo and Delahunty, 36; Memorandum for Alberto R. Gonzales, Counsel to the President, and William J. Haynes II, General Counsel of the Department of Defense, "Application of Treaties and Laws to al Qaeda and Taliban Detainees," January 22, 2002 (same text). For customary international law, see Michael D. Ramsey, "Torturing Executive Power," *Georgetown Law Journal* 93 (2005), 1213, 1245–51.

30. For Colin Powell, see memorandum from Secretary of State Colin L. Powell to Counsel for the President, "Draft Decision Memorandum for the President on the Applicability of the Geneva Conventions to the Conflict in Afghanistan," January 26, 2002. For the first Gulf War, see David Rose, *Guantánamo: America's War on Human Rights* (London: Faber & Faber, 2005), 26–27.

31. Memorandum from President George W. Bush, "Humane Treatment of al Qaeda and Taliban Detainees," February 7, 2002, in Danner, 105–6 (emphasis added). For Supreme Court opinion, see *Hamdan v. Rumsfeld*, 2006 WL 1764793 (June 29, 2006).

32. For Biddle, see Francis Biddle, *In Brief Authority* (New York: Doubleday, 1961), 226. For confusion on Iraqi insurgency, see Mayer, "Deadly Interrogation," 44.

33. For Flanigan, see attachment to letter from William E. Moschella, assistant attorney general, to the Hon. Arlen Specter (September 20, 2005). Written answers of Timothy E. Flanigan to the Senate Judiciary Committee (hereinafter Flanigan answers) on file with authors. For Gonzales, see responses of Alberto R. Gonzales, nominee to be attorney general, to the written supplemental questions of Senator Edward M. Kennedy, January 25, 2005 (on file with authors).

34. See Flanigan answers, 3–7; Eric Lichtblau, "Democrats Press Justice Dept. Nominee Anew," *New York Times*, September 24, 2005, A16. See also September 16, 2005, letter from Captain Ian Fishback to Senator John McCain, *Washington Post*, September 28, 2005, A21.

35. Susan Schmidt, "Disclosure of Authorized Interrogation Tactics Urged, Justice Dept. Concerned about Public Perception," *Washington Post*, July 3, 2004, A3; Mayer, "Deadly Interrogation," 44; letter from Assistant Attorney General William E. Moschella to Senator Edward Kennedy, September 19, 2005 (on file with authors).

36. For Abu Zubaydah, see James Risen, *State of War: The Secret History of the CIA and the Bush Administration* (New York: Free Press, 2006), 20–22. For past use of tactics, see Brian Ross and Richard Esposito, "Sources Tell ABC News Top Al Qaeda Figures Held in Secret CIA Prisons; 10 Out of 11 High Value Terror Leaders Subjected to 'Enhanced' Interrogation Techniques," ABC News, December 5, 2005, available at http://abcnews.com; For Gonzales meeting, see Evan Thomas and Michael Hirsh, "The Debate over Torture," *Newsweek*, November 21, 2005, 26.

37. Memorandum from Jay S. Bybee for Alberto R. Gonzales, Counsel to the President, "Standards of Conduct for Interrogation under 18 U.S.C. §§2340-2340A," August 1, 2002 ("Bybee memo"). For Yoo's authorship, see Michael Hirsh, John Barry, and Daniel Klaidman, "A Tortured Debate," *Newsweek*, June 21, 2005, 50; Scott Horton Statement to Beim Bundesgerichtshof "Strafanzeige gegen den US-Verteidigungsminister Donald Rumsfeld," u.a., at paragraph 27 (on file with authors). The opinion does not mention the Convention Against Torture's prohibition on "cruel, inhuman and degrading" treatment, a class of abuse one step less severe than torture. In January 2005, Gonzales told the Senate Judiciary Committee that this prohibition had "limited reach," and did not apply to "aliens overseas." Eric Lichtblau, "Gonzales Says Humane-Policy Doesn't Bind C.I.A.," *New York Times*, January 18, 2005, A17; Douglas Jehl and David Johnson, "White House Fought New Curbs on Interrogation, Officials Say," *New York Times*, January 13, 2005, A1.

38. State Department, "Iraq: Country Report on Human Rights Practices, 2002," March 31, 2003, available at http://www.state.gov/g/drl/rls/hrrpt/2002/18277.htm.

39. Bybee memo, 36–46.

40. Bybee memo, 34–35. Courts employ the canon of constitutional avoidance to avoid losing jurisdiction. See, e.g., *INS v. St. Cyr*, 533 U.S. 289 (2001). But courts' assertions of jurisdiction do not necessarily promote *judges'* self-interest. In any case, judicial opinions are public and subject to correction by Congress.

41. Ron Suskind, *The One-Percent Doctrine: Deep Inside America's Pursuit of Its Enemies Since 9/11* (New York: Simon & Schuster, 2006), 99–101.

42. See Danner, 45–46; interview with Bob Schieffer, CBS News, with President George W. Bush, in Washington, D.C. (January 27, 2006), available at http://www.cbsnews.com/stories/2006/01/27/eveningnews/main1248952_page3.shtml.

43. See Harold Hongju Koh, "A World Without Torture," *Columbia Journal of Transnational Law* 43 (2005), 641; Jeremy Waldron, "Torture and the Positive Law: Jurisprudence for the White House," *Columbia Law Review* 105 (2005), 1681; Dawn Johnsen and Neil Kinkopf, "Letter to the Editor: How to Prevent Another 'Torture' Memo," *Wall Street Journal*, January 21, 2005; R. Jeffrey Smith, "Slim Legal Grounds for Torture Memo: Most Scholars Reject Broad View of Executive's Power," *Washington Post*, July 4, 2004, A12.

44. When Bybee resigned, another conservative law professor, Jack Goldsmith, took

over. Goldsmith concluded the Bybee memo was fundamentally flawed and told the CIA it could no longer be relied upon. See letter from Daniel Levin, Acting Assistant Attorney General to Hon. William J. Haynes II, General Counsel, Department of Defense, February 4, 2004; Daniel Klaidman et al, "Palace Revolt," *Newsweek*, February 6, 2006, 34.

45. For repudiation of torture memo, see Schmidt, A3; Klaidman et al, 34.

46. Memorandum from Daniel Levin to James B. Comey, Deputy Attorney General, re: "Legal Standards Applicable Under 18 U.S.C. §§ 2340-2340A" (December 30, 2004). For water-boarding, see Ross and Esposito, ABC News, December 5, 2005; Thomas and Hirsh, 26; Hirsh, Barry and Klaidman, 50; Risen, 32.

47. Four months after Bush's CBS interview, CIA chief nominee Michael Hayden declined to tell the Senate Intelligence Committee whether water-boarding was not "a permissible interrogation technique." In September 2006, the Administration proposed legislation that purported to decriminalize water-boarding. See editorial, "New Face, Old Evasion," *Washington Post*, May 20, 2006, A22.

48. John Barry, Mark Hosenball, and Babak Dehghanpisheh, "Abu Ghraib and Beyond," *Newsweek*, May 17, 2004, 32. For Schlesinger, see "The Independent Panel to Review Department of Defense Detention Operations" (August 2004), 5.

49. For the March 2003 memo, see Mayer, "Deadly Interrogation," 44; Mike Allen and Dana Priest, "Memo on Torture Draws Focus to Bush," *Washington Post* (June 9, 2004), A3.

50. Memo for Secretary of Defense from William J. Haynes II, General Counsel, "Counter-Resistance Techniques," November 27, 2002; Memo for Commander, JTF 170, from LTC Diane E. Beaver, "Legal Brief on Proposed Counter-Resistance Strategies," October 11, 2002.

51. Jane Mayer, "The Memo," *New Yorker*, February 27, 2006, 32.

52. For Rives, see memo from Major-General Jack L. Rives, USAF, Deputy Judge Attorney General, for SAF/GC, "Final Report and Recommendations of the Working Group to Assess the Legal, Policy and Operational Issues Relating to Interrogation of Detainees Held by the U.S. Armed Forces in the War on Terrorism," February 5, 2003.

53. "Working Group Report on Detainee Interrogations in the Global War on Terrorism: Assessment of Legal, Historical, Policy, and Operational Considerations," April 4, 2003; executive summary of report of Vice Admiral Albert T. Church, 5. For superior orders defense, see Anthony D'Amato, "Superior Orders v. Command Responsibility," *American Journal of International Law* 80 (July 1986), 604.

54. For Defense Department denial, see memorandum for the Judge Advocate General and the Staff Judge Advocate to the Commandant from William J. Haynes II, March 17, 2005 (hereinafter Haynes memo). For acceptance by Rumsfeld, see memorandum from Secretary of Defense Donald Rumsfeld to Commander, U.S. Southern Command, April 16, 2003 (adopting twenty-four measures recommended by the working group). For acceptance by Sanchez, see memorandum for Commander, U.S. Central Command, from Lieutenant General Ricardo S. Sanchez, "CJTF-7 Interrogation and Counter-Resistance Policy," September 14, 2003; memorandum for Commander, C2 and C3 U.S. Central Command, from Lieutenant General Ricardo S. Sanchez, "CJTF-7 Interrogation and Counter-Resistance Policy," October 12, 2003. For Sanchez's reasons, see "The

Independent Panel to Review Department of Defense Detention Operations" (August 2004), 10. For multiple policies, see executive summary of report of Vice Admiral Albert T. Church, 15. For posters, see Steven H. Miles, *Oath Betrayed: Torture, Medical Complicity, and the War on Terror* (New York: Random House, 2006), 51–53

55. The use of sexual humiliation as a matter of routine interrogation procedure outside Abu Ghraib is documented by Physicians for Human Rights, "Break Them Down: Systematic Use of Psychological Torture by U.S. Forces," 2005, 25, 36–39.

56. For the CIA in Iraq, see AR 15-6, Investigation of the Abu Ghraib Detention Facility and 205th Military Intelligence Brigade, MG George R. Fay, 52–53; Risen, 144–46; Douglas Jehl, "C.I.A. Cites Order on Supervised Interrogations," *New York Times*, September 11, 2004, A7 (citing order that forbade unsupervised CIA interrogations in Iraq).

57. Transcript, "Media Availability with Commander, U.S. Southern Command general James T. Hill," December 27, 2005, available at http://www.defense.gov/transcripts/2004/tr20040603-0810.html. For Iraq, see Human Rights Watch, "'No Blood, No Foul': Soldiers' Accounts of Detainee Abuse in Iraq," July 2006. For SERE, see Jane Mayer, "The Experiment," *New Yorker,* July 11 and 18, 2005, 63. Stefan Nicola, "Lost in Guantánamo," UPI, December 22, 2005. For Doolittle, see chapter 1, note 4.

58. For Miller's visit, see "Assessment of DoD Counterterrorism Interrogation and Detention Operations in Iraq" (undated report on file with authors), 1–5; Mayer, "The Experiment," 63. For Afghanistan-Iraq connection, see Douglas Jehl and David Rohde, "Afghan Deaths Linked to Unit at Iraqi Prison," *New York Times*, May 24, 2004, 1; Julian Borger, "Report implicates top brass in Bagram scandal," *Guardian*, May 21, 2005.

59. The Independent Panel to Review Department of Defense Detention Operations (August 2004), 37; Danner, 27–28.

60. Third Geneva Convention, Art. 5, memorandum from Jay S. Bybee, Assistant Attorney General, for Alberto R. Gonzales, Counsel to the President, "Status of Taliban Forces Under Article 4 of the Third Geneva Convention of 1949," February 7, 2002, 2.

61. Rose, 13–22, 33–41; Tim Golden, "Administration Officials Split Over Stalled Military Tribunals," *New York Times*, October 25, 2004, 1; Tim Golden and Don van Natta, "U.S. Said to Overstate Value of Guantánamo Detainees," *New York Times*, June 21, 2004, A1; Rose, 9–17.

62. For Rumsfeld, see Seymour M. Hersh, *Chain of Command: The Road from 9/11 to Abu Ghraib* (New York: HarperCollins, 2004). For Myers, see Golden and van Natta, A1.

63. For "intense pressure," see R. Jeffrey Smith and Josh White, "Abuse Trial Revives Old Questions," *Washington Post*, May 22, 2006, A10. For e-mail, see e-mail from Cpt. William Ponce, available at www.pbs.org/wgbh/torture/paper/ponce.html. For army reports, see Department of the Army, inspector general, "Detainee Operations Inspection" (July 21, 2004), 20; "The Independent Panel to Review Department of Defense Detention Operations" (August 2004), 36.

64. Horton statement, at paragraph 27 (emphasis added). For Miller, see "Assessment of DoD Counterterrorism Interrogation and Detention Operations in Iraq" (un-

dated report on file with authors), 1–5; editorial, "A General's Dishonor," *Washington Post*, January 15, 2005, B16. For the failure to plan in Iraq, see George Packer, *The Assassins' Gate: America in Iraq* (New York: Farrar, Straus and Giroux, 2005), 298–332; Risen, 125–47.

65. Risen, 22–23 (emphasis added); Andrea Mitchell, "Reporter defends release of NSA spy program," MSNBC, January 3, 2006, available at http://www.msnbc .msn.com.; Suskind, 229.

66. Suskind, 173–75.

67. For Guantánamo, see Moazzam Begg with Victoria Brittain, *Enemy Combatant: My Imprisonment at Guantánamo, Bagram, and Kandahar* (New York: The New Press, 2006); *Rasul v. Bush*, 542 U.S. 466 (2004).

68. For prosecutorial discretion, see *Reno v. American-Arab Anti-Discrimination Committee*, 525 U.S. 471 (1999); Rachel Barkow, "Separation of Powers and the Criminal Law," *Stanford Law Review* 58 (2006) 989, 1044–50. For Abu Ghraib prosecutions, see JoAnn Wypiejewski, "Judgment Days: Lessons from the Abu Ghraib Prosecutions," *Harper's*, February 2006, 39. For prosecutions, see Hima Shamsi, *Command Responsibility: Detainee Deaths in U.S. Custody in Iraq and Afghanistan* (New York: Human Rights First, February 2006).

69. Mayer, "Deadly Interrogation," 44. For Supreme Court decision, see *Hamdan v. Rumsfeld*, 2006 WL 1764793 (June 29, 2006). For Administration response, see memorandum from Gordon England to Secretaries of the military departments, "Application of Common Article 3 of the Geneva Conventions to the Treatment of Detainees in the Department of Defense," July 7, 2006.

70. The White House, "President Discusses Creation of Military Tribunals to Try Suspected Terrorists," September 6, 2006, available at http://www.whitehouse .gov/news/releases/2006/09/print/20060906-3.html. For al-Libi, see chapter 5.

71. Brian Ross and Richard Esposito, "CIA Harsh Tactics Described," ABC News, November 18, 2005, available at http://abcnews.go.com/WNT/Investigation/ story?id=1322866&page=1; Sheryl Gay Stolberg, "Experts Say Bush's Goal in Terrorism Bill is Latitude for Interrogators' Methods," *New York Times*, September 19, 2006.

72. Mark Benjamin, "Mixed Messages on Torture," *Salon*, September 7, 2006, available at www.salon.com.

73. For Levin, see Mayer, "Deadly Interrogation," 44. For disclosure law, see 28 U.S.C. § 530D.

74. For McCain's October 5, 2005, Statement on Detainee Amendments, see *Congressional Record*, October 5, 2005, S11061. See also http://mccain.senate.gov/ index.cfm?fuseaction=NewsCenter.ViewPressRelease&Content_id=1611.

75. For summer 2005 meetings, see Evan Thomas and Richard Wolffe, "Bush in the Bubble," *Newsweek*, December 19, 2005, 30; Dana Priest and Robin Wright, "Cheney Fights for Detainee Policy As Pressure Mounts to Limit Handling of Terror Suspects," *Washington Post*, November 7, 2005, A1; Tim Golden and Eric Schmitt, "Detainee Policy Sharply Divides Bush Officials," *New York Times*, November 2, 2005, A1; Josh White and R. Jeffrey Smith, "White House Aims to Block Legislation on Detainees," *Washington Post*, July 23, 2005, A1. For Addington, see Douglas Jehl, "In Cheney's New Chief, a Bureaucratic Master," *New York Times*, November 2, 2005, A2. For veto threat, see White and Smith,

"White House Aims to Block Legislation," A1. For Bush's record on vetoes, see Phillip J. Cooper, "George W. Bush, Edgar Allan Poe, and the Use and Abuse of Presidential Signing Statements," *Presidential Studies Quarterly* 35 (September 2005), 515.

76. See Detainee Treatment Act of 2005, Title XIV of H.R. 2683; Aziz Huq, "Obstacle Course," *Legal Times*, January 16, 2006, 42; *Hamdan v. Rumsfeld*, 2006 WL 1764793 (June 29, 2006). For the difficulty of prosecuting officials for torture, see Mayer, "Deadly Interrogation," 44.

77. For 750 signing statements, see Charlie Savage, "Bush Challenges Hundreds of Laws," *Boston Globe*, April 30, 2006; see also Cooper, 515. For Reagan era, see Terry Eastland, *Energy in the Executive: The Case for the Strong Presidency* (New York: Free Press, 1992), 73–76.

78. President's Statement on Signing H.R. 2683, the "Department of Defense, Emergency Supplemental Appropriations to Address Hurricanes in the Gulf of Mexico, and Pandemic Influenza Act, 2006," December 30, 2006, available at http://www.whitehouse.gov; Charlie Savage, "Bush Could Bypass New Torture Ban," *Boston Globe*, January 4, 2006; Jonathan Weisman, "Bush's Challenges of Laws He Signed Is Criticized," *Washington Post*, June 28, 2006, A9. For the disclosure of noncompliance, see 28 U.S.C. § 530D (2006). For Specter, see Brian Friel, "Caught in the Middle," *National Journal*, June 19, 2006.

79. President's News Conference, September 15, 2006 (transcript on file with authors).

80. Military Commissions Act of 2006.

81. For debate see, e.g., Charles Babington and R. Jeffrey Smith, "Bush's Detainee Plan Is Criticized," *Washington Post*, September 8, 2006, A9. For military lawyers, see Charlie Savage, "Military Lawyers See Limits in Trial Input," *Boston Globe*, August 27, 2006. For Congress and Sessions quote, see Rick Klein, "Congress in Dark on Terror Program," *Boston Globe*, September 23, 2006. See also Bob Herbert, "The Kafka Strategy," *New York Times*, September 18, 2006, A27.

82. Human Rights First, "Getting to Ground Truth: Investigating U.S. Abuses in the 'War on Terror,'" September 2004, 2.

83. For the official investigations, see Human Rights Watch, "Getting Away with Torture? Command Responsibility for the U.S. Abuse for the Detainees," April 2005. For abuse in Iraq, see Human Rights Watch, "Firsthand Accounts of Torture of Iraqi Detainees by the U.S. Army's 82nd Airborne Division," September 2005; Richard A. Serrano, "More Iraqis Tortured, Officer Says," *Los Angeles Times* (September 24, 2005). For soldiers' complaints, see Eric Schmitt, "Officer Criticizes Detainee Abuse Inquiry," *New York Times*, September 28, 2005, A10: Elizabeth Williamson, "Witness to Abuse Trying to be Heard," *Washington Post*, August 20, 2004, A12; Rick Scavetta, "GI Flagged for Public Comments About His Abu Ghraib Experience," May 28, 2004, available at http://www.estripes.com. For ghost detainee, see AR 15-6 Investigation of the Abu Ghraib Detention Facility and 205th Military Intelligence Brigade, MG George R. Fay, 52–53.

84. The Independent Panel to Review Department of Defense Detention Operations (August 2004), 104, Appendix B. For Formica Report, see Brigadier General Richard P. Formica, "Article 15-6 Investigation of CJSTOTF-AP and 5th SF Group Detention Operations" (declassified June 2006). The Formica report was completed in November 2004.

85. *The 9/11 Commission Report* (New York: W.W. Norton, 2004), 379; "9/11 Commissioners Fault Administration," *New York Times*, November 14, 2005, available at www.nytimes.com. For example of British call for Guantánamo closure, see statement of Lord Goldsmith, British Attorney General, available at http://news.bbc.co.uk/2/hi/uk_news/politics/4759317.stm.

86. The 9/11 Public Discourse Project, "Report on the Status of 9/11 Commission Recommendations, Part III: Foreign Policy, Public Diplomacy, and Nonproliferation," November 14, 2005, 8–9.

87. For polls, see the Pew Global Attitudes Project, "America's Image Slips, but Allies Share U.S. Concerns Over Iran, Hamas," June 13, 2006; Pew Global Attitudes Project, "American Character Gets Mixed Reviews: U.S. Image Up Slightly, But Still Negative," June 23, 2005. For Guantánamo, see Julie Hirschfield Davis, "Bush, Merkel United on Iran," *Baltimore Sun*, January 16, 2006, 1A; Michael White, "Blair Pleads Ignorance Over Torture Flights," *The Guardian*, December 8, 2005, 6.

88. Sebnem Arsu, "If You Want to Make a Film Fly, Make Americans the Villains," *New York Times*, February 14, 2006, A3; Pelin Turget, "Bad Blood on the Big Screen," *Time* (Europe Edition), February 5, 2006.

Chapter 5: "Extraordinary Rendition" and the Wages of Hypocrisy

1. For Bush's speech, see "President Commemorates Veterans Day, Discusses War on Terror," available at http://whitehouse.gov/news/releases/2005/11/print/20011111-1.html. For Hariri investigation, see Michael Slackman, "Syria Attacks Evidence as U.N. Case Turns More Bizarre," *New York Times*, December 7, 2005, A3. For sanctions, see James Bennet, "The Enigma of Damascus," *New York Times Magazine*, July 10, 2005, 28.

2. For rendition, see M. Cherif Bassiouni, "Unlawful Seizures and Irregular Rendition Devices as Alternatives to Extradition," *Vanderbilt Journal of Transnational Law* 7 (1973–74), 25, 34. For countries, see U.S. Department of State, "Syria: Country Reports on Human Rights Practices—2004," available at http://www.state.gov/g/drl/rls/hrrpt/2004/41732.html; U.S. Department of State, "Jordan: Country Reports on Human Rights Practices—2004," available at http://www.state.gov/g/drl/rls/hrrpt/2004/41724.htm; U.S. Department of State, "Egypt: Country Reports on Human Rights Practices—2004," available at http://www.state.gov/g/drl/rls/hrrpt/2004/41720.htm.

3. For numbers, see Center for Human Rights and Global Justice, "Beyond Guantánamo: Transfers to Torture One Year After *Rasul v. Bush*," June 28, 2005, 3.

4. *Arar v. Ashcroft*, 414 F. Supp. 2d 250, 255 (E.D.N.Y. 2006) (repeating Arar's allegations without reaching any conclusion as to whether or not they were true).

5. See Jane Mayer, "Outsourcing Torture," *New Yorker*, February 14, 2005, 106; Canadian Broadcasting Company, "Missing Ottawa engineer turns up in Syria," October 22, 2002, available at http://www.cbc.ca/stories/2002/10/21/arar_021021.

6. Michelle Shepherd, "Record of Syrian abuse called 'extremely poor,'" *Toronto Star*, November 10, 2005, A13; Andrew Mills and Michelle Shepherd, "Convict torturers, Syria told," *Toronto Star*, October 28, 2005, A01; Clifford Krauss, "Ev-

idence Grows that Canada Aided in Having Terrorism Suspects Interrogated in Syria," *New York Times*, September 17, 2005, A7; Thomas Walkom, "Arar's troubles rooted in the Cold War," *Toronto Star*, September 17, 2005, H01; Commission of Inquiry into the Actions of Canadian Officials in Relation to Maher Arar, *Report of the Events Relating to Maher Arar* (2006), 18, 28–30; Scott Shane, "Torture Victim Had No Terror Link, Canada Told U.S.," *New York Times*, September 25, 2006, A1.

7. See Complaint and Demand for Jury Trial in *Arar v. Ashcroft*, January 20, 2005, available at http://www.ccr-ny.org/v2/legal/september_11th/docs/Arar Complaint.pdf; Andrew Zajac, "Bush Wielding Secrecy Privilege to End Suits; National Security Cited Against Challenges to Anti-terror Tactics," *Chicago Tribune*, March 3, 2005, 1.

8. *Arar*, 414 F. Supp. 2d at 283; Bob Herbert, "No Justice, No Peace," *New York Times*, February 23, 2006, A27.

9. For broader perspectives, see Cass Sunstein, "Deliberative Trouble? Why Groups Go to Extremes," *Yale Law Journal* 110 (2000), 71; James Surowiecki, *The Wisdom of Crowds* (New York: Doubleday, 2004).

10. See Charles Fairman, editorial comment, "*Ker v. Illinois* Revisited," *American Journal of International Law* 47 (1953), 678; *Ker v. People*, 110 Ill. 627 (1884), aff'd 119 U.S. 436 (1886).

11. *United States v. Alvarez-Machain*, 504 U.S. 655 (1992).

12. Timothy Naftali, "Milan Snatch," *Slate*, June 30, 2005; *United States v. Yunis*, 924 F. 2d 1086 (D.C.Cir. 1991).

13. Steve Coll, *Ghost Wars: The Secret History of the CIA, Afghanistan and Bin Laden, from the Soviet Invasion to September 10, 2001* (London: Penguin Books, 2004), 272–75; Lawrence Ziring, *Pakistan at the Crossroads of History* (Lahore: Vanguard Books, 2004), 279–89, 302.

14. See Mayer, "Outsourcing Torture," 106; comments of Michael Scheuer, *Talk of the Nation* broadcast, National Public Radio, April 7, 2005; Michael Scheuer, "A Fine Rendition," *New York Times*, March 11, 2005, A23; Neil Mackay, "These two men are experts on rendition. One invented it, the other has seen its full horrors," *Sunday Herald*, October 16, 2005, 21; testimony of Christopher Kojm, 9/11 Commission deputy, transcript of 9/11 Commission hearings, March 24, 2004; *The 9/11 Commission Report: Final Report of the National Commission on Terrorist Attacks Upon the United States* (New York: W.W. Norton, 2004), 127.

15. Quotes from Scheuer, A23, and Roy Elleston, "CIA 'renditions' in tune with Habib claim of abuse in Egypt," *Australian*, February 14, 2005, 17.

16. Mayer, "Outsourcing Torture," 106; Shaun Waterman, "Terror Detainees Sent to Egypt," *Washington Times*, May 16, 2004, 16; Douglas Jehl and David Johnston, "Rule Change Lets C.I.A. Freely Send Suspects Abroad," *New York Times*, March 6, 2005, A1.

17. See Human Rights Watch, "Still at Risk: Diplomatic Assurances No Safeguard Against Torture," April 2005.

18. Responses of Alberto R. Gonzales, Nominee to be Attorney General of the United States, to Written Questions of Senator Richard J. Durbin, response 1(b) (on file with authors); John Barry, Michael Hirsch, and Michael Isikoff, "The

Roots of Torture," *Newsweek*, May 24, 2004, 16; DeNeen L. Brown and Dana Priest, "Deported Terror Suspect Details Torture in Syria; Canada's Case Called Typical of CIA," *Washington Post*, November 5, 2003, A1.

19. For CIA tactics, see Brian Ross and Richard Esposito, "Sources Tell ABC News Top Al Qaeda Figures Held in Secret CIA Prisons; 10 Out of 11 High Value Terror Leaders Subjected to 'Enhanced Interrogation Techniques,'" ABC News, December 5, 2005, available at http://abcnews.com. For torture memo, see memorandum from Jay S. Bybee for Alberto R. Gonzales, Counsel to the President, "Standards of Conduct for Interrogation under 18 U.S.C. §§ 2340–2340A," August 1, 2002.

20. For reports on sites, see Dana Priest, "CIA Holds Terror Suspects in Secret Prisons: Debate Is Growing Within Agency About Legality and Morality of Overseas System Set Up After 9/11," *Washington Post*, November 2, 2005, A1; Dana Priest and Barton Gellman, "U.S. Decries Abuse but Defends Interrogation; 'Stress and Duress' Tactics Used on Terrorism Suspects Held in Secret Overseas Facilities," *Washington Post*, December 26, 2002; Mark Seddon, "Is There Another Guantánamo Bay on British Soil?" *Independent*, December 13, 2002; Ross and Esposito; Yossi Melman, "CIA holding Al-Qaida suspects in secret Jordanian lockup," *Ha'aretz*, October 13, 2004, available at http://haaretzdaily/hasen/spages/488039.html; Human Rights Watch, "Human Rights Watch Statement on Secret U.S. Detention Facilities in Europe," November 7, 2005, available at http://hrw.org/english/docs/2005/11/07/usint11995.htm.

21. According to the *Washington Post*, only one-third of the hundred or so suspects who have been rendered are "considered major terrorism suspects." Priest, "CIA Holds Terror Suspects in Secret Prisons," A1. For Zubaydah's story see ibid.; Daniel Benjamin, "U.S. Excesses in the Terror War are Causing a Self-Defeating Backlash," *Time*, December 6, 2005.

22. *Rasul v. Bush*, 542 U.S. 466 (2004).

23. See Amnesty International, "United States of America/Yemen: Secret Detention in CIA 'Black Sites,'" November 2005; Amnesty International, "United States of America/Jordan/Yemen: Torture and Secret Detention: Testimony of the 'Disappeared' in the 'War on Terror,'" August 4, 2005; U.S. Department of State, "Yemen: Country Reports on Human Rights Practices—2004," February 28, 2005; Scott Shane and Margot Williams, "Yemenis Freed After Transfer From Secret Prisons," *New York Times*, April 5, 2006, A10. For details on international standards for prisons, see Andrew Coyle, "A Human Rights Approach to Prison Management" (London: International Center for Prison Studies, 2005).

24. Raymond Bonner, "Detainee Says He Was Tortured While in U.S. Custody," *New York Times*, February 13, 2005, A1; Dana Priest and Dan Eggen, "Terror Suspect Alleges Torture," *Washington Post*, January 6, 2005, A1. Habib is not the only detainee to experience extraordinary rendition before Guantánamo. See Tim Golden, "Guantánamo Terror Suspect Is Given His Say," *New York Times*, April 7, 2006, A18; David Rose, "MI6 and CIA 'sent student to Morocco to be tortured,'" *Observer* (UK), December 11, 2005, 20; Raymond Bonner, "Terror Suspect's Ordeal in U.S. Custody," *New York Times*, December 18, 2005, A14.

25. For an analysis of unilateral presidential powers outside national security context, see Elena Kagan, "Presidential Administration," *Harvard Law Review* 114 (2001),

2245; see also Jonathan R. Macey, "Separated Powers and Positive Political Theory: The Tug of War over Administrative Agencies," *Georgetown Law Review* 80 (1992), 671.

26. William G. Howell, *Power without Persuasion: The Politics of Direct Presidential Action* (Princeton: Princeton University Press, 2003), 1–7; Joel L. Fleishman and Arthur H. Aufses, "Law and Orders: The Problem of Presidential Legislation," *Law and Contemporary Problems* 40 (Summer 1976), 1; *United States v. Midwest Oil Co.*, 236 U.S. 459 (1915). For presidential orders, see Phillip J. Cooper, *By Order of the President: The Use and Abuse of Executive Direct Action* (Lawrence: University Press of Kansas, 2002).

27. Howell, passim; GAO, "National Security: The Use of Presidential Directives to Make and Implement U.S Policy," January 1992.

28. Only one of the Clinton-era presidential directives on rendition is available; see Presidential Decision Directive 39, June 21, 1995, available at http://www .fas.org/irp/offdocs/pdd39.htm.

29. Ron Suskind, *The One-Percent Doctrine: Deep Inside America's Pursuit of Its Enemies Since 9/11* (New York: Simon & Schuster, 2006), 15–20. Dana Priest, "Foreign Network at Front of CIA's Terror Fights; Joint Facilities in Two Dozen Countries Account for Bulk of Agency's Post 9/11 Successes," *Washington Post*, November 18, 2005, A1; Dana Priest, "CIA Holds Terror Suspects in Secret Prisons," A1; Jehl and Johnston, A1; Shaun Waterman, "CIA 'Too Cautious' in Killing Terrorists," *UPI Wire Service*, February 27, 2005.

30. Dana Priest, "Democrats Seek Probes on CIA Interrogations," *Washington Post*, March 2, 2005, A7; Suzanne E. Spaulding, "Power Play: Did Bush Roll Past the Legal Stop Signs?" *Washington Post*, December 25, 2005, B1.

31. For Roberts, see Dana Priest and Walter Pincus, "CIA, White House Defend Transfers of Terror Suspects," *Washington Post*, March 15, 2005, A7.

32. Priest and Eggen, A1.

33. The White House, "President Discusses Creation of Military Tribunals to Try Suspected Terrorists," September 6, 2006, available at http://www.whitehouse .gov/news/releases/2006/09/print/20060906-3.html.

34. For "assurance," see Dafna Linzer and Glenn Kessler, "Decision to Move Detainees Resolved Two Year Debate Among Bush Advisors," *Washington Post*, September 8, 2006, A1. For anonymous quote, see Dana Priest, "Officials Relieved Secret Is Shared," *Washington Post*, September 7, 2006, A7. For Human Rights Watch, see Human Rights Watch, "Bush Justifies CIA Detainee Abuse," September 6, 2006, available at http://hrw.org.

35. John Yoo, "Transferring Terrorists," *Notre Dame Law Review* 79 (2004), 1183.

36. For Colby, see William E. Colby, "After Investigating U.S. Intelligence," *New York Times*, February 26, 1976, 30. For Gerecht, see Reuel Marc Gerecht, "Against Rendition," *Weekly Standard*, May 16, 2005. Gerecht, we note, does not believe the public would reject torture or abuse. On that point, we are dubious.

37. For Rice, see Joel Brinkley, "Rice to Defend U.S. on Reports of Prisons for Terror Suspects," *New York Times*, December 5, 2005, 3. For other Bush claims, see David Stout, "Bush Offers Details of 2002 Plot in Defense of Terror Strategy," *New York Times*, February 9, 2006, A1.

38. For army interrogation tactics, see Chris Mackey and Greg Miller, *The Interroga-*

tor's War: Inside the Secret War against al Qaeda (London: John Murray, 2004), 78–83. For Cloonan, see Jason Vest, "Pray and Tell," *American Prospect*, July 2005, 47. For Gerecht, see Reuel Marc Gerecht, "Against Rendition," *Weekly Standard*, May 16, 2005.

39. See Gerecht.

40. For details of al-Libi's arrest and transfer, see Jason Vest, "Pray and Tell," *American Prospect*, July 2005, 47; Evan Thomas and Michael Hirsh, "The Debate over Torture," *Newsweek*, November 21, 2005, 26. See also Duncan Campbell, "September 11: six months on: U.S. sends suspects to face torture," *The Guardian*, March 12, 2002, 4; Brown and Priest, A1.

41. On the fact that al-Libi's information was known to be untrue, see Thomas and Hirsh, 26; Ross and Esposito. For al-Libi, see Mayer, "Outsourcing Torture," 106; Douglas Jehl, "Qaeda-Iraq Link U.S. Cited Is Tied to Coercion Claim," *New York Times*, December 9, 2005; Douglas Jehl, "Report Warned Bush Team About Intelligence Suspicions," *New York Times*, November 6, 2005; Robert Scheer, "Lying with Intelligence," *Los Angeles Times*, November 8, 2005, B13.

42. On Hamid Mir, see Peter L. Bergen, "From the Shadows: An Oral History of Osama Bin Laden," *Vanity Fair*, January 2006, 112, 151.

43. For "erroneous renditions," see Associated Press, "CIA Watchdog Looks into 'Erroneous Renditions,'" December 27, 2005, available at www.msnbc.com. See also Dana Priest, "Wrongful Imprisonment: Anatomy of a CIA Mistake," *Washington Post*, December 4, 2005, A1.

44. Priest, "Wrongful Imprisonment," A1.

45. For El-Masri, see Priest, "Wrongful Imprisonment," A1; Craig Whitlock, "Europeans Investigate CIA Role in Abductions; Suspects Possibly Taken To Nations That Torture," *Washington Post*, March 13, 2005, A1.

46. See *El-Masri v. Tenet*, No. 1:05cv1417 (May 12, 2006).

47. For the Milan case, see Craig Whitlock, "CIA Ruse Is Said to Have Damaged Probe in Milan," *Washington Post*, December 6, 2005, A1.

48. See Amnesty International, "United States of America/Yemen: Secret Detention in CIA 'Black Sites,'" November 2005.

49. For Padilla, see Douglas Jehl and Eric Lichtblau, "Shift on Suspect Is Linked to Role of Qaeda Figures," *New York Times*, November 24, 2005, 1. Mark Hosenball, Michael Hirsh, and Ron Moreau, "Odyssey into the Shadows," *Newsweek*, June 24, 2002, 28. For Lindh, see Jane Mayer, "Lost in the Jihad," *New Yorker*, March 10, 2003, 50.

50. Tim Golden, "Guantanamo Terror Suspect Is Given His Say," *New York Times*, April 7, 2006, A18; Rose, 20. In March 2006, the White House issued a very weak rule against evidence gained by torture for the military commissions. Jess Bravin, "White House Will Reverse Policy, Ban Evidence Elicited by Torture," *Wall Street Journal*, March 22, 2006, A3. The 2006 military commissions law further weakens anti-torture prohibitions.

51. For an excellent summary of this argument in another context, see Stephen Schulhofer, *Rethinking the Patriot Act: Keeping America Safe and Free* (New York: Century Foundation, 2005), 7–9.

52. Remarks of Secretary of State Condoleezza Rice upon her Departure for Europe, December 5, 2005, Andrews Air Force Base (on file with authors).

53. Dana Priest, "CIA's Assurances on Transferred Suspects Doubted; Prisoners Say

Countries Break No-Torture Pledges," *Washington Post*, March 17, 2005, A1; R. Jeffrey Smith, "Gonzales Defends Transfer of Detainees," *Washington Post*, March 8, 2005, A3.

54. For Gonzales's comments, see Responses of Alberto R. Gonzales, Nominee to be Attorney General of the United States, to Written Questions of Senator Richard J. Durbin, response 1(b) (on file with authors).

55. See Committee on International Human Rights of the Association of the Bar of the City of New York and the Center for Human Rights and Global Justice, New York University School of Law, "Torture by Proxy: International and Domestic Law Applicable to 'Extraordinary Rendition'" (2004), 3, n. 5; Foreign Affairs Reform and Restructuring Act of 1998, Pub. L. No. 105-277, div. G. Title XXII, S 1242(a) (emphasis added).

56. Priest, "CIA's Assurances Doubted," A1.

57. For Goss's statement, see Tracy Wilkinson and Bob Drogin, "Missing Imam's Trail Said to Lead From Italy to CIA; Prosecutors in Milan Are Investigating Whether an Egyptian-born Suspected Militant Was Spirited Away by the U.S. Using a Disputed Tactic," *Los Angeles Times,* March 3, 2005, A1. See Human Rights Watch, "Still at Risk"; Priest, "CIA's Assurances Doubted," A1.

58. For Arar, see Shane, "Torture Victim."

59. See Convention Against Torture Art. 3 (1) and (2). Diplomatic assurances also violate the Geneva Conventions—see Geneva Convention Relative to the Treatment of Prisoners of War, August 12, 1949, 6 U.S.T. 3316, 75 U.N.T.S. 135, Art. 13; Convention Relative to the Protection of Civilian Persons in Time of War, Geneva, August 12, 1949, 6 U.S.T. 3516, 75 U.N.T.S. 287.

60. See Human Rights Watch, "Still at Risk," 7.

61. U.S. Department of State, "Egypt: Country Reports on Human Rights Practices—2004," available at http://www.state.gov/g/drl/rls/hrrpt/2004/41720 .htm; see also U.S. Department of State, "Syria: Country Reports on Human Rights Practices –2004," available at http://www.state.gov/g/drl/rls/hrrpt/2004/41732 .html; see also U.S. Department of State, "Jordan: Country Reports on Human Rights Practices—2004," available at http://www.state.gov/g/drl/rls/hrrpt/2004/ 41724.htm.

62. Richard Bernstein, "Skepticism Seems to Erode Europeans' Faith in Rice," *New York Times*, December 7, 2005, 25; Bronwen Maddox, "Tough Words from Rice Leave Loopholes," *Times*, December 6, 2005, 34. For a perceptive and pithy rejection of Secretary Rice's position, see editorial, "A Weak Defense," *Washington Post*, December 6, 2005, A28.

63. For foreign reactions and editorials, see editorial, "Tortured Logic," *Miami Herald*, December 11, 2005; David Crossland, "Europe Skeptical of U.S. Assurances," *Newsday*, December 9, 2005, A48; Anne Gearan, "U.S. Admits Botched Detention, Merkel Says," WashingtonPost.com, December 6, 2005; Rose. For EU's reaction, see Glenn Kessler, "E.U. Seeks Details on Secret CIA Jails," *Washington Post*, December 1, 2005, A16.

64. See Bernstein; "A Weak Defense," A28; Luke Hardin, "CIA's secret jails open up new transatlantic rift," *The Guardian*, December 5, 2005, 14 (detailing tensions with Germany); Wilkinson and Drogin, A1. For the House of Lords' judgment, see *A (FC) v. Secretary of State*, 2005 UKHL 71, paragraph 83. On the UK press reaction, see editorial, "Tortured Logic," *Times of London*, December 9, 2005

(noting that it was "strange" that so "basic" a principle as the refusal to use evidence from torture had to be confirmed).

65. John J. Mearsheimer, "The False Promise of International Institutions," *International Security* 19 (Winter 1994–95), 5–7.

66. Ibid., 48.

67. For reports of diplomatic friction, see Glenn Kessler, "E.U. Seeks Details on Secret CIA Jails," *Washington Post*, December 1, 2005, A16; Ian Fisher, "Reports of Secret U.S. Prisons in Europe Draw Ire and Otherwise Red Faces," *New York Times*, December 1, 2005, A1; Steven R. Weisman and Ian Fisher, "U.S. to Respond to Inquiries Over Detentions in Europe," *New York Times*, November 30, 2005, A3.

68. For Europe's attitudes, see Olivier Roy, *Les illusions du 11 septembre: Le débat stratégique face au terrorisme* (Paris: Editions de Seuil, 2002), 22–25. For Kagan, see Robert Kagan, "America's Crisis of Legitimacy," *Foreign Affairs* 83 (2004), 65, 72. For importance of nonmilitary power, see Joseph S. Nye Jr., *The Paradox of American Power: Why the World's Only Superpower Can't Go It Alone* (New York: Oxford University Press, 2002), 8–9.

69. "Torture by Proxy," 9–10; Victor L. Simpson, "U.S. Allies Resist Secret Deportations," WashingtonPost.com, June 19, 2005; *Agiza v. Sweden*, Committee Against Torture, Communication No. 233/2003, U.N. Doc. CAT/C/34/D/233/2003.

70. *A (FC) v. Secretary of State*, 2005 UKHL 71; Statement of Eliza Manningham-Buller to the House of Lords in *A (FC) v. Secretary of State*, paragraph 6; see also Elaine Sciolino, "Spanish Judge Calls for Closing U.S. Prison at Guantánamo," *New York Times*, June 4, 2006.

71. Richard Bernstein, "German Court Convicts Man of Qaeda Ties," *New York Times*, August 20, 2005, A6; Mark Landler, "German 9/11 Trial Gets Exculpatory Evidence from U.S.," *New York Times*, August 12, 2005, 16; Richard Bernstein, "Germans Free Moroccan Convicted of a 9/11 Role," *New York Times*, April 8, 2004, 18.

72. Whitlock, A1; Tom Hundley and John Crewdson, "Wife Was Left Behind with the Children," *Chicago Tribune*, July 3, 2005.

73. Stephen Grey and Elisabetta Povoledo, "Italy Arrests 2 in Kidnapping of Imam in '03," *New York Times*, July 6, 2006, A1. Whitlock, A1; Hundley and Crewdson. On the hotel bills, see Craig Whitlock and Dafna Linzer, "Italy Seeks Arrest of 13 in Alleged CIA Action," *Washington Post*, June 25, 2005, A1.

74. For Egypt, see Nathan J. Brown, *Constitutions in a Nonconstitutional World: Arab Basic Laws and the Prospects for Accountable Government* (Albany: State University of New York Press, 2002), 122–29; Milton Viorst, *In the Shadow of the Prophet: The Struggle for the Soul of Islam* (Boulder: Westview Press, 2001), 331–77. For the 2005 elections and Nour's case, see Michael Slackman, "Testing Egypt, Mubarek Rival Is Sent to Jail," *New York Times*, December 25, 2005, A1; "Not yet a democracy," *The Economist*, December 10, 2005, 54.

75. For Jordan, see BBC Monitoring Europe—Political, "German, CIA roles in terror suspect's torture viewed by paper" November 22, 2005 (detailing *Der Spiegel* article); Ken Silverstein, "U.S., Jordan Forge Closer Ties in Covert War on Terrorism," *Los Angeles Times*, November 11, 2005, A1. For Syria, see "The Syrians are in the dock, but the murders continue," *The Economist*, December 17, 2005,

43; John Crewdson, "No Regrets in War on Terrorism," *Chicago Tribune*, July 3, 2005, C5.

76. For Egypt, see Lawyers Committee for Human Rights, "Assessing the New Normal: Liberty and Security for the Post–September 11 United States," 2003, 77. For Sudan and Zimbabwe, see Human Rights Watch, "The United States' 'Disappeared': The CIA's Long-Term 'Ghost Detainees,'" October 2004. For the UN Human Rights Commission, see Warren Hoge, "Zimbabwe's Role in U.N. Human Rights Panel Angers U.S.," *New York Times*, April 28, 2005, A9. For UN Committee Against Torture, see http://www.ohchr.org/english/bodies/cat/cats36.htm.

77. For 9/11 Commission, see *The 9/11 Commission Report*, 376. For Powell, see letter from General Colin L. Powell to Senator John McCain, September 13, 2006 (on file with authors). The Church Committee had warned against and urged banning covert "support for police or other internal security forces which engaged in the systematic violation of human rights." *Bk I*, 448. For President Bush, see press conference of the President, September 15, 2006, available at http://www.whitehouse.gov/news/releases/2006/09/20060915-2.html.

Chapter 6: Bringing War Back Home

1. The reporting requirement in FISA is at 50 U.S.C. § 1808 (a) (1).
2. For Patriot Act and quotes, see the Uniting and Strengthening America by Providing Appropriate Tools Required to Intercept and Obstruct Terrorism (USA PATRIOT) Act, Public Law No. 107-52 (2001); John Lancaster, "House Approves Terrorism Measure; Bill Grants Bulk of Bush's Request," *Washington Post*, October 25, 2001, A1; Stephen J. Schulhofer, *Rethinking the Patriot Act: Keeping America Safe and Free* (New York: Century Foundation, 2005). For a discussion of the information sharing permissible under the Patriot Act, see *In re Sealed Case*, 310 F.3d 717 (FISA Ct. of Review 2002).
3. See *The 9/11 Commission Report: Final Report of the National Commission on Terrorist Attacks upon the United States* (New York: W.W. Norton, 2004) 273–76; Patricia L. Bellia, "The 'Lone Wolf' Amendment and the Future of Foreign Intelligence Surveillance Law," *Villanova Law Review* 50 (2005), 425.
4. For Patriot Act reauthorization, see USA PATRIOT Improvement and Reauthorization Act of 2005, Public Laws 109-177 and 109-178 (March 6, 2006).
5. "President Bush: Information Sharing, Patriot Act Vital to Homeland Security," remarks by the President in a conversation on the USA Patriot Act, Kleinshans Music Hall, Buffalo, New York, April 20, 2004, available at www.whitehouse.gov/news/releases/2004/04/print/20040420-2.html.
6. Remarks by President Bush: Ohio State Highway Patrol Academy, Columbus, Ohio, June 9, 2005, available at http://www.whitehouse.gov/news/releases/2005/06/20050609-2.html.
7. For Hayden, see Dan Eggen and Walter Pincus, "Varied Rationales Muddle Issue of NSA Eavesdropping," *Washington Post*, January 27, 2006, A5; Michael V. Hayden, "Balancing Security and Liberty: The Challenge of Sharing Foreign Signals Intelligence," *Notre Dame Journal of Law, Ethics and Public Policy* 19 (2005), 247–60. In April 2005, FBI Director Robert Mueller also denied that NSA was

spying on American citizens, in a Senate hearing on Patriot Act renewal. See James Risen and Eric Lichtblau, "Bush Let U.S. Spy On Callers Without Courts," *New York Times*, December 16, 2005, A1.

8. Rather than backtrack or apologize from his 2004 campaign statement at Buffalo, Bush made the implausible claim that he had not really intended to speak of "any" and all wiretaps, but only roving wiretaps, then a hot-button Patriot Act issue. At the very least, the President's statement had been misleading—and extraordinarily careless, given that he knew what the NSA was doing. Eric Lichtblau, "Bush Defends Spy Program and Denies Misleading Public," *New York Times*, January 2, 2006, A11.

9. For NSA origins, see *Bk. III*, 736; *Bk. II*, 104, 170. For statute, see Intelligence Authorization Act for FY1993, Pub. L. 102-496 § 705. For Johnson, see Loch K. Johnson, *America's Secret Power: The CIA in a Democratic Society* (New York: Oxford University Press, 1989), 52. For Cold War abuses, see *Bk. III*, 739–40; James Bamford, *Body of Secrets: Anatomy of the Ultra-Secret National Security Agency* (New York: Anchor Books, 2002) 437. For more on NSA, see James Bamford, *The Puzzle Palace: Inside America's Most Secret Intelligence Organization* (New York: Penguin Books, 1983).

10. Eric Lichtblau and Scott Shane, "Files Say Agency Initiated Growth of Spying Effort," *New York Times*, January 4, 2006, A1.

11. Risen and Lichtblau, A1; Andrea Mitchell, "Reporter Defends Release of NSA Spy Program," NBC News, January 3, 2006, available at http://www.msnbc.msn.com/id/1069784/page/2. For quote, see James Risen, *State of War: The Secret History of the CIA and the Bush Administration* (New York: Free Press, 2006), 52–54.

12. See Risen, 49–52; testimony of James Bamford, January 20, 2006, to democratic members of the House Judiciary Committee; Jon Van, "Phone Giants Mum on Spying: In Past, Industry Has Cooperated with U.S.," *Chicago Tribune*, December 29, 2005, C1.

13. For Negroponte, see Dan Eggen, "Negroponte Had Denied Domestic Call Monitoring," *Washington Post*, May 15, 2006, A3. For NSA's activity, see Lesley Cauley, "NSA Has Massive Database of Americans' Phone Calls," *USA Today*, May 11, 2006; Shawn Young and Dionne Searcey, "Nacchio Confirms Rejecting Request from NSA," *Wall Street Journal*, May 13, 2006, A3. Negroponte's "absolutely not" might refer only to the *contents* of domestic calls, not the external data around such calls. *USA Today* had originally reported that BellSouth and Verizon were involved in this program, but these companies contested that assertion. See John Diamond and Leslie Cauley, "Pre-9/11 Records Help Flag Suspicious Calling," *USA Today*, May 23, 2006, 6A.

14. Van, C1; L. Britt Snider, "Recollections from the Church Committee's Investigation of NSA," available at www.gwu.edu/~nsarchiv/NSAEBB/NSAEBB178/surv18.pdf. For EFF, see Ryan Singel, "Stumbling into a Spying Scandal," *Wired News*, May 17, 2006; John Markoff and Scott Shane, "Documents Show Link Between AT&T and Agency in Eavesdropping Case," *New York Times*, April 13, 2006, A17. For the companies' law violation, see Stored Communications Act, 18 U.S.C. §§ 2702–3. For Fourth Amendment, see *Smith v. Maryland*, 442 U.S. 735 (1979).

15. See also Patrick Radden Keefe, "Can Network Theory Thwart Terrorists?" *New York Times Magazine*, March 12, 2006, 16.

16. See U.S. General Accounting Office, "Data Mining: Federal Efforts Cover a Wide Variety of Uses," No. GAO-04-548, May 2004, available at http://www.gao.gov/new.items/d04548.pdf; John Markoff, "Taking Spying to Higher Level, Agencies Look for More Ways to Mine Data," *New York Times*, February 25, 2006, C1; Daniel J. Steinbock, "Data Matching, Data Mining, and Due Process," *Georgia Law Review* 40 (2005), 1, 10–15.

17. For Able Danger, see Shane Harris, "Intelligence Designs," *National Journal*, December 2, 2005; Keefe, 16. For endorsements, see Philip Bobbitt, "Why We Listen," *New York Times*, January 30, 2006, A23; Richard A. Posner, "A New Surveillance Act," *Wall Street Journal*, February 15, 2006, A16; Richard A. Posner, "Our Domestic Intelligence Crisis," *Washington Post*, December 21, 2006, A31.

18. Shane Harris and Tim Naftali, "Tinker, Tailor, Miner, Spy," Slate.com, January 3, 2006.

19. For dissemination, see Risen and Lichtblau, A1; Mitchell, 2. For DIA spying and "suspected of posing a threat," see Walter Pincus, "NSA Gave Other Agencies Information from Surveillance," *Washington Post*, January 1, 2006, A8. For Bolton, see Mark Hosenball, "Spying: Giving Out U.S. Names," *Newsweek*, May 2, 2005, available at http://msnbc.msn.com/id/7614681/site/newsweek; Patrick Radden Keefe, "Big Brother and the Bureaucrats," *New York Times*, August 10, 2005, A21.

20. For FISA court, see Risen, 54; Carol Leonnig, "Surveillance Court Is Seeking Answers: Judges Were Unaware of Eavesdropping," *Washington Post*, January 5, 2006, A2; Carol Leonnig and Dafna Linzer, "Spy Court Judge Quits in Protest: Jurist Concerned Bush Order Tainted Work of Secret Panel," *Washington Post*, December 21, 2005, A1.

21. For TIA, see Tom Regan, "NSA Continues Controversial Data Mining Program," *Christian Science Monitor*, February 24, 2006, available at www.csmonitor.com; Shane Harris, "TIA Lives On," *National Journal*, February 23, 2006.

22. For information overload, see Richard A. Best Jr., "The National Security Agency: Issues for Congress," Congressional Research Service, January 16, 2001, 3. For pre-9/11 leads, see Bamford, *Body of Secrets*, 616–17. *The 9/11 Commission Report* (New York: W.W. Norton, 2004), 262.

23. For FBI complaints, see Lowell Bergman, Eric Lichtblau, Scott Shane, and Don van Natta Jr., "Spy Agency Data After Sept. 11 Led F.B.I. to Dead Ends," *New York Times*, January 17, 2006, A1. For figures, see Barton Gellman, Dafna Linzer, and Carol D. Leonnig, "Surveillance Net Yields Few Suspects," *Washington Post*, February 5, 2006, A1.

24. For Faris and British plot, see Mark Hosenball, "Did It Work?" *Newsweek*, January 4, 2006; Jerry Markon, "Spying Cited in Bid to Ease Terror Plea," *Washington Post*, February 4, 2006, A7.

25. Press conference of the President, December 19, 2005, available at http://www.whitehouse.gov/news/releases/2005/12/print/20051219-2.html; "Cheney Roars Back on Spying, Torture, Iraq," ABC News, December 18, 2005, available at http://abcnews.go.com.

26. See press briefing by Attorney General Alberto Gonzales and General Michael

Hayden, Principal Deputy Director for National Intelligence, December 19, 2005, available at http://www.whitehouse.gov/news/releases/2005/12/print/20051219-1.html.

27. For Hayden, see Press Briefing by Gonzales and Hayden, December 19, 2005; Douglas Waller, "A Better Way to Eavesdrop?" *Time*, February 2, 2006. For difference between "probable cause" and "reasonable suspicion," see *Ornelas v. United States*, 517 U.S. 690, 695–96 (1996), and *Illinois v. Gates*, 462 U.S. 213, 235–38 (1983). For Tribe, see letter from Professor Laurence H. Tribe to Hon. John Conyers, January 6, 2006 (on file with authors).

28. Charles Babington and Dan Eggen, "Gonzales Seeks to Clarify Testimony on Spying: Extent of Eavesdropping May Go Beyond NSA Work," *Washington Post*, March 1, 2006, A8. For financial data, see Paul Blustein, "Financial Search Raises Privacy Fears," *Washington Post*, June 24, 2006, A12; Eric Lichtblau and James Risen, "Bank Data Secretly Reviewed by U.S. to Fight Terror," *New York Times*, June 22, 2006, A1; Arshad Mohammed and Sara Kelaulani Goo, "Government Increasingly Turning to Data Mining," *Washington Post*, June 15, 2006, D3.

29. Chitra Ragavan, "The Letter of the Law," *U.S. News and World Report*, March 27, 2006, 27; letter from Louis F. Giles, Director of Policy, NSA, to Thomas H. Nelson, January 27, 2006 (on file with authors).

30. Walter Pincus, "Pentagon's Intelligence Authority Widens: Fact Sheet Details Secretive Agency's Growth From Policy to Counterterrorism," *Washington Post*, December 19, 2005, A10.

31. For CIFA, see Department of Defense Directive No. 5105.67, "Department of Defense Counterintelligence Field Activity," February 19, 2002; *Report to Congress on the Role of the Department of Defense in Supporting Homeland Security,* September 2003, 12. Robert Block and Gary Field, "Is Military Creeping into Domestic Spying and Enforcement?" *Wall Street Journal*, March 9, 2004. For Pentagon's view on law, see Department of the Army, Office of the Deputy Chief of Staff for Intelligence, "Collecting Information on U.S. Persons," November 5, 2001, available at http://www.fas.org/irp/agency/army/uspersons.html.

32. Pincus, "Pentagon's Intelligence Authority Widens," A10.

33. For details of CIFA and Talon, see Walter Pincus, "Corralling Domestic Intelligence: Standards in the Works for Reports of Suspicious Activities," *Washington Post*, January 13, 2006, A5; Walter Pincus, "Pentagon's Intelligence Authority Widens," A10; Walter Pincus, "Pentagon Expanding Its Domestic Surveillance Activity; Fears of Post-9/11 Terrorism Spur Proposals for New Powers," *Washington Post*, November 27, 2005, A6; Walter Pincus, "CIA, Pentagon Seek to Avoid Overlap," *Washington Post*, July 4, 2005, A2.

34. For NBC story, see Lisa Myers, Douglas Pasternack, and Rich Gardella, "Is the Pentagon Spying on Americans?" NBC News, December 14, 2005. For other examples of CIFA spying, see editorial, "Bad Targeting," *Washington Post*, January 30, 2006, A16; Pincus, "Pentagon's Intelligence Authority Widens," A10; Walter Pincus, "Pentagon Will Review Database on U.S. Citizens," *Washington Post*, December 15, 2005, A1. For University of Texas story, see Block and Field.

35. Servicemembers Legal Defense Network, "Pentagon Releases Documents Acknowledging Surveillance of Gay Groups," available at http://www.sldn.org/

templates/press; letter from Will Kramer, Chief of Defense Department Office of Freedom of Information to Christopher Wolf, Proskauer Rose, April 9, 2006 (on file with the authors).

36. See "Anti-War Group Spied On," *Daily News*, March 15, 2006, 576.

37. See Risen and Lichtblau, "Bush Let U.S. Spy," A1. For Yoo, see Dan Eggen, "Bush Authorized Domestic Spying: Post 9/11 Order Bypassed Special Court," *Washington Post*, December 16, 2005, A1. Walter Pincus's reporting is an important exception to the failure to cover CIFA's activities. For January 2006 document, see U.S. Department of Justice, "Legal Authorities Supporting the Activities of the National Security Agency Described by the President," January 19, 2006.

38. For criminal prohibition, see 50 U.S.C. § 1809 (a). For surveillance defined, see 50 U.S.C. § 1801 (f).

39. For exceptions, see 50 U.S.C. § 1802 (a) (1) (foreign powers); § 1805 (f) (emergencies); § 1811 (declarations of war). FISA protects citizens and lawful permanent residents but not other immigrants. For legislative history, see chapter 3 and H.R. Conf. Rep. No. 95-1720, at 34 (1978); Peter P. Swire, "The System of Foreign Intelligence Surveillance Law," *George Washington Law Review* 72 (August 2004), 1306, 1320–25. For flexibility, see Loch K. Johnson, "Spy Law Works, Don't Bypass It," *Atlanta Journal-Constitution*, January 30, 2006.

40. Eric Lichtblau, "Nominee Says N.S.A. Stayed Within Law on Wiretapping," *New York Times*, May 19, 2006, A20; Jane Mayer, "The Hidden Power," *New Yorker*, July 3, 2006, 44.

41. For Justice Department defenses, see U.S. Department of Justice, "Legal Authorities Supporting the Activities of the National Security Agency Described by the President," January 19, 2006, letter from William E. Moschella, Assistant Attorney General to Hon. Pat Roberts et al, December 22, 2005, Alberto R. Gonzales, "America Expects Surveillance," *Wall Street Journal*, February 6, 2006.

42. Scott Shane and Eric Lichtblau, "Cheney Pushed U.S. to Widen Eavesdropping," *New York Times*, May 14, 2006, A1; Siobhan Gorman, "Wiretapping Preoccupied Hayden at NSA," *Baltimore Sun*, May 14, 2006; Charles Babington, "Hoekstra Urges Bush to Impart Intelligence Details," *Washington Post*, July 10, 2006, A7. For refusal to disclose, see letter from Assistant Attorney General William E. Moschella to Senator Arlen Specter, July 17, 2006 (copy on file with authors).

43. For AUMF, see Authorization for the Use of Military Force, S.J. Res. 23, 107th Cong., 115 Stat. 224 (2001). For Justice Department argument, see "Legal Authorities Supporting the Activities of the National Security Agency Described by the President," January 19, 2006, 10–28. For Supreme Court, see *Hamdi v. Rumsfeld*, 542 U.S. 507, 516 (2004) (O'Connor, J.).

44. For Congress and the AUMF, see Richard F. Grimmett, "Authorization for Use of Military Force in Response to the 9/11 Attacks (P.L. 107-40): Legislative History," Congressional Research Service, January 4, 2006; Richard W. Stevenson, "Congress Never Authorized Spying Effort, Daschle Says," *New York Times*, December 24, 2005, A12; Tom Daschle, "Power We Didn't Grant," *Washington Post*, December 23, 2005, A21; John Lancaster and Helen Dewar, "Congress Clears Use of Force, $40-Billion in Emergency Aid," *New York Times*, September 15, 2001, A4; Rachel Smolkin, "Bush Close to Getting Backing; Congress Drafting Resolution of Force," *Pittsburgh Post-Gazette*, September 14, 2001, A4. See also

letter from law professor Curtis A. Bradley et al to Hon. Bill Frist et al, January 9, 2006 (copy on file with authors), 3–5.

45. See *Hamdi v. Rumsfeld*, 542 U.S. 507, 516 (2004) (O'Connor, J.) (emphasis added).

46. For Patriot amendment, see 50 U.S.C. § 1804 (a) (5), as amended by USA PA-TRIOT Act § 218; *In re Sealed Case*, 310 F.3d 717, 728–29 (FISA Ct. of Review 2002), Stephen J. Schulhofer, *The Enemy Within: Intelligence Gathering, Law Enforcement, and Civil Liberties in the Wake of September 11* (New York: Century Foundation, 2002), 33–34.

47. For other proposals, see Dan Eggen, "2003 Draft Legislation Covered Eavesdropping," *Washington Post*, January 28, 2006, A2; transcript of "U.S. Senate Judiciary Committee Holds a Hearing on Wartime Executive Powers and the National Security Agency's Surveillance Authority," WashingtonPost.com, February 6, 2006.

48. For DeWine legislation, see Dan Eggen, "White House Dismissed '02 Surveillance Proposal," *Washington Post*, January 26, 2006, A4. For Baker testimony see www.fas.org/irp/congress/2002_hr/071302baker.html (the full testimony has been deleted from government Web sites).

49. Press briefing by Gonzales and Hayden, December 19, 2005.

50. For Iraq comment, see Andrew Rudalevige, *The New Imperial Presidency: Renewing Presidential Power after Watergate* (Ann Arbor: University of Michigan Press, 2005), 219. See also Vice President's Remarks to the Traveling Press, December 20, 2005, available at www.whitehouse.gov/news/releases/2005/12/print .20051220-09.html.

51. For disclosure rule, see 50 U.S.C. § 413 (a) (1). The exception is 50 U.S.C. § 413a (a). For its use, see Ron Suskind, *The One-Percent Doctrine: Deep Inside America's Pursuit of its Enemies Since 9/11* (New York: Simon & Schuster, 2006), 39–41.

52. For Administration's comments, see press conference of the President, December 19, 2005, available at http://www.whitehouse.gov.news/releases/2005/12/print/ 20051219-2.html. For details of the reporting requirements, see National Security Act of 1947, 50 U.S.C. §§ 413–13 (b). See also Alfred Cummings, "Statutory Procedures Under Which Congress Is to Be Informed of U.S. Intelligence Activities, Including Covert Actions," Congressional Research Service, January 18, 2006.

53. See Suzanne E. Spaulding, "Power Play: Did Bush Roll Past the Legal Stop Signs?" *Washington Post*, December 25, 2005, B1 (article by former CIA lawyer).

54. Eric Lichtblau and Scott Shane, "Files Say Agency Initiated Growth of Spying Effort," *New York Times*, January 4, 2006, A1.

55. Associated Press, "Bush Says He Was Within Law to Authorize Spy Program," January 23, 2006, available at http://www.nytimes.com. For partisan division, see Eggen and Pincus, A5; Dan Eggen, "Gonzales Echoes Defense of Wiretaps," *Washington Post*, January 25, 2006, A7; Scott Shane, "Democrat Says Spy Briefings Violated Law," *New York Times*, January 5, 2006, A16; Lichtblau, "Bush Defends Spy Program," A11; Spenser S. Hsu and Walter Pincus, "Goss Says Leaks Have Hurt CIA's Work, Urges Probe," *Washington Post*, February 3, 2006, A3.

56. For Rove's argument, see Adam Nagourney, "Seeking Edge in Spy Debate," *New York Times*, January 23, 2006, A1; Adam Nagourney, "Rove Lays Out Road Map for Republicans in Fall Elections," *New York Times*, January 21, 2006, A11; Eric

Lichtblau and Adam Liptak, "Bush Presses on in Legal Debate for Wiretapping," *New York Times*, January 28, 2006, A13. See also David E. Sanger and John O'Neil, "White House Begins New Effort to Defend Surveillance Program," *New York Times*, January 23, 2006, available at www.nytimes.com; Scott Shane, "Democrats Say Spy Briefings Violated Law," *New York Times*, January 3, 2006, A16. For Democrats' response, see Walter Pincus, "Spying Necessary, Democrats Say," *Washington Post*, February 13, 2006, A3. For Cheney, see Jim VanderHei, "Cheney Says NSA Spying Should Be an Election Issue," *Washington Post*, February 19, 2006, A7.

57. For Senate Intelligence Committee, see Charles Babington, "Senate Intelligence Panel Frayed by Partisan Infighting," *Washington Post*, March 12, 2006, A9; Charles Babington, "White House Working to Avoid Wiretap Probe," *Washington Post*, February 20, 2006, A8; Charles Babington and Carol D. Leonnig, "Senate Rejects Wiretapping Probe," *Washington Post*, February 17, 2006, A6. For Frist, see letter from William H. Frist, Majority Leader, United States Senate, to Harry Reid, Minority Leader, United States Senate, March 3, 2006 (on file with authors). For Roberts, see letter from Pat Roberts to Arlen Specter and Patrick J. Leahy, February 3, 2006 (on file with authors); see also Scott Shane, "Senate Session on Security Erupts in Spying Debate," *New York Times*, February 3, 2006, A16; Eric Lichtblau, "Republican Who Oversees N.S.A. Calls for Wiretap Inquiry," *New York Times*, February 8, 2006, A12.

58. For ethics investigation, see Scott Shane, "With Access Denied, Justice Department Drops Spying Investigation," *New York Times*, May 11, 2006. For executive secrecy generally, see Louis Fisher, *The Politics of Executive Privilege* (Durham: Carolina Academic Press, 2004). For need to investigate and "must address," see Terry Eastland, *Energy in the Executive: The Case for the Strong Presidency* (New York: Free Press, 1992), 199. Eastland hedges his bets by implying there may be an exception on "national security" grounds.

59. Carl Hulse and David Johnson, "To Ease Standoff, Bush Seals Files F.B.I. Seized in Congress," *New York Times*, May 26, 2006, A1; Shailagh Murray and Allan Lengel, "Return of Jefferson Files Is Sought," *Washington Post*, May 25, 2006, A1; *In re Search of the Rayburn House Office Building, Room 2113, Washington, D.C., 20515*, 2006 WL 2006107 (D.D.C. July 19, 2006).

60. *Rumsfeld v. Padilla*, 542 U.S. 426 (2004) (Stevens, J., dissenting). For habeas corpus, see Gerald Neuman, "The Suspension Clause After *INS v. St. Cyr*," *Columbia Human Rights Law Review* 33 (2002), 555, 563–64; William F. Duker, *A Constitutional History of Habeas Corpus* (Westport: Greenwood Press, 1980).

61. See *In re Guantanamo Detainee Cases*, 355 F. Supp. 2d 443, 450, 475 (D.D.C. 2005).

62. For early laws, see Alien Enemy Act of 1798, Ch. 66, § 1, 1 Stat. 577, codified at 50 U.S.C. § 21; Act of July 6, 1812, Ch. 128, 2 Stat. 777. For Marshall case, see Gerald Neuman and Charles Hobson, "John Marshall and the Enemy Alien: A Case Missing from the Canon," *Green Bag 2d*, Autumn 2005, 39.

63. For Lincoln, see Geoffrey R. Stone, *Perilous Times: Free Speech in Wartime From the Sedition Act of 1789 to the War on Terrorism* (New York: W.W. Norton, 2004), 68–123; Stephen I. Vladeck, "The Detention Power," *Yale Law and Policy Journal* 22 (2004) 153.

64. For the Emergency Detention Act and its repeal, see 64 Stat. 987, 1019-31 (1950); 18 U.S.C. § 4001 (a) (Non-Detention Act).

65. For 1942 case, see *Ex Parte Quirin*, 317 U.S. 1, 31 (1942); Pierce O'Donnell, *In Time of War: Hitler's Terrorist Attack on America* (New York: The New Press, 2005); Louis Fisher, *Nazi Saboteurs on Trial: A Military Tribunal & American Law* (Lawrence: University of Kansas Press, 2003). For Scalia quote, see *Hamdi v. Rumsfeld*, 542 U.S. 507, 569 (2004) (Scalia, J., dissenting). For "enemy combatant" category, see Major Richard B. Baxter, "So-Called 'Un-privileged Belligerency': Spies, Guerrillas, and Saboteurs," *British Yearbook of International Law* 28 (1951) 323, 332.

66. For the Geneva Conventions, see Michael Byers, *War Law: Understanding International Law and Armed Conflict* (New York: Grove Press, 2006), 69–90, 132–33. For Supreme Court, see *Hamdan v. Rumsfeld*, 2006 WL 1764793 (June 29, 2006).

67. But only about one in twenty of the Guantánamo detainees are battlefield captures. See Corine Hegland, "Empty Evidence," *National Journal*, February 3, 2006.

68. "Detention, Treatment and Trial of Certain Non-Citizens in the War Against Terrorism," 66 Fed. Reg. 57,833 (November 13, 2001). Alberto R. Gonzales, "Martial Justice, Full and Fair," *New York Times*, November 30, 2001, A27.

69. Neal K. Kaytal and Laurence H. Tribe, "Waging War, Deciding Guilt: Trying the Military Tribunals," *Yale Law Journal* 111 (2002), 1259, 1295–96.

70. See Department of Defense Fact Sheet, "Guantanamo Detainees by the Numbers," August 31, 2005, available at http://www.defenselink.mil/news/Aug2005/d20050831sheet.pdf; Brief for the Respondents in *Hamdi v. Rumsfeld*, 542 U.S. 507 (2004), no. 03-6696, 3; Jesselyn A. Radack, "You Say Defendant, I Say Combatant: Opportunistic Treatment of Terrorism Suspects Held in the United States and the Need for Due Process," *New York University Review of Law and Social Change* 29 (2005), 525, 536–40.

71. See *Rumsfeld v. Padilla*, 542 U.S. 426 (2004); Benjamin Wittes, "Enemy Americans," *Atlantic Monthly*, July 1, 2004, 127.

72. *Al-Marri v. Hanft*, 378 F. Supp. 2d 673 (D.S.C. 2005); Andrew Zajac, "Al Qaeda Liked Family Man Ploy, Declassified Papers Show," *Chicago Tribune*, April 7, 2006, C6; Andrew Zajac, "Justice Moves at Glacial Pace for 'Enemy Combatant,'" *Chicago Tribune*, February 10, 2006, C6. (Authors' disclosure: the Brennan Center for Justice, our institutional home, represents al-Marri in his habeas action.)

73. For the Wolfowitz definition, see *In re Guantanamo Detainee Cases*, 355 F. Supp. 2d 443, 450, 475 (D.D.C. 2005). For an earlier definition, see letter from William J. Haynes II, General Counsel of the Department of Defense to Carl Levin, November 26, 2002 (on file with authors).

74. Michael Powell, "No Choice but Guilty: Lackawanna Case Highlights Legal Tilt," *Washington Post*, July 29, 2003, A1.

75. For authority quote, see Brief for the Respondents in *Hamdi v. Rumsfeld*, 542 U.S. 507 (2004), no. 03-6696, 27. For justification quotes, see Brief for the Petitioner, *Rumsfeld v. Padilla*, 542 U.S. 426 (2004), no. 03-1027, 27–30.

76. Unofficial transcript of oral argument in *Padilla v. Hanft*, No. 05-6396 (4th Cir. 2005), 40–41, available at http://www.wiggin.com/db30/cgi-bin/pubs/Transcript%20of%20Oral%20Argument.pdf.

77. For legal claims, see Brief for the Petitioner, *Rumsfeld v. Padilla*, 542 U.S. 426 (2004), no. 03-1027, 13–15; Brief for the Respondents in *Hamdi v. Rumsfeld*, 542 U.S. 507 (2004), no. 03-6696, 25–27; Respondent's Answer to the Petition for

Writ of Habeas Corpus, in *al-Marri v. Hanft*, No. 02:04-2257-26AJ. For review process, see Brief for the Petitioner, *Rumsfeld v. Padilla*, 542 U.S. 426 (2004), no. 03-1027, 6–7.

78. For Hamdi, see *Hamdi v. Rumsfeld*, 542 U.S. 507 (2004); Michael Isikoff and Mark Hosenball, "Terror Watch: Out of the Brig," *Newsweek Web Edition*, September 15, 2004, available at http://msnbc.msn.com; Joel Brinkley, "A Father Waits as the U.S. and the Saudis Discuss His Son's Release," *New York Times*, October 10, 2004, A15.

79. For Padilla, see memorandum from President George W. Bush to Secretary of Defense, "Transfer of Detainee to Control of Attorney General," November 20, 2005; *Padilla v. Hanft*, No. 05-6396 (4th Cir. December 21, 2005); Viveca Novack, "Hooray, I've Been Indicted," *Time*, December 5, 2005, 27. For black sites' use, see Douglas Jehl and Eric Lichtblau, "Shift on Suspect Is Linked to Role of Qaeda Figures," *New York Times*, November 25, 2005, A1.

80. *Padilla v. Hanft*, 126 S. Ct. 1649 (2006) (Ginsburg, J., dissenting).

81. David Cole, *Enemy Aliens: Double Standards and Constitutional Freedoms in the War on Terrorism* (New York: The New Press, 2003), 6.

82. *Hamdi v. Rumsfeld*, 542 U.S. 507, 544 (2004 (opinion of Souter, J.).

83. George Will, "The Next War Resolution May Be a Long One," Townhall.com, February 16, 2006.

Chapter 7: Kings and Presidents

1. See Christopher Hill, *The Century of Revolution, 1603–1714* (New York: W.W. Norton, 1980), 54–55; Carolyn A. Edie, "'Tactics and Strategies: Parliament's Attack Upon the Royal Dispensing Power, 1597–1689," *American Journal of Legal History* 29 (1985), 197, 198.

2. There are two residual executive powers. First, the president has a limited "protective" power to respond to sudden threats before Congress can act. See Henry P. Monaghan, "The Protective Power of the Presidency," *Columbia Law Review* 93 (1993) 1; Robert Scigliano, "The President's 'Prerogative Power,'" in *Inventing the American Presidency*, ed. Thomas Cronin (Lawrence: University of Kansas Press, 1989), 253. Second, there are certain specific acts textually committed to the president by the Constitution, such as the veto and the nomination power, that Congress cannot remove.

3. See, e.g., Saikrishna B. Prakesh and Michael D. Ramsey, "Foreign Affairs and the Jefferson Executive: A Defense," *Minnesota Law Review* 89 (2005), 1591.

4. See Andrew Rudalevige, *The New Imperial Presidency: Renewing Presidential Power after Watergate* (Ann Arbor: University of Michigan Press, 2005), 57–100; Arthur Schlesinger Jr., *The Imperial Presidency* (Boston: Houghton Mifflin, 1973), 101–38.

5. Quoted in Derek Jinks and David Sloss, "Is the President Bound by the Geneva Conventions?" *Cornell Law Review* 90 (2004), 97, 149.

6. Vice President's remarks to the traveling press, December 20, 2005, available at http://www.whitehouse.gov/news/releases/2005/12/20051220-9.html; see also Bob Woodward, "Cheney Upholds Power of the Presidency," *Washington Post*, January 20, 2005, A7; Dana Milbank, "In Cheney's Shadow, Counsel Pushes the Conservative Cause," *Washington Post*, October 11, 2004, A21.

7. Caroline Daniel, "Cheney Leads the Fight for Presidential Power," *Financial Times*, December 14, 2005, 12.

8. *Bk IV*, 166. For Ford's proclamation on Japanese American internment, see 3 CFR Proc 4417, "An American Promise," February 19, 1976.

9. *Bk. II*, 205, 208.

10. Nixon quoted in Jinks and Sloss, 149 (emphasis added). For Nixon's statements to the Church Committee, see "Appendix: Select Committee Interrogatories for Former President Richard M. Nixon," in *Bk. IV: Supplementary Detailed Staff Reports on Foreign and Military Intelligence*, 157–58.

11. See Rudalevige, 101–38. For openness, see the Freedom of Information Act, 5 U.S.C. § 552b. For war powers, see John Hart Ely, *War and Responsibility: Constitutional Lessons of Vietnam and Its Aftermath* (Princeton: Princeton University Press, 1993). For foreign affairs, see 1 U.S.C. §112(b).

12. Jeffrey Rosen, "Power of One," *New Republic*, July 24, 2006, 8.

13. For "three powers" and following quotes, see presentation of the Honorable Charles Fried, *American Criminal Law Review* 29 (Spring 1989), 1669. For Meese on "unitary executive," see Edwin Meese III, "Bicentennial Program of the University of Dallas," February 27, 1986, in *Major Policy Statements of the Attorney General Edwin Meese III, 1985–1988*, 22–30 (on file at New York University School of Law Library); Douglas W. Kmiec, *The Attorney General's Lawyer: Inside the Meese Justice Department* (Westport: Praeger, 1992), 47–68. For debates on removal power and independent agencies, see Geoffrey Miller, "Independent Agencies," *Supreme Court Review* (1986), 41; Peter L. Strauss, "The Place of Agencies in Government: Separation of Powers and the Fourth Branch," *Columbia Law Review* 84 (1984), 573.

14. For "degree of seriousness" quote, see Fried, *American Criminal Law Review*, 1669; cf. Lincoln Caplan, *The Tenth Justice: The Solicitor General and the Rule of Law* (New York: Alfred A. Knopf, 1987), 176–234.

15. For "impetuous vortex" quote, see Theodore B. Olsen, "The Impetuous Vortex: Congressional Erosion of Presidential Authority," in *The Fettered Presidency: Legal Constraints on the Executive Branch*, ed. L. Gordon Crovitz and Jeremy A. Rabkin (Washington, DC: American Enterprise Institute for Public Policy Research, 1989), 225–28.

16. Terry Eastland, *Energy in the Executive: The Case for the Strong Presidency* (New York: Free Press, 1992), 10–14.

17. Fried, *American Criminal Law Review*, 1669. For Eastland, see Rosen, 8.

18. For the "original intent" idea, see Edwin Meese III, 22–30; Kmiec, 19–28. For Fried, see Charles Fried, *Order and Law: Arguing the Reagan Revolution: A Firsthand Account* (New York: Simon & Schuster, 1991), 147–49. For Scalia, see *Morrison v. Olsen*, 487 U.S. 654, 697 (1988).

19. For the legislative veto, see *Immigration and Naturalization Service v. Chadha*, 462 U.S. 919 (1983). For the independent counsel, see *Morrison v. Olsen*, 487 U.S. 654 (1988). For the presidential control of information, see *Public Citizen v. United States Department of Justice*, 491 U.S. 440 (1989). For personnel control, see Eastland, 144–64.

20. Charles Fried contends that the "unitary executive" theory of the 1980s does not necessarily lead to the Bush Administration's post-9/11 positions. (See letter to the editor, *New York Review of Books*, April 6, 2006, 67.) True, but predicate no-

tions of 1980s unitary executive theory are the same as those of the recent OLC memos.

21. For Meese, see Meese, "The Law of the Constitution," *Tulane Law Review* 61 (1986), 979, 983; cf. Frederick A.O. Schwarz Jr., "The Constitution Outside the Courts," *The Record of the Association of the Bar of the City of New York* 47 (1992), 9; Frank Easterbrook, "Presidential Review," *Case Western Law Review* 40 (1990), 905 (noting that when the Supreme Court collaterally invalidates a law, the executive has an obligation to not enforce that law because it is no longer valid).

22. *Report of the Congressional Committees Investigating the Iran-Contra Affair, with Supplemental, Minority, and Additional Views*, S. Rep. No. 100-216, H. Rep. No. 100-433 (1987), 457 ("Iran-Contra minority report"). For Cheney's subsequent remarks, see David S. Broder, "Cheney Essay Assails Congressional 'Overreaching'; Nominee Urges Repeal of War Powers Act, Rejection of Covert-Action Notification Proposal," *Washington Post*, March 14, 1989, A4.

23. Iran-Contra minority report, 432. For Addington, see Jane Mayer, "The Hidden Power," *New Yorker*, July 3, 2006, 44; Dana Milbank, "In Cheney's Shadow, Counsel Pushes the Conservative Cause," *Washington Post*, October 11, 2004, A21; Dana Priest, "CIA Puts Harsh Tactics on Hold," *Washington Post*, June 27, 2004, A1; Tim Golden, "Tough Justice: A Policy Unravels," *New York Times*, October 25, 2004, A1.

24. Iran-Contra minority report, 437. The minority report evasively describes the Reagan administration as being in "substantial compliance" with sanctions laws. Ibid., 451; see also "Remarks of C. Boyden Gray," *Houston Journal of International Law* 11 (1988–89), 263, 269 ("Lt Colonel North was not completely forthcoming").

25. See Thomas Frank, *What's the Matter With Kansas? How Conservatives Won the Heart of America* (New York: Henry Holt, 2005), 113–56.

26. Iran-Contra minority report, 448–52, 457–60, 467 (emphasis added)

27. For Cheney, see Dick Cheney, "Covert Operations: Who's in Charge?" *Wall Street Journal*, May 3, 1988. For Cheney "no justification," see Sara Fritz and Karen Tumulty, "The Iran Contra Hearings: Iran-Contra Hearings at an End; No Evidence Found of Reagan Wrongs But a Scar Remains," *Los Angeles Times*, August 4, 1987, 1; see also Peter Osterlund, "GOP Congressman Warns Against Presidential Power," *Christian Science Monitor*, November 24, 1987, 4. See Bruce E. Fein, "The Constitution and Covert Action," *Houston Journal of International Law* 11 (1988–89), 53, 54.

28. For war powers quote, see Nancy Kassop, "Expansion and Contraction: Clinton's Impact on the Presidential Power," in David Gray Adler and Michael A. Genovese, eds., *The Presidency and the Law* (Lawrence: University of Kansas Press, 2002), 5. For Yugoslavia, see David Gray Adler, "Clinton, the Constitution, and the War Power," in Adler and Genovese, 19; Abraham D. Sofaer, "John Ely, War, and Responsibility," *Stanford Law Review* 57 (2004), 785, 787. For Clinton era, see Elena Kagan, "Presidential Administration," *Harvard Law Review* 114 (2001), 2245.

29. For Guantánamo, see memorandum for William J. Haynes II, General Counsel, Department of Defense, from Patrick F. Philbin and John C. Yoo, "Possible Habeas Jurisdiction over Aliens Held in Guantánamo Bay, Cuba," December 28, 2001, 8; *Rasul v. Bush*, 542 U.S. 466 (2004).

30. For treaties, see memorandum to the President from Alberto R. Gonzales, "De-

cision re Application of the Geneva Conventions on Prisoners of War to the Conflict with Al Qaeda and the Taliban," January 25, 2002, 28, 33.

31. For international law against treaty suspension, see Vienna Convention on Treaties, Art. 60. For U.S. views, see memorandum to the President from Alberto R. Gonzales, January 25, 2002, 31–33.

32. Ibid., 15; memorandum opinion for the Deputy Counsel to the President from Deputy Assistant Attorney General John C. Yoo, "The President's Constitutional Authority to Conduct Military Operations Against Terrorists and Nations Supporting Them," September 25, 2001, 3–5.

33. See John C. Yoo, "War and the Constitutional Text," *University of Chicago Law Review* 69 (2002), 1639, 1677–78; John C. Yoo, "Clio at War: The Misuse of History in the War Powers Debate," *University of Colorado Law Review* 70 (1999) 1169, 1173, 1198–99; John C. Yoo, "The Constitution of Politics by Other Means: The Original Understanding of War Powers, *California Law Review* 84 (1996), 167, 188–296.

34. For Locke, see John Yoo, *War by Other Means: An Insider's Account of the War on Terror* (New York: Atlantic Monthly Books, 2006), 119, 122. For "wrongheaded or obsolete," see John Yoo, "How the Presidency Regained Its Balance," *New York Times*, September 17, 2006.

35. John Yoo, "Transferring Terrorists," *Notre Dame Law Review* 79 (2004), 1183, 1202–3; John Yoo, *The Powers of War and Peace: The Constitution and Foreign Affairs After 9/11* (Chicago: University of Chicago Press, 2005), 45–54, 65.

36. See memorandum from Jay S. Bybee for Alberto R. Gonzales, Counsel to the President, "Standards of Conduct for Interrogation under 18 U.S.C. §§ 2340–2340A," August 1, 2002 ("Bybee memo"). For the working group memo, see *Working Group Report on Detainee Interrogations in the Global War on Terrorism: Assessment of Legal, Historical, Policy, and Operational Considerations*, April 4, 2003, 33; Jane Mayer, "The Memo," *New Yorker*, February 27, 2006, 32. For September 25, 2001, opinion, see Mayer, "The Hidden Power," 44.

37. Bybee memo, 36–38, and n. 22.

38. Memorandum from Daniel Levin to James B. Comey, Deputy Attorney General, re: "Legal Standards Applicable Under 18 U.S.C. §§ 2340–2340A," December 30, 2004. Attorney General Gonzales's hearings before the Senate Judiciary Committee are transcribed at http://www.washingtonpost.com/wp-dyn/content/article/2006/02/06/AR2006020600931.html.

39. Letter from William J. Haynes II, General Counsel to the Department of Defense, to Carl Levin (undated) (on file with authors); Brief for the Petitioner in *Rumsfeld v. Padilla*, 542 U.S. 426 (2004) (No. 03-1027).

40. See "Legal Authorities Supporting the Activities of the National Security Agency Described by the President," January 19, 2006, 30–35; letter from William E. Moschella, Assistant Attorney General, to Hon. Pat Roberts et al, December 22, 2005; Alberto R. Gonzales, "America Expects Surveillance," *Wall Street Journal*, February 6, 2006.

41. See Ely, 3–5; cf. Yoo, *Powers of War and Peace*, 147; Cass Sunstein, "The 9/11 Constitution," *New Republic*, January 16, 2005.

42. Daniel Farber, *Lincoln's Constitution* (Chicago: University of Chicago Press, 2003), 115–43; Clinton Rossiter, *Constitutional Dictatorship: Crisis Government in*

the *Modern Democracies* (New Brunswick: Transaction Publishers, 2002), 225–30; Geoffrey R. Stone, *Perilous Times: Free Speech in Wartime From the Sedition Act of 1798 to the War on Terrorism* (New York: W.W. Norton, 2004), 72–82; *Ex Parte Merryman*, 17 F. Cas. 144 (C.C.C. Md 1861) (No. 9487) (Taney, C.J.).

43. Quoted in Rossiter, 228–29; see also Scigliano, 248; William H. Rehnquist, *All the Laws But One: Civil Liberties in Wartime* (New York: Vintage, 2000), 3–58.

44. Farber, 117–18.

45. For Lincoln's speech, see Farber, 118. For the Act, see 12 Stat. 326 (1861); Louis Fisher, American *Military Tribunals & Presidential Power: American Revolution to the War on Terrorism* (Lawrence: University of Kansas Press, 2005), 41–42. The Indemnity Act of 1863 provided a retrospective defense to damages actions brought against federal officials based on presidential orders. See Act of March 3, 1863, ch. 81, 12 Stat. 755, 756.

46. The "protective power" cases are *In re Neagle*, 135 U.S. 1 (1890); *In re Debs*, 158 U.S. 564 (1895). The law-violation cases begin at *Little v. Barreme*, 6 U.S. (2 Cranch) 170 (1804), and *United States v. Smith*, 27 F. Cas, 1192, 1230 (C.C.D.N.Y. 1806) (No. 16, 342); cf. Monaghan, 61–74.

47. For quotes, see Bybee memo, 39; letter from William J. Haynes II, General Counsel to the Department of Defense, to Carl Levin (undated) (on file with authors).

48. For "central prerogatives" quote, from a case that did settle the boundaries of presidential power, see *Loving v. United States*, 517 U.S. 748, 757 (1996); see also *Bowsher v. Synar*, 478 U.S. 714 (1986); *INS v. Chadha*, 462 U.S. 919, 954–55 (1983); *United States v. Klein*, 13 Wall. 128, 147 (1872).

49. For debate on "original meaning," see Jack N. Rakove, *Original Meanings: Politics and Ideas in the Making of the Constitution* (New York: Vintage, 1996), 3–22; Keith E. Whittington, *Constitutional Interpretation: Textual Meaning, Original Intent, and Judicial Review* (Lawrence: University of Kansas Press, 1999), 35; Yoo, "War Powers," 1639–60. For piercing criticism of Yoo's historical scholarship, see Martin S. Flaherty, "History Right? Historical Scholarship, Original Understanding, and Treaties as Supreme Law of the Land," *Columbia Law Review* 99 (1999), 2095.

50. We share professional historians' skepticism about the possibility of recovering one, and only one, meaning for each terse phrase in the Constitution. See Jack N. Rakove, "Constitutional Problematics, circa 1787," in John Ferejohn et al, eds., *Constitutional Culture and Democratic Rule* (Cambridge: Cambridge University Press, 2001), 41–42; James H. Hutson, "The Creation of the Constitution: The Integrity of the Documentary Record," *Texas Law Review* 65 (1986–87), 1–39.

51. For separated powers, see Richard E. Neustadt, *Presidential Power and Modern Presidents* (New York: Free Press, 1990), 29. For Madison, see *The Federalist Papers*, No. 47, Clinton Rossiter, ed. (New York: Signet, 1961), 304.

52. For Madison, see *Federalist* No. 51, 322. See also Akhil Reed Amar, "Of Sovereignty and Federalism," *Yale Law Journal* 96 (1987), 1425, 1443, n. 71.

53. Charles L. Black Jr., "The Presidency and Congress," *Washington and Lee Law Review* 32 (1975), 841, 843.

54. See Bob Eckhardt and Charles L. Black, *The Tides of Power: Conversations on the American Constitution* (New Haven: Yale University Press, 1976), 3, 12–38.

55. See Bybee memo, 37.

56. Ibid., 33 (emphasis added).
57. See U.S. Constitution, Art. I, § 8. Letters of marque were legal authorization for private parties—privateers—to use force to harass or prey upon a nation's enemy. Reprisal was the legally authorized act of securing redress for a debt incurred by a foreign government by forcibly taking the private property of its subjects.
58. See Bybee memo, 31. For Jackson quote, see *Youngstown Sheet and Tube Co. v. Sawyer*, 343 U.S. 579, 643–44 (1952) (Jackson, J., concurring). See also Louis Henkin, *Foreign Affairs and the U.S. Constitution* (New York: Oxford University Press, 1996), 45–46.
59. For the OLC position, see memorandum from John Yoo, Deputy Assistant Attorney General, and Robert J. Delahunty, Special Counsel, for William J. Haynes II, "Application of Treaties and Laws to al Qaeda and Taliban Detainees," January 9, 2002, 15. For torture, see *Filártiga v. Pena Irela*, 630 F. 2d 876 (2d Cir. 1980). For the Supreme Court case, see *United States v. Curtiss-Wright Export Corporation*, 299 U.S. 304 (1936). For the "secret reservoir" quote and criticism of *Curtiss-Wright*, see David M. Levitan, "The Foreign Relations Power: An Analysis of Mr. Sutherland's Theory," *Yale Law Journal* 44 (1946), 467, 493; Charles A. Lofgren, "*United States v. Curtiss-Wright Export Corporation*: An Historical Reassessment," *Yale Law Journal* 83 (1973), 1.
60. See U.S. Constitution, Art. I, § 7, Art. II, §§ 1, 2, and 3. Executive power advocates would point out here that the "Law" includes the Constitution, and thus that the "Take Care" clause does not stop the president from setting aside laws he believes are unconstitutional. See Michael Stokes Paulsen, "The Constitution of Necessity," *Notre Dame Law Review* 79 (2004), 1257, 1260–67. At a very minimum, the "Take Care" clause includes laws passed by Congress and establishes a presumption that the president will follow these laws.
61. See U.S. Constitution, Art. I, § 9; see U.S. Constitution, Art. II, § 3; *Ex Parte Bollman*, 8 U.S. (4 Cranch) 75 (1807); Christopher May, "Presidential Defiance of 'Unconstitutional' Laws: Reviving the Royal Prerogative," *Hastings Constitutional Law Quarterly* 21 (1993–94) 865, 875–76.
62. For state constitutions, see Martin S. Flaherty, "The Most Dangerous Branch," *Yale Law Journal* 105 (1996), 1725, 1765; Gordon S. Wood, *The Creation of the American Republic: 1776–1786* (New York: W.W. Norton, 1972), 132–61. See Fried, *Order and Law*, 147–49. For Locke, see John Locke, *Two Treatises of Government and A Letter Concerning Toleration*, Ian Shapiro, ed. (New Haven: Yale University Press, 2003), 171–75. For Locke's reading by Founding Generation, see Isaac Kramnick, "Republican Revisionism Revisited," *American Historical Review* 87 (1982), 629, 661. See also Fried, *Order and Law*, 147–49. Fried's interpretation of Locke is, at best, debatable. See Ross Harrison, *Hobbes, Locke, and Confusion's Masterpiece: An Examination of Seventeenth-Century Political Philosophy* (Cambridge: Cambridge University Press, 2003), 216–18.
63. See Bybee memo, 37; memorandum from Yoo and Delahunty for Haynes, 15.
64. Forrest McDonald, *Novus Ordo Seclorum: The Intellectual Origins of the Constitution* (Lawrence: University of Kansas Press, 1985), 1–8.
65. For the British constitution, see McDonald, 80–81; Rakove, *Original Meanings*, 245–47.
66. For prerogative, see Hill, 54; J.W. Gough, *Fundamental Law in English Constitu-*

tional History (Oxford: Clarendon Press, 1955), 64, 67–68; Edie, "Tactics and Strategies," 197, 221–23. The dispensing power was a "royal warrant excepting certain persons from 'the Obligation of the Law.'" Ibid., 198. For James I's quotation, see Ernst H. Kantorowicz, "Mysteries of State: An Absolutism Concept and Its Late Medieval Origins," *Harvard Theological Review* 48 (1955) 65, 69, 70.

67. May, 865, 872–73; Edie, "Tactics and Strategies," 197, 224, 230–31; Carolyn Edie, "Revolution and the Rule of Law: The End of the Dispensing Power, 1689," *Eighteenth-Century Studies* 10 (1977), 434. For James II, see Patrick Dillon, *The Last Revolution: 1688 and the Creation of the Modern World* (London: Jonathan Cape, 2006), 73–76.

68. For Adams, see John Adams, "Thoughts on Government" (1776), in Robert J. Taylor, ed., *4 Papers of John Adams* (Cambridge: Belknap Press, 1979), 65, 89. For Jefferson, see Monaghan, 15. For Wilson, see Rakove, *Original Meanings*, 257. For Paterson case, see *United States v. Smith*, 27 F. Cas. 1192, 1229-30 (C.C.D.N.Y. 1806) (No. 16342). For Supreme Court case, see *Kendall v. United States ex rel. Stokes*, 37 U.S. (12 Pet.) 524, 638 (1838). For other examples, see Curtis S. Bradley and Martin S. Flaherty, "Executive Power Essentialism and Foreign Affairs," *Michigan Law Review* 102 (2004), 545, 574–75.

69. For Declaration, see Pauline Maier, *American Scripture: Making the Declaration of Independence* (New York: Alfred A. Knopf, 1997), 97- 153. For the military context of 1776, see David McCullough, *1776* (New York: Simon & Schuster, 2005). For Jackson, see *Youngstown*, 343 U.S. at 641 (Jackson, J., concurring).

70. For state constitutions, see Flaherty, "Most Dangerous Branch," 1764–71; Gerhard Casper, "An Essay in Separation of Powers: Some Early Versions and Practices," *William and Mary Law Review* 30 (1989), 211, 212–17; Bradley and Flaherty, 571-85. For Jefferson quote, see Wood, *Creation of the American Republic*, 136. In the *Federalist Papers*, Madison observed that the shift from the Articles of Confederation to the new Constitution "consists much less in the addition of New Powers to the Union than in the invigoration of its *Original Powers*." *Federalist*, No. 46, 293.

71. *Federalist*, No. 37, 228.

72. For theorists' conflicts, see Bradley and Flaherty, 560-71, Rakove, *Original Meanings*, 245–51; McDonald, 57–96. For Montesquieu on excessive power, see Albert O. Hirschman, *The Passions and the Interests: Political Arguments for Capitalism before Its Triumph* (Princeton: Princeton University Press, 1977), 76–78.

73. For Locke, see Locke, *Two Treatises of Government*, Shapiro ed., 172–73. Locke also treated the judiciary as part of the executive; his "prerogative power" thus resembled the "equity" powers of the English courts. For "odious" quote, see Lucius Wilmerding Jr., "The President and the Law," *Political Science Quarterly* 47 (1952), 321, 322 (citing British parliamentary record). For Madison, see Scigliano, 247 (citing the 1789 volume of the Annals of Congress). For a selective use of Locke, see Fried, *Order and Law*, 147–49.

74. For quotes, see McDonald, 247; see also Rakove, *Original Meanings*, 256–68. For James Wilson, see Brief of *Amicus Curiae* Jack N. Rakove et al, in *Hamdan v. Rumsfeld*, (2006) (No. 05-184), 19–23.

75. For Wilson's speech, see *Founding the American Presidency*, ed. Richard J. Ellis (Lanham: Rowman & Littlefield Publishers, 1999), 148–49. For its relevance, see

Rakove, *Original Meanings*, 143–45; Scigliano, 248. For the anti-Federalists, see Rakove, *Original Meanings*, 270–75.

76. For quotes see *Federalist* Nos. 48, 69–70, pp. 309, 415–31 (emphasis added). For the *Federalist Papers'* role, see Rakove, "Constitutional Problematics," 44. For Oml's omission of *Federalist* No. 69, see Charlie Savage, "Scholars Are Split on the Bush Administration's Use of the Federalist Papers to Justify Its Position on Presidential War Power," *Boston Globe*, June 11, 2006, E1. For 1980s use of "unitary executive, see Rosen, 8.

77. For Hamilton-Madison debate, see Ellis, 173–79.

78. *Federalist*, No. 69, 422–23.

79. *Little v. Barreme*, 6 U.S. (2 Cranch) 170 (1804); Yoo, *War by Other Means*, 239.

80. *Youngstown*, 343 U.S. 579 (1952); Alan F. Westin, *The Anatomy of a Constitutional Law Case* (New York: Columbia University Press,1990), 186–87. Eugene C. Gerhart, *America's Advocate, Robert Jackson* (Indianapolis: Bobbs-Merrill, 1958).

81. *Youngstown*, 343 U.S. at 635–38.

82. Ibid., at 646–47 (Jackson, J., concurring).

83. *Youngstown*, 343 U.S. at 654–55 (Jackson, J., concurring).

84. *Korematsu v. United States*, 323 U.S. 214, 246 (1944) (Jackson, J., dissenting).

85. *Federalist*, No. 51, 322.

86. *Federalist*, No. 37, 229.

87. "[W]e have an *unwritten* Constitution in the United States. This is not altogether a matter of custom. It is also to a great extent a matter of law. . . ." Eckhardt and Black, 8–9.

88. For the Reconstruction Amendments and their legacy, see J.J. Gass and Nathan Newman, *A New Birth of Freedom: The Forgotten History of the 13th, 14th, and 15th Amendments* (New York: Brennan Center for Justice, 2004); Eric Foner, *A Short History of Reconstruction, 1863–1877* (New York: Harper & Row, 1990). For Ackerman on transformative moments and the Great Depression, see Bruce Ackerman, *We the People: Foundations* (Cambridge: Belknap Press, 1991), 47–56.

89. See Bybee memo, 31; "Legal Authorities Supporting the Activities of the National Security Agency," 1–4.

90. "Legal Authorities Supporting the Activities of the National Security Agency," 35.

91. Yoo, "War and the Constitutional Text," 1683.

92. Stone, 41–45.

93. *Duncan v. Kahanamoku*, 327 U.S. 304, 328–29 (1946).

94. For the O'Connor quote, *see Hamdi v. Rumsfeld*, 542 U.S. 507, 536–37 (2004) (O'Connor, J., concurring); the other cases are *Rumsfeld v. Padilla*, 542 U.S. 426 (2004), and *Rasul v. Bush*, 542 U.S. 466 (2004). For Stevens and Breyer, see *Hamdan v. Rumsfeld*, 2006 WL 1764793 (29 June 2006).

95. For historical context, see Frank Lambert, *The Barbary Wars: American Independence in the Atlantic World* (New York: Hill and Wang, 2005).

96. For Condorcet quote, see Emma Rothschild, *Economic Sentiments: Adam Smith, Condorcet, and the Enlightenment* (Cambridge: Harvard University Press, 2001), 14 (quoting Condorcet's "*Réflexions sur le commerce des blés*").

Chapter 8: The King's Counsel

1. Frederick A.O. Schwarz Jr., "Becoming a Real Lawyer," keynote address, November 2002, Convocation on the Face of the Profession, *Journal of the New York State Institute on Professionalism and the Law*, Vol. 3, No. 1, Spring 2003, 14.

2. For Napoleonic Code, see John Henry Merryman, *The Civil Law Tradition: An Introduction to the Legal Systems of Western Europe and Latin America* (Stanford: Stanford University Press, 1985), 59–60. For excellent discussions of the kinds and scope of disagreement on the American Constitution, see Richard H. Fallon Jr., "Legitimacy and the Constitution," *Harvard Law Review* 118 (2005) 1787, 1809–13; Richard H. Fallon Jr., "Implementing the Constitution," *Harvard Law Review* 111 (1997), 56, 61–67.

3. For de Tocqueville, see Alexis de Tocqueville, *De la Démocratie en Amerique* (1835; Gallimard, 1985, J.-P. Mayer, ed.), 166; John Lukas, *Democracy and Populism: Fear and Hatred* (New Haven: Yale University Press, 2005), 9–10. The British jurist and historian James Bryce, in his historical and constitutional study *The American Commonwealth*, 1888, also confirmed the central role of lawyers in America. See James Bryce, *The American Commonwealth* (New York: Macmillan, 1917). For critical remarks about lawyers in America today, see Philip Howard, *The Death of Common Sense: How Law Is Suffocating America* (New York: Warner Books, 1996); Anthony Kronman, *The Lost Lawyer: Failing Ideals of the Legal Profession* (Cambridge: Belknap Press, 1995).

4. For special duties of government lawyers, see Steven K. Berenson, "The Duty Defined: Specific Obligations That Follow from Civil Government Lawyers' General Duty to Serve the Public Interests," *Brandeis Law Journal* 42 (2003), 13; See also Frederick A.O. Schwarz Jr., "The Constitution Outside the Courts," *The Record of the Association of the Bar of the City of New York* 47 (1992), 9; Robert H. Jackson, "Government Counsel and their Opportunity," *American Bar Association Journal* 26 (1940) ("Fundamental things in our American way of life depend on the intellectual integrity, courage, and straight thinking of our government lawyers"). For the solicitor general's role, see Lincoln Caplan, *The Tenth Justice: The Solicitor General and the Rule of Law* (New York: Alfred A. Knopf, 1987), 3–50; see also Cornelia T.L. Pillard, "The Unfulfilled Promise of the Constitution in Executive Hands," *Michigan Law Review* 103 (2005), 676, 704–9; Seth P. Waxman, "Foreword: Does the Solicitor General Matter?" *Stanford Law Review* 53 (2001), 1115. For Biddle quote, see Francis Biddle, *In Brief Authority* (Garden City, NY: Doubleday, 1962), 97. For OLC appointments, see John O. McGinnis, "Models of the Opinion Function of the Attorney General: A Normative, Descriptive, and Historical Prolegomenon," *Cardozo Law Review* 15 (1993), 375, 421–22.

5. Judiciary Act of 1789, Ch. 20, § 35, 1 Stat. 73, 93, codified as amended in 28 U.S.C. § 511 (1994).

6. For Root, see W. Bradley Wendel, "Legal Ethics and the Separation of Law and Morals," *Cornell Law Review* 91 (2005), 67, 111–12.

7. For Gillers, see remarks of Stephen Gillers, *The Torture Debate in America*, Karen J. Greenberg, ed. (Cambridge: Cambridge University Press, 2006), 27.

8. For OLC's unique role, see Pillard, 676; Randolph D. Moss, "Executive Branch Legal Interpretation: A Perspective from the Office of Legal Counsel," *Adminis-*

trative Law Review 52 (2000), 1303, 1309–10. For the reasons why OLC opinions are the final word, and for Reagan-era lawyer, see McGinnis, 375, 421–29.

9. For examples, drawn almost at random, see *Clackamas Gastroenterology Associates, P.C. v. Wells*, 538 U.S. 440 (2003), and *United Dominion Industries, Inc. v. United States*, 532 U.S. 822 (2001).

10. For Edmund Randolph and Cushing quotes, see Moss, 1303, 1308–9.

11. McGinnis, 375, 430 (quoting Rehnquist opinion).

12. For Olsen, see Pillard, 676, 727. For Kmiec, see Douglas Kmiec, "OLC's Opinion Writing Function: The Legal Adhesive for a Unitary Executive," *Cardozo Law Review* 15 (1993), 337, 373. For Moss, see Moss, 1303, 1330. For contrary theorists, see Geoffrey P. Miller, "The President's Power of Interpretation: Implications of a United Theory of Constitutional Law," *Law and Contemporary Problems* 56 (1993), 35; Nelson Lund, "Rational Choice at the Office of Legal Counsel," *Cardozo Law Review* 15 (1993), 437, 447; Geoffrey P. Miller, "Government Lawyers' Ethics in a System of Checks and Balances," *University of Chicago Law Review* 54 (1987), 1293. Judge (now Justice) Samuel A. Alito Jr., a former OLC lawyer, described OLC's function (somewhat narrowly) as "preserving the constitutional powers of the executive branch." (Samuel A. Alito Jr., "Change and Continuity at the Office of Legal Counsel," *Cardozo Law Review* 15 [1993], 507.) While lawyers in the executive branch certainly should be attuned to the interests of the executive branch, their ultimate responsibility, particularly for lawyers in the OLC, is more broadly to the Constitution. Harold Hongju Koh, also a former OLC lawyer who is now dean of the Yale Law School, made a similar point in warning that the OLC "must be protected from its own eagerness to please" the administration of which it is part. Harold Hongju Koh, "Protecting the Office of Legal Counsel from Itself," *Cardozo Law Review* 15 (1993), 513, 523.

13. Bruce Fein, "Data-mining Doubts," *Washington Times*, January 24, 2006. For defenses of the OLC's views, see Eric Posner and Adrian Vermeule, "A 'Torture' Memo and Its Tortuous Critics," *Wall Street Journal*, July 6, 2004, A22; see also David B. Rivkin Jr. and Lee A. Casey, "Inherent Authority," *Wall Street Journal*, February 8, 2006, A16.

14. For the Sedition Acts, see Geoffrey R. Stone, *Perilous Times: Free Speech in Wartime From the Sedition Act of 1798 to the War on Terrorism* (New York: W.W. Norton, 2004) 58–60. For the Japanese American internment case, see *Korematsu v. United States*, 323 U.S. 283 (1944); Stone, 306 and 630, n. 346; Peter Irons, *Justice at War: The Story of the Japanese-American Internment Cases* (Berkeley: University of California Press, 1983), ix–x, 278–92. Four decades after *Korematsu*, federal courts vacated the decisions against Korematsu and another Japanese American for "manifest injustice" because of deceit by the government in its presentation to the Supreme Court. *Korematsu v. United States*, 584 F. Supp. 1406 (N.D. Cal 1984); *Hirabashi v. United States*, 828 F.2d 591 (9th Cir. 1987).

15. For Bush Administration lawyers, see the interviews conducted with John Yoo and Bradford Berenson by the PBS show *Frontline*, available at http://www.pbs.org/wgbh. For the pre-9/11 positions of John Yoo, see Paul M. Barrett, "A Young Lawyer Helps Chart Shift in Foreign Policy," *Wall Street Journal*, September 12, 2005, A1. Daniel Klaidman, Stuart Taylor Jr., and Evan Thomas, "Palace Revolt," *Newsweek,* February 6, 2006, 34.

16. The December 28, 2001, memo by Patrick Philbin and John Yoo is an excep-

tion. This early memo not only set forth the arguments in favor of excepting Guantánamo Bay from federal court jurisdiction, it also explored possible strengths in an opposing position.

17. For Yoo quotes, see Peter Slevin, "Scholar Stands by Post-9/11 Writings on Torture, Domestic Eavesdropping," *Washington Post*, December 26, 2005, A3; John Yoo, *War by Other Means: An Insider's Account of the War on Terror* (New York: Atlantic Monthly Press, 2006), 173–82.

18. Memorandum for Alberto R. Gonzales, counsel to the president, from Jay S. Bybee, assistant attorney general, August 1, 2002, reprinted in Mark Danner, *Torture and Truth: America, Abu Ghraib, and the War on Terror* (New York: New York Review Books, 2004), 115; letter from Daniel Levin, Acting Assistant Attorney General, to Hon. William J. Haynes II, General Counsel, Department of Defense, February 4, 2005, 8, n.17 (on file with authors).

19. For the necessity point, see *United States v. Oakland Cannabis Buyers' Cooperative*, 532 U.S. 483 (2001). The opinion was even written by Yoo's old boss, Justice Thomas. Martin Lederman made this point, and many others, in the superlative Balkinization blog. See http://balkin.blogspot.com

20. For the March 2003 memo, see Jane Mayer, "A Deadly Interrogation," *New Yorker*, November 14, 2005, 44.

21. For "equivalent in intensity," see Bybee memo in Danner, 115. For "burning detainees with cigarettes," see W. Bradley Wendel, "Legal Ethics and the Separation of Law and Morals," *Cornell Law Review* 91 (2005), 81; see generally Kathleen Clark, "Ethical Issues Raised by the OLC Torture Memorandum," *Journal of National Security Law and Policy* 2 (2006), 455.

22. For example, see Mayer, 44.

23. Memorandum from John Yoo, Deputy Assistant Attorney General, and Robert J. Delahunty, Special Counsel, for William J. Haynes II, "Application of Treaties and Laws to al Qaeda and Taliban Detainees," January 9, 2002.

24. For example, Solicitor General Erwin N. Griswold in 1968 handled a case before the Supreme Court in which the briefs prepared did not reflect a key fact. The case had to do with a challenge to a draft board order, and the key fact omitted showed that "the order to report for induction was invalid on its face." Griswold filed a brief saying so, even though the draft board tried to file its own brief arguing in favor of its arbitrary (and likely unconstitutional) action. See Erwin N. Griswold, *Ould Fields, New Corne: The Personal Memoirs of a Twentieth-Century Lawyer* (St. Paul: West, 1992), 268–69; *Oestereich v. Selective Service Board*, 393 U.S. 233 (1968).

25. See *Little v. Barreme*, 6 U.S. (2 Cranch) 170 (1804); *United States v. Smith*, 27 F. Cas, 1192, 1230 (C.C.D.N.Y. 1806) (No. 16, 342).

26. See *Youngstown Sheet & Tube Co. v. Sawyer*, 343 U.S. 579, 641 (1952) (Jackson, J., concurring). For a nice explanation of *Youngstown's* canonical states, see Sanford Levinson, "Introduction: Why Select a Favorite Case," *Texas Law Review* 74 (1996), 1195. Chief Justice John Roberts referred to *Youngstown* in his confirmation hearings as the definitive framework for asserting that "the President is fully bound by the law, the constitution and statutes" (see transcript: Day Two of the Roberts Confirmation Hearings, September 13, 2005, at washingtonpost.com).

27. For "near consensus," see David Luban, "Liberalism, Torture, and the Ticking Bomb," *Virginia Law Review* 91 (2005), 1425. For the "statement of principles," see Walter E. Dellinger et al, "Principles to Guide the Office of Legal Counsel,"

December 21, 2004, available at http://www.acslaw.org/pdf/OLCGuidelines Memo.pdf. For Waldron, see Jeremy Waldron, "Torture and the Positive Law: Jurisprudence for the White House," *Columbia Law Review* 105 (2005), 1681. For Koh, see Harold Hongju Koh, "A World Without Torture," *Columbia Journal of Transnational Law* 43 (2005), 641. See also Dawn Johnsen and Neil Kinkopf, letter to the editor, "How to Prevent Another 'Torture' Memo," *Wall Street Journal*, January 21, 2005; R. Jeffrey Smith, "Slim Legal Grounds for Torture Memo: Most Scholars Reject Broad View of Executive's Power," *Washington Post*, July 4, 2004, A12.

28. For vetted quote, see Dana Priest, "CIA Puts Harsh Tactics on Hold; Memo on Methods of Interrogation Had Wide Review," *Washington Post*, June 27, 2004, A1. See Douglas Jehl, "In Cheney's Chief, a Bureaucratic Master," *New York Times*, November 2, 2005, A22. See also Klaidman, Taylor Jr., and Thomas, 34; R. Jeffrey Smith and Dan Eggen, "Gonzales Helped Set the Course for Detainees," *Washington Post*, January 5, 2005, A1; Dana Milbank, "In Cheney's Shadow, Counsel Pushes the Conservative Cause," *Washington Post*, October 11, 2004, A21. For small policy circle, see Evan Thomas and Richard Wolffe, "Bush in the Bubble," *Newsweek*, December 19, 2005, 30. For Yoo's role, see Scott Shane, "Behind Power, One Principle as Bush Pushes Prerogatives," *New York Times*, December 17, 2005, A1; Barrett, A1. For "protégé" and the "Bybee, Yoo, Addington" quote, see Chitra Ravagan, "Cheney's Guy," *U.S. News and World Report*, May 29, 2006, 32.

29. For quotes, see Smith and Eggen, A1. For the military commissions, see Tim Golden, "Tough Justice," *New York Times*, October 24, 2004, A1. For books on how the Iraq war and postwar planning were hurt by limiting discussion to narrow circle of decision makers, see Michael R. Gordon and Bernard E. Trainor, *Cobra II: The Inside Story of the Invasion and Occupation of Iraq* (New York: Pantheon, 2006), and George Packer, *The Assassins' Gate: America in Iraq* (New York: Farrar, Straus and Giroux, 2005). For absence of State Department input, see Ravagan, 32.

30. For denial of access to information, see exchange between William Haynes and Admiral Donald Guter in Tom Golden, "Tough Justice," *New York Times*, October 24, 2004, A1. For Mora's story, see Jane Mayer, "The Memo," *New Yorker*, January 7, 2006, 32. Unclassified FBI memo, "Legal Analysis of Interrogation Techniques," November 26, 2002 (on file with authors); memo from Major General Jack L. Rives, USAF, Deputy Judge Attorney General for SAF/GC, *Final Report and Recommendations of the Working Group to Assess the Legal, Policy and Operational Issues Relating to Interrogation of Detainees Held by the U.S. Armed Forces in the War on Terrorism*, February 5, 2003.

31. For secrecy, see Golden, A1. For bypassing Comey and Goldsmith, see Evan Thomas and Daniel Klaidman, "Full Speed Ahead," *Newsweek*, January 9, 2006, A22; Eric Lichtblau and James Risen, "Justice Deputy Resisted Parts of Spy Program," *New York Times*, January 1, 2006, 1.

32. For Comey, see Klaidman, Taylor Jr., and Thomas, 34; Lichtblau and Risen, 1. For speech, see James B. Comey, "Fighting Terrorism and Preserving Civil Liberties," *University of Richmond Law Review* 40 (2006), 403, 418.

33. See Confirmation Hearing on the Nomination of Alberto R. Gonzales to be Attorney General of the United States, United States Senate Committee on the Judiciary (Washington, DC: U.S. Government Printing Office, 2005).

34. For discussion of principles relating to making OLC opinions public, see Harold Hongju Koh, "Protecting the Office of Legal Counsel From Itself," *Cardozo Law Review* 15 (1993), 513, 515, 517–523. See also Walter E. Dellinger et al, "Principles to Guide the Office of Legal Counsel," December 21, 2004, principles 5 and 6, available at http://www.acslaw.org/pdf/OLCGuidelinesMemo.pdf. These principles include a "special responsibility to disclose publicly and explain any actions that conflict with federal statutory requirements."

Conclusion: A Republic, If You Can Keep It

1. "Papers of Dr. James McHenry on the Federal Convention of 1787," *American Historical Review* 11 (1906), 595, 611; cf. *Federalist Papers*, No. 10, Clinton Rossiter, ed. (New York: Signet, 1961), 77–84 (distinguishing *republicanism* from *democracy*).
2. The quote is from President Abraham Lincoln's November 19, 1863, Gettysburg address. The full text of the address can be found at http://www.loc.gov/exhibits/gadd/images/Gettysburg-2.jpg.
3. *Bk. II*, 205, 208.
4. John Winthrop, "A Modell of Christian Charity," text available at http://history.hanover.edu/texts/winthmod.html.
5. See John Lewis Gaddis, *Surprise, Security and the American Experience* (New Haven: Yale University Press, 2005), 28–29; Joseph S. Nye Jr., *The Paradox of American Power: Why the World's Only Superpower Can't Go It Alone* (New York: Oxford University Press, 2002), 11; Gary Hart, *The Shield and the Cloak: The Security of the Commons* (New York: Oxford University Press, 2006), 150–51.
6. For al Qaeda, see *The 9/11 Commission Report: Final Report of the National Commission on Terrorist Attacks upon the United States* (New York: W. W. Norton, 2004), 374–77; Jason Burke, *Al-Qaeda: The True Story of Radical Islam* (London: I.B. Tauris, 2003), 254–76. For Kepel, see Gilles Kepel, *The War for Muslim Minds: Islam and the West* (Cambridge: Belknap Press, 2004), 292; Ron Suskind, *The One-Percent Doctrine: Deep Inside America's Pursuit of its Enemies Since 9/11* (New York: Simon & Schuster, 2006), 296.
7. For quotes, see *Federalist*, Nos. 47 and 51, 301–3; Forrest McDonald, *Novus Ordo Seclorum: The Intellectual Origins of the Constitution* (Lawrence: University of Kansas Press, 1985), 261–62, 322.
8. *Federalist*, No. 10, 82–84 (emphasis added).
9. Bruce Ackerman, *Before the Next Attack: Preserving Civil Liberties in an Age of Terrorism* (New Haven: Yale University Press, 2006), 14–15.
10. Hart, 133.
11. Bob Eckhardt and Charles L. Black, *The Tides of Power: Conversations on the American Constitution* (New Haven: Yale University Press, 1976), 25, 36.
12. Jim VanderHei, "Cheney Says NSA Spying Should Be an Election Issue," *Washington Post*, February 10, 2006, A7; Billy House, "Shadegg Endorsements Raise National Profile," *Arizona Republic*, January 23, 2006, 8B.
13. For political party affiliation quote, see Daryl J. Levinson, "Empire-Building Government in Constitutional Law," *Harvard Law Review* 118 (2005), 950–60. For 1800 election, see Bruce Ackerman, *The Failure of the Founding Fathers: Jefferson,*

Marshall, and the Rise of Presidential Democracy (Cambridge: Harvard University Press, 2005), 6. For "impairs deliberation," see Robert A. Dahl, "Myth of the Presidential Mandate," *Political Science Quarterly* 105 (1990), 355, 371.

14. See Thomas E. Patterson, *The Vanishing Voter: Public Involvement in an Age of Uncertainty* (New York: Vintage Books, 2003); Samuel Issacharoff, "Collateral Damage: The Endangered Center in American Politics," *William and Mary Law Review* 46 (2004), 5426–27.

15. For "unity" and "duration," see *Federalist*, No. 70, 424. For intelligence budget, see Mark Mazzetti, "Spymaster Tells Size of Secret Spy Force," *New York Times*, April 21, 2006, A21.

16. For 9/11 Commission, see Thomas H. Kean and Lee H. Hamilton, *Without Precedent: The Inside Story of the 9/11 Commission* (New York: Alfred A. Knopf, 2006), 41–42, For Truman, see David McCullough, *Truman* (New York: Simon & Schuster, 1992), 259–91.

17. See, e.g., *Bk II*, 298, 304. *The 9/11 Commission Report*, 407–20.

18. For the Administrative Procedure Act, see 5 U.S.C. § § 500 et seq.

19. See Neal Kumar Katyal, "The Internal Separation of Powers" *Yale Law Journal* 116 (2003), 103. For blogger, see Dana Priest, "Top Secret World Loses Blogger," *Washington Post*, July 21, 2006, A15.

20. For Bok, see Sissela Bok, *Secrets: On the Ethics of Concealment and Revelation* (New York: Vintage Books, 1983), 177. For wiretapping without warrants, see "President Bush: Information Sharing, Patriot Act Vital to Homeland Security," remarks by the President in a conversation on the USA Patriot Act, Kleinshans Music Hall, Buffalo, New York," April 20, 2004, available at www.whitehouse.gov/news/releases/2004/04/print/20040420-2.html. For President Bush on torture, see http://www.whitehouse.gov/news/releases/2005/01/2005012263.html. For Rice, see remarks of Secretary of State Condoleezza Rice upon her departure for Europe, December 5, 2005, Andrews Air Force Base (on file with authors).

21. See Eric Alterman, *When Presidents Lie: A History of Official Deception and Its Consequences* (New York: Viking, 2004), 12–20.

22. Editorial, "Bad Targeting," *Washington Post*, April 26, 2006, A24. For evidence that criticism of the executive branch need not be a partisan matter, see Gene Healy and Timothy Lynch, "Power Surge: The Constitutional Record of George W. Bush," Cato Institute (2006); Bob Barr, "NSA Kabuki Theater," Findlaw, February 9, 2006, available at www.findlaw.com. For 9/11 Commission, see Kean and Hamilton, 256–62; Dan Eggen, "9/11 Panel Suspected Deception by Pentagon," *Washington Post*, August 2, 2006, A3.

23. For grand jury, see Dan Eggen, "Grand Jury Probes News Leak at NSA," *Washington Post*, July 29, 2006, at A2. For excessive secrecy, see John Podesta, "Need to Know: Governing in Secret," in *The War on Our Freedoms: Civil Liberties in an Age of Terrorism*, Richard C. Leone and Greg Anrig Jr., eds. (New York: Public Affairs, 2003), 220. For informed questions, see Suskind, 97–98. For selective declassification, see David Johnston and David E. Sanger, "Cheney's Aide Says President Approved Leak," *New York Times*, April 7, 2006, A1. A federal statute demands reporting on executive branch classification authority. See 5 U.S.C. § 552 (e) (1).

24. *Assassinations*, 285.

25. Learned Hand, *The Spirit of Liberty* (Chicago: University of Chicago Press, 1977), 189–91.

Index